THE WIZARD OF MGM

Ben-Hur: A Tale of the Christ, MGM Production #1724, Released 1959, AAG Contribution: Special Effects.

THE WIZARD OF MGM

Memoirs of A. Arnold Gillespie

Art Director / Head of Special Effects

from 1924-1965

(Oct. 14, 1899 - May 31, 1978)

Edited by
Philip J. Riley
&
Robert A. Welch

Introduction

by

Spencer Tracy & Katharine Hepburn

BearManor Media
P.O. Box 1129
Duncan, OK 73534-1129
Phone: 580-252-3547 (Sandy Grabman)
Fax: 814-690-1559
benohmart@gmail.com

Copyright ©2011 by Albert Arnold Gillespie and Robert Arnold Welch
Primary Title: "Wizard of MGM"
Alternative Title: "Big Ones Out Of Little Ones"
All rights reserved, including the right of reproduction in whole or in part.
All photographs are from the collection of A. Arnold Gillespie, unless otherwise noted in caption.

Cover Art - ©2012 By Keith Kaminski

ISBN: 1-59393-292-8

First Edition
10 9 8 7 6 5 4 3 2 1

ILLUSTRATIVE
MATERIAL ACKNOWLEDGEMENTS

Most of the photos in this book were gathered over the years for my personal records. Many contain "dirt" and "scratches" which for their original purpose, that of keeping filed records, was of no consequence. These blemishes will not, I hope, detract from their illustrative value. Their use is gratefully acknowledged and the credits go to many cameramen assigned to the Effect sequences. Among them are Max Fabian, Harold Wellman, Clarence Slifer, Bill Williams, Mark Davis, Harold Lipstein, Harold Marzorati, Ed Snyder and perhaps a few whose names are buried in a fading memory.

Several "still" photographers are also represented in these pages and if a few remain incognito, my apologies. Those I recall whose contributions do or might appear, are Virgil Apger, Kenneth Bell, Eric Carpenter, William Creamer, Milton Gold, Eddie Hubbell, S.C. 'Jimmy' Manatt and Frank Shugrue

Thank you, gentlemen, each and all.

A.A.G.

Original A. Arnold Gillespie illustrative material acknowledgement and tribute above.

EDITOR'S NOTE

This manuscript, initially conceived some 46 years ago, is finally available in print. Folklore no more. Referred to over these many years as "Big Ones Out Of Little Ones" or visa versa in texts such as "Hollywood Speaks! An Oral History" by Mike Steen. "Big Ones", as Buddy explains, are the result of a lots of "Little Ones"; miniatures that contribute to block buster movies, or little ideas and bits of knowledge that, put together, add up to experience. Or, in the case of this book, a pound of history, slice of technical reference, a dash of personal perspective, and a pinch of humor, in only 360 pages! Big one? Little one?

A. Arnold "Buddy" Gillespie, my grandfather, began writing this very manuscript back in 1965; outlining the details of his life lessons, accomplishments, whimsical stories, technical "know how", all the while acknowledging the contributions of others. These are his words, his captions, un-edited. Buddy, using his draftsman skills, meticulously identified the size and placement of every photo. Buddy's extensive photographic archive, a fraction of which is referenced within these pages, is now cared for by the Margaret Herrick Library, Academy of Motion Pictures Arts and Sciences, in Beverly Hills, California. Of great interest to me are the "Form 48s" used to catalog the shot, cost of the effect, details of how each was achieved, scale, camera speed, and cameraman. These "Form 48s" reveal that an M.G.M. effectsman was truly an artistic and mechanical wizard.

Buddy, or "Papu" as the family knew him, sought to find the right publisher for many years. Technical books!. Not stories about personalities! Down to the minute detail! A "how to" book with diagrams, camera angles, film speeds, details about Process, calculations! That's what the publishers were interested in. But that was not what Buddy intended. Close friends such as Francis Coppola were provided copies for review. A few or these original manuscripts still exist, tucked away in family archives. Eight different revisions have been identified and recovered thus far. It was only just recently that events occurred willing this project back into motion, reuniting the layout pages, photos, manuscript revisions, and notes, seemingly orchestrated by the Art Director in the sky. And now, here is his book, his words of wisdom, for you to enjoy.

The presentation of this material would not have been possible if it were not for the contributions of several key individuals. First, to my grandmother Nell, "Mimi" as we called her. She had the foresight to preserve Buddy's archive. A very patient woman, giving, practical and loving. She is missed. A very special tip of the hat to Philip J. Riley, who not only worked with Buddy at M.G.M. many years ago, and collaborated on the original manuscripts with him, but is also the current co-editor. It is an honor to be working with him on this project. A prolific author and editor, historian, and now good friend. Erik C. Andersen, who's friendship, industry knowledge, and patience were invaluable. And to Arnold Kunert, who provided the extra incentive (kick?) to ensure Buddy didn't have to wait another dozen or so years to realize his words in print. And lastly, to my very significant other, Sunnie, who would rather that I not mention her here, but without whose encouragement, patience, support, and those many late, late night pots of coffee, this project would never have been completed.

It was an honor to step into Buddy's shoes for a while. I truly hope that you enjoy this book as much as we do.

ACKNOWLEDGEMENTS

Erik C. Andersen, Craig Barron, Steven Bingen, Kathy and Bob Burns, Brian Chanes (Profiles in History), David Conover, Peter Cook, Robert Gillespie, Sunnie Gonzalives, Sue and Del Howison, Keith Kaminski, Tim Keegan, Marlene and Arnold Kunert, Bill Malone, Corrado Neri, George Nolta, Robert Parigi, Ed Poole (LAMP), Michael Stein, Margie Weisner, Van Welch, and the entire staff at, especially the Special Collections section of, The Academy Margaret Herrick Library; Stacey Behlmer, Barbara Hall, Meredith Shea, and Faye Thompson.

Grateful acknowledgement to Warner Brothers for making available most of the original M.G.M. films referenced within these pages as part of the Warner Archive Collection. And to Turner Classic Movies (TCM) for screening these classics.

Thanks!
-Robert Welch
Co-Editor

The Gillespie family Christmas (1946) Van, Tommy, Buddy, Nell (Mrs. Gillespie), Robert and Margie

From the desk of . . .

A. A. GILLESPIE

DEDICATION

This book is devotedly dedicated, especially to the memory of Thomas Scott Gillespie - our Tommy, who left us just a few days before his Seventeenth Birthday.

And certainly also to my dear wife Nell, for her tedious readings, constructive criticisms and thoughtful deletions of unfunny corn which might have in some instances resulted in calamitous legalities, my loving thanks.

And lastly its dedication should and does include the host of those with whom I have been so pleasantly associated through these many years.

A. A. G.

BIG ONES — OUT OF LITTLE ONES

42 DISASTER YEARS AT MGM
OR DISASTROUS

A. ARNOLD GILLESPIE

One of three original concept cover designs by A. Arnold Gillespie in 1965.
Publicity photo with Leo the Lion was taken upon retuning from vacation to Rhode Island which featured an automobile mishap.

Dragon Seed, MGM Production #1350, Released 1944, AAG Contribution: Miniatures.

Table of Contents

FOREWORD 11
ABOUT THE AUTHOR 16
CHAPTER ONE ~ "1922 NEOPHYTE" 20
CHAPTER TWO ~ "GALLEYS AND JUTTING CHINS" 28
CHAPTER THREE ~ "PERSONALITIES - EARLY FOUNDATIONS" 44
CHAPTER FOUR ~ "UNIONS–HIPPOS–CONTROL" 56
CHAPTER FIVE ~
  "FULL-SIZED EFFECTS MASCULINE AND FEMININE" 64
CHAPTER SIX ~
  "MATTE PAINTINGS AND UNRELATED INCIDENTALS" 98
CHAPTER SEVEN ~ "MINIATURES AND MUSTACHES" 124
CHAPTER EIGHT ~ "MINIATURES SANS MUSTACHES" 178
CHAPTER NINE ~ "OPTICAL AND ANIMATION" 254
CHAPTER TEN ~ "PROCESS THE WHYS AND HOWS" 282
CHAPTER ELEVEN ~ "RAMBLING RANDOMS" 318
FILM CREDITS 368
NAMES INDEX 372
MOVIE TITLE INDEX 374

Tarzan and His Mate, MGM Production #645, Released 1934, AAG Contribution: Art Director.

FOREWORD

Author posing at his M.G.M. Studios office.

We had just concluded a three-hour evening lecture at the University of So. California. There were various items and materials to be toted back to my car including film illustrating the subject of the lecture, "Special Visual Effects in Motion Pictures." A young student offering a hand which was gratefully accepted, asked me where he could obtain a book or books devoted to the subject upon which we had just lectured. I explained that to my knowledge nothing very comprehensive re Special Effects had ever been written. "Why don't you write a book, Mr. Gillespie - write just what you told us tonight," he suggested.

Whereupon the seed was planted and after surviving a drought of procrastination it finally sprouted, was nourished by many dreams and an urge to tell "just what you told us tonight," and has now become a ripe and sometimes mellow fruit.

It has become, I believe, a textbook with sufficient moisture added to relieve the dryness and boredom of many textbooks, with their formulae, procedures, technical problems and solutions. To do this it has chronicled many amusing and true tales such as the hippopotami in Lake

Sherwood on an early Johnny Weismuller *Tarzan*, epic, the locusts of *Good Earth*, Wally Beery's aversion to water and many others, unfortunately, some tragic.

The span of years in retrospect, seems not possible. Forty-three of them, the last forty-two of which have been spent solidly here at Metro-Goldwyn-Mayer. That's a year older than M.G.M. itself! And now perhaps an explanation of the title of this book. "Big Ones out of Little Ones," or "Forty-two Disastrous Years at M.G.M." The second half of the title should perhaps have included the word "delightfully" immediately preceding "disastrous" as indeed many of our chores which fell in one or more of the Special Effect categories, involved the manufacture and filming of varied disasters, such as earthquakes, tornados, sinking ships, crashing airplanes and what not, even and including a set of angel wings for Jeanette MacDonald in a super-super *I Married an Angel*. Though often rugged and again in retrospect, these disasters were more frequently than not, truly delightful.

So, dear student, may the chapters that follow, either steer you away with a shudder from ever becoming involved in that which we lovingly refer to as the "grief department" or in the event your decision is to heed not the above warning, may their contents assist you in traversing the rocky path towards success in this highly challenging facet of picture making. And to the layman, the casual reader whose groceries are not dependent on depth bombing a submarine or coaxing a huge rubber crocodile into an underwater fight (again with heroic Johnny) well, the pages and pictures and illustrations and anecdotes to follow should have high interest and perhaps be instrumental in making you, our casual reader, at least an arm chair authority when the "how in the world did they do that!", question is asked when discussing the *Ben-Hur* chariot race or those confounded *Good Earth* locusts (coffee grounds they were, a good many of them) or the *Wizard of Oz* tornado, or on and on and on!

A whole chapter of people would be necessary to give proper credit to all connected with these "delightfully disastrous" years; all whose contribution has been so absolutely necessary and to whom the author is gratefully indebted. These were, and are, dedicated and resourceful men (and occasionally women) running the gauntlet of talents from powder men to naval architects to water men to hydraulic engineers to remarkably talented artists to loving mothers of tiny babies to mechanics and stunt men, you name it. For a happy career and the few Oscars in our collection, "thanks gentlemen (and ladies) thanks to all of you!" I know that those lovely gold plated bronze statuettes which I proudly display are all partly yours. And I also know that your loyalty and friendship is a possession prized above all else. My deep thanks to you all. And as King Vidor might have said, "it's nice for you, you knew me too!"

King had once autographed, at my request, a still of a set we had done for Johnny Mack Brown's *Billy the Kid* as follows, "To Buddy, the man who designed the set, from King Vidor, the man who designed the set." Whatever did you mean, Mr. Vidor?

Qu'est-ce que c'est que

"Special visual effects"?

Two questions have been asked the author numerous times during the past years. "Just what are 'Special Visual Effects' and what training and talents are a must?" The answer to both, if they were to be all-inclusive, would require reams of fine print. The wide and varied diversification of Special Effects behest, in all of their five category divisions (a sixth, Animation, with specified limitations has recently been added) pretty well cover the waterfront of a writer's, many writers', ability to dream-up and type-out scenes and sequences from the plausible possibles to the at times seemingly impossibles. The term "Special Effects" may apply to anything of a physical nature, ranging from 'rain' outside of a movie set window or fire in the fireplace to a hurricane's devastation or a journey into outer space or whatever – you name it.

We will, in later Chapters, devoted to documentations and examples in each category, define in more detail each of the six divisions. The Academy of Motion Pictures Arts and Sciences enumerates them as follows: Full-sized Mechanical, Matte Paintings, Miniatures, Optical, Process and Animation. The latter is not to be confused with straight cartoon or puppet animation recognized as such by an audience. Mickey Mouse may collect his laurels outside the realm of Special Visual Effects.

The aim of this art is most generally to achieve the illusion of live-action-reality. Exceptions could include a dream fantasy or perhaps some of the 'way out' demands of Science and Fiction subjects but our techniques even in these off-beats, strive principally for believable acceptance.

The student and the lay reader will have ample opportunity to digest method determinations and brief 'case histories' of the many of the problems thrown our way by those pesky writers, God love 'em. So, for a more complete answer to both questions, it is hoped that the chapters to follow will be of instructive interest.

The second question, "what training and talents are a must," carries with it no single simple answer. Men, at present involved in one or more of the six categories throughout the industry, are so completely varied in background and training and talent, they could be likened to a jig-saw puzzle with enough parts missing that it would be quite impossible to complete a standard representation depicting a single Special Visual Effects Department Head or participant. Ideally, all should have a fairly general knowledge of all aspects of picture making. Ideally, all should have a reasonably well rounded education and be able in their contacts with the whole spectrum of movie makers, to impress whatever individual he is facing with not just the knowledge of his own specialty, but a fair ken of that person's particular bent as well. And, hopefully, he should have at least a nodding acquaintance with a host of perhaps totally unrelated subjects. Conversational tangents during a particular Effect problem confab may shoot off in many directions and confidence is gained when a producer, a director, or whomever, is aware that he is talking not just to a single-track expert, but that he is facing an individual well rounded in experience other than his own particular activity.

With the above in mind, the student should make every effort possible to seek out and take advantage of the wide range of usual and unusual happenings that present themselves generally in the routine of day by day living. Many such, perhaps around the corner, but make those turns with your sensibilities alert and your memory genes available for long range storage.

In my opinion one of the most important and applicable rungs in the Special Effects ladder, regardless of categories, is to include architectural and mechanical drafting in your curriculum. Even an elementary knowledge of these two will prove value. Certainly designing engineers and more highly trained draftsmen, Navel architects, hydraulic men, etc., are available, but the ability to design and draw reasonably well and to savvy a more sophisticated layout or working drawing is highly desirable.

If you possess any native ability at all in the field of Art, that talent should be developed. A quick readable sketch will often portray your thinking far better than words and will convey to the professional illustrator or sketch artist, also available in the studios, your idea, if it is to be further developed as a more refined sketch in the presentation of a solution or concept to a producer or director.

It is obvious that specialized training in other areas, depending on Effect category selection, is mandatory. Cinema Arts courses in many educational institutions throughout the country offer this training. I wish to stress, however that though these highly valuable more technical aspects are essential, a creative, inventive, and imaginative mentality is the all important key. This particularly applies to the man who shoulders the overall responsibility of concept, method, determination, execution, delivery, and cost. This latter quite naturally raises its ugly presence usually at the outset, often in the middle, and occasionally after the job is done. I underline it because periodically in my experience this phase of an Effect problem has been the most unpleasant part of a difficult solution. Special Visual Effects of certain types come not cheap though we often refer to them as 'inexpensive' - costly yes, but definitely inexpensive as compared to alternate methods and quite often to their out-standing value in delivering solid punches to a filmed story.

Students interested in any phase of Special Effects should learn and become proficient in one or more of the crafts pertinent to whatever category is their choosing.

In **Optical Effects** as a starter, the job aspirant should be thoroughly versed in the tools of this division, principally camera, optical-printers and film, with its varying characteristics inherent in both negative and positive stock. His duties often involve extremely tight tolerances and built-in patience is a "should be" when dealing with one-ten-thousandth of an inch. The successful operator must respect precision to the nth degree. As a matter of fact some training as a precision machinist would not be amiss. Nor would that of a good housekeeper be found wanting. A speck of dust in this exacting department should not ever be viewed with alarm simply because it should never be viewed.

There are many off-shoots to routine procedures in Optical Effects, split screens, reductions, and enlargements of subject matter, superimpositions, traveling mattes, most film distortions, animation and others. Some may be elementarily covered in school but the graduate course is generally attended in the Optical Department of a working studio or in one of the several commercial facilities existent.

The personnel of a **Matte Painting Department**, as the name implies, must include Artists of a high caliber whose sensitiveness to light, shade, and color must be balanced by a thorough adherence to the rules of perspective and the depiction of reality in the majority of their renditions. They should know architecture in all of its forms from classical to modern to the imaginative structures of the future. They should be good landscapists and cloud-populated-sky painters. The diversifications of Matte Painting demands may necessitate two or more matte artists who excel in perhaps one or two but not necessarily in all of these directions. They should learn of film and its idiosyncrasies and they will be exposed to the more technical mergings of their efforts with the previously shot other half of the composite. Here the department's cameraman and his assistants with their assortment of intricate printers, precise camera setups, easels, and lighting arrangements, become the 'merger pilots.'

So, artists, cameramen, electricians, photo enlargers, grips, optical experts, precision machinists, and an imaginative Head of the whole array, cross paths constantly in the well functioning Matte Painting category of Special Visual Effects.

A third Effects branch is **Process**. Photographically, successful results are dependent upon the know-how through experience in Process of a cinematographer who must savvy not only his camera, but he must have an excellent eye for color and density balance in order that foreground and background (projected on to a translucent screen) become an acceptable 'single' scene. He should know perspective and realize that there exist common vanishing points relative to both foreground and background. A kindergarten course in perspective would be of value to all cameramen, particularly those involved in composites of any kind. Process is a form of composite photography. Process projectionists, electricians, and grips compose the balance of the crew and all increase their value to this category as they work and learn with it.

Perhaps the key person as far as the overall mechanics of the operation are concerned, is the 'Process Director.' He should have a fairly inclusive knowledge of all the requirements indicated above but his duties in addition are manifold. They include direction of all effect equipment such as wind, rain, dump tanks, set movement, and correct scale relationship between foreground and background, projected picture size, camera lens choice, camera movement during shooting. He works closely with the director and cameraman, pointing out proper or improper procedures. Training for this man? Again and ideally, the whole gamut of movie making, familiarity with Production office procedures, fairly conversant with the camera and its lenses, Process projectors and their lenses, and a thorough understanding of picture composition and scale. Here we stress again the value of a healthy smattering of art education. And at the top of his list of talents should be a sensitiveness to taste and wise uses of his effect tools, good judgement and the ability to communicate with diplomacy. His contacts with actors, directors, producers and others of many varied temperaments in the pursuit of his Process duties, make this last a prime requisite. The above hoped for competency applies of course to most endeavors certainly it applies to all of those heading each Special Effect category.

Full-sized Effects, deals, as the term implies, with full or normal sized ingredients generally including people. The student preparing for this division has a goodly variety of choices, quite a few of which he should master as stepping stones to the gang-boss, foreman, or eventual supervisory level. Practically all of the construction and mechanical crafts are involved. Structural, mechanical, electrical, and hydraulic engineering, in part or in toto, are often needed to solve the mélange of Full-sized Effects problems which may present themselves to the harried Head of this category. A knowledge of powder and explosives, physics, and chemistry, hydraulic ram installations for 'rockers,' and on and on. In this band of set and effect operators, mostly propshop men, grips, and electricians bear the operative responsibility load.

The initial determination of methods, layouts, type of effect equipment needed, old or newly designed, and the practical feasibility of any approach to a full-sized effect problem falls within the mental concept of this category's head man. He will have help from many other sources and should avail himself of that assistance. It will come from the Construction Department chief, heads of the Propshop, Paint Department, Staff Shop, Machine Shop, Electrical Department and others, depending on the specific problem. He seldom goes it alone although in most instances, he will originate and devise a problem's answer, an important part of which is to minimize elements of danger to actors and operating crew, and then follow its development on paper through layout and design, to actual construction and completion. He will be present during testing stages and company shooting. And as you will discover in later pages, he will attempt to muzzle the 'doom predictors.'

Qualifications and advance preparation for this demanding task are in general those which merit repetition; the seeking out and experiencing of our pet preachment, the usual and the unusual, as ever continuing ventures, and a broad awareness of all the techniques and characteristics enumerated heretofore which constitute the basic elements of a successful Effects Department Head. He may not of necessity be a master of all or any of the specialized crafts. A healthy knowledge- ableness, however, of them, is obviously of benefit. Primarily he must be imaginative and inventive and lastly his close association with an Art Director assigned to the picture is a very important must.

The **Miniature** category of Special Visual Effects will embrace all of the craftsmen mentioned in the paragraphs on Full-sized Effects. A Few more specialists, particularly 'water men,' will wend their way.

The cameramen assigned to Miniature shooting are or should be specialists in this area. Their photographic problems are often more demanding than those of a production cinematographer in spite of the gloomy possibility of a Star's 'good side' turning out on film as though it were her 'bad' side. In any event the man whose choice of a career encompasses the 'shooting' of miniatures must be prepared to wheedle out of his camera fantastic focus stretches at above normal camera speeds. His margin of photographic tolerance is considerably less than average straight production shooting. He will do well to know a speed camera from top to bottom, forward to aft, inside and outside. If he has studied composition, (Art schooling again) he will have increased his value, and if he develops the patience of a Mexican burro, he will have added to that value. As is true of the Process cameraman, he is unique in his qualifications and should be given preference as a choice for this type of assignment over the standard production cameraman regardless of the latter's probable excellence.

If the question were asked the author as to who becomes the leading light from the outset through to the finish and what educational preparation is necessary to qualify as the chief pilot of Miniatures, he would have no easy answer. The jig-saw puzzle with its missing pieces applies here perhaps more than in any other branch of Special Effects. There is no assembly line fabrication which turns out these gentlemen. They differ widely but I am sure, if successful, they have a common trait, that of being good guessers. Too many wrong guesses will promote a fast 'pink slip'. Much of scale determination, camera speed choices and myriad other details are predicated from the original conception to its completion, on educated guesses. There is no hard and fast formula for decisions that must be made which will result in a miniature looking not like a miniature - and that of course is the goal.

How do we become <u>educated</u> guessers? Mainly, and this is a <u>graduate</u> guess, through experience in the field when coupled with a peculiar perhaps inborn sense or aptitude relating to the mostly uncharted routes of how to make "little ones look like big ones." This faculty is somewhat like mental depth perception. It's there or it isn't. True, experience in the handling of miniature problems over a period of years may develop this necessary proficiency, but just as truly, the individual who seeks the top level of responsibility and who possesses that nebulous 'hunch judgement' will tread the paths more easily.

A general awareness of mechanics and engineering, an adeptness in the demanding field of Art Direction, a fluid knowledge of the camera, a willingness to ask for help, and the ability to weigh carefully proffered answers, are a few accessories well worth the time and effort for attainment. 'Crazy thinking' as I term it, about which numerous references will be made in the pages to follow, can often unlock vaults stacked with sane solutions.

Hence, two and two is not just a simple four in advance preparation for, nor long time actual contact with, this interesting challenging category, designated Miniature, which would seem to indicate littleness. Seldom are the physical or mental processes small.

We will skip **Animation**, the last category, other than its earlier reference and a later perusal, and with the reader's indulgence devote the next Chapter or two to the author's early years in this business and his elbow-rubbing with knowns and unknowns. I know me considerably more intimately than I know my contemporaries and the whole backlog of those early doings and contacts have, I feel confident, a direct or indirect bearing on whatever success has been attained in the 'physical' field of motion pictures, both as an Art Director and in the diversified realm of Special Visual Effects.

END OF FOREWORD

London After Midnight, MGM Production #330, Released 1927. AAG Contribution: Set Decorator.

Adam's Rib, MGM Production #1457, Released 1949, AAG Contribution: Special Effects.

ABOUT THE AUTHOR
By
SPENCER TRACY
&
KATHARINE HEPBURN

The place – Metro-Goldwyn-Mayer. The time – the twenties, thirties, forties, the fifties. This was a very special place – a very special time. And I am speaking not only for myself but for many others. For Clark Gable and Garbo and Norma Shearer and Jean Harlow, Wally Beery, Joan Crawford, Marie Dressler, Freddie Bartholomew, Bob Montgomery, Bob Taylor, Mickey Rooney, Bill Powell, Myrna Loy, Judy Garland, James Stewart, Lionel – Ethel – Jack Barrymore, Katharine Hepburn, Gene Kelly, Greer Garson, Frank Sinatra, Jimmy Durante. Shall I go on? You can see for yourself that it was special. Like a small college. None of us ever graduated. We were there year after year after year. And along with us were the directors, writers, cameramen, and the heads of departments with their talent – laden crews. The deans? Irving Thalberg and L.B. Mayer and their unique group of producers. It was like a village where you were baptized, married, buried with the protection of all the Chiefs. There were experts in every field. Their job was to make the best pictures in the world. Every means of making these pictures was available at M.G.M. and they had the money whereby top talent could and did blossom.

You would surely cross paths during a hypothetical prolonged tour of M.G.M. with great directors, George Cukor, Victor Fleming, Jack Conway, Woody Van Dyke, Clarence Brown, Ernst Lubitsch, to name a few. And a host of producers, of apex cameramen and the people of wardrobe, hair dressing and makeup, construction, props, art direction endless departments, and perhaps you might spot one individual about whom you should know if it is your intention to read his book ~ this book.

Though "A. Arnold Gillespie" is his former moniker, few if any have every addressed him thusly. It has been "Buddy" Gillespie for all his forty-two years of uninterrupted residence at M.G.M.

My friend, "Kate" Hepburn, called on Buddy the other day, sort of pinch-hitting for me, and this is what she has written as a result of that hour or so chat. Buddy may not take too kindly to some of her extollings. He is pretty adamant anti-personal-horn-blower and has taken great pains to include fellow crew members as an integral part of the outstanding success he has enjoyed in the field of Special Visual Effects. Anyway, Buddy, here's what your good friend, Miss Hepburn, says as she continues that hypothetical tour.

"People passed you on the lot. Jack Dawn, Bill Tuttle, Sidney Guilaroff, hair and makeup men, the one and only Cedric Gibbons, Art Department Head. And here comes Howard Strickland and Eddie Lawrence, Publicity, with Norma's brother, Doug Shearer, Sound Department Director. The other two? L.B. Mayer and Eddie Mannix, skipper and first mate."

"And who is that?"

"Oh, you mean the one with the pipe. That's Buddy Gillespie, Head of Special Effects. Yes, very down-to-earth, the Scottish-American male. Only he isn't. No, no, don't misunderstand me, he is certainly Scottish-American, and he is indubitably male. But somehow not entirely down-to-earth. Let me tell you about Buddy Gillespie. "

Katie goes on...

"... He is a magician. There's nothing he can't do. There's nothing too odd, too strange. Nothing surprises him. He is entirely unacquainted with a negative answer. Yes, we can do that. Burn down Rome. Destroy San Francisco by earthquake. Provide a swarm of locusts, a hurricane, a typhoon, an air battle, a sea battle. He is a wonder worker. He combines great technical skill with imagination and invention."

"His is not a routine job. He's got to know about many things. He must be unorthodox, unconventional, cool. He's got to be an expert cutter. He' got to be an expert cameraman. He's got to be able to build miniatures. And he will stress that all of the above is dependent on expert help from many sources. He knows and is emphatic that everyone should know that Effects are never one-man job. Modesty? No, just sense."

"Buddy perhaps belongs to a different breed. And if so, he was in on the creation of that breed. At twenty-three, after an eight-months' first baptism into the movies with C.B. DeMille's Art Department, he joined the then Goldwyn Studios in February of 1923. His job as a draftsman in Gibbons' Art Department led to a self-paid trip to Italy late in 1923, whereupon he joined the original *Ben-Hur* troupe. Returning as a Unit Art Director in the spring of 1925, he was later offered and accepted the position of Head of Special Effects, which he has held until retirement in March of 1965."

"His background pre-DeMille? Well, from his early start in Texas, October of 1899, through boyhood to early manhood in Oklahoma City, Buddy was athletically prone, with football his favorite sport. He enlisted at eighteen and it was in France that he met "Hezi" Tate, an assistant to C.B. DeMille. At World War One's end he attended Columbia University in New York. Special studies were advertising and journalism and a life class under George Bridgman at the Art Students League."

Other bits of Buddy's early life evolved as we talked. Loving parents, devoted sisters, a talented mother who could well have become a concert pianist, a 1910 introduction to airplanes which planted a determination to learn to fly (he did in 1928, owning his own plane for many years), the always insistent urge to swim across, not just in a lake or river; the love of horses, dogs, all animals. A pretty active normal boyhood with any and all sports occupying first call after such interfering inconveniences as lawn-mowing and other chores.

A pet preachment of this book's author which you will find throughout its pages, "Do the unusual and reap dividends," has been practiced by its preacher on numerous occasions, two of which he told of and which prove the point. On a twenty-five cent bet ~ but let Mr. Gillespie tell it . . .

"Well, the bet was made that I couldn't climb the face of a building, to, up and over the projecting cornice. Quite a crowd collected here on 113th Street between Broadway and Riverside Drive. The reach-out-grab, free swing and pull up over this last obstacle was perspiringly negotiated. A telephone call the following Fall extended to me a dinner invitation from a Mrs. Brown. Who was Mrs. Brown? I accepted and found that she had been one of those milling below during my death defying building climbing stunt. The dividends? Many wonderful meals and two charming daughters."
"Ample proof" says Buddy, "of values often gained by doing

the unusual."

The second episode had to do with an unorthodox climb up a vertical wall at the Grand Canyon. No easy Bright Angel trail route for Buddy. This on his first trip from New York to California and to his post-Columbia first California job, selling automobiles. At the top, a lookout point, three people, one a woman, gazing out at grandeur unsurpassed, were suddenly startled by the appearance of one hand coming up over the ledge to grasp a pipe railing. Buddy followed, the lady fainted and after revival, this little unusualness led to his first car sale to one of the three. The dividend here, a nice fat commission.

It was through his army pal, "Hezi" Tate, that Buddy initially affiliated himself with the movies. He tells of this early C.B. DeMille schooling in a later Chapter.

The reader may be interested in a "figure" log of Buddy's career from the first 1922 DeMille *Manslaughter* with Leatrice Joy and Thomas Meighan, to his last post-retirement donation to M.G.M. of a few days work on *Glass Bottom Boat* with Doris Day. *How the West Was Won*, *Ben-Hur* and *Mutiny on the Bounty* were three of the late bigger ones - Effectswise. His Art Direction credits to 1963 total 84 and Special Effects credits total - quite a backlog of experience represented here. Well do I remember personally *Test Pilot* and *Captains Courageous*, among many others. Particularly a wet episode in the latter.

Academy of Motion Picture Arts and Sciences recognition includes, in the Effects category, thirteen nominations (two pictures only are nominated annually) and four "Oscars."

Miss Hepburn told me of a large picture in Buddy's office of a St. Bernard. "That was Joppa," Buddy explained, "A wonderful dog - my constant companion during the early days at M.G.M. --- no, he's gone."

"'But not really gone,' Buddy Explained. 'Solitary walks in the quiet mountains back of our home, usually at night become wonderful memory treks. My mother and father and a sister are there, Joppa is there and our young son Tom is there. We seem to walk together ---.' And there it is, really. That's Buddy Gillespie. Nothing stumps him. I wonder if the solid foundation of love and security which gave him life did not also give him the nerve to springboard into the realms of the impossible. Is that why George Cukor, when I asked him, what do you know about Buddy Gillespie?, replied, 'Well, you know - men in that job - they're not like anybody you ever met. There's a faraway look in the eye. They act as though they had a secret - like the Sphinx. And they have.'"

Perhaps knowing some of the facets of the author's life make the perusal of his book a bit more personal. I know the student will receive instructive benefits and I believe I can vouch for Buddy's hopes that movie personnel in whatever bent, and layment wherever, will find that its reading affords enjoyment. I use the word "enjoyment" because Buddy has stressed every time we've talked, what enjoyment his career has given him. And I, in my career, have felt great, great enjoyment. It is when all is said and done, a wonderful business - fun to do, fun to write about and he hopes fun to read about.

Spencer Tracy & Katharine Hepburn, 1965

Adam's Rib, Paramount Production #461, Released 1923, AAG Contribution: Assistant Art Director.

Manslaughter, Paramount Production #437, Released 1922, AAG Contribution: Set Design.
- Courtesy The DeMille Special Collection

CHAPTER ONE
~
"1922 NEOPHYTE"

Manslaughter, Paramount Production #437, Released 1922, AAG Contribution: Set Design.

For the record and in the interest of accuracy, "Eight Months with C.B. DeMille" should have preceded the "Forty-two Years at M.G.M." in the title of this book. It was my first "exposure", those eight months in 1922, to that which proved to be a totally unanticipated plunge into this fascinating, glamorous, challenging, demanding, crazy, idiotic and rewarding business of picture making. Choose any adjective. It will apply.

The eight-month association with Mr. DeMille started as a two-weeks' lark. A job as draftsman for Mr. Paul Irebe, C.B.'s talented and excitable French Art Director who was then engaged in the preparation of *Manslaughter*, to star Leatrice Joy and Thomas Meighan.

I had known Mr. DeMille's assistant, Cullen Tate, or Hezy as he was more commonly known, during mutual sloughing through the 1917-18 mud of France in order that the World might be made "safe for Democracy..." (Historians, please note!). On a visit to the old Paramount, Famous Players Lasky lot, early in 1922, I jokingly asked Hezy if there was an opening of some kind at the studio. There was, as a T-Square pusher (draftsman), for two weeks and two weeks only! With no further ado and for twenty five dollars a week plus no overtime, I went to work.

Eight months later, (not two weeks!) but eight months of seven-day weeks, twelve to fourteen hour days, many eighteen and twenty hours and with two pictures, *Manslaughter* and

Adam's Rib completed, Hezy's war-time friend had run quite the most diversified gamut pertaining to the "physical" facets or Art Department functions of a major picture making unit that it would be possible to conceive. From kindergarten through grade, prep, college, graduate course and I would presume the equivalent of a Doctorate. I was at least exposed, generally involved and always a part of Mr. Irebe's operation, which, being a DeMille operation was, to understate it, quite an operation!

Yes indeed those eight months proved to be a cauldron of seething, purifying, molding, heartbreaking, wonderful experiences; a full course of strong back and strong mind activities during which we rested sparingly, ate hurriedly and worked the clock around and around.

We did many things. We designed and drafted at night; we "interior decorated" at night; we slept little at night. We were trouble shooters for Mr. DeMille by day; we would attend Miss Joy's flowing, diaphanous costume in the decadent Roman sequence of the production *Manslaughter* by day, always whenever or wherever she sat, lolled or reclined so that the folds of her skimpiness were graceful and lovely and would please the censors.

We did this by day and other things less enrapturing, such as piano moving. Once we "animal moved", I having grasped at the request of his trainer, one end of a six foot leash the other end of which was firmly attached to the jeweled collar of a full-grown, well-toothed tiger! This also during the decadent Roman sequence, as at eventide the trainer was attempting to coax with the help of the Art Department, or rather one representative of that department, this beautiful, but big animal into his too small cage. The resultant lunge, not toward his cage, tested extremely well the agility of one A.A.G. In later years during multiple "Tarzans", this proved to be a lesson well learned.

We watched and served the Master by day, fulfilling his multiple whims. I use the word "Master" not facetiously, for C.B. was truly the master, overflowing with top talents, not only as a picture maker, but quite often as an expounder of "wise words" to various members of his staff, usually delivered in oratorical fury, often with an open-mouthed gathering of visitors, complete crew and always that one poor, luckless, culprit.

I recall vividly being that culprit on one occasion when dear old Cecil in rare and violent form expressed loudly his hope that "~whoever moved that rock, I hope he dies of snake-bite!, and I hope his cousins die of snake-bite!, and his uncles and his aunts die of snake-bite!, and his, etc., etc., etc., die of snake-bite!~" This tirade having been launched, because at the request of Theodore Kosloff, I had moved a small boulder in a running stream during the shooting of a prehistoric sequence in Adam's Rib. Kosloff was a satyr or something and came dancing and flitting through our sylvan set, hopping across the stream enroute. That rock move gave Ann Bauchens, C.B.'s script girl, some good material to feed the Master at the end of the shooting day. She must have observed it early in the morning for that is when it was moved. Knowing it would really make no difference, she waited until the day's work was done so that Mr. DeMille could claim it would not match the previous day's shooting.

These vehement discourses were always highly dramatic elocutionary masterpieces, full of intended venom; a preachment designed to plant the fear of the great leather-putteed "god" firmly into each quivering fiber of everyone on the payroll. C.B.'s success in this department pretty well matched his many other successes and he was respectfully detested by many. Including yours truly.

It was years before I came to know that these tirades were mostly tongue-in-cheek. Mr. DeMille did achieve unwavering discipline and a sense of humor, I presume, albeit a bit unusual, was served. Perhaps the same ego that demanded these shows of personal authority, was mainly responsible for the great record of this very remarkable man. I am as sure that he really wanted no one to "die of snake-bite", as I am of the great respect and admiration he commanded from all, throughout his long and outstanding career. He probably is at this moment, from his formidable director's chair somewhere in that land of harps and flowing white robes, in the midst of delivering a heavenly bombast to his own crew of Angels. At the same time undoubtedly leaving instructions for the purchase of brand new eighteen carat wings for each and every one of them. A belated thank you, Mr. DeMille, for a liberal education, a most rewarding eight months and a highly developed capacity for growing a thick skin and for having learned to function sans sleep while fending off the wolf with that weekly twenty-five dollar check. I have always considered those eight months a bargain. The tuition was free.

And what has this to do with Special (Visual) Effects? The casual reader or the serious student will both be subject to many diversions from straight technical detail during the perusal of this volume. In fact such detail will be purposely minimized.

I am convinced, after these many years, that practically all experiences in whatever field can play a profitable part in the "thinking out of solutions" pertaining to the vast scope of demands covered by the variety of problems which wend their way sooner or later into the often confused mind of the so-called Head Special Effector. He must come up with a practical, three-dimensional, photographable solution ~ at a price! ~ and as per a schedule!

The latter two items have usually been at least half of our headaches and the "War" that has waged hot and heavy between the "small" bookkeepers and the Effect creators could many times have been recorded into really outstanding and <u>very special</u> effects, particularly of the Audible variety. For limited release only, however, and usually recommended for Adults only. These conflicts are generally among at least semi-friends and there is seldom a winner. Vindictiveness rarely develops. If it does occasionally soil the atmosphere, seldom does it last. In my long experience only once has this stupid state persisted and I share the blame for its continuance. As a matter of fact I relished its continuance and nourishment, probably because somewhere in the early history of my forebears, the memory genes of an elephant became somehow imbedded. I heartily condemn this school-girlish indulgence and I hope you young men and women who are considering a career in this phase of M. P. or T. V., will never be confronted with a like situation. Unless of course you do meet such an aforesaid "small" individual, in which case, have fun!

The reference to any and all experiences being of possible value in the "<u>how</u> do we do <u>this</u> one" department, can perhaps be more thoroughly understood by jotting down a few of the Effect problems that have come our way. Before doing this, however, may I delay these specifics for a paragraph to point out that the word "our" in the preceding sentence has special significance. As in the Foreword, I again stress the fact that our chores are seldom a one-man job. The successful skipper usually is showered with most of the plaudits and far be it from any normal skipper not to accept his share. But never has <u>this</u> one forgotten the abundance of help, both mentally and physically, available to him. This help is essential and prospective Effect tyros will please note that totally "do-it-yourself" attitudes will become the most efficient grave-digging tools of which I can think. The only detail to be added would be your own epitaph which perhaps might be engraved on a remote tombstone as follows:

"MAY HE LIE, THIS GUY – STIFF AND PRONE
AS HE TRAVELLED AND WORKED,
ALONE, ALONE
IT'S AN ODDS-ON BET HE SHUNS COMPLETE
ANY OFFER OF HELP FROM EVEN HELP
FROM ST. PETE."

<u>Our</u> problems have ranged from a sequence in an oldie, titled *Yellow Jacket* whereby a malaria-laden mosquito is close-upped as he crawls through a hole in a screened window to the 'Bomb' over Hiroshima in one not so old, released under the title, *The Beginning or the End*, a story of the development and use of the Atom Bomb. We built both the mosquito and the bomb. The mosquito in this case was <u>not</u> a miniature. He was mechanized and some thirty times full-sized. The bomb <u>was</u> a miniature and although it and its delivery represented in scope one of the most expansive of scenes we had yet done, the method finally used involved a scale much, much smaller than that used in most miniatures of all types and categories.

Following chapters will document these and many other problem sequences in, I hope, a manner interesting and instructive. In fact generally, the format of this book will be to chroniclize in some detail the many unusual Special Effect stints which have found their way into the author's domain in activity during his long association with M.G.M. As indicated heretofore, there will be a dearth of out-and-out technical formulae simply because this kind of information is almost always available from the many specialists employed by the average studio or obtainable on the outside. It should be obvious that the mind which is cluttered with too much "how" detail will be severely handicapped in its thinking of what <u>should</u> be done. Imaginative creativity, with its fluid and elastic approach to an effect sequence, should never be completely dominated by the "how" problems. That is why we often turn to specialists.

It may be, and often is, necessary to compromise for practical reasons ranging from cost and schedule (those two ugly words again) to a possible lack of availability of one or more individualized experts. Other than having in mind a reasonably clear preliminary determination of method, the man at the helm must be free in his initial approach to these problems, to let his fancy fly free and his dramatic inventiveness run absolutely unhindered.

Often the solution is born out of a seemingly nonsense whirlpool of ideas ranging <u>really</u> from the sublime to the ridiculous. An example; how could a crocodile have anything to do with our sequence which dealt with the atom bomb? Or why did coffee relate to locusts in the production of *Good Earth*? Well, it and they did as you will discover in later chapters.

The point of this digression, one which I cannot too strongly stress to any potential aspirant who may be regarding these contents as a serious text book and guide towards a Special Effect career, is the importance of the above-described "loose" approach. Any athlete knows that a prelude to top performance entails this physical (and mental) state. There will be "milk-the-grey-matter-dry" advice, repeated many times in the detailed telling of many step by step effect sequence histories described hereafter. This totally uninhibited and thorough, even sometimes wild, thinking process, is the real key. A few simple examples could be that if the camera normally would be thought of as in an upright position, what would happen if it were inverted? Perhaps an "upside down" set might better solve a problem such as sudden loss of earth gravity, or whatever. Maybe doing things backwards and reversing film. Should the object move or should the camera move? Why does "level" have to always be level? Which way is up? When can horizontal become vertical? And day become night? Suppose the negative (film) becomes the positive. Would <u>that</u> help? And on and on. Never fear to think real crazy. The unorthodox approach <u>sometimes</u> works.

C.B. directing our 'dinosaur' bones in *Adam's Rib*. - Courtesy The DeMille Special Collection.

Before closing this chapter and while we are still back in 1922 a bit of the DeMille lore should be included herewith. A sequence in the modern portion of his *Adam's Rib*, was to be staged in the Dinosaur Hall of a Museum of Natural History. It had been my job to make working drawings of the skeletons of several of these prehistoric monsters. One was a Triceratops Elatus or Horned Dinosaur, about twenty-four feet long; one a Stegosaurus Ungulatus of the approximate same length; a huge Tyrannosaurus who, standing on his hind legs, towered some twenty feet above the floor of Stage 4; several other smaller inhabitants of this prehistoric era and a magnificent Brontosaurus Rex some sixty-odd feet in length, startlingly impressive in its white, bony, monumental bulk. Altogether a striking achievement, a tremendous and effective set which drew lunch-hour visits from every department on the Lot. I was proud. Mr. DeMille was proud and Mr. Irebe was proud and the gentlemen of the Plaster Shop (the actual bone builders) were proud. Perhaps the only un-proud person in the organization was John Fisher, Mr. DeMille's assistant-in-charge of the Exchequer, who, typical of his type, was generally reduced to convulsive sobs at the sight of <u>any</u> cost. And here was a lot of cost!

So, as was bound to happen, Mr. DeMille alerted the Publicity Department and a big thing was brewed, (as Publicity Departments are wont to do) entailing among the ingredients,

a party of scientists from the local institutions of higher learning, the tallest in learning of whom was the most eminent archeologist obtainable in the area, a Doctor What-ever-his name-was, who, though statuesque in his knowledge of his subject, was physically puny. The large horn-rimmed glasses proved not to be an affectation. They were there for a purpose and that purpose was to see. We all soon saw!

As the party, the Doctor with Mr. DeMille, entourage et al, plus Paramount's' top ladies and gentlemen were ushered grandly into <u>our</u> set, the "ahs" and "ohs" elicited by the sudden revealment of these tremendously commanding assemblages of plaster bones, (an electrician, on cue, had switched on the kliegs) were definitely in the upper "ah and oh" class category. The reaction of all present, particularly Mr. DeMille was pleasant to behold -- but short-lived! In fact so short-lived that scarcely had the flicker of the lights settled, before those thick lenses revealed to the Doctor that much was amiss!, that grave errors were in evidence!, that apparently "Pre-historia" had been dealt with much too lightly and that Mr. DeMille didn't know a vertebra from a ~, from a ~, well, his knowledge of a vertebra was emphatically nil.

Quickly the little professor conveyed those large horn-rimmed specks to the nearest dinosaur and, oblivious to a reddening-faced C.B., pointed to a handy vertebra and in a how-could-you-have-done-it manner, described to his host what really constituted a proper bone in <u>any</u> spinal column! Yes, the spine part was fair, but what about the rib facet?! And the pedicel! ~ totally malformed; the lamina, Mr. DeMille, the lamina resembled more the lamina of an enlarged nightingale! The body of the vertebra was perhaps possible but the transverse and articular processes were in such a shape as to have never served their normal functions even abnormally!

Our Brontosaurus Rex would have been not only a hopeless cripple but the laughing stock of all the other dinosaurs in the neighborhood, except of course, the others depicted in all their bony splendor, standing there, now rather dejected looking, on the shiny floor of the Museum set on Stage Four.

There became audible in the sudden silence of our set, (silent because the doctor had stopped lecturing and was now headed determinedly towards number two, momentarily speechless) a few embarrassed clearings of the throat noises from the uneasy invited guests.

Now the word Brontosaurus comes from "bronto", combining form of the Greek "bronte", thunder, plus "saurus" which has something to do with a lizard. Well, no Greek thunder could have ever been generated with greater potential than the thunder being at that moment generated in the heart, the soul, the mind and the very being of Cecil B. DeMille. I barely heard, during a hastily determined and acted upon decision to leave by a little known utilities door exit, C.B.'s controlled stentorian as he explained to the honest Doctor that in the movies the camera seldom sees these details and for the sake of expediency (certainly not expense) his designers had "purposely omitted a few pedicels, a lamina or two, etc., etc." On the last "etcetera" I thought I detected a quavering distant rumble in the Master's voice ~ and I was right! But why at this late date, some forty-three years later, recall unpleasantnesses, disasters and tragedies? The sequence <u>was</u> shot and not one fan letter of protest was ever made public.

There were other skirmishes, many more orations beautifully detonated and never repetitious, delivered by the Head Man with yours truly never being neglected too long during that eight months' attendance at the DeMille Academy. One was the ordering of a brand new material to cover some fifteen thousand square feet of a prehistoric forest set in the same Adam's Rib. This was an artificial grass, newly invented and made in San Francisco. It was trade-marked "grass-mat" and just exactly what Mr. Irebe and his first assistant Art

Our green-dyed excelsior 'grass' as C.B. instructs Elliott Dexter as he and Pauline Garon set out cave man scene. "This lady cave girl has tripped and fallen out of a tree into your arms. You have laid aside the world's first bow and arrow long enough to revive her." - Courtesy The DeMille Special Collection.

Director, Chester Gore, needed for their primeval, tree covered, hill and dale set, again on Stage Four.

I was the patsy. I signed the order. The four dollars a square foot was not only in fine print but even had it been legible-sized type, it seemed cheap. Four dollars? Four dollars for grass for Mr. DeMille? In today's vernacular it would have seemed to be strictly "no sweat!" Or so I thought, until literally steaming and flying and fuming and skidding down the corridor waving a purchase requisition for SIXTY THOUSAND DOLLARS' worth of grass with the signature "Arnold Gillespie" modestly engraved thereunto in the proper place, came the nervous Mr. Fisher. He had not been reduced to just sobbing at this one. He had been elevated to a degree of seething, smoking pressure which exploded into a snorting bellow, "What's this?!!!", which, though John's voice would be normally classified in the high pitched category, was for the instant a penetrating, rasping and grating angry, deep-throated roar.

Distance in time as well as miles often develops a tendency towards exaggeration. Suffice it to say that Mr. Fisher was at least mildly upset! And suffice it to say that Mr. Fisher was of course right. His dedicated thoroughness in perusing all the figures in the right hand column saved a quick sixty thousand and probably had the grass really materialized, a quicker finish to the budding career of yours truly. Occasionally, I must confess, the knights of the dollar sign are not only essential, they are downright provident. A belated thanks, Mr. Fisher.

The order was cancelled and we covered the area with green-dyed excelsior held down by chicken wire which in turn was cover-dressed by grass clippings, sawdust, some moss, everybody's old leaves raked from anybody's home lawn for free, plus bits of bark and five thousand six to eight feet long fern fronds per day, supplied by Joe Evergreen, a Japanese who did this sort of thing for studios ~ at a price. These latter came from San Francisco vicinity; and were trucked nightly into our prehistoric forest.

The trees, the bark of which, like the bones of our dinosaurs, was also by the Plaster Department. They were from nineteen to twenty-four feet in diameter, the working drawings for which, were drawn by the same member of Paul Irebe's Art Department as the one who had drawn the bones. No botanist, no arboreal professor or expert, was suggested by Mr. DeMille to the Publicity Department nor by the Publicity Department to Mr. DeMille, as a possible invitee to Stage Four, this time! The set was beautiful, however, and quietly serene and peaceful. Only once did it echo to those imaginative phrases, "I hope they all die of snake bite!"

In concluding the 1922 DeMille era of the author's

Theodore Kosloff - C.B. - Jeanie and Paul Iribe - Courtesy DeMille Special Collections.

initial baptism into the movies, a quote from the Motion Picture News of September 30, 1922, might well have been a prediction of things to come. In the review of *Manslaughter* by Laurence Reid, he goes on to say "~The pretty, wealthy and high-strung disciple of speed and jazz; has been arrested for stepping on the gas. She bribes the officer. And when he attempts to arrest her again~to give her back the bracelet, she swerves the car into a side road and he is catapulted through space when he is unable to make the turn on his motorcycle. Here is the outstanding scene of the picture. A tremendous punch.— " End quote.

The underlining is mine, but it serves to show that special effects often do walk away with top or near top laurels. This particular one was a dilly ~ "outstanding scene in the picture" ~ and I had been a part of it! What the reviewer failed to note was the fact that at the crossroad where Miss Joy swerved her high-speed vehicle was a large 24 sheet "break-a-way" billboard which we had erected to intercept the hurtling stunt man's body as it soared over the hood and beyond her Dusenberg. I don't recall whether his flight carried him through our billboard or not, but I do recall my contribution to this early "full sized" effect, I had drafted the sign and composed the copy, a huge ad which blazoned forth, "Gillespie Candies ~ Sold exclusively at - Albert Arnold and Sons." The fact that my name was (and is) Albert Arnold Gillespie probably had some bearing on the brand name of the product and the name of the exclusive retailer. My choice of the product was undoubtedly a fondness for candy. The difference between its consumption then and now, however, is dictated by an ordinary, inexpensive yellow tape measure.

In any event this was a first introduction to the staging of a particular piece of physical dramatics. And though the author's association was limited primarily to that of a sweet-toothed and successful attempt at publicity, the scene and sequence did move Mr. Reid in his review to a most complimentary coverage of one of the then untitled skills and crafts to be later known as Special Visual Effects. And, may I add that throughout the making of the many motion pictures requiring "effect sequences," often the real star has turned out to be the earthquake, the tornado, storm at sea or whatever, in its newsreel realism and the exciting audience interest which well done Special Effects generate.

So lessons in this first chapter probably include: be not afraid of long hours and short pay; think, think and think; seek any and all experiences; don't be ever a "know-it-all"; share credit and "sail a happy ship"; beware of thick-lensed professors and above all never underrate the box office power of top Special Effects. ~And thoroughly analyze all purchase requisitions before signing!

END OF CHAPTER ONE

Elaborate *Manslaughter* set design complete with bejeweled tigers and a lesson learned about agile handling of the canine filled cats. - Courtesy The DeMille Special Collection

Ben-Hur: A Tale of the Christ, MGM Production #200, Released 1925, AAG Contribution: Set Design.

CHAPTER TWO

~

"GALLEYS AND JUTTING CHINS"

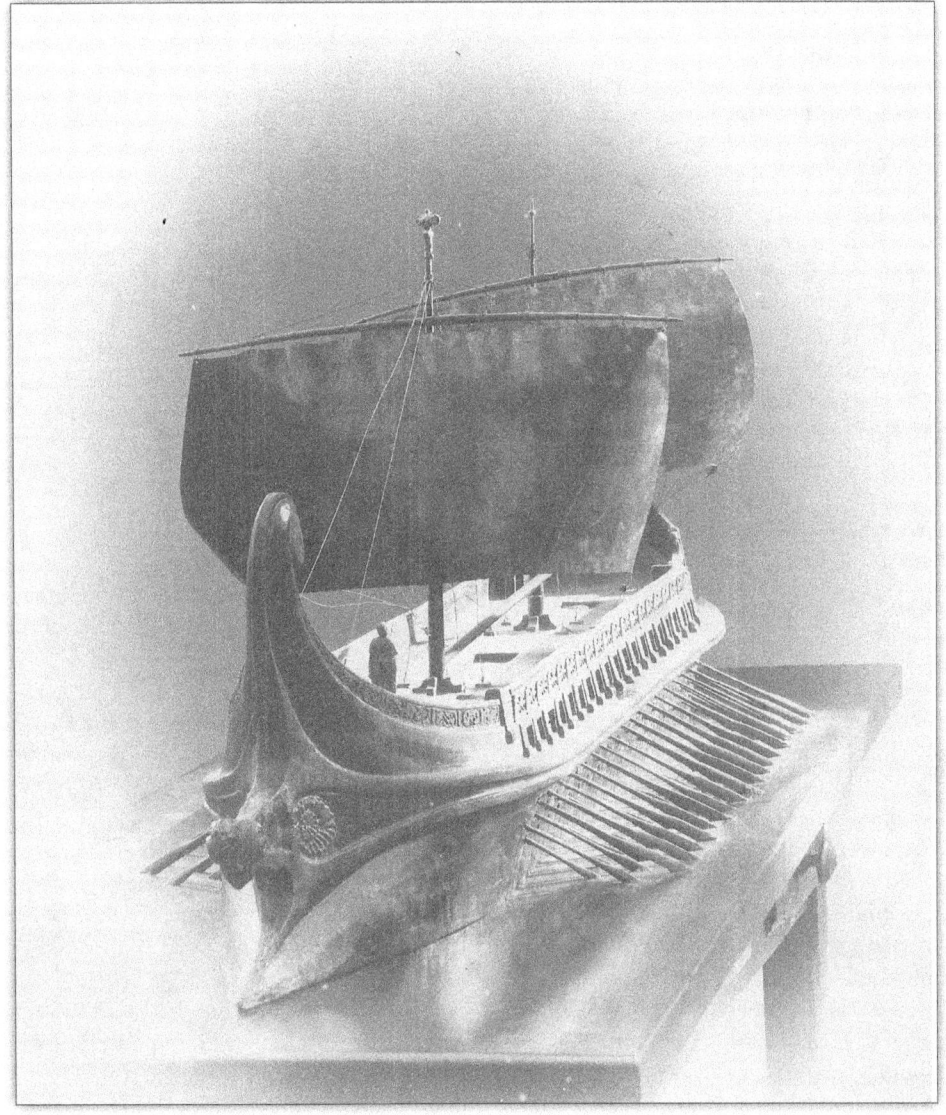

Reference model used during building of full size flagship.

As heretofore indicated, the terra "Special Effects" came into being long after some quite remarkable examples of the art had been accomplished in many early motion pictures. Crude but effective camera tricks, often ingenious, would today have found their way into the Optical Effects category, one of the five categories into which the Special Visual Effects science or art is divided. These categories were determined by a committee appointed by the Academy of Motion Picture Arts and Sciences (the progenitors of the now very famous "Oscar") consisting mostly of Effect men. I was privileged to serve on that committee which originated in 1938, and as of this date in 1966, am still a member.

Our breakdown of categories was as follows: Miniatures, Full Sized Mechanical, Transparency Projection Process, Optical and Matte Paintings. A sixth category, Animation (with limitations) was adopted by the Committee in 1964. These categories will be fully explained during the course of this volume as they apply to actual documented problems and solutions.

However, as mentioned at the beginning of this chapter, many of the then unnamed "effect methods" were used. A particular one I shall never forget, occurred during the making of *Ben-Hur*, the early 1923, '24, '25 version. Off the coast Livorno, Italy, as we were shooting the Galley sequence in which the Roman fleet is attacked by a pirate fleet of Macedonians, an Effect sequence of quite some magnitude was staged.

Fred Niblo was the Director and, as perhaps a few of you may remember, Ramon Novarro played Ben Hur, Francis X. Bushman was Messala, May McAvoy played the daughter of the Hur's trusted "C. P. A.", Carmel Myers, Kitty Key, Ben Hur's sisters, and Claire McDowell, Ben's mother, were some of the cast. Numerous cameramen, among them John Boyle, Percy Hilburn, Karl Struss, and Ben Reynolds, exposed many feet of black and white <u>and</u> color negative. (The last half of the picture was in color – an unusual combination, though years later *Wizard of Oz* started in black and white). The Art Director was Horace Jackson who had been sent to Italy in the Fall of '23 by Cedric Gibbons, M.G.M.'s famous Art Department Head, to act as an assistant to an Italian art director who had been contracted to design the picture. It was not long after Jackson's arrival in Rome that the Signore faded and Jackson became chief. I was made his assistant and from late 1923 clear through to March of 1925, Italy was our stomping ground.

It was in March of the year 1924, that M.G.M. was born. One of the determining factors of this birth had to do with our struggling *Ben-Hur* and that ugly word "cost." The then-called "Goldwyn" Studio in Culver City, California, M.G.M.'s future and only home up to the date of this writing, had started the project on a budget of four hundred thousand dollars. A completely different director, cast and staff than the ones previously mentioned, had been given the responsibility of this tremendous undertaking, but within a very short time the whole caboodle were shipped back State-side, and most of the four hundred thousand had dwindled. The lone exceptions to those sent back were H. Jackson, Art Director, his assistant, (that was I) and Harry Edington, Business Manager. And by the way, what a swell person was Harry! Not at all in the "small" bookkeeper class. We three stayed in Rome and greeted contingents from Culver City arriving almost daily on practically every incoming ship. In addition to Mr. Niblo, et al, was Carey Wilson and Bess Meredith, writers who were there to tidy up the original June Mathis' script. We who had stayed started anew if not afresh with our recently-arrived compatriots.

This is not a complete saga of the first *Ben-Hur* movie, although mighty interesting reading it could be, so we'll get back to Livorno and the Galleys. I had been sent by Jackson to Livorno with instructions to have all the Galleys ready, ship-shape and straining at their anchors within twelve days. The shooting company would arrive at that time to start the cameras grinding, etc.

I must interject at this moment the fact that we had started the sequence with the first group previously in Anzio where our original fleet had been built. When the extensive studio and management switch occurred it was decided to add a flag ship to the fleet. The facilities of Fratelli Neri in Livorno, some two hundred miles up the Mediterranean

Testing to see if the pirate ships were seaworthy.

north of Anzio were chosen for this addition, and also because they were better equipped to handle the actual shooting of the sequence.

In Anzio, before the first attempt at shooting, however the authorities had questioned the stability of our various craft and outlined a test procedure. They were particularly concerned as to what would happen if a hundred or so milling Roman and Macedonian actors and extras would inadvertently congregate on one side of the deck. Several of the port officials were confident that "she'd turn turtle and a big tragedy would happen."

So they put one hundred nice healthy Italians aboard one of the vessels, towed it out into the harbor and the brave one hundred were instructed to run from port to starboard to port to starboard to port until a "rocking chair" motion was generated. It was generated all right, and it almost did succeed in putting her on her beam's end. I think the uniformed observers, safely aboard a nearby tug, were disappointed that their prediction of chaos and calamity was not fulfilled.

And, they were still not satisfied. What, they asked, would happen if one of the Roman marines, resplendent and weighty in his studio-made armor and helmet, should fall overboard? He would surely sink, said they. So they tested this prediction by shoving overboard a fully armor-plated volunteer, helmet and all, and this time they were right. He sank. Fortunately someone had had the foresight to attach a small hawser about mid-section, just below the breast armor, and he was hoisted

Per gentile concessione di Corrado Neri e la famiglia Neri.

within a reasonable length of time from the cool muddy waters of Anzio harbor.

In the end, the stability doubters were proved at least partially right, because upon my arrival in Livorno I found our entire fleet in the water just off the Neri boat works, resting serenely on the bottom. Only the masts and parts of the superstructures were visible. That they had not withstood the two-hundred mile tow was quite evident!

Our large new "flagship" was still in the early stages of construction, resting unconcernedly on its ways, not yet aware that in twelve (12) days she must be afloat, fully seaworthy, thoroughly shaken down and ready for the cameras of a brand new organization which had been christened Metro-Goldwyn-Mayer. Nor did the rest of the fleet whose keels rested quite peacefully on and in the bottom mud of the harbor know what was in store for them. And as for Mr. Tito Neri, head of Fratelli (Brothers) Neri, his reaction upon my informing him of the proposed schedule, was one of aghast shock. But only for a moment. Then he smiled and shrugged his shoulders and waited for more. "How many men do you have employed on this job?" I asked. "One hundred and fifty" he answered. "Double it," said I.

That was the beginning of one of the most rewarding relationships of my entire life. He loves to tell the story to this day, of Sig. Gillespie saying, "Double it!", and then Tito's old eyes sparkle just as they did that first of the twelve days allotted to us in which to float a fleet in late September, 1924.

We doubled and we tripled and we spent twenty-four hours a day on the job sleeping on straw ticks on a cold concrete floor. Tito Neri, the head of an important boat and salvage operation, with a fleet of tug boats and small cargo craft that plied the Mediterranean; a big man in Livorno, but not too big to take his cat naps on that cold hard floor during those days and nights, alongside an enthusiastic tyro assistant to the Ben-Hur Art Director who had said simply, "Have 'em ready to shoot in twelve days."

We did not succeed. It took us, and four hundred opera-singing, non-clock watching, wonderful Italian workers, fourteen (14) days! On that day the Rome contingent, headed by Fred Niblo accompanied by his charming wife, former actress Enid Bennett, Novarro, Bushman, and the rest, arrived in Livorno.

Our proud Fleet, the new Flagship, and every last muddy-keeled Anzio-fabricated galley, was stretched pretty majestically across the Mediterranean, this time on top of the water. An absolutely remarkable accomplishment for which Tito and his men, particularly his top foreman, Penco, deserve ninety-eight percent of the credit. The remaining two percent I claim, if for no other reason than partial compensation for attempted sleep on that lumpy straw tick. The chill noisy draft-laden cement also was not conducive to comfort or slumber.

Such problems as where to paint the huge designs on the new galley's sails, largest ever fabricated in Italy we were told, were always somehow solved. In the case of the sails, the Livorno Opera House floor was chosen, necessitating the tedious removal of all the seats. But remove them we did and the big pieces of canvass were ready for the painters. After all the trouble and expense of preparing this improvised sail loft I thought it would be wise to produce an extra set of sails, in case of an emergency. The order, sans an authorized go ahead from either Rome or Culver City, was given. The duplicate set was made, stowed aboard and my expensive secret remained secure with the top man of Fratelli Neri, dependable Tito.

One brisk day after some two weeks of shooting, it became no longer necessary to keep this dark and wasteful deed under cover. I was below deck trying to keep three tiers of rowers, a total of seventy-five starboard and seventy-five port, in some degree of unison as they propelled our ship during the shooting of scenes, when the largest of the two sails split with a bang and a long r-r-r-i-i-p! And did this prove to be my day in the sun!

Before Mr. Niblo's frantic launch arrived 'long side, the culprit sail was being unbended (which is salty language meaning "removed"). The calm smile with which I greeted the arrival of the gentlemen of the brass (which included along with Mr. Niblo and his script-girl, 'Stan' Partridge, the Latin American Al Lena, our unit Production Manager, and others) not only must have seemed, under the circumstances,

The flagship in it's full majesty and a new sail.

Filming the "Flag Ship" - Courtesy of Photoplay Productions.

Tito's salvage crew at work on a sinking galley. -Per gentile concessione di Corrado Neri e la famiglia Neri.

incongruous, it apparently added fuel to the agitated despair of the white faces staring up at my Cheshire cat grin. "What'll we do?!" ~ "This is terrible!!" ~"How many days' delay?" ~ "Call Rome!!" ~ "Call Culver City!", and finally, "Why are you smiling?!!!"

This last was well timed as at that moment the spare in all its secret glory was broken out of its hideaway locker and a very efficient crew was proceeding to "bend" it properly to the mammoth yard which had been lowered to near deck level. "Bend" is just as salty as "unbend" and I revelled in nautical delight as I proclaimed to those below, "We are now bending the SPARE mainsail abaft the mainmast, Sir. Only a few minutes delay, Sir, and it will be bent!"

Mr. Niblo was naturally delighted and although I am sure Mr. Lena really shared his feelings, I am equally sure that an inner controversy raged at least mildly within the bookkeeping, production cost innards of Al's breast as to just what did those extra sails cost and who authorized them. I am sure Mr. Lena's thoughts were somewhat like, "The day was saved, yes, but I must make a note of this. I must find out about this. I must, etc."

On another day during the shooting of the battle, we rammed (by design) Arrius' Flagship with one of the smaller Pirate Galleys. The resultant hole in her side, just above the waterline, became "just below" the water line by the time we had towed the vessel back to Neri's shipyard. When she arrived at her berth the decks were awash and not only was the large, newly-rammed hole totally immersed, but also one-hundred and fifty oar holes were well below the water line!

Another calamity, or so it seemed to all of us, I had not ventured so far in my unauthorized daring as to have had a spare Flagship handy. However a reputation had been established, albeit out of "sail cloth" and at twenty-four years of age the fool rushed in where wiser angels would certainly have feared to tread. (I must admit that before my comment to Niblo and Company, all of whom were there, again shaken, I had been given by Sig. Neri, an encouraging nod.) In any event a cheerful "We'll have her fixed by morning, Mr. Niblo, Sir," was my parting remark as they all left, including the dubious Mr. Lena, drawn face and all. We, Tito and company stayed and went to work.

Our badly wounded Flagship had to be patched, pumped out, repaired and refloated. This entailed first the removal of one-hundred and fifty oars, all of them tied in a network together 'tween decks and all of them nicely submerged in the cold October night water of Tito's boat basin. Out came the divers with their old-fashioned round copper-helmeted suits, each with its own air pumper; out came the underwater tools and out came the large coffee pots that were ever-present and never emptied - just replenished. The ingredients, half coffee and half cognac. Always there was Tito and Penco directing, organizing, accomplishing.

That night's job is a treasured remembrance. All the facilities of a modern shipyard concentrating on the mending of a damaged two-thousand-year-old Roman Galley. A replica, to be sure, but the romance of those long, dark, cold hours of muffled, eerily lit activity seemed to make her just as real as though her keel had actually been laid in the days of the Caesars.

By 7:30 a.m. the ship was again whole, the pumps had done their job, the oars reinstalled and linked and again a shooting schedule emerged unscathed - saved, not by the bell, but by Tito Neri and his fabulous crew.

Tito Neri (center) dressed in black, Corrado Neri (his first son), Ilva (Corrado's wife), their four sons: Tito, Piero, Algerina, Luisa and the author - circa 1950s.
Per gentile concessione di Corrado Neri e la famiglia Neri.

If there are any lessons in these two episodes, the damaged ship and the wind-split sail, certainly one is that a relationship between the givers and the takers of orders must be one of great mutual respect. Tito's men worked as a prideful part of Fratelli-Neri as was evidenced throughout my association, and particularly whenever an emergency developed. These fellows always seemed to put the job ahead of any other consideration and I am sure an important part of their reward was their own sense of self-satisfaction. And if this sounds "square" lets all hope for less roundness.

Loyalty was a condition which prevailed and it was as honestly practiced by Tito as by his men. We should each of us, in any field, but especially one that requires as much cooperative effort as does this branch of movie making, be very aware of always honestly assuming this attitude. It cannot be successfully faked.

Another small lesson, relating to the "spare" sail incident, is perhaps a dangerous one, but one that should always be remembered. It could be titled "The unauthorized go-ahead" lesson. So often I have heard remarks such as, "Why should I take a chance?" or "So what! I wasn't told to do it," and many other like observations. Naturally judgment (your very best) should balance any gambles, but the old boy who said "Nothing ventured, nothing gained" said a big important mouthful.

There will be times and situations when you (I am addressing this particularly to prospective "effectors", although its application is unlimited) must rely and act on your own honest hunch or well thought-out judgment of what is best for the company in a particular situation, in spite of the fact that often the boss and the company may have withheld permission. They just plain don't always know, so you must occasionally, and honestly, move on your lonely own. You will rarely suffer as a result of the consequences. More often you will bask in well-deserved laurels. Further, you will find that most of your solution decisions and procedures are gambles anyway. No kind hearted genie, to my knowledge, has ever appeared offering a guaranty that your method determination is the right one. And those laurels, in which it is so pleasant to bask, will be few and far between, if your chin never protrudes. The fortitude it usually takes to place that chin in this vulnerable position can, however, be also monetarily rewarding to the extent that the "basking" is not confined solely to back slaps and bouquets. The weekly "green stuff" is most pleasant. And then, of course, it is within the realms of possibility that you might lose your job! This is highly unlikely, however, and in the long run well worth the gamble a jutting jaw entails.

But back to Livorno and the final big near tragic day when we burned and sank the large galley with some four hundred Italians and one lone Scotch Irish American assistant Art Director aboard.

For many days we had been casting (hiring) the four hundred to be divided about half and half between Roman Soldiers and Macedonian Pirates. They were to be paid an extra one hundred lire because of the hazards involved, and were thoroughly informed that it would be necessary to exit from the burning ship via the Mediterranean which would require a knowledge of swimming in deep water.

Apparently that extra hundred lire made many doubt our sincerity. And before the day was over it was discovered that quite some few non-buoyant Italians had yielded to temptation. Though they were almost totally inept at swimming or floating, they were remarkably vociferant in their pleadings, through dampened vocal chords, that they

had "non capisco!", and that "please would the Madonna or M.G.M. save them!" None offered to return the bonus of extra lire because they couldn't swim, though they had solemnly promised that they could.

The day had arrived and we anchored our humanity laden Flagship about a mile off the entrance to the harbor so that the prevailing wind blew from stern to prow. The purpose of this unorthodox positioning of the ship relative to wind direction was to restrict our planned fire to the forward part of the ship, as she sank aft.

The "company," cameras and all, were in various areas chosen for full photographic coverage and as two of us later discovered, a hasty retreat just in case! Signal flags from shore were to wave colored messages. Number three, green, meant all ready, start the fire, knock out the pre-weakened planks in the hull aft and commence the action on deck. The final one, red, was to signify that the cameras had finished and the rescue craft could move in to fulfill their mission. That red one must have been forgotten in the confusion. I think it was never flown.

It was my chore to manipulate the sequence of all preplanned physical steps, and to give the words "Go to it!" to the actors. (For some reason all assistant directors had turned up missing on this day. At least none were aboard.) Dressed as a Pirate, in order that the camera would not detect a usually plus-foured, sport-shirted individual running about the deck, and having duly observed the "go ahead" green flag vigorously waving some few thousand feet away, I descended quickly into the lower bowels aft, gave the order to a trembling 'Roman soldier' armed with a crowbar to knock out the planks already about three-quarters sawn through, so that the sea could enter. He did and it did, ~ with a white roar.

We both quickly climbed up to a point about midships where the maze of those three tiers of oars, interlaced and tied together in the vast interior below the main deck, created in the dimness, a web-like labyrinth of timber which though it was intended to burn later, became immediate fuel as we were very soon to find out.

We had filled the prow of the ship below decks with crates and barrels and inflammables, all thoroughly and freshly soaked with a mixture of naphthalene and benzine. A volatile tinder box, placed to ignite the forward part of the ship as water flooded the stern so that the final sight of her would be a blazing hundred feet or so of her beautiful eagle bow as her stern parts underwater would be pulling this flaming torch along with it to a watery grave, the surface of which would be generously dotted with the four hundred bobbing heads of those four hundred "expert" swimmers plus one M.G.M. employee dressed as a Pirate.

Another gentlemen, this one costumed as a fellow Macedonian had been stationed at a midship spot below decks armed with an ordinary Fourth of July Roman Candle, the kind that squirts fire balls for a hundred feet or so. This was our "igniter." Point it toward the fuel-soaked makings of that bonfire forward, light it with a match and the second part of the two steps necessary to put into high-gear the sinking flaming climax, would be completed.

I, in good Southern California Italian, gave him the order to light up. He smiled somewhat nervously, but pleasantly, and remained motionless as he wished me a good day too. My Southern California pantomime likewise failed, but with water rushing through the large hole that had been made aft, I had no choice but to risk hurting the feelings of my holder-of-the-fuse, by lighting the candle myself. (Fortunately no union jurisdictions were involved.) There was a swoosh, swoosh, swoosh, as the fireballs swished off in many directions, <u>none</u> towards the target. Finally, however, with a bit of steadying and directional aiming, one did get home, the resultant explosive roar of which was sufficient to cause us both to leave with alacrity. A hurried, over-shoulder running glance, as we raced for a stern hatch, assured me that any concern as to whether our ship would burn or not need not be at all worrisome.

As we emerged topside onto a sunlit area crowded with battling extras, (they had started "acting" without cue) the deck, even that far astern was already smoking and hot. This was <u>not</u> according to plan! What had happened was that our careful anchoring of the ship, intended to contain the fire forward because of the wind blowing from stern to prow, proved to be reacting in an exactly opposite manner. All of the oar holes, one hundred and fifty of them, served to create a reverse draft inside the ship and the fire raged very quickly towards the stem and throughout the vessel.

Our noble Livornese were doing the big fight scene with vigor and (as we had found out at the last minute) political intent. Only the previous day it had been discovered that in casting those extras to be Romans and those to be Pirates, there had been some dark doings. It seems that a fairly equal division of pro-Mussolinians wound up as Romans and anti-Mussolinians as Pirates. The alertness of one of the property crew, uncovered the startling fact that these gentlemen had been sharpening spears, swords and other weapons in preparation for the melee. Normally props such as these are purposely blunted in order that they be rendered as harmless as possible, but our gentlemen of rather opposite political views had other ideas. Fortunately we were able to restore the weapons to their original less lethal state but it was quite impossible to totally blunt the enthusiasm of the combatants as the four hundred went at it. Our burning ship proved to be the equalizer.

The seriousness of what was happening became increasingly apparent shortly after my arrival on deck. I recall vividly the duels being fought everywhere, many all too realistically, and I hoped my Macedonian costume would not mistakenly classify me as a supporter of either group. But all of this was short lived as real tragedy seemed to be in the making. Both pros and antis were quite suddenly faced with a common enemy, fire, and although this was known by all of them in advance, it was now that I became aware of those non-swimming, non-floating percentages of the four hundred.

Many were afraid to jump overboard, literally caught between fire and water. The flames, however, were always the prime mover. Over they would go, often with smoking wardrobe, and then immediately proceed to scramble, dogpaddle fashion, back to a hand hold somewhere on the side or stern of the sinking ship. As she slowly slipped further and further into the water the wild struggle for a higher something, <u>anything</u>, to grasp, became truly frightening.

Two huge rudders shaped like giant oars, the shafts of which were about the size of small telephone poles, extended from the stern on either side into the water. These soon became covered with a brawling, twisting, grasping mass of humanity. It seemed to me that here in the making, could be motion pictures' worst catastrophe. Many were still aboard in areas where the fire had not yet gained complete control. They were continuing the contest valiantly, either politically or histrionically. But even the die-hards were soon put to rout within varying short periods of time as heat, smoke and raw conflagration took over.

The red flag signal, which would have alerted the rescue craft, failed to wave. I prepared to personally abandon ship, as she seemed about ready to make her final fire laden plunge. I had no desire to be drawn down with her as she sank into the briny.

At this moment who should appear out of chaos, calmly removing his black business suit and vest, his black Homburg and his black shoes, piling them neatly, clothes carefully folded, on the hot, awash deck, just outside of the sail locker in which he had remained completely out of sight until then, but <u>Tito Neri</u>! Faithful Tito! He knew that I was to be aboard, the only actual M.G.M'er present and he had anticipated the probability of danger. Nothing was going to happen to his American "son" if he could help it and he was there for that purpose.

Stripping down to his long Italian underwear, my self-appointed protector smilingly suggested <u>immediate</u> departure and just as the tail end of our gallant Flagship, the Galley of Arrius, hissed and sizzled and sputtered into her fiery, watery grave, we dove overboard and headed for shore a mile or so away.

Many chapters could be written about this man Neri, none of which would do him full justice. I have seen him several times in recent years, the last time in April of 1967, and he is still the sturdy, straight, clear-eyed, remarkable person, though well in his eighties, that he was during those wonderful three months in the Fall of 1924. I doubt if this work will finish without further reference to Tito.

It was when I arrived ashore that I discovered the entire company, sensing the possibility of loss of life, had headed pell-mell for Rome. A strange law, existing at that time, was to the effect that a suspected culprit could be thrown into the dungeon with no immediate recourse, if apprehended within forty-eight hours of the supposed crime. After that time had elapsed he could appear with counsel to arrange bail or whatever and take steps for his defense, etc., etc. Knowing this, M.G.M's *Ben-Hur* contingent, complete except for two of us, had chosen to disappear. Little did they know that several carloads of Carbonari trailed them all the way to Rome, ready to make the forty-eight hour nab if and when actual loss of life was proved.

Dripping wet and cold, I was greeted by the lone remaining member of the troupe, (the other of the two M.G.M.ers left) Adolph Sidel, our man in charge of wardrobe. His was the responsibility of checking in all costumes and returning to their owners their rightful clothes and belongings. And hereby hangs the climactic finish of the events surrounding the day's activities. It was several days later that he told me what had happened.

Adolph was a smallish man, old-country accent, red goateed with red-hot piercing eyes and a large bald head. He had been in the Wardrobe for some years and became a member of M.G.M. at its birth, one of the many byproducts of the merger in March of 1924. He continued with the organization in Culver City for many, many years thereafter.

Late on this memorable evening there were still several unclaimed and unaccounted for civilian outfits left over and various costumes which had not been turned back to wardrobe. Sidel, in his loyalty to the organization and his desire to protect it and the individuals who by now were probably re-gassing their Lancias and Isotta Franchinis in Civitavecchia or thereabouts as they fled south, decided to destroy any remaining evidence. Alone, he burned the unclaimed apparel of those missing; shoes, hats and all. Only a scattered pile of ashes remained. But there was still a job to do. Bodies sometimes float and, again alone and with no witnesses, Sidel started his mission number two on that night at midnight.

He loaded a rowboat with chains and weights and proceeded silently from Tito's boatworks, oars and oarlocks making only muffled noises insufficient to disturb the sleeping harbor. He headed for the spot where the galley had burned and sunk. It was again his plan to destroy, or rather "sink", with those weights and chains, the evidence – if any.

A full hour of rowing brought him to the "disaster" area and his ghoulish task began. Back and forth he ranged in the still darkness, poking into and investigating the considerable debris still floating. Often he thought he had spotted one who had given his all for this *Ben-Hur* tremendo, only to be disappointed, weights and chains remaining useless in the bottom of his boat. I am sure the word "disappointed" is ill-chosen as I am equally sure that Adolph's midnight prowl was fraught with dread at the possibility of actually finding some poor unfortunate. I even question had he been successful, that he would have followed through with his "weighty" intentions. Still, maybe! Adolph was loyal.

Suffice it to say that no one, quite miraculously, was lost, as was proven within the next few days when the several whose regular clothes were now in ashes, arrived to claim them, still dressed as Roman Soldiers or Pirates! It seems they had been picked up by a fishing boat and landed down the coast a few kilometers from Livorno. Their story and their costumes made them some kind of heroes and apparently vino had flowed and flowed until the villagers finally lost their appetite for hero-worship and the costs which this entailed. This resulted in our wayward Thespians being somewhat forcibly transported back to Sidel's wardrobe department. He made a quick deal allowing them to remain Romans and Pirates in return for their clothes, shoes and hats (which "unaccountably" had disappeared!) gave them each some extra lire and bid them happily a fond "Arrive derci!"

So endeth this episode in the early laying of a foundation upon which experience is erected. Many lessons here, of which friendship is perhaps the most important. Number two is, to repeat, probably that hard work sans clock watching should be kindergarten. Test your "swimmers" is another, and again may it be stressed, never, never forget to thoroughly think! If I had really thought it out, the wind would not have taken over against our advance planning. In spite of this, however, the fire and sinking sequence was successful, and all's well that ends well. But not always will fortune smile as benignly as she did that day. And please never forget the "jutting chin" philosophy. Gambling (with judgment) often gains. As for Adolph Sidel, a rare brand of loyalty has been documented.

END OF CHAPTER TWO

BEN-HUR (1925) PRODUCTION #200

The Camera Crew on truck, filming close-ups of Francis X Bushman during the chariot race on the MGM LaCienega Boulevard set. - Courtesy Photoplay Productions.

Ramon Navarro (Ben Hur) faces off with Mesala (Francis X Bushman) near the climax of the Chariot race. Note amphitheater upper level hanging matte not visible at this angle. Courtesy - The Academy Margaret Herrick Library.

CHAPTER TWO

The Galleys awaiting action in Tito's shipyard.

On the ship to Italy in 1924. Crew listens to the radio to pass the time.

(Above) the hanging set of the Amphitheater. Note proximity to the rail and upwards tilt of the shot. Hanging matte used instead of glass matte for continuity with live audience. Hanging matte participants were wooden dowels animated using gears to push them up and down. Floating cork would not have worked for this effect.

(Below) as it appeared through the camera's 'eye' - Courtesy - Photoplay Productions.

(Above) All production was stopped and the company moved to the MGM lot in Culver city. "Stone" Amphitheater wall construction.

(Below) Tito's Italian crew digging the sunken galley out of the mud in his shipyard.

Yours truly with Penco, Neri shop foreman, making sure the Galley is sea worthy.

Tito Neri in his shipyard with the pirate vessels - Per gentile concessione di Corrado Neri e la famiglia Neri.

"Tito's" tug boat pulling the seven galleys. Demonstrating the might of the Neri workhorse.
Per gentile concessione di Corrado Neri e la famiglia Neri.

The Road to Mandalay, MGM Production #275, Released 1926, AAG Contribution: Art Director.

CHAPTER THREE
~
"PERSONALITIES - EARLY FOUNDATIONS"

Louis B. Mayer - Courtesy of Bison Archives.

Director Fred Niblo, director of *Ben-Hur* (1925) with Jackie Coogan and MGM founder Marcus Lowe.

It was during this sojourn in Livorno that I met Mr. Louis B. Mayer, head man of the embryo Metro-Goldwyn-Mayer Studio, and as it developed, my Number One Boss for the rest of his active studio life.

He had arrived in Livorno ostensibly to send the whole *Ben-Hur* company back home. He was also the purveyor of many expressive words (mostly re the quantities of lire being spent) to Mr. Niblo and others of our group. Many of these words inadvertently came through to me "loud and clear" because my room in the Palace Hotel in Livorno was adjacent to Mr. Mayer's suite and somehow my ear seemed to always be positioned next to the adjoining wall during most of the late P. M. conferences. Not that this close proximity of ear to wall was necessary in order to hear distinctly every well-enunciated syllable of L. B. discourse, but it was paramount if I wished to hear Mr. Niblo's subdued replies. The walls were not quite that thin.

Inasmuch as I was an uninvited listener, I will not disclose details other than that Mr. Mayer orated for some time on the subject of "Masterpieces." He felt that Michelangelo was pretty good at it and a few others, "~but Fred!, we, M.G.M.! a newborn infant!, still in swaddling clothes!, an innocent lamb of which I am the protecting Shepherd, Fred!, we cannot afford a masterpiece, Fred!!~" and on and on would Mr. Mayer expound. Mr. Niblo, I am sure, got the point though as I recall, he continued his *Ben-Hur* stint with little or no veering from the goal predominate in his mind, that this picture would be the greatest, and to the tune of some Four Million Dollars. It eventually turned out to be just that. A tidy sum in those days.

The evening Mr. Mayer and his two daughters arrived in

Livorno was October 14th, 1924. I remember because that was my birthday. I was eating a lonely dinner about 7:00 P.M., a little sorry I had let no one know of the great event, when into the hotel dining room came two well dressed, well muscled and sinister looking men. A quick glance about the room and they headed determinedly for my table. With no delay whatsoever, I found myself snugly fitted between the two of them, feet scarcely touching the floor as we exited, followed by the astonished gazes of perhaps a hundred other guests ~ none of whom offered help. At the hotel entrance I was unceremoniously shoved into the back seat of a large ominous-looking black sedan and screeching tires got us out of there in a hurry. The doorman stared. A quavering question or two in my particular brand of Italian was answered only by the engine's steady roar.

We finally arrived at a dark, distant dock, unrecognizable to me, where I was forcibly ejected and pushed along to the end of a dilapidated, deserted, unlit pier. A plank spanned the few feet from the end timber of the pier to a craft barely discernible in the dark as a sea-going tug. One of my companions pointed the route to be taken as the other gave me a rude shove and I walked that plank! On deck I was hustled to a small hatch and almost literally thrown down a steep companionway into absolute-silent blackness.

For a timorous (to understate it) moment or two I remained motionlessly sprawled ~ and then came the light! Someone hit a switch and there in shadowy dimness sat circle of grinning faces which, on cue and in several keys, rendered "Happy Birthday to You" in broken English, broken Italian, and because of the confined quarters plus their combined lung power, the danger of broken eardrums.

Harry Oliver, who had arrived with the second group from Culver City, and Tito had doped this one out. Al Raboch, Niblo's assistant, was there, Penco, Tito's foreman, was there, Horace Jackson and Engineer Veinier and one or two others in addition to Harry and Tito were there, including the Tug boat Captain. And I was there!

Quite an evening, this one, and quite a prelude to being introduced to Mr. L.B. Mayer. There were presents and toasts, food and talk, emotion, and a moon that just happened to be framed by the square open hatch above, and there was a beautiful birthday cake baked and decorated by Tito's tug boat Captain. His entrance with this work of art I will never forget, his wrinkled face wreathed in the proudest most embarrassed smile I have ever seen. And there was champagne and a final beautiful speech.

Tito Neri had the floor. Tito was short, but his straightness and his greatness made him seem to loom large wherever and with whomever he stood. His speech, in vibrant Italian, was not long. It said mainly and simply that I was "one of them" ~ sort of like being inducted into an Indian tribe. To make it official he blew the cork out of still another large bottle, and with a request that I stand beside him, he proceeded to pour the entire champagne contents on top of my head. This was how I met Mr. Mayer. Soaked inside and outside!

Upon our return to the Palace Hotel about midnight, Carey Wilson, the newly assigned writer, happened to spot my wavy entrance and insisted that I come into the ballroom for an introduction to the Mayer party. You simply did not refuse one of Carey's "insists." So it was done. Mr. Mayer was most gracious. It was explained to him that there had been a birthday party and when he asked "Whose?", I, in all honesty, could not recall "whose." At this instant of my dilemma I was rescued by the younger of Mr. Mayer's two daughters, Irene, who suggested that we dance!

I shall be eternally grateful for this maneuver on her part, a sacrifice certainly beyond the call of duty. A sodden clothed, emotionally unstabled victim of wonderful friends weaving in appreciative retreat from the King, accompanied and steadied by one of his Princesses. In a very few moments my composure partially returned, the music suddenly had tempo, we danced, and I remembered <u>whose</u> birthday it had been. Thank you, Irene!

Not that this has too much to do with the above, but Harry Oliver, long with the M.G.M. Art Department after this date in 1924, is now known throughout the Palm Springs Desert area as the publisher of the "Desert Rat," the only five-page newspaper which a one-armed man can read in the wind. His fine, philosophical bearded old self, still hale and hearty, resides in Thousand Palms, California, in his own adobe diggings which he has christened Ft. Oliver.

Harry could dress a character set with cobwebs like nobody in Hollywood, and never will I forget a particular masterpiece of those cobwebs plus dust and litter and mess and filth (the clean kind) and clutter upon which Harry had slaved all day. This "character" set really had character. When the shooting company arrived the following morning, Harry, rarely late, this morning was late. The set had changed. It now sparkled In its cleanliness and the Director sputtered in his efforts to simply say, "W-w-w-where's Oliver!!! A very conscientious and thorough night janitor had only done his job by whistle cleaning everything. I have heard variations of this story through the years, but this one I will underwrite as the original.

I subscribe to Harry's "one-armed" newspaper which occasionally even excels in excellence his immortal cobwebs. Take it easy Harry, old boy ~ perhaps somewhere, many years from now, in the Happy Hunting Grounds, we may one day again have as fine an evening as that one in Livorno long ago. And Tito will be there. Sentiment? Why not?

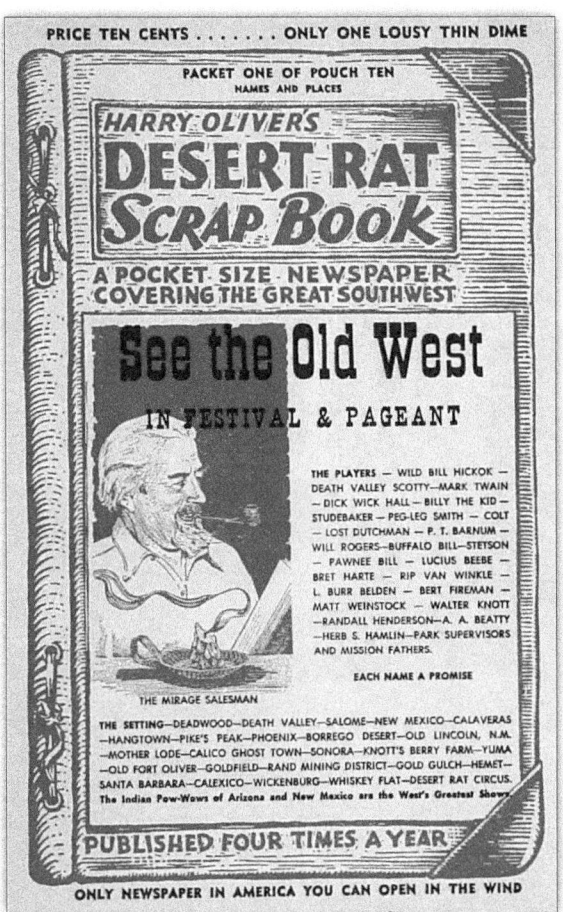

Harry Oliver's "Desert Rat" Scrap Book

Be patient, dear students. Dusting the archives has a bearing on things to come. These experiences and episodes will never duplicate themselves in your lives but others of equal influence can and will happen with benefit to you, if you are wholly open to them. Stretch out your willingness to be exposed to anything reasonably honorable and grab all opportunities to become involved in the unusual as well as the usual. Ideas can come from the strangest sources and a good effects creator files them away and survives through them. Remember that crocodile!

Christmas Eve, 1924, in Rome at the Excelsior Hotel on Via Veneto, was the time and place of another well remembered experience. Our *Ben-Hur* group were hosts to themselves on this occasion, as well as to quite a few of our Italian friends and several Americans who were visiting or living in Rome at the time.

Walking through the lobby early in the festivities, I was hailed by Carmel Myers, the sultry vamp of our picture who did her "wiliest" best to undo Ramon Novarro before the big chariot race. She introduced me to, among others present, a very blond young creature who would draw a second or third or fourth glance anywhere in any company. Even a fifth! "Buddy," said Carmel (that's me), "I want you to meet Mrs. Scott Fitzgerald. Zelda, this is Buddy Gillespie." The dialogue continued; "Nice to know you, Mrs. Fitzgerald," from me. "Oh! I just lov-v-v-v-e you!" from Mrs. Fitzgerald, in the most honeyed Peachtree accent it had been my privilege to hear almost ever.

Scarcely was this pleasant little incident over before Scott appeared, reasonably well along in his determination to support the Italian wine industry single-handedly, and sporting a glorious "shiner." My introduction to him proved to be routine and polite until I inquired as to his black eye. "None of your blank business! How'd'ja like a punch in your blankity blank nose!" retorted Mr. Fitzgerald. Being young and sound, I suggested that the lobby of the Excelsior was a poor spot for such goings on. "Let's proceed outside ~ now!" replied I. And then suddenly he, like Zelda, also had "lov-v-v-v-e" for me. "You're a great guy!", he now proclaimed, interspersing a few "esses" in this statement, particularly in the word "great." "Thank you. But what did happen to your eye?" I mistakenly again inquired. "I'll punch in your blankety blank blank nose! S'none of your business!" came heatedly and threateningly from Scott. Repeating my invitation to go outside, I immediately again became a "great guy." After a few more encores of this byplay we joined the rest for dinner and so started my Christmas Eve.

As the evening became midnight, I found that somehow I had been elected guide and protector for Mr. and Mrs. Scott Fitzgerald as we wended our way into and out of many of Rome's late, late spots. By 3:00 A.M., it was usually necessary to fight our way out as Scott would make a wild pass at some native for ogle-eyeing Zelda who just lov-v-v-ed to be ogle-eyed. I would usually manage to talk my way back into the hat-check department to retrieve our wraps, leaving Zelda and Scott outside word-battling in the chill Christmas drizzle, safely propped up and wedged into any handy vertical object I could find. Once it was the Coliseum.

A very expensive three-foot glamour doll which he had bought for her in one of our night club forays, was a brunette glamour doll and Zelda was just a one-hundred percent blonde, possessed of most of the attributes gentlemen prefer. How could he have chosen a brunette doll! He no longer loved her!! He this and he that and with each this and that she would throw the doll into the wet rainy street.

I had managed to get them into a horse-drawn carriage previous to these toss-out proceedings in order that I could deposit them where they lived. At each hurtling of the now soggy, muddy doll, Scott would stop the carriage, step out into the cold rain and fetch back his gift. Zelda would then be properly dressed down by her husband who with controlled violence never once was at a loss for very expressive words with which to do the dressing. I sat dumbfounded. This was not the kind of Christmas I, in my sheltered life, had ever experienced.

They knew not where they lived, but after about two hours of jogging along Rome's deserted streets with periodic dollstoppings, I finally found the right hotel, placed them safely inside the front door in the capable, experienced hands of the night porter and with an un-cheery "Merry Christmas," was on my exhausted way.

Two or three days later a note from the Fitzgeralds inviting me to tea, came to my office at the old Cines Studio. I accepted and upon arrival at their suite in the Russie Hotel I found that the invitation meant just what it said, tea ~ and that was certainly fine with me.

Two very charming people greeted their guest with all the engaging attractiveness they both possessed, and each overflowed with honest humiliation over the evening we had spent together. Very little did they remember, but they had apparently pieced together enough to know that I had played the role of a good Samaritan. They apologized just the right amount and their thanks were humbly sincere.

Our paths crossed several times shortly thereafter in Rome, and years later, subsequent to Zelda's tragic death. Scott, much older, white faced and gaunt, black overcoat too large for his shrunken shoulders, took on a writing assignment at M.G.M. His sensitive eyes seemed then to have been pierced with hurt, though they continued to burn searchingly into all detail, all reasons why, all of life. There was just less sparkle than that afternoon tea in late December of 1924.

Perhaps it was this sparkle that day which I recall most vividly about taut, finely tuned Scott Fitzgerald. It was not limited to his eyes, however. His listening, his attitude, his words, and his sophistication all shone with the cold, hard, intense glint of a diamond. And I gained much from this afternoon's tea during which we covered a waterfront of topics in our conversation.

In retrospect I realized how much Scott had just listened. I noted his occasional scribbling in an always handy notebook as he fired many questions in my direction on a great variety of subjects some quite personal. I was flattered, and only later when I asked about his note-taking did he reply in some such words as, "What you say you already know. What you hear, may be news and you <u>may</u> use. I make notes."

So we learn another lesson. And how does the above have any bearing on an effect sequence such as an earthquake or a tornado, synthetic and studio made? Well, directly perhaps not at all, but indirectly, probably. I have tried, not always successfully, but ever since that Fitzgerald tea, to listen better and to remember "~What you hear may be news and you <u>may</u> use ~." To repeat an earlier thought, ideas come from the strangest sources. You <u>will</u> eventually hear about that crocodile!

F. Scott Fitzgerald and Zelda - Courtesy John Springer.

Frank Williams, one of the originators of "traveling mattes," developed and patented his own method of this very useful use of composite photography, some time in the 20's. The term "Traveling Matte" is used to identify a method whereby foreground action of whatever nature can be photographed against varying types of solidly painted backdrops, black, white, blue, etc., depending on the system used. Newer developments often use translucent screens illuminated by Ultra violet, Infra red or Mercury Vapor as the "backdrop." The foreground now registered on one piece of film can be later combined "into" a second film upon which has been registered the background.

This "combining" is accomplished by using the first piece of film with its foreground action, to optically produce solid mattes which when printed in unison with the second film, leaves "holes" in the background film, <u>into</u> which the foreground is later optically inserted or "combined" with the background. This is a form of composite photography which generally falls in the Optical Effects category.

Its use, as will be discussed in the chapter on Optical Effects, serves a similar purpose to the Effects category known as Transparency Projection or Rear Projection Process, in that foreground action is combined with previously shot background action. The difference is that in Process the two are combined in one operation, the background being projected from the rear onto a translucent "process" screen and rephotographed from the front of the screen where is played the desired foreground action. Many examples of this latter tool are forthcoming.

CHAPTER THREE

Ben-Hur 1923 - Frank Williams very first traveling matte shot.

Among Williams' very first matte jobs for the new M.G.M. organization was a long shot showing the Palace of Pontius Pilate at the time of Christ's crucifixion, as its earthquake-activated, crumbling walls came down, crushing the milling hundreds at its base.

I mention the above at this point primarily because it is an early example of combining two of the categories of Special Effects which are today classified as Miniature and Optical Effects. In this early example they were used in conjunction with a "full sized" lower portion set of the Palace along with those milling hundreds, who, at about five dollars a head, were willing to "mill" and then fall down on cue as the "tons of stone and marble" clobbered them unmercifully, until ready for Take Two. I would be remiss in leaving the *Ben-Hur* Number One era without devoting a sentence or two not only to this "Williams shot," but also to other accomplishments which were an interesting and instructive part of the author's early exposure to "tricks" as such.

Certainly the chariot race included some fanciful thinking and unique rigging and doing which would now be known and fall into the Full Sized Mechanical Effects classification. Breezy Eason directed much of this race, to him, to the prop shop craftsmen, and very much so to the stunt men who participated, should go most of the credit.

These "stunt" individuals, by the way, cross paths often with the Effects creator, particularly in the full sized field and they deserve high praise. Certain risks at times cannot be avoided and serious, occasionally fatal, accidents do happen. On the whole "stunters" are about as capable and pleasant a group with which to deal as can be found. The "cost" boys may disagree, as stunt rates are high, but I certainly value the contacts I've enjoyed with many of them through the years.

One, Yakima Canutt, has long been a Second Unit Director specializing in thrill episodes and (like Breezy Eason on the first *Ben-Hur*) directed, along with Andrew 'Bundy' Marton, the chariot race in the second version of this epic, made also in Italy in the late '50's. My first glimpse of Yak in Nineteen Thirty Something was as he stood on the wing of a low and slow flying biplane, one hand holding a megaphone, the other gripping a wing strut, as he was flown back and forth over the Studio at roof-top level, shouting ~ could it have been imprecations? ~ at or to someone on the lot. Yakima Canutt ~ one of a great bunch of guys. I call him "Back Light" now ~ have for several years. He's a bit touchy about this and one day I fully expect him to revert to some of his early-day stunt tactics, whereupon I'll wind up crumpled and shaken in a fifteen or twenty-foot distant corner.

The "back light" cognomen has to do with how <u>not</u> to shoot background plates for the Effects category just mentioned in the paragraph about "traveling mattes," known as Rear Projection Process. This handy tool also rates a chapter which is forthcoming. A thumbnail glance at this point however, will give the reader at least a sketchy understanding of its function.

It would be impractical, as an example, to transport an expensive actor to Paris for one solitary shot of him standing in front of the Eiffel Tower. So, a shot of the Tower is obtained and shipped back to the studio. This is called a "Process plate" or "Process background." A proper print is made which, when the scene is to be shot is projected on to the rear of a translucent screen (a Process Screen) in front of which stands the actor. Both are then photographed together and our man has been transported to Paris the easy, cheap way. There are of course many variations, not always easy, not always cheap.

"Back light" refers to light position or direction as related to the subject to be photographed. If the sun, for instance, is directly "behind" the subject, this is "back light. Behind but off to one side or the other is termed "back cross" light. "Front or "front cross" light naturally means the opposite. In this latter case the main light source is on the subject, and particularly in color photography when the film is to be used as a Process plate, the results are <u>always</u> better. That "always" will raise one or two skeptical eyebrows from a few hard nosed cameramen and perhaps others, but from our general experience, that well known pudding is stuffed with "front" light proofs. And it <u>is</u> the exception that establishes the authenticity of the rule. Hard noses notwithstanding!

Enos Edward "Yakima" Canutt, a.k.a, "Back Light", circa 1920s. Stunt man, wrangler, and second unit director.

Ben-Hur #2 - Horse trainer Glenn Randall, Yakima in the chariot, and Charlton Heston. Yakima's son Joe was Heston's double in the chariot race and drove the quartet of white horses. Canutt's autobiography notes that stuntman Joe Yrigoyen was handling the reins of the four black horses, doubling actor Stephen Boyd.
Courtesy - Nancy and Donn Moyer.

CHAPTER THREE

Tarzan And His Mate - Swinging "vine" contraption.

Yakima, directing a unit during which Process plates were to be shot, was, through no real fault of his own, forced to photograph some in back light. Old Yak's batting average has always been so doggone close to One Thousand that I could not resist the temptation (even though I knew this slip was not of his doing) to make a good-natured issue of it. Dubbing him "Back Light" seemed proper and I presume it is only due to his good nature that I haven't wound up in that far away corner long ere now.

I wish I could name many or all of these unsung heroes in this volume, as they have often been the keys to the success of certain "effects," in that they have contributed life to what could otherwise have been an inanimate though possibly spectacular scene such as the burning of the Bounty in M.G.M.'s second edition of *Mutiny on the Bounty* to be subsequently detailed herein. Space simply does not permit.

Probably another reason for the soft spot in my heart for these fellows (and gals) is a carry over from my early amazement and pleasure in watching Doug Fairbanks (senior) cavort all over a castle, sword in hand or teeth, making those impossible leaps and sensational swings to save Lady Whoever. He was just great, and his outstanding gymnastics early inspired me with a burning ambition to go to Hollywood and obtain for myself a castle-cavorting job.

During the Art Direction days on the Johnny Weismuller "*Tarzans*," I had the opportunity of putting into practice this hidden youngish ambition of mine. Johnny was essentially a swimmer, world records and all that, but not necessarily a vine swinger, stockade leaper or myriad others of the many prodigious feats of athletic prowess the script writers dreamed up for him. He eventually became pretty much all of these things and many of them were gleefully tested by yours truly on behalf of the loin-skinned "You Jane, me Tarzan" holder of Olympic Gold Medals.

Often the contraptions which enabled Johnny to defy gravity like a moon jumper, flitting effortlessly through forest, were the product of that Doug Fairbanks inspired mind, which, coupled with the mechanical know-how of legions of prop-shop men and enthusiastically tested by the possessor of that enthusiasm, almost always worked. Mr. Weismuller generally had complete faith in our contrivances, if first, I would try them on for size. Again being young and sound, still retaining those visions of the mighty Doug, this was heady stuff.

Along with many other facets of those early *Tarzans*, that period has remained in my memory as of outstanding benefit in the learning of lessons on many diversified problems in the realm of physical dramatics. A few were painful ~ most were fun. Some of these lessons are to be chronicled later, such as the hippopotami in Lake Sherwood (mentioned in the Foreword). And it was Tarzan who in fighting that big rubber crocodile, gave us a clue on how to do the Hiroshima bomb in M.G.M.'s *The Beginning or the End*.

My meeting with Mr. Mayer kicked off this chapter so a word or two more about this fabulous man as I knew him may be a fitting conclusion to it.

A few weeks after the Livorno "birthday" introduction I was back in the Cines Studio in Rome, and one morning while walking in opposite directions on the lot, we passed. There was an exchange of "Good mornings," then he stopped and said, "What was it, Bud, you wanted to see me about?" Well, there had been nothing I had wanted to see him about and I so replied with an added and polite, "Thank you, Mr. Mayer." It was only after pondering this relatively insignificant occurrence that I realized this was his way of letting me know that if I wished to talk to him about anything, he was available. And Mr. Mayer always seemed to remain available throughout the many years of our association.

Somehow this little incident has filed itself away in my memory and to this day I interpret it as a pretty good character study of "Uncle" Louis. Much has been written about L.B. Mayer, not always in a complimentary vein.

My own views are very much in variance with this "tear-down" type of writing. No one is faultless, but this fine and successful gentleman who built and headed an empire within the motion picture industry, possessed qualities of leadership excelling, in my opinion, that of any of his contemporaries.

Outstanding among his many attributes was his innate judgment of talent and his knack of surrounding himself with top craftsmen in all of the creative and executive branches of picture making. I certainly prefer to remember these admirable aspects of this man's unique success story rather than to point out and stress occasional temper tantrums or rare slips in philosophical or business acumen.

Generally, at least in my opinion, those tantrums, if indeed they could be classified as such, were merited and excusable.

In the early days Mr. Mayer had two "right arms"; Irving Thalberg and Eddie Mannix. It is typical of Mr. Mannix that I should refer to him as "Eddie." As General Manager of the Studio and Nick Schenck's man at the time of, and for years subsequent to, the merger, Eddie was not only the most capable and respected of Studio General Managers, he was everyone's friend and helpmate. Irving Thalberg, L.B.'s other "right arm," probably more nearly represented the absolute apex of a successful, high caliber picture maker than any other top executive producer before or since. These two men were totally different in their natures, their backgrounds and natural aptitudes. Thalberg, sensitive, idealistic, shy; Mannix fearless, robust, true diamond in the rough. They, in partnership with Mr. Mayer and Mr. Schenck, proved to be an odds-on combination spelling success.

Many years later there were "back lot" rumors of an L.B.~Irving feud and this proved to be true, and relatively unimportant as far as I was concerned. I remember each as outstandingly remarkable men, both of whom have my lasting admiration. Irving Thalberg passed away in September of 1936, much too young and valuable a man for the industry to lose. Mr. Mayer, having resigned from M.G.M. in August of 1951, passed on in October of 1957. And dear old Eddie Mannix followed on August 30th, 1963. Those three carved an enviable niche in the saga of Hollywood and I am grateful for having been privileged to share a long and, for me, rewarding association with these men.

There are many other individuals whom I am tempted to "biograph" as important cogs in my own individual wheel of experience. But I must limit this very strong inclination to brief references only, during areas in the telling of these experiences, where people were either a helpful integral part of a problem or when a pardonable, I hope, digression from the principal subject of this book seems to me to be of more than ordinary interest. Usually any departures from strict adherence to text will be prompted by humorous incidents or by the desire to personalize and often to give the reader occasional rest periods in which to share behind-the-camera happenings and insights, many of which are completely non-technical.

The reference to "technical" brings us to what has perhaps been learned in Chapter 3. Mainly, I think, the example set by Mr. Mayer of surrounding himself with top talent and using it! This may not always be as successfully possible as in Mr. Mayer's case, but be sure to make a big effort in this direction and when you uncover exceptional craftsmen, fight to keep them. Use them to the fullest and always share with them, if credit is due. They usually deserve it anyway and your gain is that you wind up with a crew working <u>with</u> you rather than <u>for</u> you. True, you are supposed to be and are the General. It becomes your lot to absorb the rude shocks of misses, big or little, but the misses will be fewer, if the above attitude is assumed and "glory basking" as a result of combined and willing effort is far from unpleasant. Love your crew, mate! Credit-sharing is not always too easy, what with studio regulations re Screen Credits and Academy rules as to "Oscars." In any event, make the attempt.

The paragraphs devoted to the "grabbing" of any and all experiences, exposing oneself with relish to the unusual as well as the usual, should once again be remembered. Also the reference to "listening." "~What you hear, may be news and you may use.~", partial quote, Scott Fitzgerald. And long live the stunt man.

END OF CHAPTER THREE

The Fair Co-Ed, MGM Production #329, Released 1927, AAG Contribution: Art Director

The Divine Woman, MGM Production #332, Released 1928, AAG Contribution: Set Decorator.

Women Love Diamonds, MGM Production #296, Released 1927, AAG Contribution: Set Design.

Tell It To The Marines, MGM Production #266, Released 1926, AAG Contribution: Set Design.

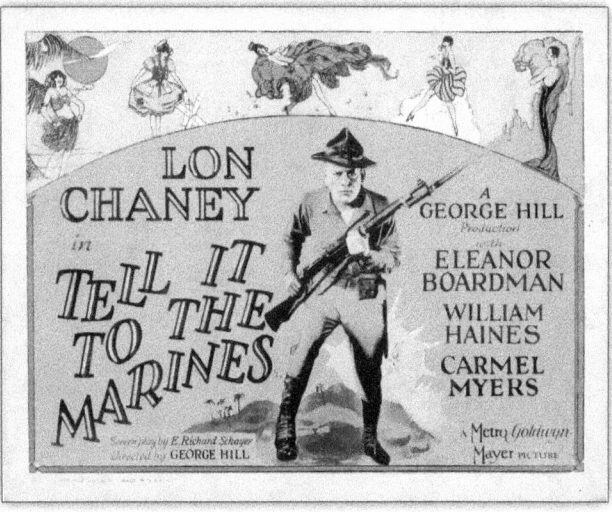

The early years; some of the titles credited for Set Design and Art Direction.

"PERSONALITIES - EARLY FOUNDATIONS"

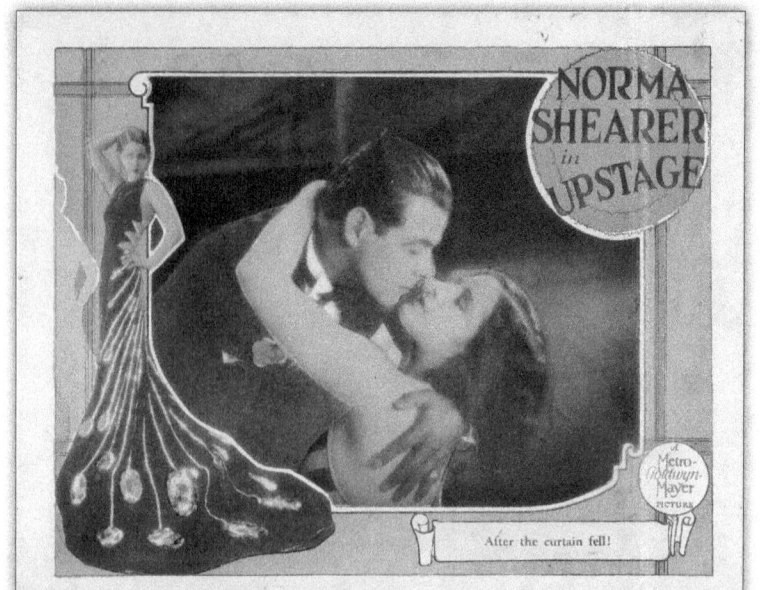

Upstage, MGM Production #279, Released 1926, AAG Contribution: Set Design.

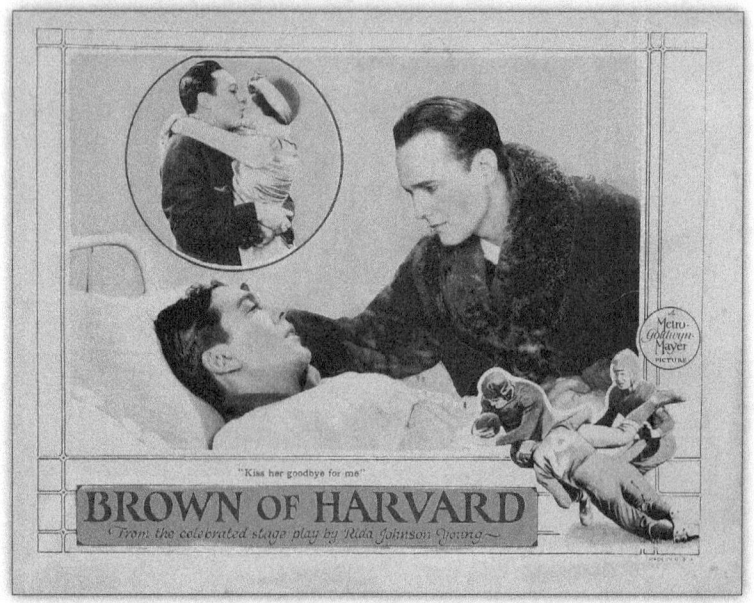

Brown of Harvard, MGM Production #258, Released 1926, AAG Contribution: Set Design.

The Demi-Bride, MGM Production #298, Released 1927, AAG Contribution: Art Director.

Naughty Marietta, MGM Production #801, Released 1935, AAG Contribution: Associate Art Director.

Mutiny On The Bounty, MGM Production #817, Released 1935, AAG Contribution: Associate Art Director.

CHAPTER FOUR
~
"UNIONS—HIPPOS—CONTROL"

Tarzan Escapes, MGM Production #856, Released 1936, AAG Contribution: Associate Art Director.

Though I am aware that the following is repetitious, the count down of this chapter will blast off with a very sage remark, to wit, "Son, when you are young and young in your job, you do two to ten times more than that for which you are paid; when you are old, you get paid for much more than you do." Unfortunately "organized" regulations often toss snags at the entrance to this path; such rules as, "If you stay after punch-out time, they gotta pay ya' son. Or else!"

Well, it is trite to say that Unions have many worthwhile purposes, but none of them should ever interfere with a beginner's willingness to add as many of his or her own helpful openings as desired, when opportunity knocks at that wonderful door. I know the usual, "the boss will take advantage" rebuttals to this philosophy, as well as I know that often the boss does take advantage. But who is the gainer? Sometimes both, but at all times, you. Why? By now you should know, if you read carefully in the "Neophyte" Chapter of that early DeMille exposure to work far beyond the call of the pay check.

Advice along these lines was given to a young friend of mine several years ago who was employed as a sort of junior draftsman in M.G.M.'s Art Department. "Stick around at night, Milt," I suggested, "and come in an hour or so early every morning. One day, maybe even months from now, but one day, someone will notice that morning, noon or night, Milt is always around, always at hand for those occasional after or before hours' emergency jobs." Continuing, I added, "And one day, that someone or another someone will decide that this young man could make a good assistant, never watches the clock!" This, I said, might be a pretty good way to help open that door whenever those opportunity knocks might occur.

He was enthusiastically willing and he thoroughly understood that much time might pass before such a forward advancement might be forthcoming. But both of us had neglected to reckon on what reaction his Union steward would have to this unorthodox (but pretty old and well founded) method of being not only ambitious, but also in letting "opportunity" know that honest willingness was eagerly available. So, as you have guessed, our best laid plans went up in short (union) sighted smoke. Milt could not do this, said the Steward, unless "they pay ya, kid."

Why labor should have the right to impose upon an individual's wishes in this respect, I do not know. And we speak of Freedom? There are probably many answers, most of them I am happy to say I know not and happier to say did not apply in my own experience.

Quite aside from rules, and on the other hand, the hard working new employee should never assume a milk-toast attitude towards his boss. Far from it! Tiffs with management are par for almost any course, particularly when that time comes for, shall we say, an increase in earnings. But a background of having done much more than that miserable weekly check would seem to call for, is a powerful prop with which to be shored in confronting the usual pain-faced gentleman sitting at his busy, secretarily-house-kept desk, when he expounds, as did Al Aronson on an occasion in Rome when I had the temerity to present such a request to him; a raise in pay.

Al was our very popular and capable Paris representative. During the finishing 1925 *Ben-Hur* days (can't seem to get away from that picture) he was the "Mr. Pain Face" I had to confront, because he had been delegated Business Manager by Mr. Mayer to wind up our Rome activities. I shall always remember his tear-laden arguments, one of which was an oracular gem in addition to being a unique new slant on how to say "No!" This one should have received some kind of an award for both delivery and originality. It went thusly ~ with a quiver (or is it quaver) in his voice, Al Aronson began bluntly. "No, you shall not receive what you ask, Buddy. It's out of the question, Buddy, as well as being preposterous. But not, Buddy, for the reason you may suppose, Buddy. It's <u>not</u> the money." (And now the first saline tear appeared. How these fellows do this I'll never know. Mr. Mayer, many years later, literally streamed tears during a notification of a slack-period-imposed general salary cut. His voice also quavered ~ or is it quivered?) Mr. Aronson continued his defense of M.G.M.'s young treasury. "No, it's <u>not</u> the money! We could afford twice what you ask, Buddy, but for your own good, Buddy, for your own future, you must be <u>curbed</u>, Buddy. Like a young (and here it comes) <u>mustang</u>!" He forgot to add another "Buddy."

Well, no one in my experience has ever quite equaled <u>that</u> approach since. It didn't entirely work, however. Now that I was likened to a bronc, I bucked, and I remember Al's biting the dust to the tune of at least certain parts of my requests.

This example is an important one for all those fortunate enough to do their own bargaining in their early "mustang" years, particularly when that bargaining is backed by that "two to ten parts work, one part pay" theory. Labor should lax up a bit and give the youngster a chance to fill his early storehouse by following more frequently the old axiom of "it's the exception that proves the rule." Milt should have been allowed that hour or so extra, without being required to charge for it.

Expounding theories related to Union control of certain crafts was not my intention at the outset of this book, nor were random ramblings on unrelated other subjects a part of the outline I had vaguely established, for myself. I see no harm, however, in these wanderings, particularly when strong feelings that something is amiss keep raising large question marks. By occasionally passing them on to the reader, a corrective seed may be planted. Who knows?

One such question mark, has to do with hiring an individual just because he happens to be qualified, you need him and he needs you. It's not all that easy. An example. During World War Two days, a young man was sent to me through a mutual acquaintance, seeking employment. He was 4F physically, and had been turned down by the various Services. He had worked in the Kaiser's model ship building department and was then employed in the experimental "wood" department at Howard Hughes' Aircraft Plant, where daily fist fights among members of management, had discouraged his wish to stay. He had completed courses in plastics (an industry infant at that time) and was attending night classes in synthetic rubbers and various other chemical compounds. He was a good craftsman and knew hand and machine tools. He was not asking for a white collar job. He wanted to work as a propshop man in our Construction department. We needed propshop men, good ones. But we could not hire this young man, directly, and he in turn could not be assured of M.G.M. employment.

Yes, a work permit could be obtained but he would receive his work calls, if and when, from the local union office. This meant that <u>if</u> all the regular card carriers were placed and somebody needed a man, he, depending on his permit number, might get the job at any one of a dozen different studios, and for no assured number of days. In simple language a man we wanted, who possessed qualifications we needed, could not be hired by us. And from his viewpoint he had no specific choice of employers except that maybe in time his union status might allow his eventual M. G. M.

employment. He couldn't wait ~ and continue to eat!

There's something awfully smelly here and it may be that there is no practical roll-on or spray-on eradicator in the rules and structure of a Union. Older, long dues - paying members must be and generally deserve to be protected ~ they <u>should</u> get the calls. <u>But</u>, and what a big "but" <u>this</u> one is, what about the situation just described? How can we continue to countenance this very formidable obstacle in the path of free choice? Too many great men in our history achieved top positions in all fields by simple willingness to "donate" that little, often liberal, extra. Let us hope this trait, because of rules and regulations much too inflexible, is not murdered, buried and forgotten. Rather, Union membership should give this problem (granted, a real tough one) a long hard look with the thought that a fair solution is mandatory.

One more detail before we leave the subject of "rules," is the abuse of jurisdictional "rights." Again, the principle of the old precept, "it's the exception that proves the rule," should be much more generously applied in actual studio production than is generally the practice. The idea that <u>everyone</u> may push to un-stick an emergency, just makes common decent sense. And it very much makes economic sense too. May I say in deference to the great majority of members of my many crews through the years, and in grateful tribute to them, that we all "pushed" when necessary. Even the non-card-carrying boss was allowed to push.

Exceptions to the above unique and wonderfully pleasant and productive way of working, are the following two examples of which many more could be cited. One was the need for a crude small sign, the kind an unskilled person might crudely paint on a rough board, for a scene suddenly dreamed up by the Director. The troupe was on a twenty-mile distant from the Studio location. A standby painter was present. He, or for that matter any member of the crew, could have painted the sign satisfactorily. But jurisdiction raised its righteous (and impractical) head and it was necessary to send a standby car the forty mile round trip to the Studio in order that a sign writer with his proper credentials, could do the job. Which he did, satisfactorily ~ and at considerable unnecessary cost, particularly in time.

The second example involved a long used technique of passing a small leafed branch in front of the key light when shooting Rear Projection Process where moving backgrounds were involved, to create the illusion of moving shadows on the foreground action, people in a vehicle, on horseback, walking, or whatever, so that added realism be given to this particular medium. One of the electrician members of the crew had always done this chore, particularly because it was necessary for him to tend the key light source at all times and often there was only convenient room for one person. He passed the piece of brush, cued by the projected background plate, in front of his key arc-lamp to create the shadows.

Then out of the blue descended the "Green" men's local. All green stuff, foliage, trees, plants, grass, <u>must</u> be handled by their card carriers. Our shadow twig, they claimed, fell in this category so one more gentleman was added to a shooting crew and placed in an inconvenient spot where two was a crowd. This, so that his jurisdictional rights, even if only in shadow, were not infringed upon. I believe that is questionable grammar, but you will get the point. So did we. Whereupon with great strategy we built a little pierced cut out irregularly perimetered paddle-like object, discarded our "green" branches along with their "green" wielders, and handed the new shadow maker back to the electrician. This victory was but momentary. It seems the propshop had made our wiggly-holed contraption and their <u>local</u> claimed and <u>got</u> jurisdiction. Hence that one-man ladder was again re-populated. A new set of shadow creators were diplomaed and superfluous cost was for the second time added.

This childish short sightedness on the part of the negotiators for competing Union Locals when such demands are made, won and enforced, is not only regrettable, it is economically unsound and helps to kill the "Goose that laid the Golden Egg." Today, neither "green" men nor propshop men are in charge of shadows. Grips have taken over, and this is fine because firstly they "operate" all shooting sets and secondly we now mostly use unattended "inky" lights and that much maligned ladder supports only, as originally, one person. The term "inky" refers to Mazda or "bulb" lighting as opposed to "arc" lighting which requires attendance.

Management is of course a party to all of this as they are on the other side of the table when labor contracts are drawn. However, an important part and parcel of that contract, should include provisions to change and correct obvious faults by means of further discussion on a lower level with the personnel directly involved, when comparatively petty problems, such as those described, arise. Many times in the past I have heard comments from working members, the <u>real</u> workers, agreeing with this opinion. By now, adult thinking should certainly dictate the elimination of costly unreasonableness, triggered generally by selfishness, in these disputes. And why not form the habit of using a bigger dose of horse-sense in thinking it mandatory that every last "i" be dotted and every last "t" be crossed in literally following the letter of the jurisdictional law.

John Bossart, friend, the best and most thorough hydraulic and mechanical engineer M.G.M. ever had, once told me that a good engineer could be split, in analysis, into three even parts; one part education, one part experiences and one part horse-sense, and that of all three thirds, the last was the most important. You'll hear more of John when we touch on Clark Gable's and Spencer Tracy's *Test Pilot*, and productions such as *A Guy Named Joe*, *Green Dolphin Street*, *Plymouth Adventure*, *Mutiny on the Bounty* and others, Bossart's "children" always worked with a refreshing minimum of "bugs". Horse-sense played an important part and its practice should never be confined to just engineering. Labor <u>and</u> Management could well take note.

To relieve the tenor of seriousness which seems to have permeated this chapter with its "Go West Young Man" type of unasked for advice and its gentle hints to Labor and Management, a recounting of the saga of Lake Sherwood and the Hippos should be a welcome breather. I believe the story qualifies as a "saga" because one of the dictionary definitions of saga is "legend" and its telling has become legend, which also has the word "unverifiable" as part of <u>its</u> definition. From me, however, you will get a factual report, because I was there, Charley.

Tarzan again! The scene called for Johnny and his Jane with two or three "denizens" of Africa's deepest jungles (whose address and telephone number was in the Los Angeles listings at Central Casting and whose "Bwana raumbo jumbo" was often spoken with a U.C.L.A. accent) to cross a hippo infested stretch of water on a flimsy bamboo and baling-wire raft.

We had the stretch of water, which was an arm of Lake Sherwood, on a location not far away from the studio and so named, I believe, because it was the spot where much of Doug Fairbanks Senior's *Robin Hood* was shot. But we didn't have the hippopotami. Out went the call, to zoos and circuses across this broad land of ours. And hippos began to arrive!

Publicity departments are not about to pass up a meaty tidbit (pun not intended) such as this weighty one, and ours, under the expert guidance of Howard Strickling, was no exception. Howard, by the way, still heads, as of today, this highly important area of picture making and picture selling. He has, like the author, survived many M.G.M. regimes and for years was, if not another of Mr. Mayer's right arms, at least an important left one. It was decided to cover thoroughly this unusual occurrence. Captive, absolutely genuine, African hippos, released to nature in a reasonable facsimile of what they might have expected in their native haunts, had not Ringling, Barnum and Bailey and countless other outfits and zoos backed up with sufficient cash their wishes to possess one or more of these big-mouthed brutes.

The day arrived. All news media were gathered on the banks of the arm of our location lake. Quite an assemblage was there which included trucks holding thirty odd of the big animals and smaller trucks brim full of newsreel cameras and equipment and studio furnished limos for the gentlemen of the Press, local <u>and</u> national. This was a big thing! The cameras would record these large herbivorous mammals as they lumbered and frolicked about, ecstatic in their new found freedom, marred only by the cluttered presence of Howard Strickling's army.

The signal was given, truck gates opened to heavy ramps already placed, cameras whirred, flashlights popped, the more timid of the reporters present stayed close to their chauffeur manned cars as thirty-odd hairless, thick skinned, short legged, enormous muzzled, lumbering and frolicking beasts waddled clumsily down into the lake and disappeared! But completely! And they just <u>stayed</u> disappeared as anticipatory hopeful cameras continued to devour film at the rate of ninety feet a minute waiting for the day's star performers to again show their bulky selves. Our own cameras wound up with several thousand feet of placid Lake Sherwood water, disturbed only by sporadic hippo produced air bubbles and occasional small ugly bumps breaking the surface. The many newsreel cameras also recorded this total lack of creature cooperation!

Well, early afternoon became evening; then night arrived and the fact that no one had provided for lights and generators made it pretty obvious that all present could go home. The hippos were already in theirs ~ their newly found one, on the bottom of the arm of the lake, where grazing was plentiful and virgin, having previously never even been touched by almost any hippos.

These beasts are mammals, and as such must breathe. To breathe they must surface, but what we didn't have was information re their long windedness, which we discovered to be an average of seven minutes between air gulps. And we knew not their surfacing characteristics. With a built in and perfectly balanced system of controlled buoyancy all they had to do to breathe was to poke two nobby nostrils (balance of Hippo continuing to remain totally out of sight) just above the surface, expel any lung residue, inhale quickly and again completely disappear to resume feeding on the bottom. The result was that before nightfall, and at seven minutes multiplied by ninety feet of film per minute per camera, of which ten were on the job, each seven minutes produced in simple mathematics, seven thousand feet of negative of lake surface with those air bubbles and a plus or minus thirty times two hippo noses that would protrude suddenly in pairs, looking like medium sized gray pine cones and then just as suddenly withdraw from view leaving only ever widening circles which intermingled with other circles produced by other pine cones and always more and more air bubbles.

This was hardly fare for newsreel theater patrons and though many seven to ten minute intervals of expectant grinding were executed by the cameramen, the sum total of useable, though questionable, footage consisted of thirty tremendous rear end views, swaying down grade and into Lake Sherwood and out of sight. Cameras using long focal length lenses produced magnifications that were not even questionable ~ they were quickly deleted.

Howard was heartsick and his Publicity Department's *Tarzan* budget was severely dented. Nothing to show for the day's activities but the west end of our Hippo herd as they headed eastward. And so the stage was set for Act Two of this quandary, which developed into quite an act.

We had had the foresight to construct a steel cable supported fence across the arm in which we wished to shoot our scenes. We were quite sure our animals would return ashore where full-course hay, mash and bran dinners had been temptingly placed, as soon as the "bottom" feed was exhausted. But again we were caught short in our knowledge of Hippopotomology. They <u>did</u> exhaust the bottom food. They <u>did</u> contact the sturdy restraining fence along the bed of this confined arm of water, and then they <u>did</u> a very unsportsmanlike thing. They all trundled out of the water at the far end of our fence, climbed the bank, skirted the tree which tethered that end of our steel cable, came back down the bank and one after the other, like amphibian submarines, sank beneath and into the waters of beautiful resort populated Lake Sherwood ~ on the <u>lake</u> side of the fence!

The main body of the Lake represented perhaps fifty or more times the area of the arm which had been selected for our scenes. Quick calculations indicated, of course, that there must be fifty times or more bottom, all of which undoubtedly offered the same delicious assortment of nourishment as had been their diet for several days now. So fifty or more multiplied by several days, in relatively simple finger counting, meant that many disastrous things could happen to this *Tarzan* production while we waited ~ principally cost (once more that ugly word). Or Jane, lovely Maureen O'Sullivan (Mrs. John Farrow) might become again pregnant, always a schedule disrupting possibility, particularly when scanty jungle wardrobe prevailed. Yes, all kinds of imbroglios could develop. The Hippos <u>must</u> be retrieved!

Well, we hired cowboys, top ropers, and put them in rowboats, one rower and two cowboys per boat. They rowed and rowed and rowed. Seldom were they sufficiently near when targets appeared which would give them a reasonable shot. It quickly developed that attempting to lasso wet slippery noses or an occasional ear, was not going to be successful. The Production Office became desperate and after more expensive days had passed, the conclusion was reached that more <u>must</u> be done. So Studio propshop powder men were added to each rowboat crew.

Now powder men come not lightly laden. Their paraphernalia weighs. When the small crafts' gunnels began to ship water, one cowboy was removed from each vessel and our fleet ventured forth with a bagfull of new tactics, which in reality consisted of a bag full of dynamite sticks and caps. These were to be, and were, discharged here and yon so that the inconsiderate greedy gorgers below would be disturbed, rise to the surface, look around to see who had the temerity to interrupt their continuous salad course, charge the boats and get themselves lassoed.

Well the spare cowboy was not missed. The hippos were disturbed, alright. They just beat it, <u>underwater</u>, towards any direction of the compass away from the small explosions, and then, when safely out of range, up they would come, head and shoulders dripping, look around, spot their tormentors and ~ charge? Not quite. Hippos apparently forgive quickly, like your faithful inadvertently stepped upon dog whose yelp of pain is immediately followed by a wagging tail and brown-eyed adoring pardon. Whether their eyes were adoring or not could not be determined as no one got close enough to find out. Probably their glance was full of disdain, but certainly not for long as they somehow continued to be hungry and disdain melted into appetite. The nether regions of this diabolical lake was their pantry, and they continued to systematically vanish. So neither the cowboy left ashore nor his lariat slinging pal aboard, ever tossed a fertile noose. It seemed not practical to drain the lake.

At this point, and deserving a paragraph all its own, came the "yellow" of all yellows. A "yellow" is an order originating in the Production Office and issued to all departments or persons concerned. It takes its name from the color of the paper upon which it is mimeographed. Some studios may have "purples" or "pinks." I don't know. M.G.M. had "yellows," and many copies were made of this one because Frank Messenger had concluded that a Production Office yellow was akin to a mandate from the Pope, and he wished no one to be exempt from his, her or their responsibility in this case. Frank was the Unit Production Manager, his duties having mainly to do with foreseeing snags that might delay production and instituting methods and procedures for their removal. If all tried methods and procedures seemed enveloped in haziness, a surefire "get off the spot" and "for the record" move, was to issue a "yellow." This one read, "As of tomorrow morning, by 9:00 A.M. have all of the Hippopotamuses OUT of Lake Sherwood," no more, no less, not even "please." Needless to say this particular "yellow" quickly became a collector's item in addition to having no effect whatsoever on the problem at hand.

One weekend resident who had heard nothing of his infested lake, arrived late one Saturday evening with a few merry making friends. The night was long and noisy and wet. Early the next morning (about 10:00 A.M.) our host crept out of the debris, attired in bathing trunks, and headed for a cranium-clearing dip in the waters of Sherwood. None too sure footed, he descended the several steep stairways from his house on the cliff to a float moored below, upon which had been installed a diving board. Shakily he balanced on the end of the board, his mind probably solely intent on a determination to not wait for New Year's resolutions. Just before push-off, one of our lost menagerie parted the waters directly in the path of the gentleman's contemplated dive!

Now whether this particular hippo's immediate and tremendous jaw stretching was a giant yawn, a request for breakfast or an amicable greeting will never be known by our friend. He executed instant retreat! His ascent of those precipitous stairs and headlong disappearance through the handiest opening his shocked eyes could find, would only have been recorded and analyzed by resorting to slow motion photography. Shortly thereafter, following signs of protesting activity, three cars were seen to be leaving, weaving zig-zag trails of dust which originated at this white with green trim cottage high on the cliff and overlooking a bit of dark, dark Africa. Someone has said that within twenty-four hours a "For Sale" sign appeared near the front stoop with instructions to call such and such a number and "make an offer!"

Other stories, such as the one about the boy and his father fishing from a rowboat were told. The boy, facing his rowing parent, noticed one huge protruding head a hundred feet or so directly behind his father, and yelled, "Hey! Dad!! There's a hippopotamus!" "Yes, Son, I know. Sure, sure." "But Dad, it is! Look!" And of course by the time Father twisted around for an unamused look, only a widening circular ripple was visible. "Some fish!, Son. Wait'll I tell your Mother that you saw a fish that looked just like a hippo," and with a mildly sarcastic guffaw, on they rowed. Son, of course, had the last guffaw as the news eventually got around.

<u>Finally</u> the Hippos <u>did</u> lumber out, a "blessed event" being directly the reason. The baby was netted, placed on the bank near all that tempting hay, the fence across the arm was removed and "mother" soon was coaxed into and corralled alongside her infant in plain view of her pals, if they cared to look. They must have cared, because they all followed the bait she apparently represented, within the next day or so.

They were speedily trucked into the studio, placed in a concrete bottomed fire reservoir, firmly restricted to the twenty-seven inch deep area of the tank and with Tarzan and crew manfully poling a four wheeled dolly-mounted raft alongside the concrete lip, all close shots (cameras high, shooting down) of the dangerous hippo-infested crossing, were filmed. They (the hippos) just couldn't sink out of sight in this shallow water and though they had gorged themselves for several weeks, a few days of enforced diet enabled the trainers to wheedle them into opening their huge chops, by holding aloft, just out of camera range, handfuls of tidybits, thereby adding the desired ferociousness to the scenes.

Long shots at the Lake were done with hydrocal-cast hippos, full upper bodies and heads, and some just heads. They floated and were <u>never</u> hungry. Each was fastened to a long cable which passed through a weight-anchored sheeve or pulley on the bottom from whence it and all the other cables stretched several hundreds of feet away to camouflaged teams of horses, who upon commands of "Back-up," "Giddy-up" and "Whoa," gave our inanimate counterparts very lifelike submergings and surfacings.

The silver lining to this cloud proved to be in the final editing of the sequence. As occasionally happens, adversity paid dividends. The very necessity of "doing something else," once the hippos finally decided to leave the lake, resulted in adapting more intelligent methods of control, which in turn gave us a much better sequence.

If there is a lesson to be pondered here, it lies in that one word "control." Its reference here is to animals but in the field of Special Effects it is equally significant. Particularly when dealing with the elements in a sequence calling for nature's fury. <u>Manufacture</u> these "elements" so that reasonable control is at all times exercised, and whether humans are exposed, or inanimate objects suffer the brunt of mother earth's violence, results will be usually much more realistic and chances of harm or fatal accident greatly reduced. We have sad proof of the latter which should perhaps be left undetailed. No one ever is <u>intentionally</u> to blame.

The early pages of this chapter contain, in my opinion, some worthwhile hints. Namely, a young man's attitude towards his new position and Union restrictions on his free exercise of that attitude. Also the often immature rulings and letter-of-the-law adherence to jurisdictional disputes which should call for a more general use of, "it's the exception that proves the rule." Raise in pay requests, strengthened by the "two to ten" theory and job openings, based on right to hire ~ this latter an enigma, but solvable. <u>And</u>, the rediscovery and reactivation of just plain horse-sense thinking in its application to practically all problems. Lastly, control. <u>Control</u>, and you avoid possible disaster, you may by-pass frustrations and, who knows, you may not lose a herd of hippopotamuses.

END OF CHAPTER FOUR

The Girl From Missouri, MGM Production #750, Released 1934, AAG Contribution: Associate Art Director.

San Francisco, MGM Production #870, Released 1936, AAG Contribution: Associate Art Director and Special Effects

CHAPTER FIVE
~
"FULL-SIZED EFFECTS MASCULINE AND FEMININE"

The Wizard of Oz, M.G.M. Production #1060, Released 1939, AAG Contribution: Special Effects.

The Academy of Motion Picture Arts and Sciences is the cultural and technical sounding board of the industry. "Oscar" is a cherished by-product. Academy committee memberships and their related activities can be quite rewarding — a common stomping ground for all industry compatriots.

The Special Visual Effects Award Committee convenes early in January for the first of its two annual get-togethers, the second usually taking place in February. At this meeting, Effect film excerpts from every preliminary nomination are viewed and through certain voting procedures, two productions are chosen which constitute the final nominations from which the winner is later determined by the entire Academy membership.

Category selections are also decided at this meeting and only those deemed worthy are retained. In no case can more than three out of the six eligible, qualify, and the winner or winners are limited to the one, two or three people whose responsibility lies within these categories. Because of varying studio-set-ups, it could be possible that one person only is solely responsible for two or more categories in which case he alone might be the potential recipient of an "Oscar." Or with other set-ups two or three individuals might be so honored.

A portion of the "Special Rules for the Special Visual Effects Award," governing procedures up to final nomination choices, follows:

> 1. Achievements being considered for nomination for the Special Visual Effects Award shall be judged on the basis of:
>   a. The necessity of the special visual effects employed to overcome economic infeasibility and/or physical impracticability.
>   b. The skill and fidelity with which the illusion of reality and/or fantasy is achieved so that the effect mechanisms or methods are not apparent in the final results.
>   c. Consideration of the effects achievements which contribute the most to the overall production.
>
> 2. The Academy President shall annually appoint out-standing visual effects technicians and qualified art directors and cinematographers to serve on the Special Visual Effects Award Nominating Committee. This committee shall be charged with the responsibility of nominating two productions, representing in their judgment, the best special visual effects work of the year.
>
> 3. Entries for this award may be made in one or more of the following visual effects categories: Full-Sized Mechanical, Matte Paintings, Miniatures, Optical, Transparency Projection Process and Animation. However, animation may only be considered under the following conditions: (a) two dimensional animation (cartoon or painting) is eligible only when used as an adjunct to, and included in, live action scenes; (b) three dimensional animation is eligible only if its purpose is to achieve a result sufficiently realistic to be accepted as though it were not stop-motion and it must relate to live action scenes or sequences only. Motion pictures or sequences that are principally cartoons or three dimensional animation are not eligible for this award.
>
> 4. Representatives of each production under consideration shall prepare excerpts and provide a brief written description of the special visual effects in the picture. The description shall indicate which of the effects categories are being submitted and shall name the one person principally responsible for the work in each category. Categories retained through committee balloting will thus automatically indicate who shall receive the award, or awards, when the winning picture is selected by the final vote of the full Academy membership. Copies of the descriptions of the special visual effects will be made available to the committee in advance of a meeting at which the Nominations voting will be conducted.

Instructions re preparation of written excerpt descriptions, viewing and voting and certain other formalities to be followed, conclude the "rules."

Close attention and a careful perusal of the basis upon which Visual Effects should be judged, as indicated in Number One - a, b, and c above, is recommended to the student or serious reader. In these few words the reasons and purposes are clearly outlined. To the adept Effects designer and director, the conscientious creator of the myriad extra ordinary demands fired directly at him through the years, those A B C concepts become a fixed formula of approach - a well adhered to Bible.

The following brief descriptions and examples, which might fall in any of the six Effects categories, should help the student to gain a gleaning of the actual make-up and function of these divisions. Let's take them one by one in alphabetical the reader to gain a gleaning of the actual make-up and function of these divisions. The exception to this order is "Animation" which is a late and limited arrival in the realm of Special Visual Effects and will be dealt with last.

"FULL-SIZED MECHANICAL"

As this heading implies, the job of the full-sized category is to supply a working method whereby real people become integral parts of, and photographed in conjunction and "within," the Effect. Many offshoots of this generalization develop, often overlapping into one or more of the other Effect categories.

Scenes confining themselves to the effects supplied by this one category, would be such as those showing, for instance, any part or parts of a ship, from keel to topmast, constructed on rockers operated ordinarily with hydraulic rams, and usually involving a storm at sea, or, a small craft handled also generally hydraulically, for the same purpose, often actually in water. The "in" water may be activated by wave-machines, dump tanks, underwater propeller agitators, pump-supplied water jets and sprays, and wind which mostly is generated by airplane engines driving airplane propellers. Additional examples in this category would include fire and people, explosions and people, earthquakes, floods, avalanches, always with people; tornadoes, outer space and weightlessness, airplane mounts which enable the craft (with people) to bank, climb, roll, loop and dive, in the safety and on the floor of a studio stage.

Further included, are hurricane swept atolls, chariot and automobile races, mechanical horses, mechanical elephants, mechanical anything; and on and on - as long as it is done full-scale and includes, customarily, actors or actors and/or stunt people photographed directly in conjunction with the Effect.

Contrivances such as treadmills, human and horse, fall within this full-sized classification, or "wire" jobs for "flying" whatever, including people. Synthetic clouds, turntables, tidal waves; the conception, method, design, manufacture and use of any device for the delivery of all of the above and countless more, falls also into the proper administration and the intelligent, imaginative employment of this highly usable and tough branch of the Special Effects Art.

Because it is less than cricket to endanger or maim (even actors) the Full-sized category is a sensitive one and really worrisome. Of necessity, there have been and will be times when calculated risks were and must be taken. Average backfires have, in our case, been considerably less to personnel involved, than those caused by normal routine activities, such as Freeway driving - if this can be considered normal, or bathtub slips.

An example of the "overlap" into one or more of the other categories, could include such situations as a hydraulically operated boat rocker, such as described above, combined with Rear Projection Process upon whose process screen are projected background plates, possibly made in Miniature, of which a part might (though rarely) be Matte Painted. Something or other might be added to the "plate" which could be, for instance, jagged lightning and tracer bullets produced through Animation and Optically printed into the background.

So here, in a hypothetical case, all six Special Visual Effects categories have been included to achieve the physical requirements of one scene which, again hypothetically, could read as follows:

```
"SCENE 193, EXTERIOR DECK OF AIRCRAFT CARRIER, NIGHT PROCESS..... 'Miles
Standish (that could be his name) stood braced on the pitching flight deck. The
treacherous rain-laden wind, at times reaching gale velocity, drenched his
clothes as did tremendous seas which all but engulfed the valiant ship.(Full-
Sized Effects) He looked off into the black storm tossed water (Process with
Miniature Backgrounds) towards the distant scarcely distinguishable horizon
upon which the lights of Coney Island (it could be Coney Island) twinkled and
shone. (Matte Painting or Miniature - probably the latter) Streak lightning
(Animation and Optical) split the sky. When suddenly, tracer bullets (Animation
and Optical) hissed out of nowhere (the Writer) and did miles in!"
```

All of this played safely on a stage at considerable ugly cost entailing weeks of advance preparation and shooting. Seldom would every Effect branch be represented in one scene, though it is possible. Many times, however, two or three combine to satisfy the often wild, but fortunately, more often dramatically legitimate, whims of writer, producer, director. Scenes such as the raft, in M.G.M.'s Cinerama *How the West was Won*, whirling and dipping as it rushed headlong down the white rapids of a river, conveying Debbie Reynolds and her family to a wet havoc, were medium-shot and close-upped at the studio with a spinning ram-operated raft in a tank (F. S. Effects) against a large Process Screen, upon which were projected background plates, shot on location, by a "second unit" crew who also supplied the "long shots" with actor "doubles" (stunt people) that further augmented the sequence. So here, two categories, Full-size and Process, were involved. Again, Debbie as a six or seven months old baby, in *The Unsinkable Molly Brown*— baby in a cradle, cradle on a rocker, twisting down another white rapid, flood swollen, M.G.M. river (stage and river both heated) with the baby's doting parents in "quick grab" positions just out of camera range, much more nervous than that wonderful infant, and neither of the three as nervous as the gent whose job it was to dream up "how?," and then do it. Here also, two Effect categories, Full-sized Mechanical, and Process.

Innumerable other examples and combinations in the Full-size plus area of our subject, would require volumes to record if all were included. Even Judy Garland and her tornado in *The Wizard of Qz* depended upon, shall we say, "us." And *San Francisco*'s earthquake! That was a Full-sized Mechanical dilly. We dreamed up some firsts, I believe, on this one.

Clark Gable, Spencer Tracy, Jeanette MacDonald and several hundred others all survived, although I recall one shot which looked so realistically fatal that we could use only the start of it – a brick wall was dumped on Mr. Gable, a tall thick brick wall, and surely, it appeared, he would have perished. This would have discommoded the balance of our tale as Clark was to "get" Jeanette in the end (with Tracy's help). So the film was necessarily scissored just as the wall started to tumble. The "bricks" were by courtesy of the L.A. Paper Box Co., the "mortar" was an extremely lightweight plaster mixture, and the illusion of a gory crushed demise, much too believable for even the "King" to have scrambled smilingly out from under, resulted in the necessary film clipping.

The big theater-night-club set, for this picture, in which Miss MacDonald warbled her lovely lyric soprano, occupied all of Stage 12 at M.G.M. There had been some argument about the destructive movement of an earthquake. I supported the "horizontal" theory while others insisted that it was the vertical, rolling, "ups and downs," which caused the damage. An expert from California Polytechnic College in Pasadena was contacted, and I won. In fact, he commented that our "schematic" for the big set, actually represented the very kind of an "earthquake table" upon which, in small scale, Cal Tech experiments were conducted.

We proceeded, though confronted by the misgivings of many who made dire predictions of broken legs and ankles. But we proceeded. We built our Full-sized Mechanical Effects earthquake-table. The entire set was erected on a huge platform, supported by railroad car wheels resting on steel rails, secured to the concrete floor of the stage. Running almost the full length of the stage, 179 feet, along both side walls, were huge timber "buffers" fastened by numbers of coiled railroad car springs to solid timbers next to the walls. Powerful short stroke rams were installed, which would propel the entire set, with its cargo of those predicted "legs and ankles to be broken," a quick short distance of about three feet. Whereupon the spring buffers would instantaneously react by shoving the whole works crashing back into the other buffer which would react in the opposite direction. This gave us a lateral to and fro movement that diminished from sudden violence to zero in a very few seconds. A small rug quickly removed from underneath two unsuspecting feet is generally upsetting and our three foot floor travel, almost instantaneous, though not unexpected, did create its share of upsetting. Not one broken ankle however.

The preliminaries were purposely not entirely explained in advance to our several hundred reveling night club extras. They all knew that the set would suddenly move. Those in and under the balcony knew that it was rigged to fall and breakaway walls had been pointed out. Stunt people were placed in the more hazardous areas. Operating crews, pressures, cue lights, and all acting personnel were checked for readiness and position. Miss MacDonald started her song to a pre-recorded play-back, cameras turned and, "Action'" from the Director blared forth over several loud speakers. The scene started; dancing, drinking and general merrymaking. What they had not been told was now activated by a pressed cue button in the hands of the Director. A sound track, prepared in advance, became suddenly audible through many strategically placed speakers.

A distant but ominous rumble grew in intensity for all of about five seconds, when a deafening rat-a-tat-tat from several air driven trip-hammers, slamming against steel plates on the edge of the platform, created deafening vibrations which jiggled liquids in glasses, potted palm fronds, tables, chairs, footlights and people. Then drowning the machine gun like clangor of the trip-hammers, the sound track again took over. Came an ungodly wailing roar, which sounded like the scream of a banshee wedded to the victory cry of Tarzan and all his apes! As a matter of fact, it was Weismuller's famous yell, augmented and staggered by the "sound" boys, but having no handy banshee, they must have used sound library tracks of tire-skid squeals, steam whistles, donkey brays and boiler-factories, all combined to give a few more seconds of unearthliness before, wham!! – the rams took over! The rug was pulled! People fell, the balcony fell, walls fell, chandeliers waved and fluttered, a few unrehearsed shrieks pierced our Full-sized Mechanical Effects category din — and we had ourselves the beginning of the *San Francisco* earthquake.

The unannounced bone-chilling rumbles and screeches were designed to accomplish exactly what happened in the short interval between the first distant reverberation and the actual set destruction. Startled, shocked fear, registered itself on every suddenly blanched face. And this was vividly recorded by each of the eight or ten cameras present.

Only a few moments were required to cover the work of many weeks of planning, construction, rigging — and occasionally necessary, albeit at times filled with trepidation, poohpoohing of the usual "calamity predictors." These people, though well-meaning, are often the bane of the Effects

SAN FRANCISCO (1936) PRODUCTION #870

Right: Breakaway balcony in earthquake scene. Stunt people carefully placed away from falling balcony.

Below: Tall thick "brick" wall fall on Clark Gable in earthquake scene. Scene cut just prior to wall impact.

Raised set on railroad car wheels with breakaway balcony, faux ceiling, and "brick" walls.
Courtesy - The Academy Margaret Herrick Library.

Director and at times have thoroughly monkey-wrenched well laid plans.

Perhaps now is a suitable time to dwell for a bit on these "doubters." Having been unpleasantly tripped a few times by their mostly sincere, often stupid, pessimistic and questioning interference, activated by inexperience (generally) and their doom's day brand of thinking, I hereby forewarn all young aspirants to this vocation, that they will sooner or later run into these dissenting, enigmatical, disbelieving "experts." If you become at all worth your salt, the controversy will be generally settled your way, but hindrance will have probably already done its degree of damage.

A by-product of these "doubter" inspired intermeddlings, is the "I told you so" threat, which, in the event of failure, can and will be used. So?! Contributions of this stripe are better ignored, regardless of outcome. In an early chapter it has been pointed out that many method and procedure determinations are gambles, in varying ratios, and that no assuring "genie" is permanently ensconced on your shoulder to guarantee successful results. Hence, this tip to all supervisory skeptics and interferers. Give your man a free hand. His problem is sufficiently difficult without your "help." He is the expert in all matters, including cost. He will avail himself of any assistance he needs.

And to the interferers, particularly, this advice - stay out of the <u>details</u> of an Effects director's routine. He will have his own courses of procedure from start to finish including delivery of the finished product, on <u>film</u>, to whomsoever should see it in whatever form, and in whatever order, <u>he</u> dictates.

I seem to be stressing this unhappy subject. If so, it's because of one period during those forty-two years when miserableness became a generous part of my daily diet, due to a particular brand of hysterical stupidity. Details are of no consequence and would be boring to the reader. Suffice it to say, that having traveled quite a lengthy road, I hope recognition of a sizeable accumulation of experience will tend to accent the suggestions herein. If you don't believe in your man, or he proves too frequently incapable, get rid of him. But until then, recognize that generally on Effect problems, he starts out with two already called strikes, while endeavoring to get from behind a sizeable eight-ball.

But back to the subject — examples that fall in this Effects subdivision. So many of interest from which to choose. A fairly recent one involved the horses and riders galloping through the sky in *The Four Horsemen of the Apocalypse*, a Glenn Ford starer directed by Vincent Minnelli. How to do these scenes, practically, effectively and reasonably safely? A big "how." A treadmill seemed to be a logical start.

But for four galloping horses with riders and no protective railings or harnessings or safety wires?! A wide open gallop in simulated clouds and lightning, smoke and fire?! Another first if it worked.

Treadmills have been used many times; Mary Martin on the stage in *Peter Pan*; Jimmy Stewart on a galloping white horse in an early M.G.M.'er; <u>three</u> hitched to a Russian troika for the production *Balalaika* carrying Nelson Eddy and Ilona Massey at a dead gallop in front of a Process screen on which was projected Process backgrounds, shot day for night in the snow and pines near Idyllwild, California. The area near Idyllwild was doubling at the moment for a wolf populated forest in old Russia. Illusions, illusions — all safely though noisily executed on Stage 12 with proper wolf-yaps added later - courtesy of the Sound Department. But — Mary's horse was harnessed to the mill, and a safety wire, which had been fastened to an undergarment girdle-jacket, would enable Miss Martin to be suspended unharmed in midair, should her galloping mount stumble, fall or in any way unseat its rider. Jimmy Stewart was similarly protected and the three troika steeds could have hurt only themselves had one or the other messed things, which was practically impossible due to strong and thoughtful rigging.

Our Four Horsemen representing War, Pestilence, Famine, Death, presented a different problem. A free gallop on an open treadmill plus the added effects of smoke and fire which would further complicate the confusion.

The size of the projected treadmill, twenty-one by twenty-one feet, its method of drive, the beefiness needed to support eight pounding hooves, the problem of friction and lastly, its future use had to be determined. For the latter consideration, it was decided to fabricate into three equal parts which for later demands could be used, each part independently, or in combinations forming single units.

Schematic drawings with specifications were given to one nationally known outfit for their bid, design and execution.

It soon became obvious that they wanted no part of it as they upped price and projected time of completion, twice. Time was beginning to be of the essence and I called the old firehorse, previously mentioned and long retired, John Bossart (another of those few individuals who outshine all others in their field) back into the studio to tackle the engineering of this three-in-one behemoth. And dear old John, true to his record of success in every chore ever given to him, no matter how unusual, how difficult, came through as usual. We had a treadmill that did its job efficiently and with not one failure.

What a solid, stubborn, capable and honest soul is John Bossart. You will recall his reference to "education, experience and horse-sense" in an earlier chapter. Several times since he became "too old" to work he has been persuaded to let us avail ourselves of his great ability and dogged determination to do it only one way — right! Now, as of this writing, eighty, straight as a string, no glasses, he lives alone in Beaumont, California in a house which faces his beloved mountains. As a matter of fact, he is at this moment doing a job for us, but at his home. His drawings on graph paper are mailed to us and from them working layouts are made. His drawn lines and his neat legible printing are a bit shaky and a sadness comes over me. But the three "Rs" by which he lives, particularly the last one, "horse-sense," are in evidence just as brightly and firmly as ever. Perhaps a fourth "R" should be added — his openness and lack of false pride in listening and accepting advice, if and when it passes his rigid code. Gentlemen of this character are real gems. There have been quite a few in my experience, and as this book unfolds you will hear of most of them. And you will probably hear of John Bossart again. Though I could be accused of maudlin sentimentality, the honest affection and gratefulness I feel for these co-workers, is pretty well without bounds.

Mr. Minnelli went a bit batty in his glee over our toy and he shot beautiful and <u>bountiful</u> footage of horses galloping from every conceivable camera angle. If the rest of the "Apocalypse" had fared as well as the Four Horsemen or for that matter (and modesty stops me not) the rest of the Special Visual Effects in the picture, M.G.M. would not have had to write off a few million dollars loss on the effort.

Before closing this episode, my plaudits to the four cowboy "stuntmen" riders, who not only braved and mastered this hazardous assignment, but who with true cowhand stoicalness, endured patiently and executed without complaint the whims and demands of Director Minnelli whose whims and demands had also made the Ballet in that wonderful *American In Paris* an outstanding artistic triumph. But cowboys on horses? All due credit, Vince, the shots were magnificent!

Wallace Beery's aversion to water often presented problems. What he used in his bath to overcome this antipathy, we did not know, but storms at sea are wet as is water generally and Wally's rubber, liquid proof underwear was always a part of Wardrobe's budget. Face splashes and moist hands he would endure but neck trickles, or worse, usually erupted into noisy, petulant, complaints. "Petulant" is perhaps an unfair adjective. I think Wally was really allergic to just plain water. To overcome this, it would have been impractical to introduce into the city's system a softener or oil or whatever he used at home, whenever the script dictated H2O contact. It seems that writers took fiendish delight in including damp or damper sequences in almost every Beery script.

previewed in Washington for approval by top Pentagon brass – as was the custom whenever films were produced involving cooperation from any of the military services. They loved it but for one small detail.

As everyone knows, all Carrier based aircraft have a "hook" on their tail that catches on cables stretched across the flight deck, to arrest forward progress upon landing. We had naturally included this detail, in the thrilling and very photogenic shots of planes coming aboard. The arresting gear (cables) was plainly visible at the bottom of each shot and at this Washington showing, some gentleman of authority, whose three or four striped nose must have been out of joint for some reason or other, bitterly proclaimed that M.G.M. was denuding sacred Navy secrets. The fact that none of the out of sight mechanics of the system were visible made no difference. The cables must go! And they went, through the tedious process of optically "blacking out" the lower third or fourth of every shot that showed a "hooked" airplane. The picture was released this way with those disturbing black panels popping in and out. Two weeks after the Hollywood opening of *Hell Divers*, Popular Mechanics monthly magazine came out with an article, profusely illustrated, which included detailed photographs and explanations of aircraft carrier landings, with those forbidden cables all over the pages! L.B. Mayer was a staunch Republican and possibly that Admiral was a Democrat. I don't know.

The gallant old "Saratoga" now rests peacefully beneath the waves of an ocean which was once her vast domain, and though I am not sure, the Admiral has also probably retired. Actually, 99.9% of Armed Forces individuals, when Pentagon approval has been given in advance, leave little to be desired, and final viewing of the finished product for official OK is generally characterized by sensible give and take. Though occasional producers or studios may get badly miffed over a turn-down by Washington when requesting use of tax-payer owned equipment and tax-payer paid military personnel, there is usually an excellent reason for refusal. Otherwise, through the years, Hollywood should consider itself most fortunate to have had at times, production partnership with varying branches of these Services.

Hell Divers, a George Hill directed Navy Air and Carrier vehicle starring Gable, Beery and Conrad Nagle included a "bail-out" sequence which parachuted Conrad and Wally into a rock strewn area of pounding surf.

Minor Full-sized Effects were involved here. Wave machines and dump tanks to produce the "surf", a rig to lower two chuted actors into our preheated maelstrom and many plaster rocks covered with many, many sponges, the latter to better avoid bruising the Messrs. Nagle and Beery with, as they were dashed wettily about.

Things went reasonably well. Wally's underwear sprung no serious leaks and only occasionally did "rocks" go floating off or dance merrily on top of an incoming "dump" of water, as wayward sponges were torn loose from their plaster counterparts. Details of this latter nature constitute some of the reasons why Film Editors are supplied with scissors. And through the magic of ingenuity, we kept our powder -'Beery's hide'- dry.

An interesting sidelight was our use of the original Carrier "Saratoga." A "second-unit" crew photographed landings and take-offs for use in the picture during a practice cruise to the Panama Canal. After completion, *Hell Divers* was

I personally value highly, contacts I have been privileged to make with the Armed Services during the making of such pictures as *West Point of the Air* starring Wally Beery, Robert Young, Maureen O'Sullivan (*Tarzan's* "Jane") and 'way down in the cast a Robert Taylor (1935), *Test Pilot*, with "King" Clark Gable, Spencer Tracy and Myrna Loy and much of Bossart's handiwork evidenced in the airplane mounts needed for this picture. The story of Doolittle's carrier launched raid *Thirty Seconds Over Tokyo*, written by Ted Lawson, one of Jimmy's pilots - he lost a leg on this tremendous raid - or the *Beginning or the End*, saga of the Hiroshima "bomb", and others. One such contact, Auby C. Strickland, then an Air Force Captain assigned to us as technical advisor on "West Point," stands strong in my memory as a top individual and, a tall storyteller.

"Strick" retired as a Brigadier General after a brilliant career and war record. I am sure his store of stories has multiplied many times since those days at Randolph Field and at the studio in 1935, during the making of this early Air Force picture. They were all true (true?) stories collected or experienced by the General during his lifetime career as a cadet and "flying" officer in our U.S.A.F. His factual (factual?) accounts were beautifully colored and enhanced by a southern drawl and mirth-filled blue-grey eyes. One I recall, had to do with a young lieutenant, Swede Larsen, who was on a ferrying mission from Randolph at San Antonio, to McAlester, Oklahoma. He was flying a two-place biplane and as "Strick" tells it " — this hyah soldier, asked Swede could he go 'long? His mammy and pappy had a farm near McAlester and the soldier had a leave of absence. Well they just ran into a headwind like all tarnation broke loose, which slowed 'em considerable, and they passed the Red River into Oklahoma about dusk and sure 'nuff Swede was a gittin' nervous. No McAlester. Well now, it got plumb dark and at six thousand feet, ('t'were flat country)" explains Strick, "it looked like the gas gauge was gonna peter out and it did just that, quicker than you could skin a skunk! Now 't'warn't a moon and 't'warn't practically any stars - black as your Aunt Tillie's storm cellar - and when that engine quit, Swede, having dutifully learned the laws of gravity, knew he had to just come down. Now if that dag-nabbed soldier hadn't been along, Swede could a' bailed himself out of there, 'cause he had a parachute. Instead, he just had to mush down and down slow-like as he could, through that black air which was no blacker than his ideers about that consarned hitch-hiking passenger!" In silence, down and down they went, only the swish and sing of the wind through the wing struts and wires could be heard except for occasional muffled Scandinavian oaths. And they landed! A sort of crash-bang landing in pitch darkness, but a landing. No more wind sing, everything quiet, except for a huge air exhalation from the farmer boy's lungs, followed by, and Strick continues, "'Gee! That was a mighty fine landing, Lieutenant!' and Swede, braggin' a bit replied, 'You're darn tootin' right it was, Soldier,' and I swan if he didn't climb right out of his cockpit and fall forty feet through the scratchin', tearin' branches of a tree to the dad-blamed State of Oklahoma below. And he broke his leg!"......!

Or, the time when a cadet was making practice landings somewhere in the sticks of central Texas and nosed over on his back. Hanging, unhurt, by his seat belt, he was about to release himself when the "w-h-r-r-r-r" of a husky diamondback, visible now as the dust cleared, stared right into the upside-down eyes of our "blue-yonder" boy, all of about twenty-one inches away. Strick says, "That horn-swoggled rattler was spittin' mad. Invasion of private property or somethin'. Anyway, he wouldn't move a cotton-pickin' inch. He'd quit rattlin' now and then but ever'time Cadet Laocoon — no foolin', that was his name — that Greek guy who got nipped

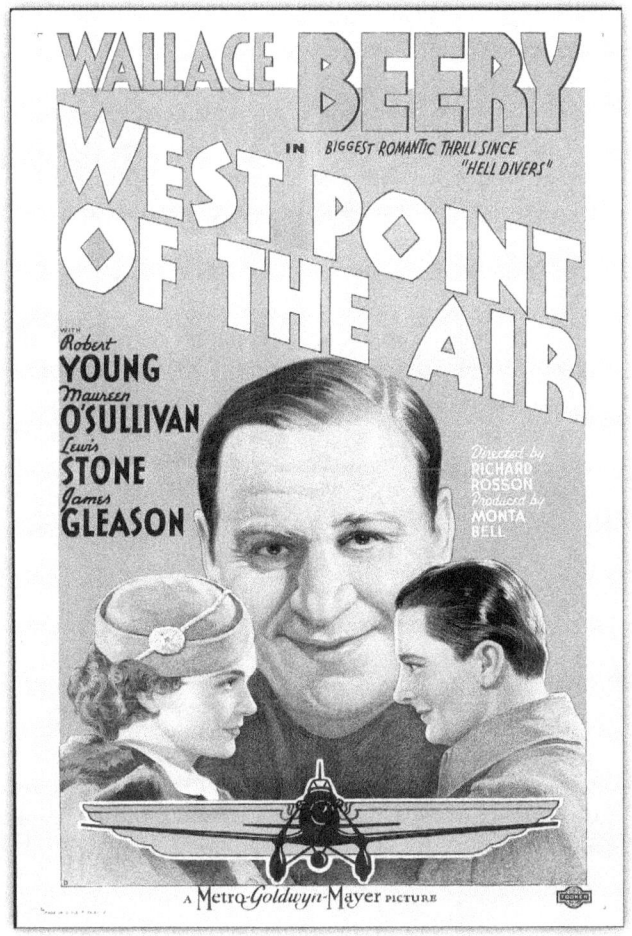

by a bunch of serpents — ever'time young 'Coonie would breathe, old diamond-back would start a'buzzin' and spit a little. He might've been a great-grandson of the snake who's on the flag of Mexico and maybe remembered the Alamo. Anyway, about two weeks later we rescued Cadet Laocoon and he'd learned to quit breathin'. Yessir, he won ever' apple-in-a-tub contest on Halloween; he could eat the whole thing 'out comin' up for air. Us'ta lie on the bottom of the Medina River an' watch th' canoes go by. We had to boot'im out'a the Air Corps, missed too many bugle chow calls, ears all plugged up with water when he'd go t'sleep takin' his bath. Guess he would've starved." The General has been Head Master of a couple of boys' schools since retirement and I envy the youngsters who have learned discipline and life and humor, and more discipline, under this stern, glint-eyed, demanding, story-telling "softie."

I'll bet no long-haired delinquency develops in any of Auby C. Strickland's boys, or their boys. Hi, Strick!

Patience! This all may have direct, or indirect, bearing on potential Effects neophytes. A good story could well be the means of winning an argument against obduracy wherever it should raise its stubborn head, even maybe at times among those keepers of the exchequer. Swede Larsen, also retired, achieved high rank like General Strickland, and I see him now and then at Quiet Birdmen gatherings. He remembers the deadstick landing story, but he claims that tree was closer to four hundred feet high than the "forty" Strick quotes. The "QBs" are a pilot organization which came into being shortly after World War One. It is national and "Hangars" (chapters) exist in most cities. Our Los Angeles Hangar meets every other Monday night and long since has Mom (Mom is Nell and Nell is my wife) long since has she learned to regretfully decline almost any invitation which falls on a "QB" night.

The reference above to airmen brings to my mind Frank Clarke, stunt pilot extraordinaire, and <u>also</u> a great story teller. It seems one day in the early thirties, a red hot crap game was in progress in a small office at a local airport when in walked an Indian, who stood staring at the group, motionless. Finally, Frank, between fades and passes, asked him what he wished. He said quite solemnly that he wanted to hang by his hair from an airplane.

Well, in those days, flying dollars were not too plentiful and anything unusual perked the economic imagination of the leather-helmeted, goggled fly boys. Momentarily the crap game stopped. Proof was needed. So the Indian was suspended by his hair from a roof truss in the hangar adjoining, as a test. He claimed he could remain so hung for thirty minutes. Someone noted the time and everyone returned to the little office to continue rolling the dice.

About an hour later Frank suddenly remembered the Indian. He was still there, kicking weakly, more purple than red, and a lot more solemn. They lowered him, got his signature on a hastily drawn contract at five dollars per thirty minutes (hanging only), called the newsreel companies and made a quick thirty-five dollar deal. The shot was made, the money pocketed, the five dollars paid to the star performer and then back to the hangar office.

A day or so later, again appeared our stoic Redskin with a new idea, "Me jump from airplane with parachute and cut um away." The dice practically stopped in mid-air! Where-upon, the Indian explained he would put on many parachutes, cutting away one after the other, free falling until the next opened, reserving the last for a gentle descent to terra firma. This was big! The phones buzzed and the original' thirty-five dollars was multiplied many times by eager competing newsreels.

Several single parachute practice jumps were made and then the final big rehearsal day arrived. Eight chutes intricately harnessed to Chief Snowdrop — some such name had been given to the tribal daredevil, — and from ten thousand feet he jumped. Like clockwork and in perfect tempo chutes one, two, three, popped beautifully and were cut away, followed by four, five, six seven, and, and, — and EIGHT!! Eight? "Well," exclaimed Frank, "there went our meal ticket. I guess he just couldn't count. And no cameras! Just a rehearsal. No dough. What lousy luck!" Chief Snowdrop was probably

inviting that trip to the "hunting ground of his forefathers" anyway. If not on this stunt, certainly he would have dreamed up another even crazier.

Frank, along with Roy Wilson, Garland Lincoln, Frank Tomick, Paul Mantz and many other pilots were the fellows who helped make such pictures as Bill Wellman's *Wings*, Hughes' *Hell's Angels*, *Dawn Patrol*, *Legion of the Condemned* and others, the exciting thrilling spectaculars which they were. Generally there are definite Effects "tieins" and the Special Effects director will become importantly involved in pictures of this type. Meetings with all personnel concerned, particularly the Director, Art Director, Cameraman, Producer and Location Manager, and often a Head Grip and Propshopman, result in flight plan layouts and breakdowns and methods determining which shots are straight, which miniature, which process with background plates to cover, and specifically,' scene for scene, how a sequence is to be fabricated so that understandable points are made and embellished with whatever thrills are required, finally resulting in a coordinated

CHAPTER FIVE

spectacular whole.

The sky becomes, in a sense, a huge blank chart upon which is planned and plotted air sequences. The preliminary tools are paper, pencils, sketches, erasers, and conversation. Best, you listen to these fellows during such a meeting and best they listen to you. The Effects Director, the Art Director and the Pilot have much to contribute to each other towards the successful organization of the handling of these often complicated air puzzles. A real pleasure to hash it out with these fellows. Many are gone, Wilson and Clark some years ago, Paul Mantz just recently. The industry will miss their multitudinous, often gallant, contributions.

There are, and will be, others to take their places. Frank Tallman, partner of Paul Mantz, is one. He is currently hobbling about due to a one-point landing from a skate board. A couple of the older ones, now less active, are John Hinchey and Floyd 'Speed' Nolta.

John earned the title of "upside-down" Hinchey due to his habit of duplicating every accomplishment of any polished stunt pilot – but more faultlessly, and upside-down! He always wore a derby, business suit, flower in lapel, spats and one Warner-powered Monocoupe high-wing airplane. This attire, including the Monocoupe, fit the immaculate Mr. Hinchey as though it had all come from a Bond Street custom tailor. His inverted flight was really something to behold. John crashed once in Arizona, enroute from Illinois, I believe, to California. His total and only comment later was, "I ran out of altitude and knowledge at the same time."

'Speed' Nolta ran a crop-dusting operation out of Willows in North Central California. World War Two saw him flying for the Motion Picture Unit of the Air Force. My introduction to Speed was in a U.S.A.F. Lockheed Loadstar, military version, as we flew towards San Francisco scouting for aerial locations which would simulate a low level, across the bay approach to Tokyo. Jack Smith, cameraman, was aboard and one crew chief. I was riding the copilot's seat and Speed discovered that I was a pilot. When he found out that Harry Ashe had been my instructor, he extended to Harry the absolute ultimate compliment. With a "What am I doing here?" he got out of his pilot's seat, made his way into the plastic nose of the airplane and went sound asleep in the warmth of the sun. I was left engulfed in the deep blue yonder. Though Harry was a top pilot and instructor, flew an airplane before he learned to drive an automobile in the early World War One days, flew a Lockheed Vega for Senator McAdoo, flew Mr. Fleischmann's "Yeast Special" for years, flew for Douglas Aircraft during World War Two, ferried C-82's to Australia and flew a typewriter so successfully that several of his stories were published; though indeed, all of this, I felt Mr. Nolta was grossly remiss in his duty towards the taxpayers, who after all did indirectly own the plane that Harry's former student was now "guiding" – Speed exhibited much too much relaxed confidence.

Publishers detest long sentences. My apologies for the above. Harry's complete career would fill not only long sentences but many long chapters. Real good guy, Harry. As a matter of fact, most people are real good guys, I find. Even those oft' maligned debit and credit gentlemen.

But, back to Speed, now at the controls, as we made a cameragrinding test-run down over Angel Island in San Francisco bay, flying "on the deck" towards Berkeley six and one-half miles away. Doolittle's boys came in low to escape Radar detection in their Tokyo approach.

We flew at roof top level across Alameda, over Oakland and Berkeley, and practically shaved the TV aerials of Richmond. Startled American faces from windows and roofs skittered past. For our purpose they became Japanese faces. This was the area you saw in the Mervyn Leroy directed, Van Johnson vehicle, *Thirty Seconds Over Tokyo* after Doolittle's B-25's had arrived over their target. The approach to the city was strictly 'on the deck' to escape radar detection and we chose a camera grinding test run over Angel Island low across the Bay towards Berkeley some six miles away. For good measure we flew under the Bay Bridge, fore and aft. Knowing the thrill value of this skimming, seagull scattering approach, I asked Speed if he couldn't fly a little lower, to which he replied, "I can't, Buddy. The tide's in." But he did and I am sure he added salt spray to our lightly loaded ship. What we didn't know was that proper clearance from the Military in Los Angeles to the Bay Area had in some

Floyd "Speed" Nolta (1929). Photo courtesy of George Nolta.

THIRTY SECONDS OVER TOKYO (1944) PRODUCTION #1316

Thirty Seconds Over Tokyo- Floyd "Speed" Nolta flying low over Oakland Bay.

Left: Richmond substituted for Tokyo in this Process shot.
Right Alameda Naval yard substituted for Tokyo bay.

Process setup on Stage 12 of "The Ruptured Duck" B-25 cockpit for Spencer Tracy and Van Johnson scenes 285-B and 302-B above.
Courtesy - The Academy Margaret Herrick Library.

manner been goofed, and though our Loadstar bore the Air Force Star-Circle insignia, every anti-aircraft gun in the vicinity followed us through its sights and range finder for every low level inch of our travels. The war was still on.

Shy not away from such assignments. Rather, insist upon planting your feet in the big middle of them from start to finish.

Active participation as well as 'paper planning' can and should be part of the well rounded Effects Director's routine. Avoid not such opportunities as the above. Elements of risk, yes. But big dividends in experience gained, in excitement, in developing a valuable closer association with the men who actually "do the stuff" and in following that previously expressed bit of sageness, "do the unusual, as well as the usual," at every opportunity.

Reference to Mervyn Leroy above reminds me that there is a dearth of Director recognition contained herein. Our association with a host of these gentlemen, occasionally a lady, has been varied and certainly most generally pleasurable. A few downright so. Mervyn is one of those; always highly interested in Effects' problems, genuinely appreciative when we deliver and charitable should a miss, but not too big a one, occur. For years, known as the "boy" director, big fat cigar always protruding, Mr. Leroy has his credit many fine accomplishments, not only in the movies but in other activities, particularly thoroughbred racing.

Additional "downright so" (pleasurable) Directors with whom we have crossed Art Direction and Special Visual Effects paths, many in the dim past and excluding those previously mentioned in the past pages, are Victor Seastrom, Charles Brabin, Mickey Neilan, Frank Lloyd (the first *Mutiny on the Bounty*), Harry Beaumont (left pictures years ago for oil), Robert Leonard (May Murray's ex, Gertrude Olmstead's happy present), Boleslavsky, Frank Bozage, George Hill (writer Frances Marion's beloved until his tragic death), George Fitzmaurice, Edgar Selwyn, Chuck Reisner, Jack Conway (a habit of slapping one ear with the speed of a machine gun while discussing a problem), Sam Wood (difficulty at times in explaining what he wanted, but knew when he got it, performance or whatever, that it was right or wrong), Wesley Ruggles (a delightful five weeks with Wes in Mazatlan on *The Sea Bat*, not one of his better ones but exciting because of our efforts to elect a Queen for an annual charity festival; we helped with potent black powder explosions along the beach in front of the Belmore Hotel; successful to the tune of some fifty or sixty window-pane replacements which were not anticipated in the movie's budget. (Our queen won). King Baggot (one of our early full Art Director's chores, *Lovey Mary*), John Stahl (*Memory Lane*, the initial baptism), "Wild Bill" Wellman (an almost all-time favorite; tough, gentle, sensitive, vehement; quite a somebody, is Bill), Ed Sedgwick (comedy and slapstick de luxe; Buster Keaton in many of Ed's early ones), Johnny Waters (also for years a second-unit director, not afraid to ad-lib and thereby improve a sequence), Tay Garnett (an old-timer still mega-phoning), Harry Bucquet, Norman Taurog (tickles with adroit comedy and equally adept in steering subjects of sadness or drama), Freddy Zinneman, Roy Rowland, Bundy Marton (he and "Backlight" Yakima handled largely, with the vary able assistance of horseman Glen Randall, *Ben Hur*'s chariot race), Frank Capra (many outstanding directorial credits), John Sturges (excels in camera use and set-ups and in owning a fast Italian Ferrari), John Huston (*The Bible* his latest), Panama and Frank (a team of laugh producers, Norman Panama and Melvin Frank), Tony Mann (mostly in Spain does Tony now hold sway), Chuck Walters, John Ford ("The script? Does anyone read the script?"), Mark Robson, George Seaton (his Williamsburg restoration activity, which includes an uncredited movie of its history, is an other feather many feathered cap), Michael Anderson, Alfred Hitchcock (he directed only one at M.G.M., *North By Northwest*).

But back to a few examples of past Full Sized Mechanical Effects. Some years ago, Fred Astaire who was as nimble mentally as he was physically, came up with a dance routine which was to take place in a rather confined room. It was to start normally on the floor (where else) and included some graceful leaps over and onto various pieces of furniture as only the incomparable Fred could do it. The number was lengthy, however, and the room was small, so to avoid too much repetition Mr. Astaire had decided to enlarge his area of activity to include walls and ceiling! Why not do a few involved rhythmical steps up and down the walls in a completely horizontal position? And why not go further with an upside down bit of terpsichorean art on the ceiling? Why not? All in split second timing to the tempo of a pre-recorded rendition which might have been entitled, "Call In The Full-Sized-Effects-Boys, Boys," That was not the released title, but we were called nevertheless.

The solution of course, was to keep Fred reasonably perpendicular at all times and rotate set and camera. This was accomplished by building the room inside a 'barrel,' a steel frame which would serve as a solid camera mount so that camera and room at all times remained in constant relationship. Simple? Well actually with Fred's athletic, well-balanced adroitness, yes. The 'barrel' consisted of giant rings fabricated from 8 inch channel iron, the open flanges of which were on the outside perimeter, so that they could be supported and maneuvered on roller-bearings. A smooth and accurate motorized control coupled with a gentle braking device, supplied the essential mechanics and having 'glued' everything in the set, including a glass of 'water,' so that horizontalness or upside-downness would mean naught, we were ready for Mr. Astaire's bounding aesthetics.

A day or so of rehearsals uncovered a 'barrel' operating propshop man who had an ear for music, instant reflexes and an instinct for timing. The gravity-defying number was shot with a minimum of tumbles and shin bruises. Perhaps the unsung hero was the camera operator who though firmly seat-belted, was required to follow Fred's gymnastics by panning and tilting his instrument, often in an inverted or 90° angle to mother earth. The chandelier required some doing as it had to 'stand' as well as hang, and our plastic 'water' spilled nary a drop. Those channel-iron rings, by the way, in a previous picture had been used as a mount for a heeling submarine interior set. Hence, Fred, and particularly the budget people, should have bowed in grateful obeisance to the Navy, to the original inventor of a submarine and to some distant writer who had had the temerity to include in his script a sub that must heel.

An interesting and I believe new though simple method of introducing 'waves' breaking over a ship in a storm, was contrived and installed during M.G.M.'s last *Mutiny on the Bounty* production. The "Bounty" had been reproduced in its entirety, except for topmasts and top-rigging, on our Stage 30. It was mounted on a Bossart designed rocker which enabled the whole ship to roll as though pounded by angry seas at the touch of two levers which activated this beautifully counter-balanced mass hydraulically, with little more manual effort exerted than that which a lullaby-humming mother might use to rock her baby's crib. The term 'rocker' has been bandied about heretofore. Perhaps we should interpose to briefly define this close friend of the Effectsman. There are many

types of rockers. Drawings of several small ones appear at the end of the 'Process' chapter. Roughly a 'rocker' is a platform on which a 'set' is built or placed and as the name implies, it rocks. A rocker with a ball pivot support in its center, will tilt in all directions. Others hinged at one end will rise or fall at the opposite end while others, like a teeter-totter, will move only longitudinally or laterally.

Power choice is usually hydraulic, though other means such as counter-weighted cables to power winches are employed. A very old one of ours is an eight or ten foot diameter half a sphere, which, when small units are aboard, may be operated manually. As the weight load shifts, a non-center balance moves to off-center during the rocking. Counterweights help to reduce the changing loads.

It is in this area that design and engineering know-how enters. The stabilizing or proper mergings of power needed, estimated load, counterweight required (the latter to vary its function the tilt increases or decreases) spells the difference between a smooth, easily operated rocker, or a dud.

Our "Bounty" rocker was an enormous steel-trussed structure with bearing point at the bottom of each inverted truss from prow to stern. Its movement was lateral. A series of hydraulic rams, interconnected in that they all received equal flow and discharge of water, provided the power transferred to them from heavy duty pumps. Counterweights in the form of huge concrete blocks and large cast iron balls were attached to each truss along both sides by chains and cables of varying lengths. When the ship was on an even keel they rested on the bottom but as she keeled to portside the starboard weights would be lifted, short lengths first, followed by the longer length to compensate for the increasing off-center load. A starboard rock reversed the procedure.

Many variation in the rocker family. Some have been vertical as was one designed for the side of a large freighter in M.G.M's *Wreck of the Mary Deare*, but the principles entailed are similar. Bossart's cradles, aided and abetted by many studio craftsmen, worked.

But we needed those seas, the white water from which must break over her starboard bow. A scenic-painted stormy sky backed up the ship, providing for shots dead ahead, straight aft and everything between, along her starboard side. No place for dump tanks with which to effect those 'seas' without their being within the camera's range.

A volume of water suddenly dumped and plunging down a steep flume to an upturned lip at the bottom, is still the best method of delivering a large quantity of water to a given area without generating excessive velocity. The sky backing forward was some thirty-five or forty feet from the prow of the ship which allowed ample room for her projecting bowsprit and for low unseen effect equipment, wind and spray, but not dump tanks. So we simply placed several of our largest high in the trusses of the stage <u>behind</u> the backing, attached steep flumes which carried the dumped water to near floor level from where it rushed in an almost horizontal <u>enclosed</u> flume <u>beneath</u> the painted sky to points near the bow where an adjustable lip projected it up and onto Captain Bligh's storm-beleaguered ship. Some doubts as to the effectiveness of this installation because of the long floor-level travel necessitated, were soon dispelled. Only the introduction of salt into our fresh water supply could have improved the seeming absolute reality of our very photogenic dump-spawned onslaughts.

Possibly this application of an old, tried and true piece of effect equipment, the dump tank, has been used before or since, but to us, this adaptation was another first, not particularly world shattering but a worthwhile "can do," to put in your memory book.

The Big Parade, an early Irving Thalberg-King Vidor World War I epic starring John Gilbert and Renée Adorée, supported by such stalwarts as Karl Dane and others, now memory dimmed, brings to mind our old 'black and white' method of marking pre-prepared artillery shell explosion locations on a 'battlefield,' so that actors and extras advancing across 'no-man's land' would be forewarned and not blown hither and yon. A piece of jagged red flannel, plainly visible to the eye but not to black and white film, was firmly pegged on the top of each neatly-filled, powderladen 'shell' hole and served as a taboo against close proximity to such markings. It almost always sufficed. But not once upon a time.

While reminiscing one day with Mladin Zarubica, ex-UCLA football player, ex-PT boat skipper, now big ditch-digging engineer and lately also successful author ("Year of the Rat," and "Scutari") he recalled an incident that had to do with another 'red-marked' battlefield of M.G.M.'s, this one I believe for *Balalaika*.

Football players from both U.S.C. and U.C.L.A., were two handy sources of supply for this rather rugged type of "extra-ing". They were often hired by the studios to help them further their educational pursuits financially - and, indirectly, to better lever from them, choice fifty-yard-line locations in the Fall.

Well, as Mladin tells it, one of his cronies, a hefty right tackle, and he himself were among those chosen for the *Balalaika* battle, and on the night of shooting distinct instructions were loud-speakered to all 'soldiers' to beware of those bits of red flannel. At "Action! Camera!", smoke pots merrily exuding, dampening visibility, and assistant directors yelling, "OK Go!, Start crawling! Get through that barbed-wire!" (the barbs were rubber) "Run! Crouch! Crawl! Run!", the 'troops' took off. In the big middle of no-man's land, several granddaddy explosions had been prepared, one of which became momentarily the resting place of, you guessed it, our two-hundred-fifty pound right tackle. Mladin nearby, suddenly saw a piece of crimson projecting from under his pal's girth about midships, and yelled, "_____" The "_____!" was drowned completely as at that selfsame instant, shell-hole number 17 was effectively detonated by a distant powder man, on cue and properly. The meticulously prepared hunks-of-cork-and-sifted-dirt 'hole', was now possessed of a third ingredient — one football player. The whole powder triggered mess rose majestically, the light weight constituents of the mixture sky-high, though somewhat less altitude was attained by part three.

A bit shaken upon landing but fortunately still intact, our unplanned 250 pound 'effect' was hurriedly approached by Zarubica who quite askance, asked, "you dumb cluck! Didn't you see that red flannel?" Through a mouth full of cork and dirt and barely audible came the reply - "I'm color blind."

How the coaches taught this man to tackle the right color on a football field, I do not know. Perhaps they had never played against red-jerseyed rivals-- although one opponent <u>was</u> U.S.C., sort of maroonish. Confusing. Of course, in those days U.S.C. always defeated their crosstown rivals. Perhaps color blindness had something to do with it.

The design of mounts for various vehicles - cars, boats, ships, planes, motorcycles, et al, are duties that fall within the scope of Full-sized Effects. Their purpose is to impart realistically acceptable action, to said vehicles while they are completely out of their element and as they 'work' in conjunction with another Effect medium, usually Process. Reference to John Bossart's many contributions in this field always aided and abetted by Eddie Stone's crew of craftsmen, has been made throughout this book. The 'dreaming-up' of their desired functions, however, generally falls within your provinces. Head Effectsman aspirant, so it will behoove you to lay out your schematic mounts so that all characteristics of the critters, be they a leaning motorcycle, a banking or diving plane, a skidding race car, a pitching boat or a rolling ship, or whatever, are included. Real value here in the ultimate delivery of such scenes and a real need for engineering and inventive help from the Bossarts, the Eddie Stones (Construction Department Head) and others.. Many have we had through the years and I count as near the top in challenge and interest this phase of Effects' work.

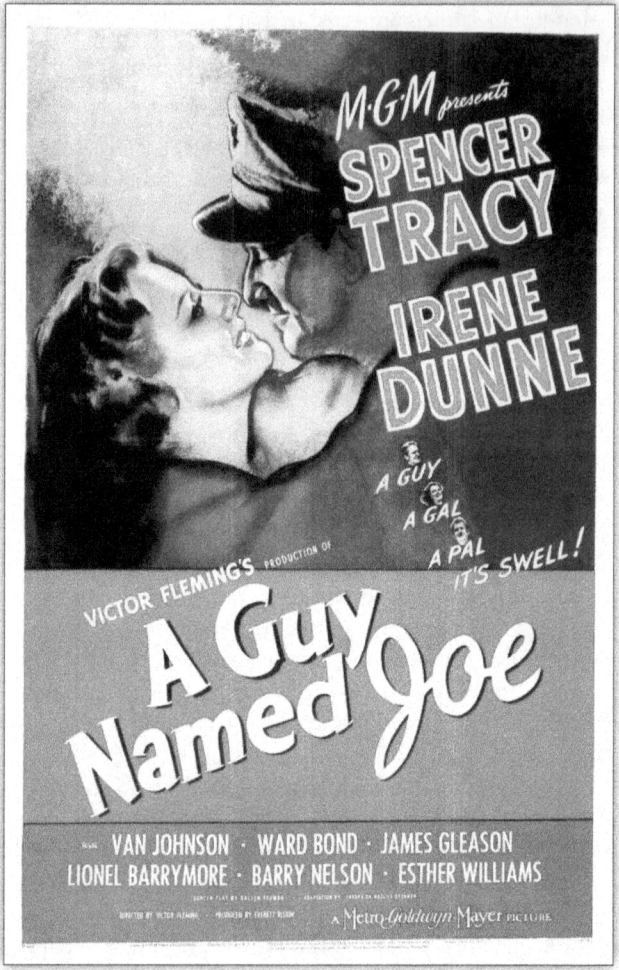

A full-sized P-38 used in *A Guy Named Joe*, with Spencer Tracy and Irene Dunn, directed by the one and only Victor Fleming, stands out as a wonderful example of teammanship in handling a pretty tough assignment. This airplane was required to 'fly' in front of a large Process Screen — and that it did, controlled off stage by a lever the size of a pencil projecting out of a box about twelve inches square and eight inches deep, which contained electrical instructions imparted to hydraulic activators. Miss Dunn banked, climbed and dove at the will of this little box. The airplane was supported at one point only, underneath and considerably aft of the pilot and this was the only area necessary to avoid in shooting. Side angles, three-quarters, ahead and back angles, produced shots which intercut beautifully with longer vistas of actual or miniature P-38's. John's 'pencil' and box, his overall design of support and control, executed perfectly by Lampkin's machine shop and Eddie's prop shop wizards, supplied one Effector's 'dream' with workable answers. As mentioned previously, throughout *Test Pilot* were many similarly to be solved enigmas and the 'team' seemed to always come through. A few more 'firsts', I believe, in this one also.

A simple quickie, though hardly qualifying as a full-sized mount, follows. Why movies with winter sequences always seem to be made in the summer, and vice versa, I do not know, but such is often the case.

One M.G.M'er, which included a ski sequence, was naturally scheduled to be made at summer's peak. Insufficient funds to send a Second Unit to snow country, much too far New Zealand or Chile, so how to photograph skiers schussing down a powder slope when all nearby mountains in our hemisphere were totally devoid of 'powder'? An inter-office 'blue', not to be confused with, the 9:00 A.M. shooting 'yellows', was duly routed to the Special Visual Effects Department along with a duplicate to the Art Director, the contents of which suggested that "we take careful note and come up with something — important considerations as to cost features are paramount".

In progress at the time in the old Pan Pacific Auditorium, was a Roller Derby, one of those six day mayhem and splinter begetting races in which the bad guys and gals were always dumping the good ones all over the track in their 'sportsmanlike' efforts to win a 'heat' or whatever those point-gaining 'rallies' were called. I had been a spectator for several nights and it was during this period that we had been recipients of the Production Office 'blue'. As so often occurs in our mental wanderings over a problem, two plus two becomes four. In this instance, however, it seemed possible that two roller skates plus two snow skis might make one pair of roller-skis. Brilliant? — and economically sound too, by golly!

Action was put into some preliminary words by contacting one of the good guys as well as a sort of cutie-pie good girl, during their respective rest periods between "jams" (Note - In line with the all-inclusive ferreting of indisputable research in order that words and phrasing be correct in this epic, it was thought that 'heat' and 'rally' might not be proper terminology, thereby casting a blemish on the otherwise pure

CHAPTER FIVE

contents of its pages. They are not proper terminology. These rough set-to's, we discovered through diligent searchings were called 'jams'). Hence, between jams a tentative deal was made with these two Roller Derbyites. A long, not-too-gentle slope was constructed and covered with sufficient marble dust so that proper 'powder' would rooster-tail behind the two 'skiers'. They were backed by a white scenic ten foot high drop, running the slope's length which bore a few painted rocks for variety's sake, and placed sufficiently distant from Judy and whatever his name was, to avoid their shadows being cast on to the backing by a frontlight sun. A bit of foreground set completed the essential wherewithal, matte painting to supply above and below that which would finally depict long shots of a girl and a boy 'skiing' in the whiteness of an Alpine wonderland.

Close up long-focal-length-lens panning shots were covered by the set itself. A slight side tilt of the camera added to the steepness and a twenty-frame-per-second camera speed provided a bit of additional dishonest velocity to the two schussers. Not that they needed it! Those well-oiled rollers barely projecting from the underside of their skis directly below each ski-booted foot, were not in the least slowed or affected by a quarter of an inch or so of marble dust. They just flew, and at the bottom we provided a level to somewhat uphill stretch of slowing area, ending with strands of shock cord encased in sponge rubber so that our good guy and his pretty companion would not splatter themselves against, or damage any of the many standing sets on M.G.M.'s Lot 3- All worked well, a. few minor stumbles followed by a few major tumbles were not at all serious — the set being easily repaired and the reactions of our two roller-skiers were simply that compared to the falls and rude shocks, so intimately peculiar to roller derby heats or rallies, or "jams". If you are a stickler for researched facts, these set shattering tumbles were a tea party. Maybe on some late late TV program you will see a re-run of this movie's episode. If so, please don't tell your children of its doing and help us maintain the faith of the innocents.

Perhaps as we approach the windup of this Chapter, we should stress the value of 'continuity sketches'. In TV they are called 'story boards' and for many years Walt Disney's product has been pre-planned, practically 'written' in sketch form, as have all cartoons for that matter, and many 'live' features. So the Idea is not new, but its application to an involved Effect sequence should be a must. Very helpful, these thumbnail drawings in which one shot may be broken down into numerous progressive parts. And always there is the hope which usually turns into realization, that the artist will add beneficial pluses of his own. Such a gent is M.G.M.'s long time sketch artist, Alexis Dukelski. Certainly we have had many other talented and adept men in this field whose sketch and illustration contributions are and have been of major importance. Duke shines above at times, and seldom below, this high standard of excellence. Of Russian birth, his early arrival in the U.S.A. was followed by the usual struggles of language and a strange new country. Success must be presumed, as he holds a B.A. from the Massachusetts Institute of Technology, a Masters Degree and Travel Fellowship in Architecture from the same Institution which gave him the opportunity of further art and architectural training abroad. Few sketch artists have this broad a background and in our many and diversified demands it has stood valiantly as a knowledgeable sponge well equipped to absorb any and all of our thrown curves. Beyond these academic excellences, Duke has inborn traits of good taste and sound judgment in fields other than those of his chosen profession. I have used and I value his opinions on many unrelated subjects and should a 'blue Monday' thrust its gloomy presence upon occasion, one of his inimitable smiles will do much to dispel so unproductive a mood. You're on the team, Duke, and not just as a bench warmer.

How could I omit Bruce Bushman (son of Francis X, our "Ben Hur the First" Messala), Dave Constable, Stan Johnson, Dave Hall, Gene Johnson, Harland Frazer, Freddy Tuch, Ernest Tonk, and others from the past, in discussing this group? I can't. All tremendous talents. All occupying unsung niches in M.G.M.'s Hall of Fame.

So we conclude this chapter. We have glanced at some of the "Oscar" rules of the Academy of Motion Picture Arts and Sciences which relate to Special Visual Effects. We have chronicled a few examples of the, in alphabetical order, first category, "Full Sized Mechanical Effects", and some indications have been given of the "overlapping" and combining of categories to solve problems. Contrivances have been mentioned, rockers, treadmills, etc., the design and often invention of which can fall in the realm of the Effects Director. Reference to the "predictors of doom", and to well meaning interferers of the routine of handling, from start to finish, the "eight ball" problems which confront the Special Effector, have been made. There has been brief documentation of one or two M.G.M., and possibly industry, firsts. Tribute has been paid to the "helpers" and particularly one, that stubborn, remarkable engineer who practices so well, horse sense!

Wally and water, Pentagon protagonists, story telling pilots, stunt pilots, and just pilots have been discussed, and the continuing suggestion to "get in the swim" regardless, has been stressed. And may I here and now add, possibly repetitiously, that each individual's formula for success must include the cooperative help of others. Even Bossart's many noteworthy achievements are usually aided by the contributions of such as Eddie Stone, M.G.M. Construction Head, Bob Staples, Ray Lampkin, Dario Mortara of the Machine and Metal Shop, and others, all of whom, in their own rights, are sufficiently expert to, upon occasion, require and accept help from others. My own lucky stars have received many personal attestations to this fortunately available storehouse. It is of equal importance, however, to know when to filter, or perhaps turn down completely, proffered and even asked-for help. This particular talent is unfortunately not inborn. No rule to follow here. Continued exposure over the years is probably the only answer and luck.

Following the above sageness we tripped the light fantastic, though indirectly, with Fred Astaire in a 'barrel'. Then we thoroughly doused the "Bounty" with dump tanks positioned neatly and unobtrusively behind a 'sky'. We extolled dump tanks as prime drenchers sans unwanted velocity and we proved that a sufficient 'head' of water will push itself for some distance horizontally with little loss in effectiveness.

Marked shell holes, armed and loaded, were related to a color blind football player and then we detailed one of many mentioned vehicle mounts, hydraulically, mechanically and electrically operated. We stressed teammanship as it relates here, and suggested that the top 'dreamer' divorce himself not from this phase of Full-Sized Mechanical Effects.

A hot August summer was converted into a white snowy winter with the help of some opportune thinking and two hardy roller-skaters. This was followed by a concluding few paragraphs anent continuity sketches and grateful recognition of the many artists whose charcoal and brushes have formulated guide lines for those of us who dabble in Effects' responsibilities — hoping for and usually getting, added dividends from all — especially one smiling individual.

So herewith the Full-Sized Mechanical Effects Category. Not complete however, without reference to a 'film clip' prepared some time ago for the Academy's Annual Oscar Awarding shindig. It befell me to produce this 'abbreviated short' of about two minutes, which was to precede the announcement of the Effects' Award winner of that year. What better than a young lady in abbreviated shorts, no less, holding a silver tray upon which 'Oscar' stood looking coolly out over the black-tied, beautifully gowned assemblage? And what better than to have him slowly turn on the tray to behold his holder? And then certainly what better in the remaining one minute (90 feet of film) to have him immediately melt into a bronze and gold glob in the middle of the tray? Indeed, what better!

Applause burst from the audience, which grew in appreciation for some reason, as our Miss Special Effects profiled her departure, camera right.

I suspect <u>OUR</u> Special Effect, that smouldering, melted Oscar, played a miserable second fiddle to the lady, as the full side view of her protruded startlingly during her slowly paced exit. At the least, we should have re-christened her "Miss <u>Extra</u> Special Visual Effects", not "Mechanical", definitely not "Miniature", nor "Optical" or "Matte Painting", but unquestionably a combination of the two remaining Categories, "Full-Sized" with "Animation!"

END OF CHAPTER FIVE

(Above) Harry Ashe, pilot instructor on left, and yours truly flew this one from Cleveland to Los Angeles in 1929.

(Left) M.G.M.'s 1928 embryo pilots. Standing Merrill Pye, Bill Daniels, Doug Shearer. Squatting, the author, Jimmy Mannat, Ray Binger.

(Below) our cattle-herding Spartan, a speedy craft which could fly up to 120 m.p.h., downhill.

TOO HOT TO HANDLE (1938) PRODUCTON #1046

Pictures from *Too Hot to Handle* in the Full Sized Effects Category. This sequence is also referred to in the chapter on Miniatures. (See illustrations in Miniature Chapter.)

A "behind-the-scenes" story follows: Permission had been obtained from the local Harbor authorities to shoot our chartered vessel with controlled piped gasoline fire aboard, stunt extras to dive into water, etc. etc., when a "method" rival of mine predicted dire consequences and imparted his story of impending tragedy to the Studio's Management. Men would drown, ship would burn and sink, who would be responsible? "Gillespie did not tell us he intended to lose the ship and drown people!" said the Harbor authorities and permission to do anything at all at sea was withdrawn.

The ship had already been chartered, protective fire-proofing applied and a goodly sum of money already invested.

What to do? Mr. Mayer knew an attorney John V. Lewis of San Francisco who knew well the ropes in Washington D.C. , and off to the Capitol he and the writer DC-3'ed. First, interview with the Secretary of the Interior who referred us to a Captain Fielding, Merchant Marines bigwig. He took a very dim view of showing any vessel afire (the "Morrow Castle" disaster had just occurred and it was apparent that they would grant nothing which might affect any development or growth of the Merchant Marines. Our sequence had actually been based on the "Morrow Castle", newsreel coverage of which was to be one of Clark Gable's experiences as a Newsreel cameraman, in the story. Again, what to do? That night I wrote a new idea synopsis of the sequence in which the ship was of a foreign registry, carrying contraband of war. A long distance call to Larry Weingarten, the Producer, the next morning and the idea was enthusiastically accepted. "Much better," said

he, "and now we can blow her sky-high - all that war material!"

"That we'll do in Miniature," said I, and off we taxied to Capt. Fielding with this new approach.

"Well, this puts a different light on your problem. I think we can allow you to go ahead." Permission was re-granted and we were Culver City bound a few hours later.

My well-meaning pessimistic friend prevailed upon Management that danger still lurked and insisted that swimming tests should be held and that no stunt men should be allowed aboard during the "holocaust." He conducted the tests, a touch lengthy course from shore around a pier and returned, considerably more trying than our planned paddling about the ship with floatable debris and life preservers. Several of the testees almost didn't make it!

Also our controlled gas fire was ruled out by M.G.M.'s fear-inspired Underwriters, although our fuel supply was to have been submerged alongside the vessel in a large steel tank. And no stunt men aboard. Too dangerous! Johnny Waters and I were aboard, along with about twenty prop-shop men who threw dummies from the decks in lieu of people. Not too dangerous for us apparently and though we received no stunt checks, soap was freely supplied to remove smoke soot and grime at the end of the day.

Past experience in controlled fire went down the drain and the though adequate, suffered from total lack of leaping flames in the areas aboard, chosen with the safety of the ship personnel paramount. Down with the interferers!

TOO HOT TO HANDLE (1938) PRODUCTON #1046

Too Hot to Handle - Miniature 'newsreel' plane shot in process against full sized plate of full sized ship at sea. Controlled fire and smoke aboard.

Ditto above, closer Ship supposedly loaded with contraband of war. Fire areas insulated with "Wylolite".

Old garbage truck bodies, brick mounted on decks were loaded with rubber tires, crude oil and gasoline.

Too Hot to Handle sequence, continued. She blows! - but in miniature. Scale, 1"=12".

She sinks. Cameras were mounted on high platform which circled area on railroad tracks some 150 feet in diameter to simulate view from circling plane.

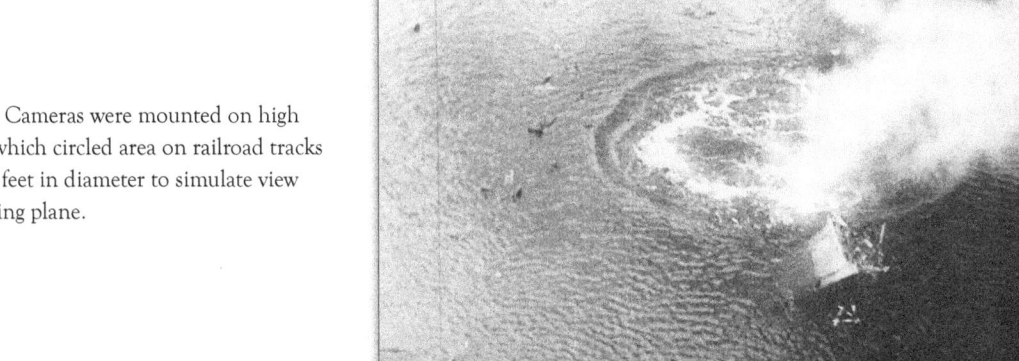

Post activity aboard full sized ship. The author removing a lot of soot. Johnny Waters on left. Not always roses these special effects jobs.

87   "FULL-SIZED EFFECTS MASCULINE AND FEMININE"

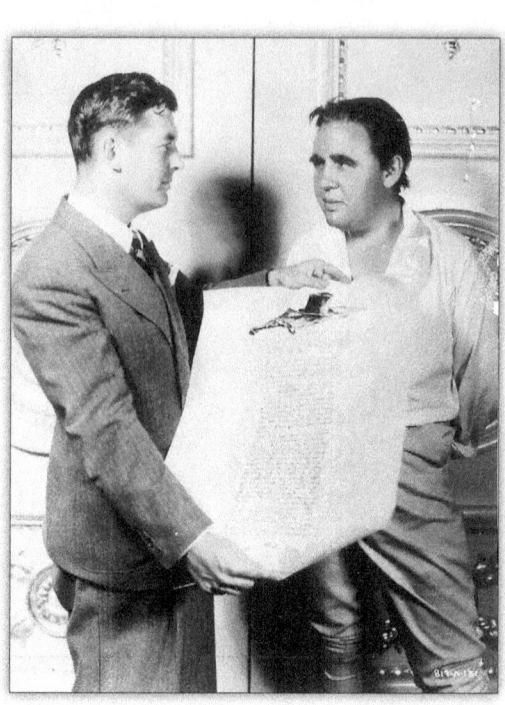

Left - Tahitian 'drafting room' 1934. First "Mutiny".

Right - 'Capt. Bligh', Charles Laughton and a youthful A.A.G.

Selling J Walter Ruben, Producer on right.

Apparently no sale. Bill Kaplan, onlooker.

The "Wizard" wicked witch, pre-backfiring smoke 'bomb'.

Cameramen Len Smith, left, George Folsey right and Eddie Hannon, Author of the "Glorified Plummer" gem.

We designed, overnight - Harlan Fengler built, this land speed racer for Lucien Hubbard's *Speed*. Early thirties.

CHAPTER FIVE

```
A.A.G.           "A TIME OF GLORY"              12-15-64
         (FULL SIZE, MINIATURE, PROCESS)              P. 1
         (SEQUENCES WHERE AIRCRAFT ARE INVOLVED)

SCENES       SET OR LOCATION       D N    GEN. NOTES

1,3          EXT. ROAD - 6 NIEUPORTS   D   TROOPS BELOW ON ROAD
                                           PLANES FLY BY-SALUTE.
                                           MIN. OR F.S.

2,4,5        EXT. COCKPIT-NIEUPORTS    D   C.U. WATERS - SALUTES
                                           LOW LEVEL FLYING
                                           SHOTS FOR TITLE
                                           PROCESS - SHOOT B.G.'S

6            EXT. AIR SHOT-6 NIEUPORTS D   FLY UP INTO CLOUDS
                                           F.S. OR MIN.

7            EXT. AIRDROME #1          D   NIEUPORTS LANDING
                                           F.S. OR MIN.

104,105,     EXT. FRENCH AIRDROME      D   THREE ANCIENT NIEUPORTS
106-111                                    ON TARMACK & TAKING OFF.
112                                        F.S. OR MIN.

117,121      EXT. SKY - 3 OLD          D   HEADED FOR AMERICAN
             NIEUPORTS                     AIRDROME
                                           F.S. OR MIN.

118          C.U. COCKPITS             D   SHOTS OF KIMBERLY
                                           MARTIN AND WATERS
                                           PROCESS - SHOOT B.G.'S

136,138      EXT. AMERICAN AIRDROME    D   3 OLD NIEUPORTS CIRCLE AND
                                           LAND
                                           F.S. OR MIN.

140,151      EXT. AMERICAN AIRDROME    D   3RD NIEUPORT CRASH
                                           LANDS - BLOWS UP.
                                           MIN.

170,172,175  EXT. AMERICAN AIRDROME    D   RECRUITS GET GROUND
                                           INSTRUCTION - THE REMAIN-
                                           ING TWO OLD NIEUPORTS AND
                                           GUNNERY PRACTICE   F.S.

183          EXT. AMERICAN AIRDROME    D   C.U. OF FARMAN ABOUT TO
                                           TAKE OFF. CASSELL AND
                                           HANNIFY - F.S.

184,185,     EXT. AMERICAN AIRDROME    D   FARMAN TAKES OFF.
186,188                                    FARMAN LANDS
189

190-196      EXT. SKY - FARMAN         D   TRAINING SHOTS -
198,199                                    F.S. OR MIN.

             EXT. COCKPITS - FARMAN    D   MARTIN AND HANNIFY
                                           PROCESS-SHOOT B.G.'S
```

```
A.A.G.           "A TIME OF GLORY"              12-15-64
                                                      P. 6
SCENES       SET OR LOCATION       D N    GEN. NOTES

614,618      EXT. AIR SHOTS - ATTACK  D    FIELD BOMBED AND STRAFED -
             ON GERMAN AIRFIELD            MANY SHOTS INTERCUT F.S.
                                           AND MIN. AND PROCESS

616,617      EXT. AIR-COCKPITS        D    WATER'S, MARTIN'S REACTION
619          AMERICAN PLANES                TO ABSENCE ON GROUND OF
                                           THE 50 GERMAN PLANES -
                                           LOW LEVEL FLYING OVER
                                           GERMAN FIELD, ETC. F.S. & M

622,625      EXT. SKY. AM. SQUADRON   D    ECHELONS OF 5 EACH HEADING
             REFORMED - CLIMBING           BACK TO OWN LINES.
                                           ACK ACK EVERYWHERE.
                                           ONE PLANE HIT   F.S. OR MI

626          EXT. WATERS COCKPIT      D    TRYING TO SPOT NEW GROUP O
                                           GERMAN PLANES.
                                           PROCESS - SHOOT B.G.'S

627,630      EXT. AIR DOG FIGHT #3    D    FROM AIR DOWN TO 1000 FEET
631,632,635  DUSK                          LEVEL, WAVE AFTER WAVE OF
636,638,639                                GERMAN PLANES.  SPOT
640,642,647                                AMERICANS AND ENGAGE.
648,652                                    VARIOUS SHOTS ALL OVER SKY
                                           SIX FOKKERS HIGH. CLOUD
                                           BANK. F.S. AND MIN. AND
                                           PROCESS.

628,629      EXT. GERMAN COCKPITS     D    C.U.'S GERMAN PILOTS
637,641      DOG FIGHT #3                  SPOT BOMBED FIELD AND AM.
                                           PLANES AND ENGAGE.  PLANES
                                           SHOT OUT OF SKY.

633,634      EXT. AM. COCKPITS        D    C.U. AM. PILOTS, VARIED
639,645      DOG FIGHTS #3                 ANGLES, EFFECTS, MEN HIT,
646,649      DUSK                          FIRE SMOKE, ETC.  F.S. AND
650,651                                    MIN., B.G.'S - CLOUD
653                                        BANK, WATERS

643,644      EXT. SKY FROM GROUND.    D    DUSK L.S. OF FIGHT
             DOG FIGHT #3                  PLANES FALLING, LEAVING
                                           SMOKE TRAILS - 10 OR MORE.
                                           BODY FALLS.  F.S. AND MIN.

656,657,     EXT. COCKPIT OF WATERS   D    DUSK, ESCAPES IN BROKEN
658,660,     NIEUPORT                      CLOUDS, SIGHTS ZEPPLIN -
662,863,864,                               HIGH ALTITUDE - PLANE
665,669,670,                               SPINS, GROUND FAR BELOW,
672,674,675,                               GETS HIT, EFFECTS - CRASHES
676,677,679,                               INTO ZEPPLIN. PROCESS-
680,682                                    F.S. AND MIN. B.G.'S
```

```
A.A.G.           "A TIME OF GLORY"              12-15-64
                                                      P. 5
SCENES       SET OR LOCATION       D N    GEN. NOTES

530,         EXT. AM. AIRDROME        D    PLANES (5) RETURN TO
531-541                                    FIELD AFTER DOG FIGHT #2
542,543,                                   F.S. OR PART MIN.
544

545,546      EXT. AM. AIRDROME        N    MOONLESS NIGHT - WORK
547,548                                    ON PLANES - PAINTING

559          EXT. AM. AIRDROME        D    FIELD ENSHROUDED IN FOG.

561,563,567  EXT. AIR-LOW LEVEL       D    HIGGINS NIEUPORT ON TAIL
                                           OF RUMPLER OBSERVATION
                                           PLANE-HITS GUNNER, HERDS
                                           GERMAN BACK TO AM.
                                           AIRDROME.  F.S.

562,564,     EXT. HIGGINS COCKPIT     D    C.U.'S OF HIGGINS DURING
565,566,                                   LOW LEVEL DUEL.
567,568                                    PROCESS - F.S - B.G'S

569,570      EXT. AM. AIRDROME        D    GERMAN RUMPLER LANDS
571,572,                                   FOLLOWED BY HIGGINS AND
573,574,                                   THE REST OF THE
575,576                                    PATROL (5) HANNIFY DEAD.
                                           F.S. OR F.S. AND MIN.

581-589      EXT. FRENCH NIEUPORT     D    FRENCHMAN FORCES GERMAN
             AND GERMAN TWO SEATER         TO LAND. OBTAINS BRIEF
                                           CASE.  F.S. - MIN.?

588,589      EXT. AM. AIRDROME        N    2:00 A.M. SEVERAL PLANES
                                           BEING WORKED ON.
                                           MITCHEL ARRIVES   F.S.

597,598      EXT. AM. AIRDROME        D    LATE AUTUMN MIST AND FOG.
                                           NIEUPORTS, SOPWITHS
                                           AND S.E. 5'S - 17 PLANES.
                                           F.S. OR F.S. AND MIN.

599,611,612  EXT. AIR AND GROUND -    D    LONG ECHELON OF KIMBERLY'S
             AM. PLANES (17)               COMMAND FLYING ON DECK
                                           ENTROUTE GERMAN AIRFIELD.
                                           F.S. OR MIN.

613,614,     EXT. GERMAN AIRFIELD     D    GENERAL ACTIVITY, 10
615,620,                                   PLANES ON GROUND.
621                                        FIELD BOMBED AND STRAFED,
                                           EXPLOSION FIRE, ETC., ETC.
                                           MACHINE GUNNERS HIT HIGGINS
                                           AND 2ND NIEUPORT.
                                           F.S. AND MIN. AND PROCESS
```

Typical preliminary breakdown, 3 of 7 pages. The picture "Time of Glory" was not produced. A World War I air story, full of effects and effect problems. Usually this type of 'breakdown' serves to consolidate ideas and methods during meetings with all departments concerned. In the notes, F.S., MIN., and B.G., indicate full sized, miniature and backgrounds (Process Plates).

77-P

A TIME OF GLORY (UNPRODUCED) 1964

As mentioned in the text, sequences Continuity Sketches are a helpful 'must' in preliminary method determinazation.

These, by Addison Hehr, Art Director, show a proposed attack, World War I, on a German Zeppelin.

Number one is straight miniature.

Number two combines process in the foreground backed by a miniature process plate into which have been matte printed 'German' gunners.

Tricky, this one, because of camera movement along miniature Zeppelin, but possible optically.

Number four is straight miniature.

78-P

These would all be straight miniatures, the exteriors probably at 3/4" or 1" scale. The interiors should scale larger, 1 1/2" or 2" = 12".

A method of adding people referred to on the opposite page might be as follows.

Both parts to be composited are shot from stationary camera set-ups. The miniature top of the zeppelin moves at proper plane speed to and beneath the camera. Ditto the full-sized platform upon which the 'gunners' are stationed.

The equivalent full-sized speed would be impractical; hence it may travel at a fraction of the desired rate. Later optical through calibrated 'printer' enlarging and vertical compensation placement will position the people '<u>on</u>' the cat-walk and avert the illusion of 'skidding'. Both parts should then 'jell' in the final composite.

A TICKLISH AFFAIR (1963) PRODUCTION #1804

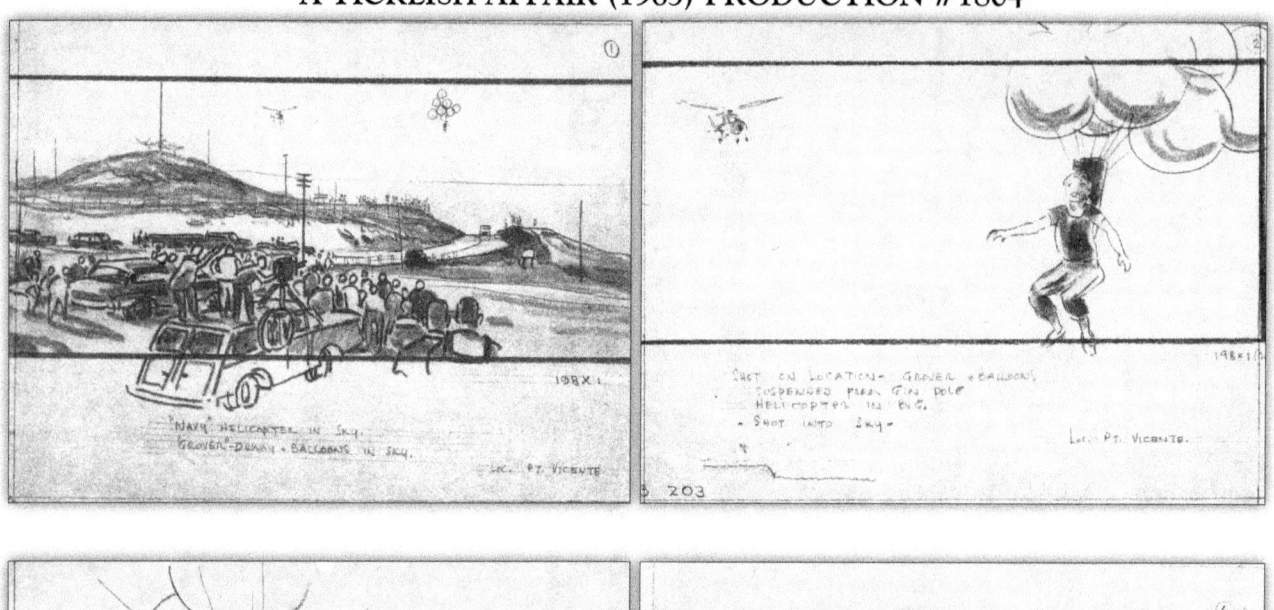

Continuity sketches by Alexis Dukelski for a sequence in producer Joe Pasternak's *Ticklish Affair*. Many combinations of straight shooting and various effect categories.

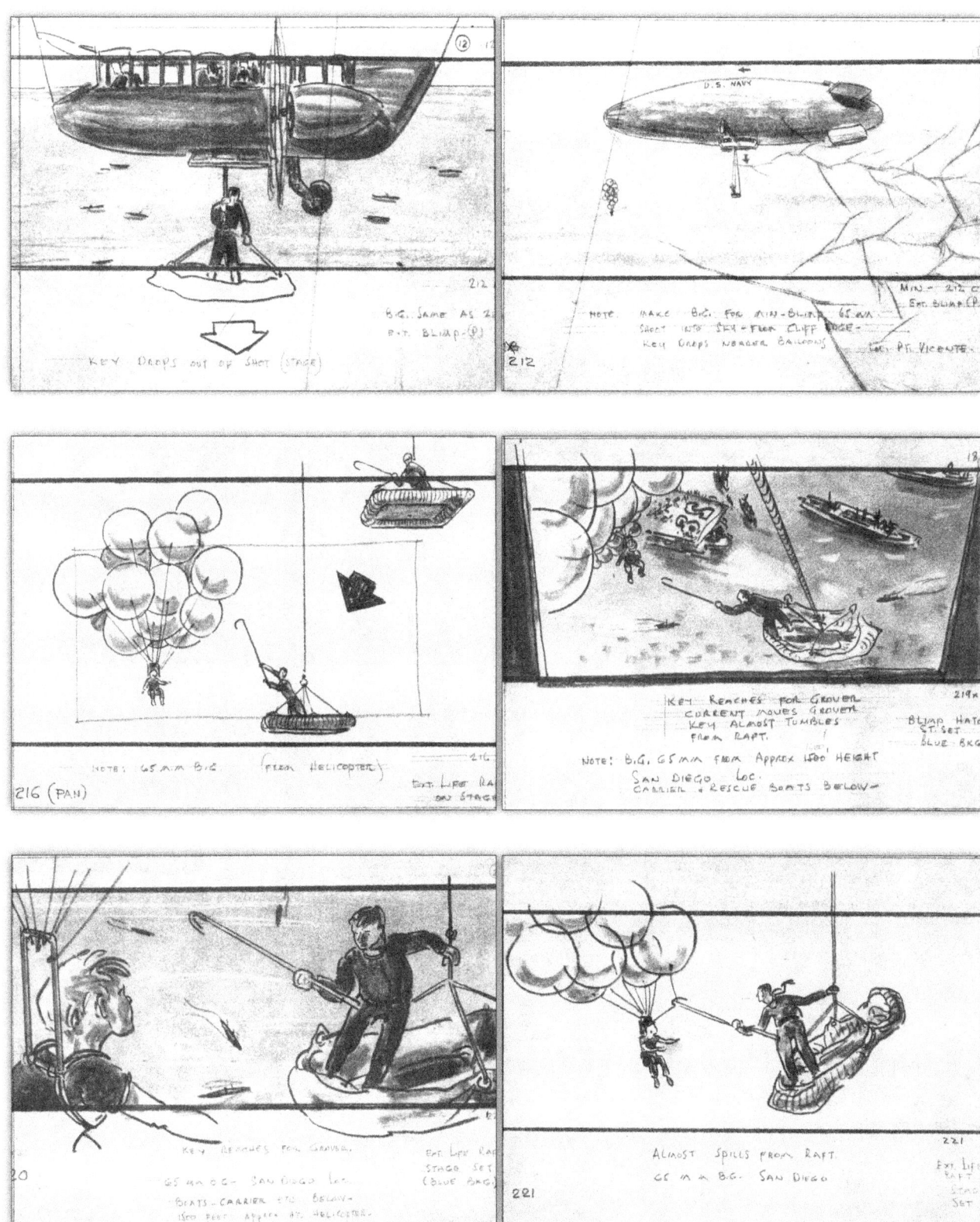

Eighteen only, of some sixty odd sketches covering the entire sequence, are shown. 'Duke' though a graduate of M.I.T., obviously was not subjected to a course on 'Blimps', Navy or otherwise.

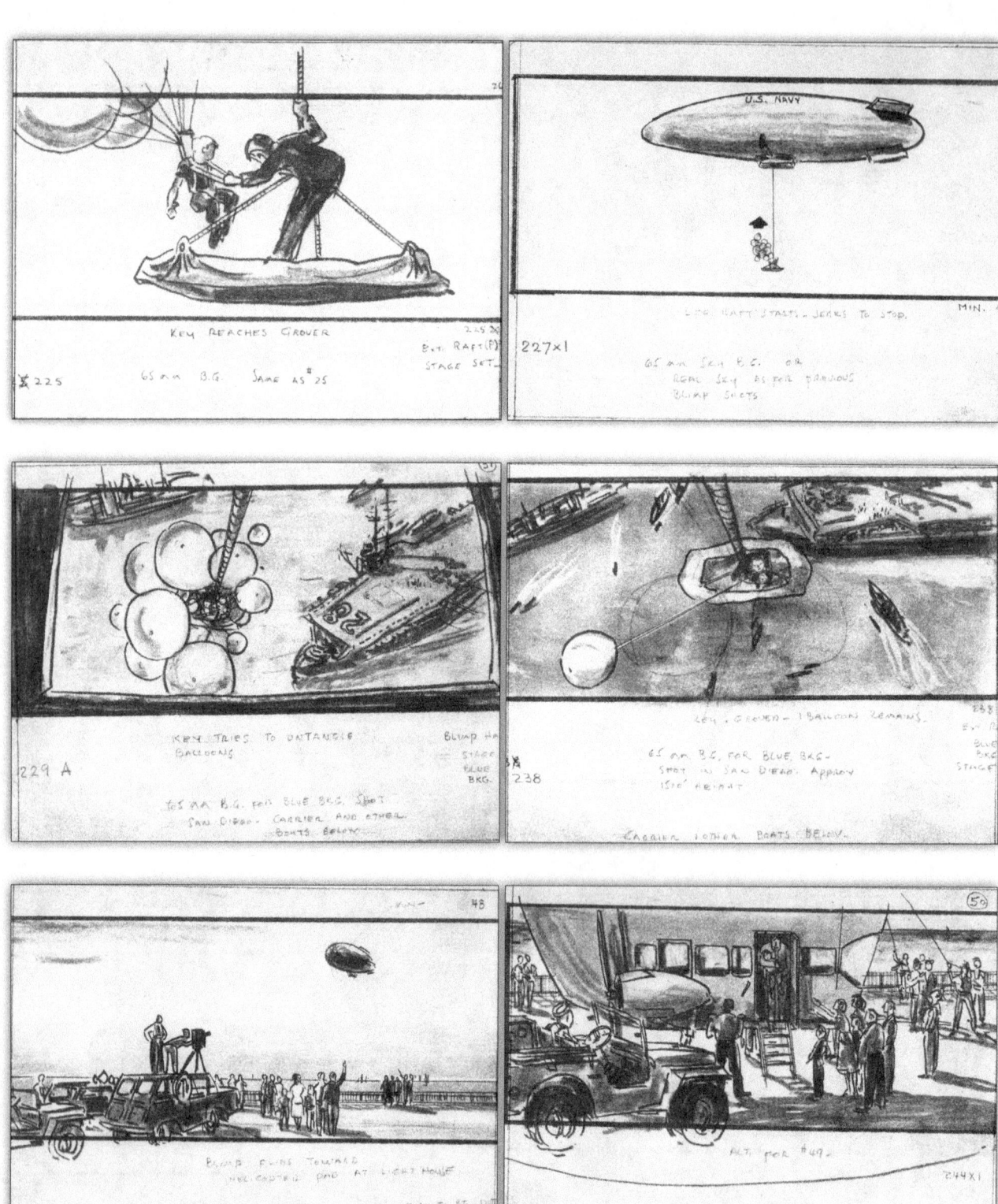

The sequence involved Miniatures, Matte Paintings Composites, Process Optical Travelling Mattes and Full Sized Effects --- all in tune with the Art Director. The value of such continuities is obvious.

THE PRIZE (1963) PRODUCTION #1808

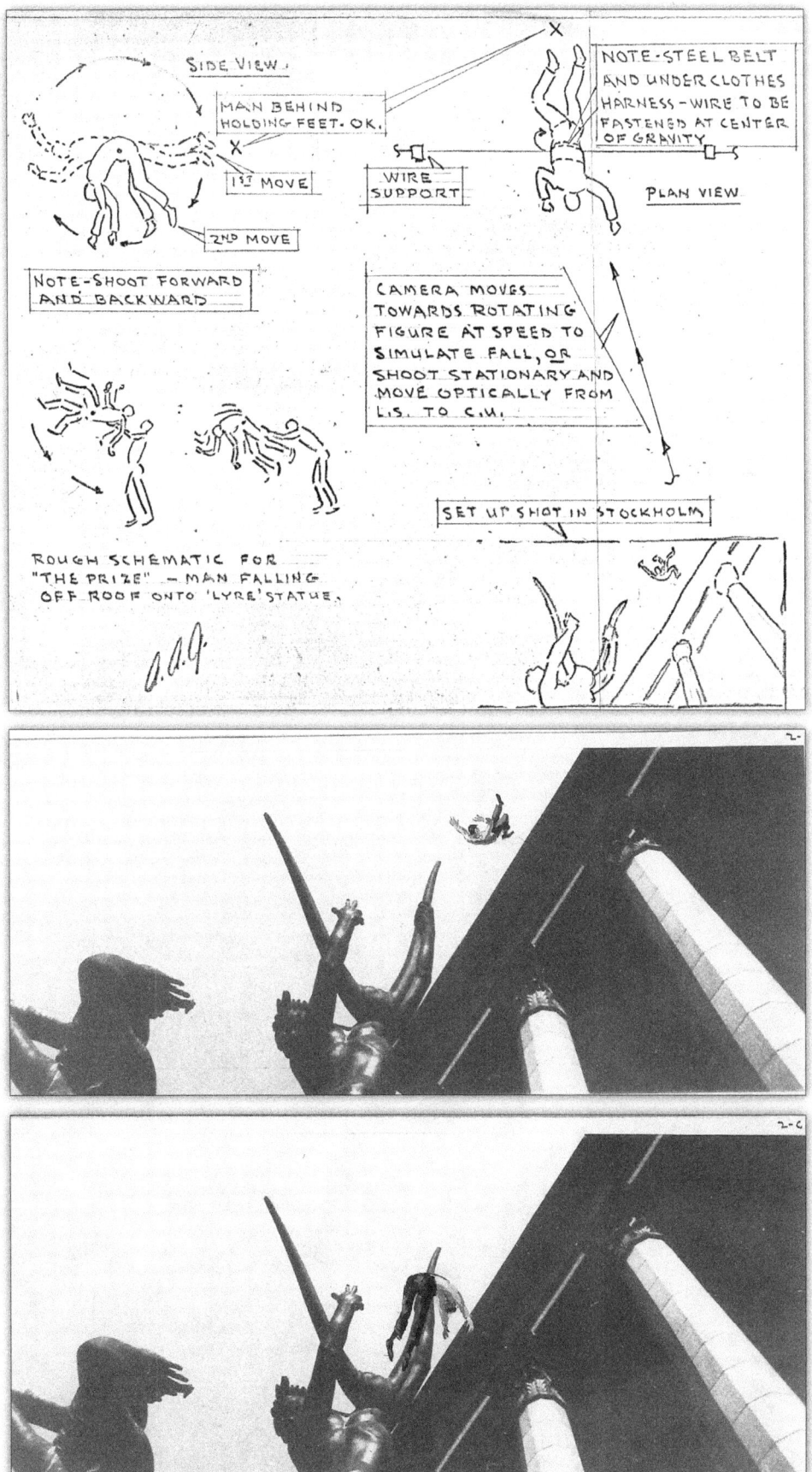

Method determining 'roughs'. (Above) Figure sketched into actual set-up.
(Below) It worked, as you will see, in *The Prize*.

(Above) a battery of 7 dump tanks and chutes. Capacity, 900 gallons per tank. Termites and dry rot eventually flattened this installation.

(Below) Elmer Dyer, one of the early 'sky' cameramen. A typical wing-mount, triggered 'on' and 'off' by the pilot.

(Above) Frank Reicher as "General Lee Wallace", "Red" Golden, and "Billy the Kid" Johnny Mack Brown on "King Vidor's" set of Lincoln N.M.
(Below) An early Studio Tournament. Top row, Tom Held, A.A.G., Jim Basevi, "Put-Put" Harold Rosson; Bottom "Wild Bill" Wellman, Frank Davis, curly-headed Robert Taylor & cinematographer Bill Daniels.

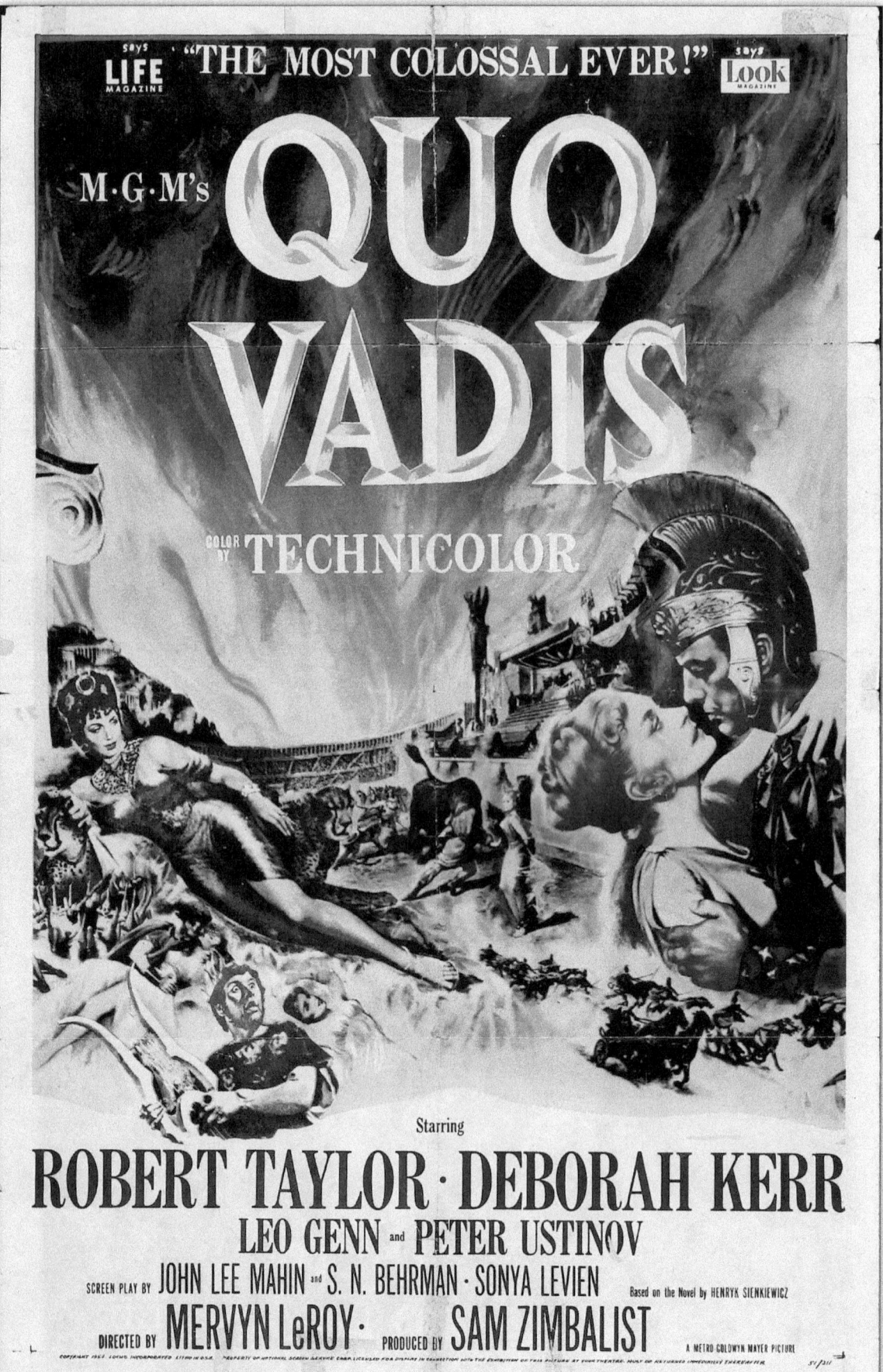

Quo Vadis, MGM Production #1312, Released 1951, AAG Contribution: Special Effects.

CHAPTER SIX

~

"MATTE PAINTINGS AND UNRELATED INCIDENTALS"

Matthew Yuricich - A *Ben-Hur* Matte painting. Matt mixes his colors with same adroitness he formerly mixed as a football player.

Again alphabetically and not necessarily in the order of their importance or unimportance, "Matte Paintings" is the next category to be discussed. This particular tool or device should be perhaps descriptively referred to as "this particular art", more than any of the other Special Effects categories. They are all in a sense special "arts", but Matte Paintings, as the name implies, needs as its prime craftsmen, painters. These highly talented people are known in their field as Matte Artists and in simple form it is their chore to be able to complete for a finished shot the "unbuilt" portion of a scene, a set, a vista, in such complete realism that the audience accepts the whole as unfaked authenticity, absolute reality.

Though this branch of Special Visual Effects could not possibly function sans artists, other experts are importantly involved, particularly cameramen. And certainly the department head whose guidance, criticism and general helmsmanship in his own department and whose ability in the selling to, and diplomatic handling of, sometimes difficult to please upper echelonites, is probably <u>the</u> most important essential towards successfully produced and accepted "matte paintings". And like all other "leaders" he must be backed by those having many additional individual talents.

Suppose the script calls for a high camera set-up of an extreme long shot of a lone figure walking slowly down the center aisle of New York's St. Patrick's Cathedral. Impractical to shoot in reality if for no other reason than the difficulty of lighting. To build as a set, also out of the question. It would be possible to duplicate the Cathedral in miniature, shoot the figure separately and matte print (traveling matte) him or her into the miniature film. Much too costly a miniature for just one shot of this type. So the decision would be to handle this problem in the most economical way possible, as a painting.

A <u>steady</u> tied down camera is set up so that the lone walker can be photographed as he heads down the aisle for the non-existent altar. The only actual part of St. Patrick's needed is that which would be built to "back up" the actor, in this case the aisle floor upon which he is walking. The necessary-to-build portion of a set, is of course a wide variable. It is usually essential however, that the action takes place in front of a prepared portion of the set. Variations to this rule, principally involving animated mattes, as well as more diversified uses of the Matte Painting category will be explained later in this chapter as other examples are detailed.

The initial part of the St. Patrick's shot has now been made. We have on one strip of film a lot of nothing except for a narrow strip of aisle down the center of the film frame along which the lone figure walks. This first step may be optically reduced to allow even greater expanses of nothing, which will later be occupied by the painted Cathedral. And now the magic. With very precise preliminary steps the material to be used on film strip number one is carefully plotted on a fairly large board (we generally use tempered masonite) upon which the area of St. Patrick's which "fits" the original shot, will be produced. Occasionally photo enlargements of the subject are used and adapted as a skeleton more or less, upon which the painting will materialize.

When completed, this realistic reproduction of the vast majesty of the Cathedral is combined with the original aisle shot, to produce a perfect illusion of the scene having been shot actually in and at St. Patrick's. The "perfect illusion" is of course dependent upon the degree of excellence achieved through each step. A photographic match of the two parts and the blend line which "weds" them together, are important must-be-rights in addition to the reproduction of the Cathedral itself which, though a painting, must look very definitely not like a painting, but rather it must absolutely duplicate the real thing.

The above example should be a very simply understood illustration of a problem solved within the Matte Painting category. As a matter of fact it is a relatively simple shot except for the actual painting itself. In this case, St. Patrick's, embodying all of its intricate detail, its perspective demands with their multitudinous vanishing points, the choice of "lighting" painted in by the artist and often his own liberty taking, to achieve perhaps beauty over reality, though always tempered by reality, represents when successful, a tremendous achievement.

In the early days of movie making a problem of this nature would have most probably been handled through what was then known as a "glass shot." I have heard even today, matte paintings referred to as glass shots. This method of supplying "St. Patrick's" also involved the painting of all but the "aisle." However, it was executed on glass, a large framed pane of which was solidly set up to "tie into" whatever area of the set had been prepared to back up the action. Through the camera lens the tie-in points were precisely established on the glass, proper perspectives laid out and the painting was completed. Only upon its completion could the scene be shot, as both parts of the finished whole were photographed in conjunction with each other and simultaneously. Once on film, no corrections or changes were possible without redoing the complete shot which would involve not only actor or actors, but an entire shooting crew as well. In contrast. Matte Paintings entail no such production office tragedies. Once the "aisle" has been shot, alterations to the painting, by contrast, become nothing of great consequence. The "glass shot" certainly was one of the forebears of the modern technique of matte painting and deserves recognition as such.

Warren Newcombe, long at M.G.M., was, if not the first, one of those to pioneer a departure from glass shot procedures. His arrival at M.G.M. in the late twenties or early thirties was accompanied by a great shroud of mystery, a special brand of showmanship which Warren nourished through the years until a "Newcombe Shot" became synonymous with hushed secrecy. A "tight tent" became almost his trademark. It was present on every shooting occasion and within its small dim interior only a chosen few ever ventured, often it was perched on high, heavy "Newcombe" parallels (platforms), but regardless and wherever there was to be a "Newcombe Shot," like the Arab and his tent, there would be Newcombe ensconced in his.

Warren Newcombe was a real character, an eccentric, talented artist, a pretty good chess player, a better ping-pong player, had a volatile temper and a heart as big as the landscapes and seascapes he painted. He was a reverent devotee of Wagner, "Tannhauser" probably being his favorite. Warren's collection of "Red Seals," the old Victor classical records, was monumental. Numbers of concerts have I enjoyed in his home, lights out and the finest equipment available blasting forth in high volume, operas and symphonies by the hour. No artificial aid to the deaf <u>ever</u> needed at these wonderful musical soirees.

Many facets of living, in addition to his painting, were very serious to Warren, including one small gold earring which resided in the pierced lobe of his right ear. This bit of eccentricity served two purposes. One, according to Newcombe, was to give rout to the evil spirits which might attack, weaponed with some sort of malady which I have now forgotten. The other unadmitted purpose was that much conversation would be generated thereto, and this I think was the real reason Mr. Newcombe sported this unusual, for Culver City, adornment. Warren played a bit at these things.

Before and after, top and bottom, of a typical Matte Painting. Photo at top shows total set needed to 'back up' action. The completed shot, about four-fifths, is shown below. A slow optical forward move added a bit of 'sauce'.

Warren Newcombe and the author at the 1947 Academy Award Ceremony - Courtesy Academy of Motion Picture Arts and Sciences.

An interestingly damp custom he long observed was that of pouring water on the tablecloth after dining, into which sogginess he would slap his hands fore and aft, smear the wetness all over his face, sometimes including the back of his neck, and then drying thoroughly with his napkin all exposed parts.

He consistently used his pocket knife to cut his meat after which the cutting blade used would receive a thorough rinsing in his water glass, following which it also would be thoroughly napkin dried.

Yes, Warren Newcombe was a character and to those who really knew him, a beloved and eventually depleted one. That big heart of his really got to his purse strings. As one of the early developers and masters of this complex art, he deserves mention.

During slack periods at the studio, anyone passing near his "building" would hear the click-clack, click-clack of pingpong balls from morning to night. Warren became quite adept and took little pains to keep this talent a secret. Upon one occasion Sam Zimbalist, one time film editor and then producer of many important M.G.M. films, including *Ben -Hur* number two, challenged Warren to a match. A big thing quickly developed, bets pro and con were wagered, one "large" one of ten dollars between the participants was deposited with a trusted stake holder.

The match was to be held at Warren's house and many guests were invited. The evening approached and Mr. Zimbalist, who played ping-pong practically not at all, became suddenly stricken with the first stages of anxious panic. The entire affair had assumed proportions far beyond his intent on that day when he had told Newcombe that he, Zimbalist, had won many laurels at the game. This had been a well-intentioned needle with which Sam kiddingly and with a straight face, attempted to deflate Warren's boasted prowess as an out and out ping-pong ace. A quick acceptance of the challenge by Newcombe ensnared Sam's foot immediately in circumstantial quicksand.

A week passed and suddenly tomorrow was the night! Sam, now desperate, yelled for help and though I was reasonably adept at producing volcanoes without mirrors, had faced shortleashed Bengal tigers and could, with help, build an oversized mosquito, Sam's predicament appeared quite hopeless. Facing the explosive wrath of one W.A. Newcombe in front of all those expected people after this elephantine build-up called for drastic action. Promptly!

Now, dishonesty is not a trait to be recommended in this volume. However, a good Special Effector should maintain a dab or two of it always available on his crowded palette. We dipped our wand into one of these dabs and came up with a sensational solution to Sam's situation! "Break your wrist," we told him, "the one you don't play ping-pong with!" You see, he really didn't play much, but the little he had played was played with his left hand, so on our technical advice, he "broke" his right wrist and proceeded to sport as professional a looking cast enclosing it as the very talented members of the plaster shop could contrive.

He arrived at the Newcombes' Brentwood address thus attired, wended his way through the many parked cars, and reinforced by this unlisted Special Effects category, pushed the button which rang the bell which led to the opening of the big front door. With only mild temerity, he entered. The "oh mys" and "too bads" of sympathy elicited by Sam's in-a-sling right arm assured me that design and execution were passing muster. The Plaster Shop boys, in spite of their dinosaur bone heritage, had ridden again. No third strike yet!

Warren didn't exactly explode, though the fuse was burning precariously close. A quick glance at the preparatory labor which had been exerted, furniture removed from the living room, championship ping-pong table with perfect lighting installed, rented seats for the guests and a moderately sumptuous buffet for afterwards. Dear Sam now really quaked. The moment to test and hopefully prove our strategy, had arrived.

Sam apologetically explained his regret over the

unfortunate turn of events and insisted that the match would be played regardless, wrist or no wrist. The script we hoped would be followed from this point on read, " ~ whereupon Mr. Newcombe, in true genteel sportsmanship, declined and instructed all bets be called off. 'We will get on with the buffet,'" was to have been said by our host ~ but Warren had not read the script. Instead he accepted Sam's completely phony and unintentional suggestion of really going through with it. Newcombe's edict; the match before the assembled guests would go on!

But, ~ and with sudden dramatic magnanimity, ~ Warren, with the same flare for showmanship which had given his "Newcombe Shots" importance even beyond their average of excellence, called for his hand, his playing hand, to be tied behind his back and he would carry on for fair Harvard and glorious Newcombe prestige. He would play left handed!

We had foreseen this possibility ~ remember a good Special Effects man thinks ~ and for this contingency we had naturally "broken" Sam's non-playing hand.

Three sets out of five would determine the victor. Three out of three did it. Poor Warren with his wrong hand was terrible and Sam with his right hand, which was his left one, though only slightly less terrible, was enough so to enable Zimbalist to emerge a shaky victor. There exists in many things, and there are upon numerous occasions, points of no return. This had developed into one of them, to grossly understate it.

Man-made orbitings were nonexistent in those days, but had anyone let Warren in on this spoof, so innocently started and now so prodigiously proportioned, a blast off with no count down would have shattered the peaceful equanimity of West Los Angeles.

At a hastily convened council of war later that night, Mr. Zimbalist and his now humbled advisor, in the interests of avoiding high blood pressure causes, and with a sense of responsibility to the Studio that we not wreak havoc on Studio property (Newcombe was considered valuable Studio property) we chose the only path to follow, valorous or not. Newcombe must never find out! At least until such time as age had mellowed him a bit, perhaps in another thirty or forty years. Hence, it was agreed, Sam Zimbalist must not shed his plaster handiwork nor the sling in which it snuggled, until

M.G.M. President Joseph R. Vogel (dark suit) stops by the *Ben-Hur* set and poses with director William Wyler, Charlton Heston, Haya Harareet, Stephen Boyd and producer Sam Zimbalist- Courtesy of John Springer.

sufficient time had passed for the bones to "mend" ~ if there had been any real broken bones to mend.

Day after day our dark secret arrived and departed from the Studio, Sam's secretary forging beautifully the Zimbalist signature whenever a "signing" could not wait for nature's time consuming bone repairing routine. Actually in this case Sam proved remarkably recuperative. A complete healing occurred on the fourth day. This was reputed to have been caused by a mishap to the plaster cast which had inadvertently come into contact with a small hammer and saw from a do-it-yourself kit in the Zimbalist home which up to then had never been cracked.

The happy ending to this tale was Sam's decision to launch a "foundation" for the benefit of starving Matte Artists by donating the full amount of his ten dollar winnings to this worthy idea. Warren was selected as the Treasurer.

In essence the above is mostly true. Both Sam and Warren are gone. Both men made worthy contributions in their field. Both men left too soon. Both men are missed.

Matte Paintings are not all "St. Patrick" problems although the great majority would follow generally the pattern outlined early in this chapter. Refinements and variations solve many otherwise economically infeasible demands.

In the great majority of cases, birth to a matte painting shot is given by the Art Director. It is usually his creation from the original concept through the design and building of the "live" portion of the set and including camera set-up and final sketch of that to be painted. This is done on an enlargement from a blow-up of the negative obtained when the "lower" or action part of the shot is photographed.

It is the actual execution that is left to the Matte Painting Department which when coupled with close advance Art Director contact may result in that execution taking various and intriguing forms. Occasionally two or more action scenes are composited into a final single shot. The word "lower" above is simply a figure of speech. It refers only to the backed up action segments of the picture which can occupy any area of the total finished whole, top, bottom or either side.

Largely because of a man whose name is Clarence Slifer, has M.G.M.'s present Matte Painting Department been able to execute many extremely complicated and demanding shots not often attempted in this particular Effects category. An Art Director, McMillan Johnson, recently appointed Head of the Department, or someone, will dream up a fanciful poser and with a "let Clarence do it," you may rest assured that Clarence will do it. His genius as a top "trick" cameraman in the use of all the sophisticated tools of his trade is well known throughout the industry.

I am quite sure Clarence could "fly" a projection printer blind! To the uninitiated and in explanation, I believe it would be possible for him to consummate the most intimate maneuver, requiring the most delicate of caresses, to that optical love of his, in total darkness while blindfolded. If Mrs. Slifer were inclined towards jealousy, that assemblage of stainless steel, nuts, bolts and glass, gauges and counter-gauges and those many beautiful, attached appurtenances, conceived by her husband, well, this exquisite hunk of metal could well constitute a serious threat to marital abidance.

They are, and for years have been, happily married. It's just that his nice wife doesn't know what goes on when Clarence is quietly alone. Reels of film wantonly scattered about in low key subdued lighting, one confidential assistant perhaps present, and the romantic throbbing and pulsating hum of excited electric motors blending with the tender, rhythmic and eager cluck-cluck, cluck-cluck, of on and off automatics. My, what does go on! All this and inter-meshed gears too.

Clarence Slifer has but one fault. He is stubborn. Like John Bossart, what a migraine (and what an asset) that stubborness can be! This trait when supported by the exceptional "know how" of such men, should be and usually is, understood. It is advisable to nurture tenderly such rare and valuable mulishness. But like that four legged creature from Missouri, it must at times be curbed, albeit delicately.

There, at times, is reached a zone of commercial sufficiency, and occasional nudges by a higher authority are needed, to get the message of "good enough" across. The great possibility of error here, lies in who is the nudger. It normally should be the gentleman directly in charge, the man whose overall responsibility is the completed shot or sequence ~ yes, including cost ~ and no one else. "Good

J. McMillan Johnson, former Art Director, now heads Matte Painting and Miniature Departments (circa 1965).

Clarence Slifer with one of his beloved printers. Dick Worsfold on the right.

Matt working on a shot in "Bounty" mentioned in the text.

enough" (when it is not) coming from someone who doesn't really know, someone whose training and inborn instincts and talents in this particular domain are deep in left field, is worse than a complete abandonment of the project. Much better a toss-out than the inclusion of a less than acceptable result in a finished film. Walt Disney has understood this criterion and has profited in many ways handsomely through adhering pretty well to this precept. Putting it bluntly, film footage that exudes malodorous emanations should be committed to the disposal and only a knowing and qualified nose should determine the degree of stink acceptable.

In this vein I have often commented that it is "necessary to protect them from themselves." Pick whom you will to fill the shoes of the "thems." It can be the Producer, the Director, the Production Manager or even the Saints. And, though rarely, it can be you. Horrors! This latter would be, of course, an utter calamity and could be attributed to that "exception-proves-the-rule" philosophy. Even a Special Effects Impresario can, in extremely remote cases, possibly fall flat upon his nose. I vaguely recall a far away, long ago, inconsequential similar occurrence scarcely worth mentioning. So I won't.

Though it is true that straight painted "fill in" completions constitute the great majority of stints executed by the Matte Painting Department, such variations as "animated mattes" are an interesting and valuable side line. This tangent or offshoot to the normal functions of Matte Painting are not practiced in all studios for varying reasons, which could include lack of equipment and a dearth of top craftsmen.

The reader will recall a brief description of "What is a Traveling Matte" in a previous chapter. You will remember that it is the combining of foreground and background through optical mattes made from the foreground action film strip which, when printed into the background, will produce "holes" in this second strip of film into which the foreground action is inserted or composited. You recollect? Well, there is a relation, in this instance, to "traveling mattes." The exception is that the technique of making the mattes, the "holes," is quite different. There remains the two or more film strips to be combined but, generally, the reason for resorting to animation is that the problem may have complications and/or features not ordinarily solvable through the use of the common traveling matte method.

To be economically sound, this procedure should not involve long footages. The reason for the latter reference to length is because of the necessity of frame by frame animation. Each frame of the action to be matted into film strip number two is meticulously projected onto a pane of glass which has been covered with white paint. It is then precisely outlined and developed into the actual matte by carefully razor-blading the paint away from the perimeter or perimeters of whatever that film frame of action has registered. The use of glass is obvious: lack of variances due to temperature changes and ease of removing the areas of unwanted white opacity, plus availability of the glass and its relative inexpensiveness. What remains is a perfectly outlined solid silhouette which is later photographed, along with many of its brothers, to produce on film the "hole maker" for film strip number two.

This is painstaking work, tedious and time consuming. Time represents that commodity so dear to the budget enforcers, so it behooves he who proposes this step to think in terms of six or eight to probably a maximum of twenty feet of film for the "animated matte" portion of a scene. A twenty foot cut, as an example, would require, at sixteen frames of film per foot, a total of three hundred and twenty separate sheets of glass, "writ by hand," so to speak.

Regardless of result excellence, the bookkeeper's computer is not likely to be plunged into a fit of ecstasy over such per-film-foot expense. But computers and ledgers and those money-mad Grooms of the Production Stables notwithstanding, it is possible to cite proofs of "Star" savings that are not to be snickered at (or to be snickered at not), pick your grammatical choice.

The point is, "Mr. Christian" of "Bounty" fame was not even singed when he stood 'midst searing flame on that Stage Thirty burning deck and got really clobbered by a blazing yardarm which free-fell from on high, downing Mr. Brando in a sickening shower of sparks and heat-laden weight. Method? Animated mattes. Procedure? The first step, from a tied down camera, Mr. Brando or Mr. Brando's "stunt" double, on cue and with flames reasonably, but not too close, hits the deck. First step completed and camera stops as the gentleman exits. Camera starts again, with combustion again rampant, and the signal for one fiery blazing yardarm to drop is given. Star at this point cozily nestled in his stage dressing room listening, perhaps, to a Tahitian record. The yard drops, the fearsome sparks shower, and our number two film strip, sans actor, has been shot.

And now in the quiet of M.G.M.'s Matte Painting Department, "holes-to-be" in the form of one well paid Thespian are plotted, razor scraped, recorded and married to the yard-descending second film strip, after which the real Mr. Brando or Mr. Brando's double, from which the "hole" was made, is inserted. Naturally, the "hole" or matte which represents the actor must "close up" as the yard covers him in order that the figure disappears "behind" the burning debris. Only one small portion of one leg and foot prone on the deck was to remain just barely visible. It did. The audience gasped.

The completed shot was made possible through this application of painting and optical talents, tedious frame by frame preparation and the availability and skillful use of unique tools and combinations of tools. Much of the latter came from the ingenious inventiveness of one Clarence Slifer.

MUTINY ON THE BOUNTY (1962) PRODUCTION #1769

Mutiny On The Bounty - Marlon Brando's stunt double hits the deck as yardarm comes crashing down. Animated matte method with tied down camera to combine both shots. Second photograph exposes matte line between shots. Final photograph as Mr. Christian's legs stretch out from underneath burning debris.

CIMARRON (1960) PRODUCTION #1763

Cimarron - Glenn Ford rushing in front of a galloping horse to rescue a small boy. Tied down camera to combine two separate shots. This required double animated matte method to completely matte Glenn and the boy into the shot.

Another "actor protector" shot handled similarly showed Glenn Ford in *Cimarron*, rushing in front of a galloping horse to rescue a small boy. As before, a tied down camera from which two shots were made. One, the galloping horse, and two, the boy in the center of a Western street with Glenn rushing out to sweep him out from under those pounding hoofs. This required a <u>double</u> animated matte method as the boy and Ford had to be completely matted into that portion of the action which placed them for a few seconds in front of and then <u>behind</u> the horse's legs as it sped past. So, for those few frames the fast moving horse's legs were inserted into the "holes" they themselves had modeled, on those white glass panes, <u>over</u> the matte of Mr. Ford and the youngster. Complicated? Yes. But well within the range of this fine M.G.M. department and, on this one, not too extensive a dent in the budget. A short footage shot, only a few glass frames to be razor scraped and shot. Actually, about thirty.

Slifer's use of the "split screen" technique on the above shot accounted for the fact that so few frame animations were necessary. Variations of split screens have been with us for a long time and usually lie within the functions of the Optical Effects category. In splits, both film strips become one, meshed down the middle or wherever desired. The right half of number one strip, in this instance, covered the horse as he thundered along on a three-quarter angle toward the camera. The left half of number two strip showed the action of Ford and the boy. The blend between the two becomes invisible when properly shot and combined. It was only at the point of contact of the two actions that the shot, of necessity, involved animated mattes.

The term "split screen" is occasionally misinterpreted as meaning that two separate subjects having no common interrelationship are simply combined into a single picture, such as two people talking to each other from separate locales on the telephone. Strictly, a "split" winds up as though it were not a split at all. It represents a single scene, but for a required practical reason is shot with a solid tied down camera in two parts.

One actor playing a double role, when called upon to talk to himself, is a common example. As "Joe," he may be placed sitting down, perhaps to the left of a predetermined "split" line, while to the right may stand <u>anyone</u> so that "Joe" will look in the right direction as he talks to his to be "standing self." This first part is photographed, whereupon "Joe" hurriedly changes into a costume which now identifies him as "Pete," Joe's twin brother. No lights on the set have been changed. Nothing has been moved. "Pete" (Joe) now stands in the position formerly occupied by Mr. Anyone, who now sits to the left of the split where Joe had been, and to a playback recording of Joe's dialogue the second part of the scene is shot. Optical Department combines the two, being cued as to matching footage by the two dialogues. The unwanted half, showing "Mr. Anyone," is <u>lost</u>. Additional types and uses of "splits" will be given in the chapter to come on the Optical Effects category.

A further use and extension of Matte Painting procedures is well exampled by a shot used early in M.G.M.'s costly late version of *Mutiny on the Bounty*. It introduces "H. M. S. Bounty" at dock in Portsmouth, England, prior to the ship's departure on its ill-fated breadfruit journey to Tahiti. The scene shows a long, comprehensive shot of the harbor, filled with square-rigged ships of the period and the usual small craft activity. The camera pans some thirty or forty degrees to the right, disclosing the distant hills, the mid-distant and near-distant buildings of Portsmouth, following which it tilts down through the rigging of the nearby "Bounty" to dockside, full of people readying the ship for its journey. Over all of this fly sea gulls. Truly an impressive introduction, full of that ingredient known in Hollywood as "production."

The elements which combined to make this shot, the art and ingenuity of their development and merging by the Matte Painting Department, is roughly as follows.

First, a shot in miniature, solid stationary camera set up, of water, miniature ships and small craft, principally a longboat type being rowed mechanically by several miniature figures. The ships were a heterogeneous lot and were to be used for their water reflections only. The small craft were properly correct and became a part of the final scene. This shot, photographed at <u>above</u> normal camera speed to lend scale and weight to the water (camera speeds and their important relation to the photographing of miniatures will be dealt with in detail in the chapter devoted to the Miniature category), was transformed by the Matte Artists into a harbor full of historically correct square rigged ships ~ all painted! Every reflection now had an authentic reason for its being.

Secondly, a high camera set up, again stationary and tied down, photographed a full-sized set on M.G.M.'s Lot 3. This set was subsequently completed in the manner described as a "St. Patrick's" type matte painting. The distant hills and buildings were the painted "fill-ins", the lower portion of the shot blending and merging with the actual built portion of Portsmouth.

Thirdly, from this exact camera location the last segment was shot, which consisted of a tilted down, also stationary view, from the same high set up, showing the full "Bounty" with its pier full of activity.

This is an oversimplification of the three preliminary steps but will serve to illustrate the underlying structure of that "<u>single</u>" shot, which so smoothly panned over a host of Britannia's sea-ruling vessels arriving at the end of the pan, to Portsmouth's hilly skyline, followed by a slow tilt-down to a luscious bevy of bustled, extravagantly hatted young things who so very much disturbed Trevor Howard, the 1963

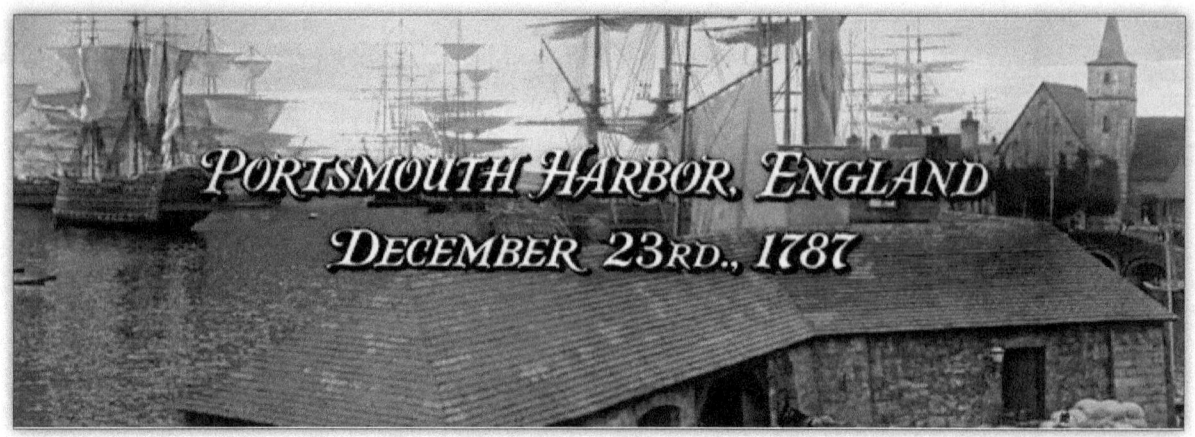

"Captain Bligh." (I am sure had our original 1935 version, the truly great Charles Laughton, been present at this one, he would have "MISTER CHRISTIAN'ED!!!" with sufficient stentorian volume to have jiggled Mr. Slifer's tied down camera perched so solidly on its high braced platform).

Perhaps I should explain the frequently mentioned "tied-down" in its reference to certain camera set ups. It is always desirable that cameras while operating, are free from vibrations, sharp jerks and waggles, or any bothersome unevenness. In "tricks," with all that that word implies, it is mandatory. It should be obvious that one part of a composite which moves will not splice itself to a second part which doesn't, or worse, which does! Hence we should always solidify as perfectly as possible all cameras and camera set-ups whenever negative is exposed which will get itself involved in some later Optical whoopee, Matte Painting skylarking or Process monkeyshines.

Back to the "Bounty". Within the polished mysterious clutterings of Clarence Slifer's diggings, so full of regulated voltages, ten thousandths of an inch tolerances and seemingly inexhaustible supplies of talent, the three strips of film aided and abetted by the all knowing, all seeing Slifer sorcery, are jelled into that "single" shot.

To explain in detail these "weddings" with their optical pans and optical tilts, Clarence's use of aerial images (someday I'm going to really learn about that one myself) his laboratory headaches, his patience and his unshakable (almost) adherence to quality, would, I am afraid, undershoot the mark. This chap represents another of those characters in an early reference to the kind of personnel you "fight to keep." And though true, having kept, you may occasionally have to "fight," best you let him win most of those academic, ivory-towered squabbles.

Oh yes - the seagulls. This, probably an afterthought, was designed to give further credence to an already excellent and easy to believe accomplishment. Whether those flying harbor habitants actually improved the shot is open to some question. They were injected into the whole, not through the "animated matte" technique, but rather by being "burned" in or "superimposed." This is a short cut method in cost and time and as a result, Portsmouth that day had black seagulls.

The point? There are two. One the obvious heretofore stressed, "do it right, at least within a reasonable degree, or do it not at all." The second, much more difficult to determine, could be labeled, "When is enough?"

It would be trite to "oraclize" the above as a brand new pronouncement. Moderation, however, is one of my professed bibles, the dictates of which are much easier to preach than to practice. Give to me one ear, particularly a young one, and I'll fill it with fervid dictums on "moderation." The sermon could be titled, "The transcendental value and rich rewards of being moderate," or possibly, "How about taking it just plain easy, kid?", or, choose any heading you wish.

The word "moderation" has rivaled if not surpassed in meaning and importance in my experience, the word "judgement." In this case, "gilding the lily" (adding the gulls) could qualify as a mild form of immoderation. How to know when to quit! This question serves to couple my two pet words into a team. The second, "judgement," is about as cantankerous a cayuse upon which to remain seated as could be found from the Ft. Worth Fat Stock Show to the Calgary Stampede with Pendleton thrown in for dessert. J.J. Cohn used to call it "opening a can of beans," when his judgement dictated that best the can opener get lost.

Joe "Judson", as we affectionately titled him, was M.G.M. Production Manager for years and more years. Though he represented the "bookkeepers" to which I so often refer and could and did fight tooth and nail to keep we spendthrift creators within certain dollar limits, Joe was the squarest of shooters and could be convinced. In all fairness, Joe often would suggest further pursuance of ideas and methods which might enhance, a sequence even though a possible fractured budget could be in the offing.

In retrospect I would conclude that J.J. Cohn's determination as to when and when not to spill additional beans, struck a pretty high average of good judgement. He always retained close communication however, with whatever native intestinal fortitude he needed, to say firmly, "No!"

Upon one occasion when additional firmness seemed necessary Joe put the ictus on his several "No's" by banging his removed wristwatch on the top of his desk in perfect tempo and smashing fervor, to further accent the positiveness of each of those strongly uttered two-lettered words. Those "no's" carried the weight of one demolished Philippe-Patek. (Privately my suspicion has always been that a reasonable facsimile absorbed those desk impacts. Like perhaps a one-to-ten-cost-ratio facsimile.)

The lesson, exemplified by those probably unneeded "seagulls" and Mr. Cohn's "can of beans," is certainly one worth an attempt at learning. While it is less of an evil to overdo than to underdo most physical dramatics and effects, it is still an evil. Gross overdoing is not only usually wasteful, though at times adding a completely disproportionate ounce or two of betterness, it can in many cases actually harm.

The old, "if one pill is good, two should be better," type of thinking must be carefully analyzed and generally curbed. Not always curbed however, and I wish not to stress this bit of practical advice so strongly that the tendency would pendulum too much in either direction. Milking a sequence that falls within the solving province of Special Visual Effects, can many times supply a film editor with material sufficiently abundant to result in the difference between a fair to good result, and an outstanding result. This latter is almost always box office.

As I re-read the above, I find a lot of words that seem to say two things - do overdo and don't overdo. Confusing, isn't it? The real answer, I would surmise, lies somewhere between Bossart's "experienced horsesense" philosophy and whatever the offspring might be called should "moderation" be mated to "judgement." We could undoubtedly christen such a progeny "Millennium the First."

The "box office" reference brings to mind our preview of San Francisco in Santa Barbara before the picture's final editing and release. "Previews" are those devices whereby a random theater audience with no advance notice is "surprised" by a picture not shown on the theater marquee. Reactions are noted, which in intent, at least, are supposed to lead to corrections of errors, livenings of dead spots and, if possible, general improvements or, may the Fates have mercy, possible sinkings into abysmal depths of out-of-pocket despair.

Now Santa Barbara had experienced a rather severe shake a year or so previous to our earthquake preview, so it is possible their reaction to our efforts in San Francisco were more finely attuned to this type of Effect fare than had they never experienced the rumble and tremor of a sizeable shock. Be that as it may, the streets of Santa Barbara buzzed the following morning with, "Did you see that picture with the earthquake last night!" "By golly, you wouldn't believe it. Darndest movie I ever saw! You gotta see that earthquake!", and many other similar buzzes, followed usually by other details of the picture like " - and we sure thought Clark Gable and Tracy and Jeanette MacDonald were marvelous. Gee, what a good picture!", etc.

But, and hark ye well, Effects aspirant, the big news, the first topic, the main subject of initial discussion and conversation was that Stage 12 born, M.G.M. earthquake! And hark ye also Mr. Producer, along with Gable, Tracy and MacDonald, that's box office!

I will never forget at a viewing of this picture after its release, sitting in back of a rather large, rawboned lady with a semi-furrowed reddish neck, who certainly seemed to get full measure out of this sequence.

With the first distant rumble she sat bolt upright and from that point on to the end of the first shake, she managed to writhe into more positions within the confines of a theater seat than I would have believed possible, even had she been the world's foremost and most gifted contortionist. Maybe that she was.

At any rate as the audible destructiveness quieted down on the screen, so did my heroine - with a long drawn quivering sigh-h-h-h. Out whisked a large handkerchief, and as she settled back limply into her sturdy seat (it must have been engineered to absorb stresses far beyond normal expectancy) she proceeded to energetically mop her sopping face, finally extending the area her now drenched handkerchief had covered, to the back of her neck and then into each ear which proceeded to get a thorough swabbing. This was my first exposure to the knowledge that the inner part of the outer ear perspires. Or possibly she was only removing from those catch-basins the drippings from the many cascading rivulets which for that minute or two had streamed from and through her thick tousled sun-tinged tresses.

I was entranced. And I knew there would be a repeat performance because I knew number two was about due. And here it came, the second shock, the distant rumble, the bolt uprightness, the twisting squirms, the profuse salty exudations, the works. And the mop up afterwards. Real sweet music to one of my ilk. This lady paid us without ever knowing it, the highest of compliments.

We seem to have swayed from the gist of this chapter's Matte Painting topic but such is the fullness of our cup. I trust a rudimentary understanding of the basic whys and hows of this category have been divulged. Much precise technical detail will be garnered by the student only in the class room, and later through discovering just how hard the earth is by sinking his own pick into it – and through guidance by men like Clarence Slifer.

A "St. Patrick's" type of straight matte painting has been sketched. Complicated multi-shot weldings into a single one, with their optical pans, tilts and aerial images have been briefed. The use of animated mattes, not always strictly a Matte Painting Department function, has been described. Early "glass shots," and the Saga of Warren Newcombe are matters upon which we have touched. And we should have learned two lessons about "putting your big foot in," as it applies to a ping-pong game.

The first lesson, "don't do it" and the second "if you do, climb out on a ladder whose rungs spell, 'honesty is the best policy.'"

We know about tied down solid camera set ups. Screwjacks are often employed between the actual camera box and the head to which it is attached, to further eliminate any movement. And we possibly were the recipient of a small inkling of "when is a seagull not needed." That was in the "judgement and moderation" department.

A tribute to Joe Cohn, a tribute to Clarence Slifer and a here and now apology for "un-contributing" to so many others in this area who merit it. Someone said, "if you try to please all, you please none." I am determined to "not please none," so that's why you and you and you have not yet been immortalized, within these expensive covers. Maybe you'll make it. We'll see.

Then we blew our trumpet a bit (again) on one *San Francisco* earthquake by detailing audience reaction -- specifically, one member of it -- in order to again point out the value of Special Visual Effects to the Specie Supervisors and all others. And we hope our snitching on Mr. Slifer about his second (second?) love will serve no tragic purpose affecting the sublimity and foreverness of his connubial state.

With the following thought we conclude this chapter. Of all of the Special Effects categories, Matte Paintings is so closely aligned with the Art Director, it is quite possible that Academy Award-wise it should be removed from the Effect categories and added as an eligible division within the Art Direction field.

Special Visual Effects are overwhelmingly thought of as falling within the spectacular, disaster class of scenes or as out and out "tricks." A matte painting is in the great majority of uses, an extension of Art Direction. Involved in execution, as are the examples noted herein, the results wind up generally as solutions to the problems which confront the Art Director as well as being usually of his own original creative thinking.

Let us continue to recognize this highly valuable medium through industry recognition within the concepts of the "Oscar" givers, but let us switch its vehicle. (The above is not an open letter to the Academy. They are already aware of my cogitations.)

Matte Painting - an economic must, a versatile answer to many Art Direction puzzles, a way out, a skillful craft and a stamping ground for exceptional talents.

END OF CHAPTER SIX

Three of over three hundred titles requiring collaboration between the M.G.M. Special Effects and Matte Painting Departments.

(Above) *High Society* 1956 - Special Visual Effects project.

(Middle) *Kismet* 1944 - Miniatures and Process. Ext. Zuleika's apartment, city scene.

(Below) *Meet Me In St. Louis* 1944 - Special Effects, World's Fair miniature - Ferris wheel, buildings, lights, etc. Technicolor backgrounds used for large process set on Stage #30.

82-P[2]

Another Matte Painting Department's 'composite' with an optical 'tilt-down'. The upper enlargement from a 'frame' of 35mm film was shot at Christchurch, New Zealand. The center, street and traffic, was shot at MGM, Culver City with corresponding 'sun' position. The two combined in lower photo near finished of optical 'tilt-down'.

CHAPTER SIX 114

THIS COULD BE THE NIGHT (1957) PRODUCTION #1708

An excellent example of composite versatility fabricated in the Matte Painting Department. Two separate scenes, top and center, become one with a move towards girl in left foreground, completing another Clarence Slifer piece of sorcery.

This Could Be The Night (1957) starring Jean Simmons just prior to entering "The Tomic" night club.

BEN-HUR (1959) PRODUCTION #1724

Before and after, from *Ben-Hur*. Note that top original was optically reduced to allow matte painting on sides and top of second photo.

THE UNSINKABLE MOLLY BROWN (1964) PRODUCTION #1815

In *The Unsinkable Molly Brown*, original was shot with added 'squeeze' (anamorphic lens) using 65mm film, so that ceiling et all shown at bottom could be painted to complete the composite. A 35mm Panavision aspect ratio was delivered.

BEN-HUR (1959) PRODUCTION #1724

Three sketches for *Ben-Hur* by the masterly artist and illustrator, Dave Hall, for Matte Painting execution. Dave passed on recently (1964). A tremendous industry loss.

David G. Hall was widely known for his early Alice in Wonderland illustrations and collaboration with Walt Disney.

CHAPTER SIX

60-P

Foreground blue backing 'travel-ling matte' set for *Ben-Hur*. Scene 208 A-4, soldiers on deck of galley.

Our fleet of 2" scale miniature galleys used as a background for full-sized action above. Scene 210 X1-2.

Another "travelling matte" set. Jack Hawkins played the role of "Arrius". Scene 220 X5A-3.

Miniature Macedonian galleys attacking. Matte background for foreground above, Shot 27, Scene 231 A-1.

119 "MATTE PAINTINGS AND UNRELATED INCIDENTALS"

BEN-HUR (1959) PRODUCTION #1724

Catapulted 'smoke signal'. Prepare for battle! Our Miniature Roman fleet. Extreme distant galleys were profiles.

The 'Pirates", two of them engaging. Figures were modeled and cast in rubber with flexible wire armatures for 'positioning'.

During the early stages, a 2" scale, 1/6th lineal full-sized, helped the scale of smoke, fire, and water.

Closer shot. To avoid 'staticness' our miniature 'people' were coil-spring-mounted and a few 'walked' about the deck.

See shooting schematics at end of Chapter Eleven for scene planning detail.

CHAPTER SIX

Additional examples of full sized foreground which were matte printed into miniature backgrounds. Charlton Heston, "Ben Hur" and "Arius" on some 'floating debris in these.

An amusing incident, nothing to do with "Traveling Mattes", occurred during the Galley Miniature shooting. All activity aboard, moving oars, miniature people, etc., were triggered by a radio signal. At 2:00 A.M. one black night the dozing watchman was awakened by strange noises coming from inside a huge covered 'hangar' which berthed the galleys at night. Stealthily entering, his eyes popped as he observed all oars operating and 12" people traversing the decks. Some wayward midnight frequency had tripped all switches.

Thoroughly aghast in the eerie dimness one now wide-awake watchman finally headed for the phone and eventually an electrician was roused, sleepily drove to the Studio and disconnected many batteries.

121   "MATTE PAINTINGS AND UNRELATED INCIDENTALS"

DRAGON SEED (1944) PRODUCTION #1305

Two *Dragon Seed* examples of combining Miniatures and Matte Paintings. Areas of action, people pulling locomotive, heavily laden vehicles and barges, below, are miniature. Balance of set was matte-painted. Note bad match in lower enlargement which was corrected later.

HIGH BARBAREE (1947) PRODUCTION #1385

High Barbaree "The Great Bernadino" Marlowe Bros. Circus bicycle loop miniature. Above, prior to matte application. Below, quarter section matted out on miniature.

Captains Courageous, MGM Production #951, Released 1937, AAG Contribution: Associate Art Director

CHAPTER SEVEN

~

"MINIATURES AND MUSTACHES"

Forbidden Planet, MGM Production #1671, Released 1956, AAG Contribution: Special Effects.

A momentary yield to temptation, now and then, can be a forgivable failing, if indeed it should be termed or classified as such. The youngster who must pluck that watermelon, the grandfather who bursts into a silent mental rendition of "Memories" upon observing guardedly and repeatedly a well-provisioned bikini, the thirty-an-hour miler in a twenty-five mile zone and/or many other such yieldings, are quite human. It will be my inclination to give in to similar, harmless, I hope, enticement in this chapter. Miniatures, along with Fullsized Mechanical Effects, are two of my three favored pets. This chapter, following our alphabetical sequence of Special Visual Effects categories, will be mainly about "Miniatures."

It may be enlightening at this early point to define the term as it applies to picture making. A "miniature" is not necessarily small. A miniature is not a "model" in our terminology. We have, on many occasions, prepared "models" of "miniatures" for study before final construction of the miniature itself.

In England, miniatures are termed "models." It is probably just such a stubborn bulldog trait that led to the spilled tea in Boston Harbor some years ago. I have repeatedly protested to His or Her Majesty's Special Effects people as to the wrongness of their nomenclature, particularly to Tom Howard, our M.G.M. British sleight-of-hand hoax producer, to no avail. The British are so profoundly definite! And if Tom were not such a capable gentleman, I would have attempted to use administrative persuasiveness (we in Culver City, you see, are the parent company) to dictate to them that, "as of such and such a date, and pertinent to, etc., etc., you will mend your ways." End of ever communicated quote. Had this fiat been sent, the reply undoubtedly would have come back drafted impeccably in grammatically pure words of the King's choosing, and meaning, "mind your own bloody business!"

Enough about models. Students will refrain from

such "Crown leanings" and will do well to shy clear of any juggling of or disrespect to, our time-honored Hollywood cantankerousness -- to repeat, miniatures are not models and not always small. Smaller than full-sized, yes, but in theory and practice, anything less in size and volume than that which it represents, and which is to be used and photographed in motion pictures, qualifies as a working miniature.

The scale (size) of a miniature is dependent on many factors, the advance determination of which becomes a prized key, contributing largely to success when used correctly. A miniature may be half full-sized, three-quarter full-sized or one ten-thousandth full-sized.

In reality, varying scales are included in most miniatures, ranging from the basic principal foreground size or scale of objects or areas, to infinity. A "saucer" in space, such as in M.G.M.'s Forbidden Planet, illustrates this truism. How big is space? What scale should that indicated billions-of-light-years-away galaxy be? Within certain tolerances, our galaxy was "built" and shown properly in its relation to, in this case, a particular "spot" in space along which our vehicle was to fly. Many liberties could be taken here as we were dealing in the unbounded realm of science - as well as the limitlessness of no dimension-fiction. Such "looseness" must not prevail however, in its application to the achievement of realism or rather the successful depiction thereof.

So, near the forefront of the many early determinations, relative to miniatures, is the question "how big?". We cannot, so to speak, build small water. Hence boat, ship, water miniatures, are among the most difficult, and become increasingly more so when we "drop" the size or scale of such boat, ship or water miniatures.

The ocean-liner-in-a-bathtub cartoon, is a bit misleading. Our M.G.M. "bathtub" is three hundred by three hundred feet, some forty-two inches deep and contains three "wells" that measure from twelve feet to thirty feet in depth. These depths have removable flooring and are used only when added deepness is needed, such as that required to show the upending death plunge of a sinking ship or perhaps a surfacing submarine and in some cases, area utilization for the installment of effect equipment.

It is a tried and true axiom that when water is a component, it behooves the Miniature Director to choose as large a scale as possible within practical bounds. Those bounds are naturally influenced by available facilities, particularly miniature "tank" size, and the nature of the scene.

A storm at sea such as the "Mayflower" weathered in the picture Plymouth Adventure dictated of miniature ship consistent with the size of miniature storm waves it was within our ability to create. This essential resulted in the construction of a sturdy one-eighth full-sized ship (scale, 1 1/2

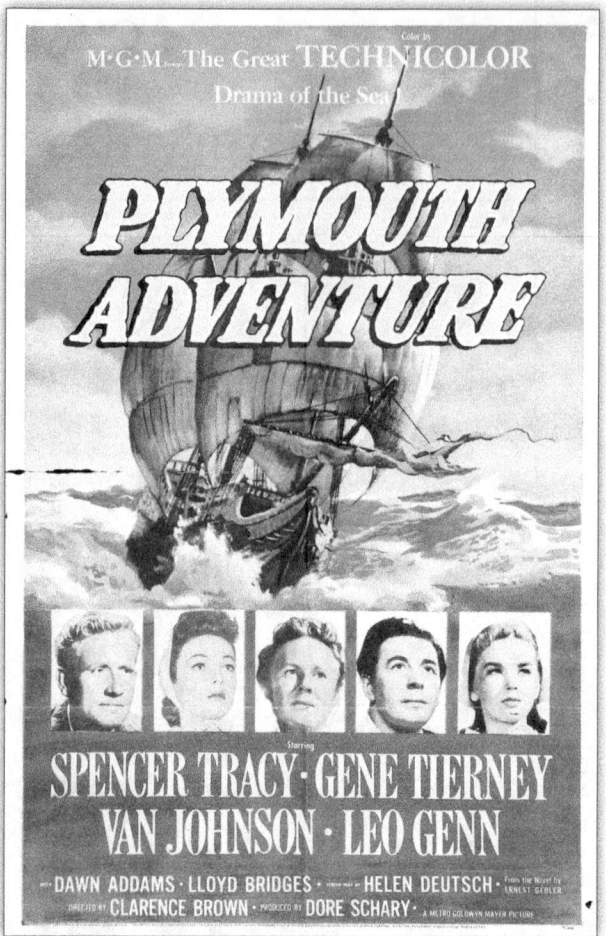

inches, equals 1 foot) which, during the shooting, was put on her beam's end at the height of the storm by a "giant wave" looming out of nowhere and bearing down on our sorely tried, pilgrim-laden vessel, right in the middle of M.G.M.'s wind-whipped, wave-agitated three hundred foot ocean.

This "special wave" was by courtesy of eight large diesel trucks which pulled on cue, from a standing start, a huge inverted chevron-shaped "shovel" riding on rails anchored to the forty-two inch bottom of the tank. This moved a wall of water with increasing speed towards our already tossed and struggling twelve foot miniature ship, and incidentally towards a tossed and struggling shooting crew, clad in armpit waders, who would be attempting to keep cameras afloat, lenses reasonably clear of driven spray, in addition to, often vainly, maintaining their own upright position. Everyone, particularly the shorties, ship water over the top of their waders from time to time in such scenes, or manage to snag a leak. Wet soggy clothes become standard wardrobe which always score unpleasantly. Much more so in cold weather.

The "giant wave" truck-pulled contrivance worked beautifully. A tremendous pelican hook (a quick release device) triggered by a carefully measured, dead-ended cable, served to detach at the last second our onrushing plow from those eight heaving snorting trucks. We preferred this surefire release to a less safe reliance on the braking reflexes of eight individual truck drivers.

Process backgrounds were made for all of the "Mayflower's" voyage, in our square Lot Three ocean. Particularly effective were the storm plates. Of these, our "wave" was outstanding. And bravely watching its approach (on a Process Screen) stood the "Mayflower's" Skipper, Spencer Tracy, astride the Poop deck at his rocking and pitching post. Gasoline-powered wind machines, firehose spray, dump tanks (all full-sized Mechanical Effects) were in total concert to make Mr. Tracy's day just another miserable one. And to produce an important part of a sequence as spectacularly believable, when intercut with straight shots of the miniature ship, as though somehow it had all been done in actuality.

An example, by the way, of Effects category overlapping, Miniature, Process and Full-Sized Effects.

As the miniature wave arrived (on the Screen) we released water generated by two ten thousand gallon pumps running wide open, from under the screen up and over the Poop deck set. Poor old Spence had to almost swim out of this one, "Poor old Spence?" A gap, perhaps, between Mr. Tracy's income and that of J, Paul Getty, but not sufficient I would conjecture, to lack in compensation for a few hours of damp discomfort.

A momentary digression induced by the mention of my good friend, "poor Spencer", is here-to-be chronicled. M.G.M.'s *Captains Courageous* starring Tracy, Lionel Barrymore and Freddie Bartholomew and including Mickey Rooney in the cast, had, as those of you who saw this notable picture will recall, a racing climax which causes the death of the beloved Portuguese fisherman in the story, Mr. Tracy. Victor Fleming, just one of the greatest, was the Director.

Many Effects in this picture, mostly Rear Projection Process. Tracy's death involved his having become entangled in some lines while aloft, as a mast of the "We're Here," a New Bedford fishing schooner, gave way. This supposedly deposited Spence overboard in a fresh heaving sea amidst rising and falling spars clashing with one broken mast and a veritable maze of twisting squirming cables. As he struggled, the weight of the underwater wreckage presumably pulling him apart was expressed in his agonized pleas to be cut loose, to be let go into and below the briny.

Full-sized category answered this call to arms with vim and relish. Our spider web of underwater hydraulic rams and hoses, rigged to manipulate all moving parts, and the protective network of below the surface steel, was a complex labyrinth designed to first, harm not our Star, and second, to deliver to the sequence the illusion of unquestioned authenticity.

An exact description of the installation with its complicated many details will not be attempted. Principal elements, however, were initially a precise layout of the underwater rig. Following this all important preliminary, a steel frame upon which hydraulic rams were to be placed to control all moving parts of the debris, was secured to the bottom of our tank 'ocean'. Half a dozen or so rams were used of varying lengths and strokes, each firmly attached to partially submerged spars and the sizeable length of broken mast. Tangled cables, sail and lines, loosely fastened to these heaving, threatening parts were realistically activated as the wreckage rose and fell. Wave and wind machines added their contribution to the over-all.

Upon completion, after testing and before Mr. Fleming was to actually shoot the scene, I took Spence to the locale of his to-be-heroics and explained in detail, item by item, every last nut and bolt involved. I stressed particularly measures we had taken for his absolute safety including an out-of-sight steel basket which had been fabricated and then placed in a spot to insure his being at all times properly and safely positioned. Number one item, no harm to our Star!! A full functioning rehearsal followed with one of our propshop men in Tracy's basket - Wind, waves, spars swaying and splashing; mast and cables alive - the works.

Spence was enthralled. "Wonderful, Buddy," said he. "Absolutely wonderful!" My question as to whether he had any concern whatsoever about any phase of the rig and its mechanics was greeted by a completely reassuring, "Lordy no! Not a thing to worry about, Buddy. Not a thing." With a parting word of praise, he left.

One hour had not yet passed when in passing M.G.M.'s Barber Shop I was hailed from within by a loud authoritative voice which said in staccato well enunciated words, "What - are - you - trying - to - do? Kill - one - of - our - Stars?" Jim the Barber nervously continued honing and stropping Mr. L.B. Mayer's personal razor. Actors? Phooey!

I really don't feel this way. That is I don't always feel this way. Or rather I am sure in some cases I never react thusly. Spence told me later he just wanted to impress the big boss! He succeeded!

It is strange to me, however, why exposure to discomfort or very minor hazards, reacts as it occasionally does to some members of this profession. A small percentage of top people, so handsomely reimbursed for their histrionic services have lost the respect of many, due to their consistent petulant quibblings over really trivial vexations. It is even stranger to me why their own pride would allow them to be placed in such positions of distaste and derision. I certainly wish not to imply that Spence qualifies in any way as one of the above. It is equally true however, that the route he travelled to touch Mr. Mayer's sensitive quick, puzzled me at the time, no end!

The subject of "scale determination" continues. Only

PLYMOUTH ADVENTURE (1952) PRODUCTION #1552

Three examples of the use of small craft in harbors to lend "life" and reality. These are from *Plymouth Adventure* and contain 'clothes-modelled-on miniature' figures. Foreground boats are larger in scale than those in background which must 'match' in scale the 'ships'. No 'people animation except in foreground row boat whose mechanized oars gave the 'rowers' a fore and aft movement. All shot in Lot Three.

Plymouth Adventure's 'Mayflower' in rough weather. Scale 3"=12". We also built a 1 1/2 scale miniature ship for rougher weather and 'giant' wave sequence.

Eight diesel trucks pulled 50' bulkhead painted like water. It made approx. 90' run at 8 MPH. 8' sq. steel plates totalling 3/4" thick used to anchor ship. Camera mounted no boom to rise and fall to increase scale of approaching wave.

Aboard the 3" scale miniature to shoot process plates for Spencer Tracy at the wheel.

Miniature 'sailors' reefing the mains'le. Figures were not animated. Sail was pulled up off camera.

in the broadest of generalities will we be able to discuss this important step. It remains one of the early decisions whereby final attainment of success will sink or swim.

A few examples out of our experiences may serve to illustrate reasons for big or little miniatures. In *Plymouth Adventure* we used two "Mayflowers", the one-eighth full-sized one (determined by storm and wave size limitations) and one twice as big, quarter full-sized. The scale of the latter (3 inches equals 1 foot) fell within our facility bounds and gave us the added advantage of a less objectionable spread between miniature ship and full-sized water. It was mentioned earlier that small water cannot be "built". But we can build large miniatures. So, within the job-it-has-to-do limitations, and of course, facility restrictions, the advantage is generally to "go big."

Added cost is not as much of a factor as might be supposed, when a sequence to be done in miniature lends itself to large scale. In the majority of cases the big cost item lies in the myriad details of rigging, operation, shooting crews, area rental, overhead, film and supervision; not whether a miniature "Bounty" is sixteen feet long or twenty-four, or a B17 Flying Fortress has a wing spread of four, six or eight feet. As in most things, there are exceptions to this rule. Not often however, so size of a miniature should be determined mainly on what is best, not what seems cheapest. Many times have I been asked if we possess such and such a miniature in stock, the "if" seeming to be regarded as the all important reason for a go-ahead decision. The real importance here of "if" is that if a jet transport, ferris wheel, gondola or destroyer or whatever, is in stock, and if it happens to be reasonably in scale for that which it is called upon to do, so much the better. But it can, and has happened, that pressured decisions to go ahead when there are basic wrongs, generally mean a waste of all that surrounding money expended in such various directions as balance of necessary set construction, operation and shooting. We Special Effectors have all been thusly trapped from time to time. Not just in the use of inappropriate "stock" but also in other related "higher", untutored, though possibly well meant decisions. Be on guard and for "their own protection" battle. For your own protection, however, battle wisely.

The aircraft carrier miniatures (again plural) which worked in our *Thirty Seconds Over Tokyo* showed a wide variance in scale. One "U.S.S. Hornet" was an actual toy about eighteen inches long which we placed next to a very small scale miniature dock around which was represented the Naval Air Station at Alameda, California. Painted "water" sufficed here because our view was from a sufficiently high circling B25 as it prepared to land. No movement of any kind other than that of the camera, mounted on a medium camera boom which was pulled around a very small scale miniature set, (one one-hundred and twentieth of an inch equalling one foot), built on the floor of Stage Fourteen. The requirement here was to give Van Johnson his first inkling of what proved to be the Tokyo mission, by showing previously landed B25's alongside and aboard the Carrier as he approached the field. No animation, no problems of storm water or fire or smoke or any feature embodying elements which would require larger scale. Hence in this case and particularly economically, a "tiny" scale was the sensible determination.

Our second "Hornet" was quite another matter. Real wet water, not scenic, was involved here. Take-offs of Doolittle's normally land-based medium bombers had to be photographed. Process background plates and all manner of straight cuts here and there about the flight deck and from higher setups on the bridge and other areas of the Carrier's "island" were required.

A "size" to be determined (the scale of our miniature) was influenced by the usual multiple considerations. Cameras must be aboard which meant that many setups would necessitate the approximation of normal level viewpoints of a standing person. These lens heights in full-sized reality would measure five to six feet from the deck. From lens center to the bottom of an unmounted motion picture camera measures approximately four and one-half inches. Hence, our five to six foot setup representation should, if possible, be no less than an equivalent number of inches, five or six, preferably more for operating and viewing convenience. At an inch and one-half scale (one eighth fullsized) the five foot six inch full-sized dimension would be represented by eight and one quarter inches. Good for the camera situation, but let's look further.

At this scale, a nine hundred foot flight deck would become just over one hundred and twelve feet long. A rather large miniature ship to float in our three hundred foot "ocean". In less than three boat lengths of travel her prow would have rammed into the huge sixty-by-three-hundred-foot painted sky. A compromise was obviously in the offing. A reduction in size of one-third appeared to be the practical limit within which to accommodate cameras. At this scale, one inch to the foot, OK for a five and one-half inch setup, we would still be confronted with some seventy-five feet plus or minus, of miniature ship. No material gain in length of travel and in addition, the uncomfortable fact that we would be shooting mostly forward and that our cameras, traveling with the ship closer and closer to a painted sky, would totally destroy the illusion of distance perspective. An added "debit" would be the decreasing distance our airplanes could fly after taking off, before butting into a scenic cloud, painted on canvas and backed up by sturdy tongue and groove siding supported by the vast structure of our Lot Three Miniature Tank Backing! Decisions, decisions! Now, as always in the life of one who has chosen this profession, was another time to think.

I don't wish to imply that we and we only have an option on the gray matter department, but I do believe we have at least a partial ownership in the "thinking real crazy" domain. You will recall the bit of advice in a previous chapter which

9-P

The 'Mayflower' under way in a brisk breeze. Note purposely inconspicuous unanimated miniature figures. 3" scale ship.

Anchored off 'New Plymouth'. "Aerosol" used along distant beach to simulate breakers.

A miniature 'Miles Standish' and his crew head for shore. Miniature figures work well in this type of shot.

dealt with occasional recourse to lunatic mind wanderings in an effort to snag elusive will-o'-the-wisps.

Well, why not keep our thirty-knot per hour "Hornet" absolutely still and move the ocean? Move the <u>ocean</u>?! "Yeah," said we, "Move the ocean <u>by</u> the ship." This was done and one more dividend was chalked up to mental looseness.

At one inch scale with about four fifths of her flight deck (all we needed) operating on hydraulic rams for pitch and roll, we were able to "feel" her progression through the water by directing our "ocean" against and by, the rolling pitching sixty odd feet of ship, by judicial use of wind and wave machines.

Aeroplanes took off and "flew," suspended by vertical piano wires attached to an ingenious car high above, which rode along on horizontal wires stretched from the top of the sixty foot high sky-backing to telephone poles planted aft of our miniature ship.

Piano or "music" wire as it is often referred to, is a high tensile strength steel wire and has been used extensively in Special Effects. Its main claim to fame lies in its load-to-diameter ratio which in simpler English, means it can be made less visible while supporting a given load than other means of support. It is usually "deadened" with vinegar or acid because of its high sheen and often painted to blend with the background. It is available in quite a range of gauges from "spider-web" on up and it is temperamental. No right angle bends will it tolerate and no kinks. Should it let go under stress, it becomes a curling whipping weapon, exceptionally anti-optic. It is cursed and blessed by every Effect man who has ever dealt with its cranky temperament.

It seems our dissertation on scale determination was sidetracked by related delvings into other puzzlements. These meanderings will continue to tangent from main topics because scarcely ever is one facet of activity unrelated to another or others. And seldom will personalities importantly involved escape without praise or gentle fun-poking, if named— or when not named, not so gentle coal-raking, fortunately, very, very few of the latter at this stage disturb the happiness and tranquility of many, many pleasant recollections.

As briefly illustrated above (our two Aircraft Carriers - one 18", the other 60'), you will see that there is no ironclad rule which designates the size of a miniature. Thoughtful analysis of the job it must do and the elements of action which surround it, coupled with facility limitations are the principal factors in advance determination of its 'scale'. If it does little or nothing, just sits for its photograph, with a scarcity of movement other than perhaps camera, a fairly small scale may be chosen, tempered always, however, by the limitation of a lens' focus stretch. Too small a scale when units of a miniature are situated from very close to the camera to some distance away, suffer either foreground, background or both, in sharpness, and size or scale must be upped.

A larger scale miniature will also be necessary if improper camera-to-subject relationships, other than focus problems are encountered. This occurs mainly when vertical space is lacking to position a camera sufficiently low so that the lens will view a miniature correctly. The example related in discussing our Tokyo carrier scale problem, indicated that a miniature 'size' must be chosen to allow space for the camera itself so that an equivalent in inches or fraction thereof from lens to 'floor,' be that which is required. Another camera-to-miniature relationship has to do with ships. Many reasons here to build as large as possible as heretofore indicated – scale of waves, etc. The camera relationship as it affects scale, is simply that a miniature ship looks less like a miniature if the viewpoint is low.

A worm's eye camera 'water' setup may become damp, if not drowned, when attempts are made to photograph a too-small ship in this most effective manner. So much for 'scale;' its determination should be based on knowledgeable judgment after analysis; the knowledgeableness ingredient flourishes principally on diet of experience.

At this point and herewith, one of the most pleasurable of my personality deviations. His name, Donald Jahraus. His position, an assistant of mine. His particular activity, Miniatures. His rating, Triple A, if that signifies the highest. My opinion of this gentleman? Don Jahraus was as fine a man as I will ever meet.

He is gone now and no one in his ken, no one who ever participated to any degree, large or small, in his field of activity, but became a better man through contact with Don. He left nothing but love and admiration from us all for his understanding, kindliness and his exceptional work qualities. Truly one of the greats.

I referred to him as an "assistant". Rather I should have said co-worker or equal partner if not indeed at times realizing that I was the cart and he the horse. Don was the best executor of miniature assignments with whom I ever came in contact. Intelligent, imaginative, artistic and patient. Another one of those whose every fiber was impregnated with "do it only right" characteristics.

To detail Don Jahraus' contributions to this difficult field of Special Visual Effects, would be to name every important miniature job we ever did during his long stay at M.G.M. Our method of an independent approach to problem sequences paid rich "result" dividends. We arrived at our solutions and method determinations autonomously so that neither would be influenced and perhaps inadvertently hobbled by the other's thinking. Then we would compare in detail, digest thoroughly, many times combining strata of each towards a whole, often choosing one or the other and in general arriving,

THIRTY SECONDS OVER TOKYO (1944) PRODUCTION #1316

Thirty Seconds Over Tokyo. Alameda Naval Air Station. Scale 1/120"=12". Extremely small.

'B-25' take-offs from the "Hornet". Note miniature crew members.

Panning camera of take-offs designed to spend minimal footage on static 'people'.

"Tokyo" sequence. Day for night process plate. Moon path from sun reflectors over backing.

We moved the 'ocean' by our <u>stationary</u> but hydraulically heaving vessel.

Miniature of the "Hornet" was set in our three-hundred-square-foot water tank. We devised a method to make it appear that the ship was moving.

We made the ship rise, pitch and roll hydraulically as we moved water past the ship with pumps and wave machines.

Approaching Japan. 'Fuji' painted on backing.

CHAPTER SEVEN

She's off. Overhead trolley controlled flight pattern.

"Doolittle" checks compass by flying over ship with known heading.

We used a scale of one inch to the foot and built about four fifths of the deck of the"Hornet". It was about 60 feet lnog, which shows that miniatures are not necessarily little.

The miniature bombers were attached to piano wires and took off with an overhead trolly controlled with little synchronized motors.

#2 ready as #1 heads for our sky backing. Scale, 1"=12".

From a 90'-0" tower. Direct 'hit' on a 1/2 scale storage tank.

Ground shot of tank. An extra dividend for our 'stock' film library.

Low level moving camera process plate for close up of one of the pilots.

to the best of our combined abilities, at the most practical and effective way of delivering a bang-up job. There was never the taint of selfishness in this working companionship. It made no difference to either of us whose solution predominated or whose might be totally ditched. In rare cases, if and when a stalemate evolved, the boss (that would be me) exercised his power of command and dear old Don would smilingly attack all of the diversified problems with the same loyal fervor as though he were executing what he had thought best (which it probably would have been).

Jahraus was particularly adept at developing mechanical and/or electronic controls. Split second timing, often made necessary because of high camera speeds, should be activated by other than human reactions to cues, if and when adherence to exact precision seldom is required. Such gadgets often grow like Topsy grew and seldom did they reach workable maturity without the help of one or more propshop or machineshop cooks. We were both acutely aware of this. Further proof of my oft repeated dogma of "ask and then listen." Two or three or more is not necessarily a crowd. To name all the cooks - many too many! A few, however, who have contributed importantly in this and all Effect directions will follow.

Glen Robinson and Robert McDonald as a team or as individuals. Glen and Bob, both at times heads of M.G.M.'s highly important and generally grief-ridden Propshop department. Both top explosive experts and remote control wizards. Both steady and ready props upon which I have many times leaned.

Bob Staples, Ray Lampkin, Dario Mortara, mentioned previously in conjunction with John Bossart, and more recently Al Sculati, denizens of the machine shop and foundry - three at the top in their difficult, exacting, calling. Always dependable and somehow, in view of the "must be done yesterday" curves we have so often thrown them, always cheerful. And to go 'way back, Jeff Smedley with his mouth full of nails. Awake or asleep, even at mealtime, Jeff carried always a whole jowl full of nails and no one ever caught Jeff sans nails. Why? Ask Jeff and get the same answer we did, a naily grin, from this long ago propshopper.

Jack Gaylord! Interior head of the Propshop for the longest span of any of them. Wonderworker deluxe and a veritable sponge when it came to absorbing anyone's and everyone's problems, including the "unsolvable" ones. Jack, one of my very closest friends among the many, many valued ones made during that long M.G.M. term, somehow always seemed to find a good or an excellent answer. No duds with Gaylord. When he left M.G.M., and because at the drop of a hat, I always seem disposed to write a poem (so-called), I managed to swing a thirty-two line effort, the first sixteen of which are reproduced below. This may give the reader an inkling of our esteem in addition to exposing him to a rare brand of versified culture. Please be charitable - no aesthetic harm to the sensitive intended.

AN ODE TO THE WIZARD
or
JACK THE GIANT KILLER
or
GRIEF SHOOTER #1

THEY TELL ME HIS MA ON THE DAY OF HIS BIRTH
TOOK A LOOK AT THOSE BIG BLUE EYES
AND SMILED AS SHE SAID "THAT'S MY BOY
AND HE'LL BE MY BOY 'TIL HE DIES."
SHE WAS PARTLY WRONG FOR AS TIME WENT BY,
THOUGH HE REMAINED HER PRIDE AND JOY,
HE FAST BECAME TO A WHOLE HOST OF GUYS
NOT JUST HERS, BUT ALSO THEIR BOY.

IT'S BEEN "JACK DO THIS" and "JACK, DO THAT",
OR, "LET GAYLORD DOPE IT OUT."
AND HE'S TACKLED THEM EACH AND EVERY ONE
WITH NEVER THE SLIGHTEST DOUBT
THAT SOMEHOW HIS EFFORTS WOULD FIND SUCCESS
AS HE DREAMED, INVENTED, CONTRIVED,
(PROVIDED, OF COURSE, THAT THE FINANCIAL STRENGTH
OF M.G.M. SURVIVED.)

ever closer, she (Esther) suddenly swerved her sweat-foamed steed towards a cliff which dropped a sheer two hundred feet into the sea below. A moment of hesitation to survey this perilous avenue of escape, a quick turn around from which to gain momentum, and at a dead gallop she (Esther) and her brave black stallion leapt into space ~ and down, down, down, in a perfect swan (horse) dive, breaking the surface and disappearing deeply into and below the wave-ruffled veneer of the blue Adriatic (or Ionian or Aegean or whichever)."

We could probably have located the two hundred foot cliff with little trouble but Esther and her "Black Beauty" (or reasonable facsimiles thereof) were a mite more of a problem. Definitely the brave black stallion wanted not even the remotest part of such idiocy. The SOS bell clanged and again Special Visual Effects hastened to the rescue. We built a three inch scale miniature cliff in our three hundred foot "ocean". We modeled and cast in rubber a pliable wire-armatured Esther Williams. Miss Williams is somewhat statuesque - hence our one quarter full sized figure measured about seventeen inches. Her clothes were modeled on her and became an integral part of the rubber cast.

This mode of handling wardrobe for miniature people, by the way, has been common practice with us at M.G.M. for many years. We have found it much more satisfactory in most cases rather than "building" actual small scale clothes. It is difficult, if not impossible, to find materials that "scale down" in thickness, texture and "loose" or "flow" characteristics. The exception we at times must face are scenes calling for wind-whipped flowing robes or hair ~ in which cases those parts are of necessity treated, with materials chosen to represent as closely as possible the predetermined scale-down.

"Bendable" wire armatures (in a sense, skeletons) enable us to shape the figure into certain desired positions. It is wise however to see that the original clay is modeled into a close representation of whatever general position is needed so that arms, legs, and body adjustments of the later cast may be minimized.

It is also wise, whenever possible, to avoid animating miniature figures. Unless very excellently done, which becomes usually, <u>very expensively done</u>, animation can detract from the illusion of reality rather than add to it. It is equally important to use "static" figures in such a manner that their inanimateness is as little noticed as possible. Figures in a moving vehicle or figures upon which the camera does not dwell too long generally should not move in themselves unless simple movements, such as rowing a boat or walking the deck of a ship, the rail of which hides completely the lower half of the body, can be devised. Once more, that word "judgement." Open not Joe Cohn's "can of beans" unless its opening has at least a Chinaman's chance and don't tempt Fate too often by over-extending the built-in limitations of miniatures. They become less like miniatures and correspondingly more

There was more of the same, but you get the point. Particularly will the bookkeepers enjoy the line enclosed in (parentheses).

There was Curly Hubbard, miniature "gang boss" who worked with Jahraus and your chronicler, for many devoted years. Curly's heart attack only seemed to make him a better man, which, in a word, indicates the character of Curly. Plaudits for these men would be unceasing, and Hubbard is no exception.

Word economy at this point or perhaps long ere now may have become a fervid wish if not a demand of and by the publisher. Those of you heretofore briefly mentioned and the host of others not credited, will I trust, be as generous and forgiving in your thoughts as I should like to be thorough in extolling your virtues. I repeat a wish that <u>all</u> could be included.

Curly Hubbard at times was another one of these stubborn people. I recall a *Jupiter's Darling* chore which befell us. Esther Williams starred in this M.G.M. one and the writer of the script had devised an escape for the lady as she was being chased by nasty individuals on horseback, somewhat as follows. "~as the rapacious brigands drew closer and

JUPITER'S DARLING (1955) PRODUCTION #1652

Esther Williams in *Jupiter's Darling* making that prodigious leap.

Not the 'Real' Esther, but the one we used. A 3" scale miniature.

believable when asked to not exceed their particular capacity and sensible usage.

Probably more of this later, but back to Hubbard's stubbornness as it was this time shown. The rubber Miss Williams mounted on her glass cloth and plastic beautifully modeled and cast horse, tresses of both glued on so that they would flutter naturally in the wind created by that one fourth of a two hundred foot dive, wave machines operating, wind machines operating, cameras set, camera speed determined, both crew and horse champing at their respective bits as they waited for the "Camera, speed, action!" command.

Came the command — "Camera'" from the miniature director. "Speed!" from the assistant cameraman. "Action!" and "HORSE!" from the Director, whereupon our animal took off and proceeded to do a perfect outside loop landing in an unheroic and violent belly flop. Nothing too <u>too</u>, here, so try again. The camera slate now bore a chalked "2" in place of the "1" in the little square over which was printed "take". (A few feet of "slate" is photographed ahead of all scenes for identification purposes). Ready for take two and again the command, "Camera, etc," This time our critter went in feet first all right, but <u>hind</u> feet first! Take three, a twisting two-thirds gainer in which Esther broke the surface first, her mount, upside down and on top, last. A few quick repairs to our latex and sponge-rubber star and we were ready for take four.

So it went with Eastman's expensive color negative purring through our two speed cameras at some four and one half feet per second. Curly had previously proposed a "launching" rig to me which he stubbornly insisted would make our plastic beast and its rider perform any reasonable maneuver we desired, I explained to Mr. Hubbard that this was hardly necessary. Why complicate a simple toss out that could be done manually, by hatching some involved mechanical contrivance. Why add needless cost. Why — and with a final, "do it my way, Curly," he slouched off and proceeded, to go right ahead with his own simple pendulum swing launching device.

This was a couple of days before we were scheduled to shoot and Curly had simply followed my own so often preached advice to "stick out fearlessly, and hopefully with judgment, one's chin." He was quite sure I was wrong and thanks to this wonderful kind of stubbornness, backed up by intelligence and experience, had done what he was reasonably sure should be done. Had I not once ordered a spare set of sails?

When finally resorted to, (at about take 7) Curly's horse launcher, which he with a big grin brought out from its hiding place, delivered nicely.

He always remained fearless though not always faultless — who is ~ in pursuing to the fullest what he thought was right.

And if he thought it was right to throw body blocks into an unreasonable or possibly unscrupulous "whoever", woe be to that ill-advised gentleman. Curly took great delight in this latter activity if and whenever he felt justified. And those who were bruised, mostly a particular "he" who was bruised, knew not from whence those bruises came. His confidants knew, however. I was one of them.

Having broached the subject of water setups, let us get on with more about our saltless miniature 'ocean' and certain techniques used to make it behave photographically so that it resembles one of its big brothers. To repeat, water miniatures are among the toughest.

The dimensions of physical generalities of our Lot 3 'tank' appear early in this Chapter. So let's start with the instrument that 'sees' – the camera, although it rightfully belongs at the kite-tails extremity. It records only that within its range after all the disciplinary measures to make water, ships, whatever, behave properly, have been installed. But how it sees is a point worth remembering. Float your camera! Be they straight shots of a ship in a storm or a ship in a calm, and certainly be they Process plates to be used in conjunction with a full-sized section of that ship. Float your camera, mates!

Seldom have we violated this rule, as the illusion of actually being at sea an enhancement to be importantly added to the whole and quite worth the misery and difficulties inherent. Our camera 'platforms' that work when a water miniature is ordained, are small, square 'tubs' which normally house only the camera, the wader-clad operator in back of the tub, panning and tilting when necessary. They (the tubs) are steadied somewhat by from two to four like-garbed grips per tub, depending on the water's intended violence. This, to avoid total loss of control and to hopefully avert complete submergence. The latter has upon occasion occurred, which as elicited dim-view reactions from the Camera Department. Gains in realism, however, far overshadow such dousings.

Our practice of crew in water, not happily and dryly aboard a craft of some kind, makes for more effective and efficient handling of water miniatures. Discomfort often, particularly in sunny California's so-called 'warm' winters. Armpit waders, like Beery's waterproof underwear, are standard wardrobe. Seldom however are waders entirely waterproof and they mostly resemble patchwork quilts from many unsuccessful attempts to stay leaks. Adding to the soggy discomfort of underthings is the inevitable shipping of water over the chest-high limits of these waders.

Frequent lost footings also donate waderfulls of cold water when a victim goes completely under. Discomfort yes, but tempered whenever the latter happens by boisterous laughs from all present and more importantly, by the realization that a water job is better done through following this dampish procedure.

Jim Vesey, stand-by painter, ager par excellence, and champion "in-the-drink" stumbler. Jim could trip in our miniature tank and go under more regularly than any other three of our "wader crew" combined. Someone would yell "There he goes again!" and it would be Vesey. Occasionally one arm holding a can of paint would be all that was visible above water, until a sputtering drenched Jim would flounderingly emerge, not having spilled a drop. Martin Schreiner who succeeded Vesey upon the latter's retirement never equaled Jim's proficiency below the water. He did carry on, however, with the same talents and loyalties above it.

Joe Regan. Rough, tough, kindly Joe Regan can "play" wind machines like an organist plays an organ. Joe is a "gaffer" electrician, sort of like a top-sergeant. In addition to his duties of set lighting, seeing that cameras are supplied with proper current, generators operating and more, was our wind and wave machine impresario.

During such rough weather as the "Bounty" encountered attempting to negotiate the Horn, or that mid-Atlantic storm and wave which nearly did the "Mayflower" in, Joe would be out in the big middle of it all, coaxing, cajoling, threatening, pleading over his soaked inter-com to maybe eight, ten or twelve operators, to "up number three to <u>fourteen</u> hundred, down baby, <u>down</u> you on number five, up six ~ y'hear me! up! up! ~ OK start your wave machines to the count of one every four and keep 'em going and hey! you on number three! - didn't I tell you <u>fourteen</u> hundred? Watch your tach——" and with a final "They're all goin' Buddy, what d'y'think?", maybe, just maybe we could shoot.

The "maybe" is stressed because so many elements are involved in miniature shooting of this nature, any one of which can malfunction, that often the tedious advance preliminaries up to actual "Camera!" go for naught. In which case we correct, amend, repair, put out the fire, reload the camera, retrieve someone's racing form which has blown out of the cockpit of one of our Douglas Dauntless Dive Bomber war surplus wind machines and is floating wetly in the center of our ocean, or a cigarette, or matches or Jim Vesey. Or and more "or's". Sometimes seemingly endless "or's".

So patience becomes of prime importance. To avoid over-taxing this commodity, however, so that a breaking point be not reached, requires the institution of strict discipline in order that some of the above can be controlled. Meticulous policing of the premises and stern housekeeping rules can avert costly and frustrating invasions of unwanted debris. Joe Regan acquired, in addition to his many other accomplishments, the proficiency of a Holland housewife backed up and enforced by a vocabulary of which she had not the remotest acquaintance.

Joe's one great disappointment, which grew to be increasingly dolorous as the years passed, was climaxed on the day of my retirement from active execution, by the fact that I had somehow completely avoided, during those years, our principal occupational hazard of being dunked, submerged, soused, engulfed, in the waters of M.G.M's ocean. Walking backwards, a habit I early formed, would always bring out the anticipatory gleam in Regan's eyes. Sorry to disappoint you, Joe. The suppression of that granddaddy of all "guffaws" must have taxed you sorely. In retrospect from the dryness of my desk, I must admit, <u>now</u>, that I would have enjoyed rating the loudness of that never uttered "Ha Ha!" against the decibels generated when all six World War Two Wright R200 airplane engines plus all three World War One Liberty engines were turning at top R.P.M. Without the benefit of amplification, I am sure such an unseemly and undignified happening would have racked up a most impressive total.

Very high on my list is Olof Olsson. As you could surmise from that name, Olof is a Swede, born on a little island in the Skagerack, north of Goteborg. As a boy he worked and he fished. And as a man the two top passions which have always run a dead heat in Olof's life and activities, were to be a good fisherman and a better workman. I cannot vouch for his piscatorial transcendence from first hand viewing but I can underwrite his attainment of passion number two. Olof was not only an excellent workman, he was just plain superb. He is a member of that group of "stubborn" fanatics who <u>know</u>. His field was watercraft, the whole fleet from dinghy to one of the "Queens." Particularly, he knows about sailing ships - full-sized <u>and</u> miniature.

I have often said that when a certain few individuals such as "Ole" would decide to leave the confines of M.G.M. for good, I would have little choice but to follow. It is an axiom that people are not irreplaceable but as far as my feelings are concerned, that truth would be severely stretched in an attempt to replace the likes of Olof Olsson.

Olof became a New Bedford fisherman in this country and somehow got himself involved in sailing the two-masted Gloucester fishing schooner "We're Here" from Massachusetts through the Canal to California. She had been purchased by the studio for *Captains Courageous*, mentioned earlier in this chapter, the vehicle in which Spence Tracy's <u>two</u> performances were so exceptionally outstanding ~ one throughout the picture and one in the privacy of L.B.'s office. The latter could have been titled, "Tracy versus A.A.G., the Sanguinary, Slaughterous, Slayful, Special Effector." All is really forgiven, Spence.

Olof Olsson delivered the ship and was prevailed upon to desert the fat cod of the Grand Banks off Newfoundland and stay in Hollywood. This rates as one of the best "prevailings" ever swung by M.G.M.'s help hirers. Give Ole a hawser to splice, a ship to rig, a sail to sew, a pound or two of lead to balance a square-rigged miniature which heels too far to starboard, ask him any salty "how" and watch him scoot!

His great joy on a not-to-be-interfered-with yearly vacation consisted of lonely trips in his small boat, far to sea for days, sometimes weeks on end. Lonely? Not for Olof Olsson. What more could any man want than a sturdy keel between him and the deep, a three hundred and sixty degree horizon of dawns and sunsets and midnight star-sparkled skies, noiseless calms to laze in and sudden waspish little squalls to test one's at-homemanship in the vast world of ever changing water so magnificently domed by an equally ever changing cosmorama of violent hues, to leadenness, to tempest – this was and is Ole's beloved home. And never underrate a "square-head's" willingness to lift an honest dollar. That two or three or four week jaunt always saw Olof's craft return laden to the gunwales with top quality, marketable, long-finned tunny. I thank you, Ole, as should all of M.G.M., for your loyal and invaluable aid through these many years. I timed my retirement pretty well, didn't I?

Paraphernalia employed to properly harness water for a miniature is varied. Photographic speeds, to be explained in more detail later are an indispensable adjunct. They slow or 'scale down' water movement, waves, spray, currents, to register properly within the selected scale of the miniature, all of the water effects generated by an array of wind and wave machines, paddle wheels, dump tanks, pump exudations, gravity activated rapids, whatever.

The use of paddle wheels, similar to the Mississippi stern-wheeler, mounted on pontoons for mobility may operate to advantage against oncoming wind and waves and dump-tank dumpings, thereby building wave height. Though shortening wave travel. Two or more may also be placed in various areas, directing their outflow at different angles to create eddies, cross currents, whirlpools and other simulations of treacherousness. When you couple all of this with proper wind treatment, which will include (and this in all miniature water situations) 'small' wind, in close camera vicinity, (we use four or five foot electric fans for this purpose) to create scaled-down ripples or 'texture' visible at close range, you will have milked well the techniques of converting ordinary full-sized water to miniature water so that on film it appears to be ordinary full-size water.

A dividend paying plus during the design stage of M.G.M.'s miniature tank was that of sloping the sides. This feature tends to absorb and disseminate waves traveling from one side to the other, whereas vertical sides would cause a reverse reaction on such water movements resulting in a choppy, confused, no purpose surface. As a matter of practice, it is always well to delay the kickoff of waves and wind until just before all is ready to shoot so that even with sloping sides, choppiness does not have time to develop.

We have referred to dump-tanks in the preceding Chapter, their employment to send white water high over the prow of our full-sized "Bounty". Generally in miniature use, their function is to release singly or in multiples hundreds of gallons of water from twenty-five or thirty feet in the air down a steep flume into a storm-tossed sea, that a relatively much larger wave or swell results. The lip at the flume's bottom is adjusted to that the force is exerted more or less horizontally. The ship or object receiving this engulfment must be positioned reasonably close in order that the outcome may be one of maximum impact. Very effective, dump tanks, for this purpose.

A 'wave machine' may be any contrivance which displaces or pushes a volume of water at the surface in a controllable 'beat.' The ideal one has not yet been built, at least to my knowledge, although on paper we think we have designed a somewhat better one. Its principle consists of a powerful fast-acting air-ram-operated vertical 'plow' which pushes as much water as the face of the vertical plane is large – width and depth – returning immediately with face louvers automatically opening on the back stroke to allow back water to replace the theoretical void. One day a capital expenditure budget will include an O.K.'d item – "Six (or hopefully more) better mouse-traps.

One of the two remaining features of our 'ocean,' aside from our deep holes, is an absolutely level horizon-straight-edge, over which surface water flows into a full length large catch-basin trough. Some fourteen feet behind the 'horizon' is located the second of these two features, a 60' by 328' slanting structure which supports scenically painted backings. An apex of skill is needed here and a few words of its arrangement and the artists who ply their talents so successfully on it, should be helpful to the student whose bent may be towards that of a scenic painter.

Firstly, the backing was placed at the North end so as to receive maximum sunlight hours. Slanting it some fifteen degrees added to its light gathering potential and a bit more of this necessary illumination commodity was gained by positioning it slightly off an East-West axis, favoring the West. This to obtain more afternoon shooting time, the early morning hours being occupied by pre-shooting rigging, a profitable use of those hours as morning haze or fog is generally present.

The real payoff lies, of course, in the backing itself. An acceptably realistic foreground chore may go completely for naught if it is not just as realistically backed. We have been blessed (and best you see to it that you are likewise blessed) by having at our beck and call a Scenic Department topped by none in the Industry.

Camera speeds, the number of film frames per second that pass through the camera and are exposed, can vary greatly. This applies particularly to the photographing of

Wind and wave conference with Joe Regen. *"Bounty"*.

Brisk weather and under way. Wakes assisted by siphons.

"Ben-Hur" - Note distance helped by smaller scale profile galleys at horizon.

'Conducting' during "Atlantis". Clarence Slifer below.

miniatures but is not limited thereto. "Undercranking" and "Overcranking," a terminology holdover from the pre-motor-driven camera days, have long been practiced to achieve desired effects. Mack Sennett's early slapstick chases, Chaplin's speedy wiggling down a dusty road and many pie-throwing cop-spilling comedy sequences were enhanced greatly by "undercranking." The result when projected in the theater at normal correct speed, was to make the scenes abnormally fast and jerky - the greater the undercranking, the faster and jerkier and funnier, in intent at least, the scene became. The reverse, when "overcranking", is of course true and can result "in slow motion" photography familiar to all. This also had applications to comedy.

I say "can" above, because "overcranking" does not of necessity always produce recognizable slow motion. It will be used, as an example, to help create an underwater effect when photographing a girl actually high and dry who is supposed to be totally immersed. Her flowing hair and garments are activated by properly directed wind and air jets, which when slowed down by projection after having been photographed at speed, give an illusion of how these features would act in water. By compositing such film footage with previously shot "under" water, the scene can become completely realistic. We did this recently in *The Outrage*, for a scene depicting an attempted suicide.

Above normal camera speeds, as they relate to miniatures, are essential in the great majority of instances for the same reason - achievement of reality. Picture a huge breaker, the kind surfers like, making its ponderous way shoreward and time it with a stopwatch. Fifteen, twenty seconds? And measure its travel. Two hundred feet, three hundred? Now to duplicate in miniature at two inch scale, one sixth full sized, A travel of two hundred and fifty feet becomes one sixth of that distance or forty-one feet and eight inches. Hence an important part of the believability of the to-be-produced oncoming miniature wave, is that it should travel forty-one plus feet in the same number of seconds its full-sized counterpart would take to travel two hundred and fifty feet. But instead of a hypothetical twenty-four seconds, suppose the mechanically produced miniature breaker covers the scaled down equivalent distance in six seconds? There is little that can be done to control the speed of water in a shot of this type but by photographing at four times the normal camera speed of twenty four film frames a second (four times six seconds equals twenty-four seconds - the time it would have taken the full-sized breaker to travel two hundred and fifty feet) we wind up with a correct determination of how much above normal the camera should turn, or in the vernacular of old timers, "grind."

The latter word is more descriptive as the film literally hums through the camera, in this case at ninety-six stop and go separate pictures per second. Faster film travels are occasionally mandatory but it is wise to preplan when possible

their avoidance, through scale choice and if feasible, speed control. There are cameras available and used mainly for scientific purposes which through the use of stroboscopic lighting can outdistance our "slow" speed cameras by many multiples. Seldom would a practical application of this wary limited use be feasible or even desired for movie miniature speed photography.

You will note in the "wave" illustration above that there seems to be no relationship between scale size of a miniature and choice of camera speed. The miniature, at two inch scale, was one-sixth full-sized but the camera speed chosen was only four times normal speed. Well, and this may be surprising to the uninitiated, there is no hard and fast relationship, no formulae of scale to camera speed, no easy slide rule answer. About the best I can offer to the novice who faces the uncontrollable actions or reactions of an explosion, a tidal wave, an avalanche, the Red Sea's parting, an H Bomb ~ is to use his noodle, borrow a small slice of Bossart's horsesense, think it out and then, if possible, test.

The latter, though not excluding the "think routine", is the best course to follow particularly in ye tyro's formative years. Always, testing entails some cost but can well serve to protect against a possible down-the-drain catastrophe. Years of experience may later develop a sixth "guessing sense", and a thoroughly thought out "feel" will dictate, "twice normal, two and a half or three and one-half, or ~". Your Uncle Dudley likes to think the years have sensitized his acumen

CHAPTER SEVEN   144

in this mystical region of choice. Part perhaps of that two to ten pay ratio preachment when you're young and learning, to the enormous overpaying enjoyed later as one treks along towards and into a career's twilight era. Lend an ear, Henry Henigson. (Henry at one time did a 'salary survey' at M.G.M.. Did I escape? I did not!)

At times a wrong "speed" guess can be salvaged by "frame cutting". A scene shot at four times normal, which proves to project unrealistically slow, can be speeded by printing only every other frame which would give the same result as though it has been photographed at two times normal. The action as a consequence, when projected, would appear twice as fast as originally shot. This may appear to be too fast, too much of a correction and it is often here that we have difficult duels with the "don't knows."

It is very possible optically to reduce this "twice-as-fast" result by eliminating every third frame, which changes our scene to only one third faster than the original too slow scene. But, two frames and a miss, two frames and a miss, two frames and a miss will, as should be easily understood, result in a series of evenly spaced "stutters", an annoying, in tempo, blink.

The same general objections are inherent in the results of attempted slow-downs from scenes originally shot at a given speed, by printing each frame twice or more. To lengthen a scene thusly which contains no movement and was shot from a stationary camera position is quite permissible. This is common practice if additional footage is needed. A moving dolly or camera car shot, a panning shot, or a scene which includes any subject matter from a stationary setup that manifests very noticeable movement, is almost always taboo. "Almost always?" Here is that exception proving the rule again. An example.

In William Wyler's wonderful *Mrs. Miniver* produced by Sydney Franklin (picture makers, by the way, these two) we needed additional footage of a Process Plate shot in miniature, of a burning English village in the near distance, preceding the swoop-in entrance from overhead of a burning two-engined airplane which was to crash in a nearby field. The flickering distant fire in front of which the village was silhouetted seemed to us as though it might survive lengthening by this unorthodox slowing of the action. Drifting smoke or violent movements such as explosions would have vetoed this thought. But there were none of these and the fact that the scene was night and the fire was the equivalent of half to three quarters of a mile away, was an advance indication that this would prove to be a valid exception. We did and it was.

The problem with these "exceptions" is that often Director John Doe or Producer Joe de Doaks remembers them. "Wha'd'y'mean you can't slow it down, bub. I did it lots'a times!" So, occasionally, in spite of efforts to explain that this situation is different than those "lots'a times" we are forced to double or triple frame print the scene in question to prove just how wrong the gentleman or gentlemen is or are. How embarrassing it can be when he or they are right! Never happened to me ~ I think.

There are occasions when "speed" compromises are necessary. Two or more elements may react in a different ratio to a determined scale down. A one-eighth full-sized blowup of an ammunition dump will measure a different speed than a one-eighth full-sized nearby waterfall. One or the other will suffer and again we oracles must tap our well of doubt and confusion and judgement to determine a speed that will jar the least.

Sometimes it is possible to control a bit, one or the other of such variables. In the above instance it is obvious that little could be done explosionwise. The waterfall? Maybe ~ let's see.

I hereby disclose a state secret. We do not use water to make a waterfall - a miniature waterfall, that is. Many years ago M.G.M.'s *A Woman's Face*, starring Joan Crawford (one of my all-time favorite people) Melvyn Douglas (whose politics irked me no end) and Conrad Veidt (a fine actor) told much of its story in and around a steel works in Sweden in midwinter. Victor Saville, British, the Producer, and George Cukor, a top Director, decided that our huge miniature of the whole works, smelter, overhead cable trolley, ore buckets continually on the move, white water rapids below which included a menacingly vortexed whirlpool and snowed-in cliffs and pine trees, should also show a power source. Why not a beautiful waterfall?

As we knew and as has been said earlier, you just don't "build" small water. Details of a miniature sea, drops, spray, surface, can be reduced somewhat by proper use of wind, and then given weight and size through a correct choice of camera speed. But a drop's a drop when dealing with falling water. A camera slow-down helps, yes, but the incorrect scale of small detail can completely destroy any illusion of fidelity.

Another opportunity to "think real crazy"! Water for a waterfall? Why? So we tested and thought and thought and tested and finally came up with a dry gypsum, coarsely granulated, with sufficient of its own dust to create a fine "mist" as it plunked from on high to a dry hard surface below. This gyp was continually fed on to a moving belt which formed the brink of the falls as it passed over and under a front roller. Two belts in fact with a small rock divider - two old M.G.M. treadmills served our purpose. The hopper feeders spilling fresh gyp just forward of the rear rollers, were hidden by a strategically placed scenic profile, the top of which showed the cutout contour of distant snow-clad mountains; the bottom, about two or three inches above the moving belts, served as a straight edge "evener" to insure a better regulated flow of our dishonesty ~ dry water!

A WOMAN'S FACE (1941) PRODUCTION #1177

A Woman's Face - Long shot of Swedish steel mill. Scale 1 1/2"=12". Camera speed 3 plus normal 80 frames per second.

Closer shot of mill. Smoke and steam. Good tree detail and excellent snow application.

Joan Crawford's 'waterfall', and our trade secret. Gypsum fed to 2 treadmills behind profile. 'Mist' created by gyp dust. Some steam added. Real water for rapids.

CHAPTER SEVEN

Miniature ore bucket, mill and plaster-skin-cast mountains, steel mill beyond. Smoke pots and steam.

Another shot of the falls shows profile clearly, behind which gyp is fed to the treadmills.

Fresh out of gypsum! Note impediments below treadmill used to break up falling gypsum.

The real white water rapids below, agitated and turmoiled by underwater air and pressured water jets, seemed to issue from the foot of our dry falls perfectly. The weir, constructed to a few inches above the surface of the rapids, was the divider at the base of the falls and was completely camouflaged by our new invention, dry dusty "mist".

About the only shortcoming this "mist" had was that it would not form a rainbow. Somehow it occurred to neither of the Messrs. Saville or Cukor that Joan, as she traversed, in one of those ore buckets, that raging ominous maelstrom and rapids far below, contemplating murder (or was it suicide), should do her contemplating against the yellow to purple-hued drama of a rainbow. Yes, somehow this idea escaped their very agile brains for which a belated praising to all the Saints.

George has accumulated many fine credits through the years, the most recent a *My Fair Lady* Oscar. Victor, richly misunderstood by bevies of M.G.M. secretaries at one time simply because he arranged for a showing of one of his late efforts for these young ladies in order that he may have their opinion. In fact he told them politely that he wanted to know what the <u>little</u> <u>people</u> thought. He was told. In spite of this innocent unassuming attitude it was a real pleasure working with Victor Saville. He was unusually astute in understanding the riddles of our peculiar jargon and he savvied, well the mechanics of our proposals.

So -back to the subject before we were sidetracked by Joan and George and Victor. Back to our explosion of which we could exercise little if any speed control and one "water" fall. What to do about camera speed.

Objects of different weights and densities and of similar shapes and sizes will, except in a vacuum, fall at varying speed rates. If granulated gypsum fell too fast for the explosion -determined camera speed, let us try a similar material lighter in weight. Ground balsa wood? Ground feathers? One of the new extremely light weight children of chemistry? Or if too slow, something heavier such as tiny marble chips with enough marble dust for simulated mist, or maybe <u>lead</u> pellets from a number nine shotgun shell painted white. We would buy the pellets without the shells, naturally; or glass beads, ball bearings, white sand, rice, perhaps smashed rice crispies and/or a continuing bunch of "perhaps", covering the waterfront of possibilities with which to help wed a powder and dynamite laden blowup of a magazine to a peaceful waterfall. The one going up in a violent whoosh, punctured and pierced by bings and pings and bangs and lesser whooshes, while the other poetically and mistily veils itself down from a one-eighth full-sized precipice.

So we have seen that there may be balance through partial control, though in actual practice this is a rarity. A compromised camera speed is the rule.

Why at this moment I should think of W.S. Van Dyke I do not know unless the word "compromised" recalled a trip to Tahiti in 1928 on M.G.M.'s early newborn sound venture *The Pagan*. Still written titles for this one, a "<u>silent</u>" except for the song "Pagan Love Song". Ramon Novarro, of *Ben-Hur* Number One, played a Tahitian native opposite Dorothy Janis, a lovely young imp, who was his light o'love. Donald Crisp, staunch Scot, an actor's actor and a crew favorite, and Renée Adorée, Jack Gilbert's French sweetheart in *The Big Parade*. Renée in Tahiti! Sigh. Palm fronds, white surf fringing and frosting the distant reef, a midnight moon glowing with sufficient luminosity to read a newspaper. Velvet water and velvet breezes and who would want to read a newspaper anyway. But this tale has to do with <u>mustaches</u>.

Ten days by ship from San Francisco to Papeete and ten days to return. Thirty days on the island would make an elapsed total of fifty days - almost two months and ample time to raise a mustache. So everyone, ladies excluded, decided to raise his own particular brand of upper lip bristles — everyone but Mr. Van Dyke.

The weeks wore on and strange looking "bushes" sprouted, some glorious handlebar shapes, others rough and scrubby, an occasional modest wisp, and one or two just simply unkempt outrages. It makes no difference to the story into which

Edgar Rice Burroughs, creator of Tarzan, on the set of *Tarzan And His Mate* (1934) with Maureen O'Sullivan and Johnny Weismuller - (Note - Large rubber ears crafted to convert Indian elephant into an African type.) -Courtesy David Conover.

classification my personal achievement fell, but its blossoming, I say with all modesty, was at least individual.

Directors, in theory at least, are supposed to have fluid, ever-seeking, idea-searching minds. Woody Van Dyke was a personification of that theory. Especially was he mentally active when three o'clock in the morning rolled around at which hour he would awaken, coughing and restless. My room at "Johnny's" in Papeete was immediately below Van's and the slap, slap, of his bare feet on the wooden floor above as he paced back and forth, continued always for the full hour preceding Tahiti's sudden burst of rooster crowing, which precluded further sleep anyway.

His idea searching bore fruit on one of these before-dawn bedroom treks about a week before we were to leave. He decided he didn't like mustaches!

Being a man of talent and action it became his immediate wont to creep stealthily into the quarters of his crew, one by one, at any ungodly hour when the victim would be peacefully snoring, pounce on top of him and proceed in whatever dimness the light happened to offer, to whittle off his mustache. Van used a small pocket knife, the tiny scissors accessory of which enabled him to sufficiently maltreat every individual's pride and joy, so that by daylight, one look in the mirror was motive enough to implement total removal. By sailing day, only one mustache remained untouched – mine!

My feelings were not hurt. In fact, my feelings about Van Dyke at this point had vacillated between this and that. At times, strongly <u>this</u>, and again overwhelmingly <u>that</u>. I was not of his crew. Pop Arnold, Harry Albiez, Lew McAfee, had been with him for several years. They were his boys, grip, propman and electrician, in and out of the studio, on tough locations, whatever and wherever ~ <u>his</u> boys. A new, fresh, Art Director was I, untried and untempered by having been doused and tested in Van's particular brand of "purifying" cauldron. One day short of docking in San Francisco I still had my mustache!

That evening after dinner, men in black-tie, ladies appropriately gowned, many of the passengers had adjourned to the ship's card-playing saloon. Two staid gentlemen from New Zealand made up a bridge foursome with Novarro and the lone remaining mustache-adorned member of Van Dyke, Inc. We were engaged in a friendly game when across the room, standing in a passageway door where she had apparently been trying to catch my eye, was Renée.

She had been a bit off kilter for a day or so and was clad in a sort of ostrich-feathered dishabille. She, from her stateroom, had apparently become aware of dark doings and had with loyalty and fortitude determined to rise from her feverish bed and wave to me a red flag of ill-boding. Her attire had prevented a closer approach but our eyes finally met. She put one finger cross-ways below her nose, pointed another one at me and vanished.

A distinct tocsin, surmised I. A noble warning, dear Renée. I thought of Paul Revere. I thought of that message from somebody to Garcia. I probably thought of Lafayette, Renée being French, and I bid four Spades while plotting sketchily the soon-to-be battleground.

I noted principally that my chair, ship fashion, was firmly fastened to the red carpeted deck and just as three fellow bridge players proclaimed, "I pass," the corner of my right eye disclosed five creeping roughly-clad creatures moving up on the starboard flank. Ten paces away, nine, eight, and at five, the cards flew as I jumped onto my firm chair and then through the air to a perfectly timed neck tackle of the leading ruffian, W.S. Van Dyke.

We hit that red carpet in a wild flurry of legs and bodies with Van's chin resting securely in the "V" of my left elbow; my right hand and arm, linked solidly in this embrace, were putting ever increasing pressure on poor Van's Adam's apple. A dirty choke hold. Dirty? <u>Five</u> to <u>one</u>, or rather counting Mlle. Adorée five to two, although she was of no immediate help at that moment.

I have always been blessed with good legs. Not the slim silk-stockinged, white-wigged Louis variety; rather resembling more the shape of nail kegs or possibly those of a concert grand.

At twenty-eight years of age, they could kick - and did! Dirty? Not at five to one, reasoned I. Poor Pop receipted for a solar plexus bull's-eye as astounded passengers gasped. McAfee's Achilles' heel must have been his shin. A wild swinging well-shod Gillespie heel, unaimed, crashed into this vulnerable stretch of thinly padded bone and Mac became a hopping, ouching, hors de combat. The audience remained fascinated. Harry Albiez wisely decided "mule tackling" was too bruising a sport and Van's fourth crony, whom I have forgotten, retreated to await orders from his Director. None came because of the simple fact that only gasping gurgles were escaping from Van's muted vocal chords and then only when that strangle grasp was eased enough for him to whisper "Uncle" ~ which he finally did, much to everyone's relief, particularly Van's.

"You win, kid. My gang went back on me," came raspingly from deep in his sorely fractured gullet. Whereupon we disentangled and the victor, mussed but still mustached, magnanimously proffered the sheepish four and their leader, a drink. People still stared, the British element, which composed four-fifths of the passenger list, reacted from disgust at the uncouthness of Americans to a few hearty expressions such as "Ruddy good go, y'know. Ruddy good!"

Never have I seen so disconsolate a loser as was W.S. Van Dyke. He simply couldn't stand it. I was smugly enjoying my triumph when within just a few minutes of its conclusion, Van suddenly blurted forth, "Your mustache or my hair!" Wow! "Tails your mustache, heads my hair," he challenged.

I had already won the first skirmish, but this one I really wanted to win. A sporting proposition and of course I couldn't refuse. Novarro was to toss the coin and I prayed for "heads". My victory-stimulated brain was already creating fantastic designs to cover all parts of the Van Dyke scalp. Not a square inch would remain unused. Wiggly worm designs, swathes, and circles and squares and the initials "AAG" would stretch from troubled brow to the nape of his scrawny neck. Make it a "heads" I silently implored. Ramon tossed, it came up "tails" and out came Van's pocket knife with the little scissors. I sat still.

Not too many miles west of San Francisco's Bay Entrance, was deposited into the Pacific one half of one mustache which was followed by the remaining half the following morning, victim (this half) of my own safety razor. It was flushed down the ship's drain just below where now stretches that loveliest of all bridges, the Golden Gate, a fitting monument to the valorous defense of those seventy or eighty odd crinkly, sunburned blondish filamentous outgrowths which had so recently adorned a patch of my epidermis.

The aftermath of this physical contact horseplay, was that I was accepted into the circle and became not only one of Van's gang, but a long time friend. Another of those "quite a guy" people. His accomplishments were many and his easy informality with top stars became a trademark. Everyone was "kid" and/or "honey". Greta Garbo's morning entrance would be greeted by, "Hi'y honey. Y'ready kid? Let's go to work," or some such.

As usual with the many outstanding individuals who creep into these pages, some by design, others by happenstance, much, much more, could always be told. A biography of Woody Van Dyke, including the spit and polish of his beloved Marine Corps, his water-filled gin bottles (in his later years, water), the playful pushes into his swimming pool, followed always by a paid-up replacement of damaged toggery, usually evening gowns complete with intimates, and details of his serious picture activities and enviable credits, would make up a sheaf of very readable pages. He could now be one of St. Peter's barbers, specializing in the removal of upper lip atrocities if and when groups of angels should be so mistakenly led as to believe that, wings and halos

CHAPTER SEVEN

notwithstanding, they could get away with any defiance of a W.S. Van Dyke whim. Happy memories, Van!

"Miniatures?" Certainly another few to come, but in a subsequent chapter. Not yet have we told the "tale of *Tarzan's* crocodile" nor "*Good Earth's* locusts". If just "people" would only quit squirming their intriguing ways between the technical and instructive paragraphs, more of value to the student might be reported herein.

Up to this point, in review, we have brushed upon and perhaps learned in this Chapter, something of the following. "Miniatures" are not "models," and the British can be "obstinate." Much about "scale," (size of a miniature) when should it be big, when little; its relation to "big" water, and its determination not by formulae, but by experienced judgment, and a few details of M.G.M.'s Miniature Tank. Storms and giant waves, the howls of wind and wave machines were described. One important item neglected there, was the "dump tank," high on a platform, from which down a steep flume, many thousands of gallons from multiple tanks are dumped on cue to form "huge" swells and to augment waves generated by other means. Giant "paddle wheels," as found on a Mississippi sternwheeler, mounted on pontoons and driven by four hundred horsepower engines, to create currents, cross currents, and at times directed against the wind and wave direction, were also neglected as part of our "ocean'" arsenal.

We found out about water inside our waders and its cold sogginess particularly in winter shooting. And we talked about some of our crew members. Actors, God bless 'em, caught with their at times temperamental idiosyncrasies down, have been mentioned. Did we extol Spence? We meant to do so. Costs of "big or little" miniatures were discussed and the wisdom of arriving at a scale based not on the relative price of a five or a ten foot airplane, but on the job it had to do, were, I hope, distinctly understood.

Pressure from well meaning "don't knows" occupied a few choice words and we also "moved an ocean", dictated by crazy, fluid thought processes. Piano wire, friend, enemy, rated a bit of recognition, and then we were sidetracked by Don Jahraus and how well the two of us teamed. Further sidetracking by many others of these "people" culprits during which leanings towards "poetical" tendencies were uncovered. Esther and her horse, pliable wire "skeleton" armatures and modeled clothes, and the inadvisability of animating of miniature figures, preceded a discourse on J.J. Colin's "can of beans," as it relates to the important "let well enough alone" theory. Generally! Not always, but generally.

Another "stubborn" individual was lauded, the champion "dunked" crew member named, and "windy" Regan, master of the "wind" revolutions per minute and the wave machine rotations per two, six or ten seconds, Joe, house cleaning enforcer sublime (at times blue), was diligently and purposefully recorded.

Patience and the great craftsmanship as exemplified in Olof Olsson was touched upon. Then we delved into camera "speeds", their life history and factors determining a choice. Again, judgment and hopefully, "tests" are the answer to this toughie. Lack of "scale and speed" relationship was stressed and optical salvage through frame cutting was detailed. A waterless waterfall, high on our secret list, was disclosed and bared for all humanity to see and judge, during which the subject of "control" once more reared its sensible head.

The "Saga of the Mustaches" could have perhaps been omitted, but omit reference to Van Dyke, in this book of mine, no! That episode might be titled "How to Strangle and Kick Enemies and Make Friends", with due apologies to Dale Carnegie. Just now, at this late writing, a terrible thought! I recall that Van made the "heads you win, tails I win" proposition. Did he hand the coin to Ramon and did it maybe have only two "tails"? No "heads"? Oh no! At this late date? If so Van, and wherever you may be, may your chuckles turn into uproarious laughter. So we wind up with one more unintended but pithy lesson, to wit: Let nary a detail escape the scrutiny and the suspicion of your otherwise trusting soul.

END OF CHAPTER SEVEN

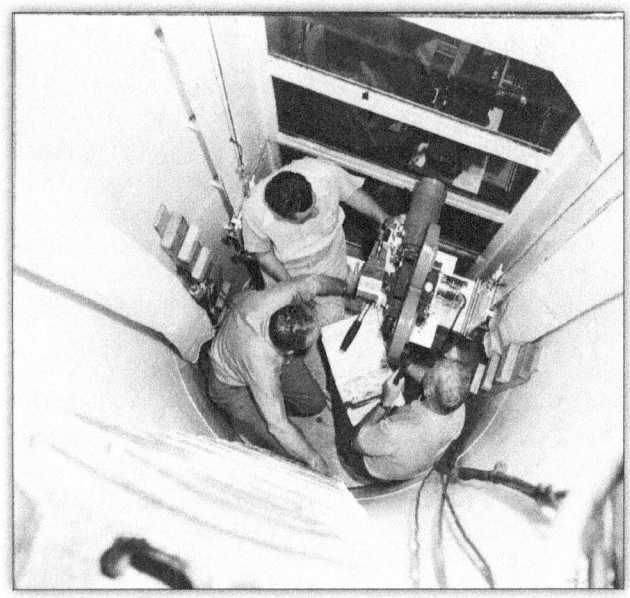

Below the surface shooting submarines or Esther Williams. Many days, many bubbles.

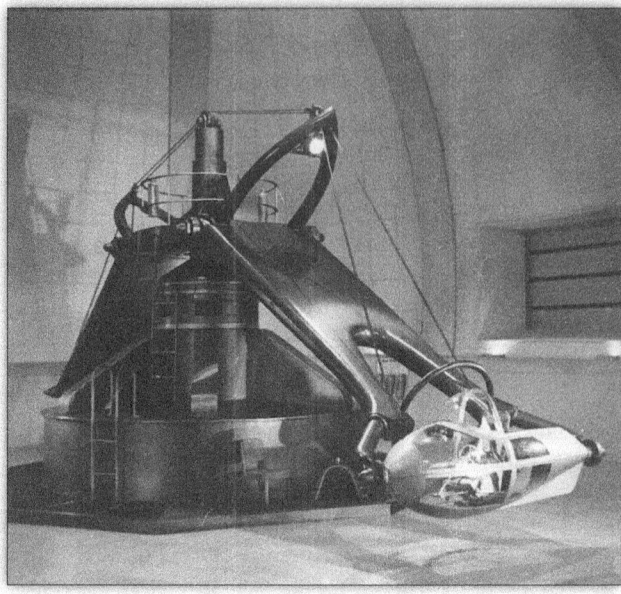

Our idea of a centrifuge for *Without Love*. 2" scale. Arms rotated and lifted, and 'car' also revolved.

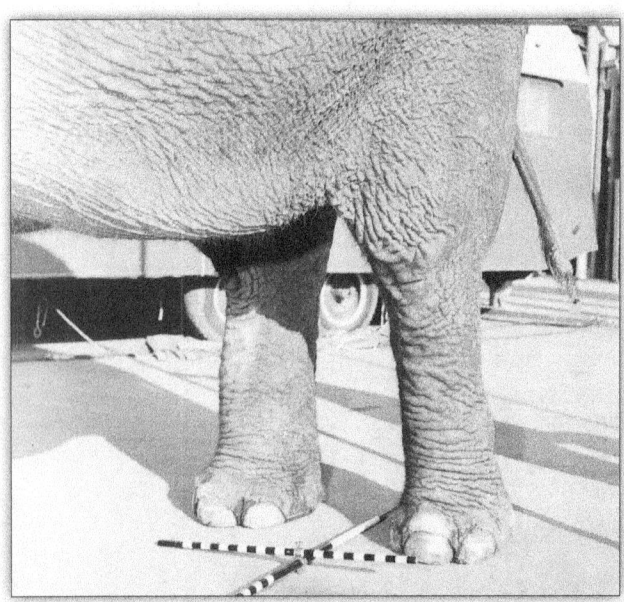

We build elephants, so we measure elephants.

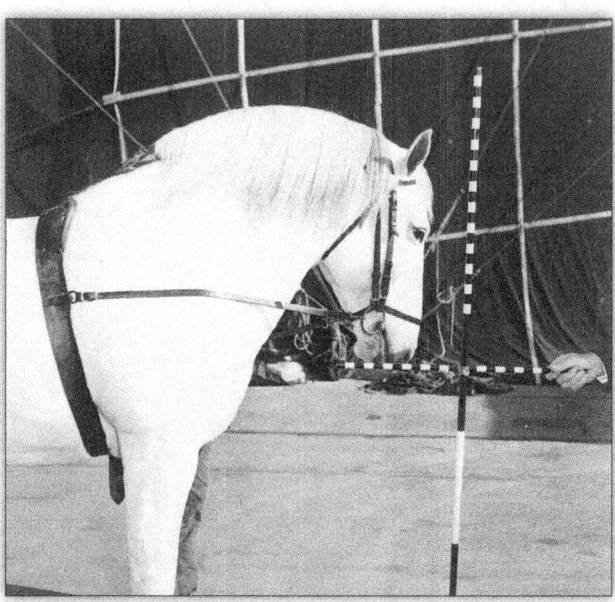

Also horses, which when modeled and cast in rubber are wedded to one of several mechanical horse mounts.

ATLANTIS, THE LOST CONTINENT (1961) PRODUCTION #1767

Miniatures are not shot in bathtubs. Stanchions at top of backing explained below.

Douglas "Dauntless" dive bomber, upper left. One of seven we used as wind machines.

Miscellaneous from *Atlantis, the Lost Continent*. 'Stanchions' in No. 1 are used to support and position large refelctors from which the sun provides 'moon' paths.

Part of "Atlantis" pre-sinking. Many miniature buildings and detail from 'Rome' in *Quo Vadis*.

Profile 'Volcano lava' was colored heavy liquid inter mingled with smoke and steam.

CHAPTER SEVEN

George Pal visiting the author on the set of *Atlantis, the Lost Continent*. Our tank in Lot 3, is three hundred by three hundred feet, some forty-two inches deep, and contains three "wells" that measure from twelve feet to thirty feet in depth. Backing at North end, slanted some 15 degrees to accommodate afternoon shooting.

Joe Regan, wind and wave impresario. "Atlantis" in background.

OUR VINES HAVE TENDER GRAPES (1945) PRODUCTION #1342

Above. Long shot, miniature dairy farm. *Our Vines Have Tender Grapes*. Good scaled detail throughout.

Below. Closer. Note miniature fence and trees. Scale of miniature was 1 1/2"=12".

CHAPTER SEVEN

Miniature dairy barn and silo - *Our Vines Have Tender Grapes*. Day shot.

Start of fire night sequence. Photographed broad daylight with bright sun at Lot 3.

Latter stage of fire - scenic night sky and foreground paint-darkened to achieve balance.

THIS MAN'S NAVY (1945) PRODUCTION #1320

(Above)- From *This Man's Navy*, Wallace Beery and William Wellman, Director. The blimp, a 'Navy K ship' scaled 1/2"=12". Foreground miniature set was 1" scale. Day for night.

(Below). Three varying scale miniatures were constructed. This one against projected clouds on a Process screen was 1"=12" scale.

(Above) Our largest 'K-ship' at 1 1/2" scale settles into MGM's lot 3 ocean. Starboard engine still functioning. She was 'hit' by shell fire. K-Ship sequence shot September 9, 1944 for process. Working title was "Air Ship Squadron #4".

(Below) The culprit, a 1" scale 'enemy' sub, eventually sunk by depth charges from 'Wally's' valiant blimp. We used prime cord on steel plates just below surface for water explosions. B.G. Perambulator shot from motorized boom 28' high with 2" and 3" lenses at 4x normal speed. B.G.s for bow and stern of blimp.

COMRADE X (1940) PRODUCTION #1159

Miniature 'Russian' tanks for *Comrade X*. Scale 1"=12". Distant hills are a scenic profile. Real Sky.

Tanks were pulled by cable from split tube which vertical rods engaged each tank. 'Split' was covered by dental rubber, slit with a razor blade to allow rods to pass.

A larger 3" scale tank fells a tree. Tubes described in center caption followed contours and varied directionally right and left.

Our 3"=12' scale tank emerging from a miniature 'river'. This tank was self-propelled and remotely controlled.

1/2" scale 'cast' tanks on miniature flat bars. Foreground oil wells are miniature. Background wells are real.

Inoperative tanks for this sequence were of a scale, 1/2'=12", to fit the scale of stock miniature flat cars. Casting was the most economical. Final tank size of 11" x 25.5" and approximately 20 lbs each.

71-P

Matte Painting supplied this bluff for *Comrade X*'s miniature tanks. There actually was none.
Example of Miniature and Matte Painting Departments collaboration.

At bottom of bridge railing, was the stage floor. Lower part of bridge 'river' and boat, shot in
miniature, and matted into the full-sized set. Scenic backing in rear.

(Above) Occasionally our Miniature 'ocean' became a full sized one. Mr. Minnelli 'borrowed' it for *Two Weeks In Another Town*. Note paddle wheel 'water mover' on right.

(Below) Same 'ocean', now miniature, during *Ben-Hur* galley sequence.

"Phanton Raiders". Initial flash of mortar installed series of explosions. Scale 3/4"=12".

Series of eruptions immediately following. Note 'force' lines in blasts. The miniature ship was scarcely damaged.

An early "Thunder Afloat" 'barge' blast. Wally Beery starred in this one. Scale 2"= 12"

An original manuscript layout page from A.A.G.

Japanese cruiser encountered by P.T. boat in *They Were Expendable*. 3/4" scale, day for late 'dusk'.

P.T. boat B.G. - Moving background shooting ahead approaching Japanese cruiser in the bgd; which appears on screen R to L after coming from behind. Headland covered with dense tropical trees.

Process plate for full sized action aboard PT boat. Note near hit and white water 'from' our fast moving camera raft.

South of the 'Philippines' (our Lot 3 'ocean'). She is torpedoed and her magazines go. Mortar installed explosions.

AMERICA (UNPRODUCED)

This is an excellent example of why 'the lily should never be gilded', or rather gilded beyond good judgement.

The six enlargements, on this and the next page, would seem to be acceptable. An otherwise tremendously detailed, beautifully operated miniature of an assembly line plane factory, was ruined by someone's insistence that <u>animated</u> miniature people be added. The original conception included the matte printing of real people into some of the shots. We were overruled and miniature figures were substituted.

This costly decision caused its elimination in the final editing.

The miniature scaled at 3/4'=12' and our own designed with fuselaged transport had a 30 foot wing span, the equivalent of 480 feet full sized. The date, 1943.

From start to finish everything moved, center section, wings, tails, props, sections of fuselage 'skin', landing gear etc., joined the slow progression of the plane's skeleton to a completed finish. And out she taxied under her own power. The picture *America*, and what a pity.

LUXURY LINER (1948) PRODUCTION #1412

Luxury Liner stage set. Much of superstructure, and life boats, were 'matte painted' and miniature water substituted later for stage floor.

Luxury Liner traveling water shots for Newcombe. Day and night and night with moonlight shots. Mounted camera on large single pontoon with outboard plow traveling 3/4 length of tank toward backing for water effects. Mounted on high paint frame which was moved across screen to tie with camera for moonlight effect.

The "Mayflower" for *Luxury Liner*. Scale 3/4" = 12". She is 54 feet long. White water from pumps and siphons in her hull. Note background for size reference at top.

In heavy weather at 'night', a sunny afternoon with a night sky.

Stock shots of liner in storm. Set-up used 3 wave machines grouped in foreground. In background 3 liberties above wave machines. 2 planes on pontoons. 4 planes on bank. Cameras in large tub and mounted on gimbals.

Another water 'vehicle'. This, a submarine in the days of *Atlantis*. Scale 1"=12".

Ext. 'Cannes Harbor' for *Mrs. Parkington*, dawn. Miniature shot on our 'tank' stage in April, 1944.

Shot by Bill Williams with camera on float drawn across tank with boat lights on and off as they pass in Harbor.

At 'night' with the same painted sky. Different lighting and exposure. 'Moon' path was arc above backing.

They Were Expendable ship torpedoed. Day for night Scale 3/4"=12".

Aboard the large scale miniature "Bounty". This became a Process Plate for full sized foreground action. Miniature figures were not animated.

At 'Pitcairn' the 2" scale "Bounty" burns. A moving Process Plate for Marlon Brando in small boat.

Continuance of above, then a cut to the full sized ship as 'Mr. Christen' and his crew boarded.

A miniature Process Plate for the full sized bridge of the "Mary Deare" scale 2"=12".

VALLEY OF DECISION (1945) PRODUCTION #1341

Long shot of Pittsburgh 'Steel Mill'. Miniature scale 3/4"=1'-0. Shot on stage 14 in November 1944 by Max Fabian.

The same, now active, at night. Both used as Process plates for *Valley of Decision*.

Set constructed for two screen projection with miniature section separating screens.

Closer shot of the 3/4 Miniature. Projected sky background.

A larger scale miniature of the 'Mill', 1"=12" people were matte printed along road.

Close shot of the idle 'Mill', People were also added. Note importance of small detail.

Another shot. Again small detail gives scale.

MINIATURE RATE OF TRAVEL CHART

Miniature Rate of Travel Chart

A helpful chart designating rate of travel of Miniatures, varying in scale and camera speeds, to simulate Full-Sized velocities. Travel Rates beyond or less than those charted, may be obtained by simple multiplication or division. Recall that one mile is 5280 feet.

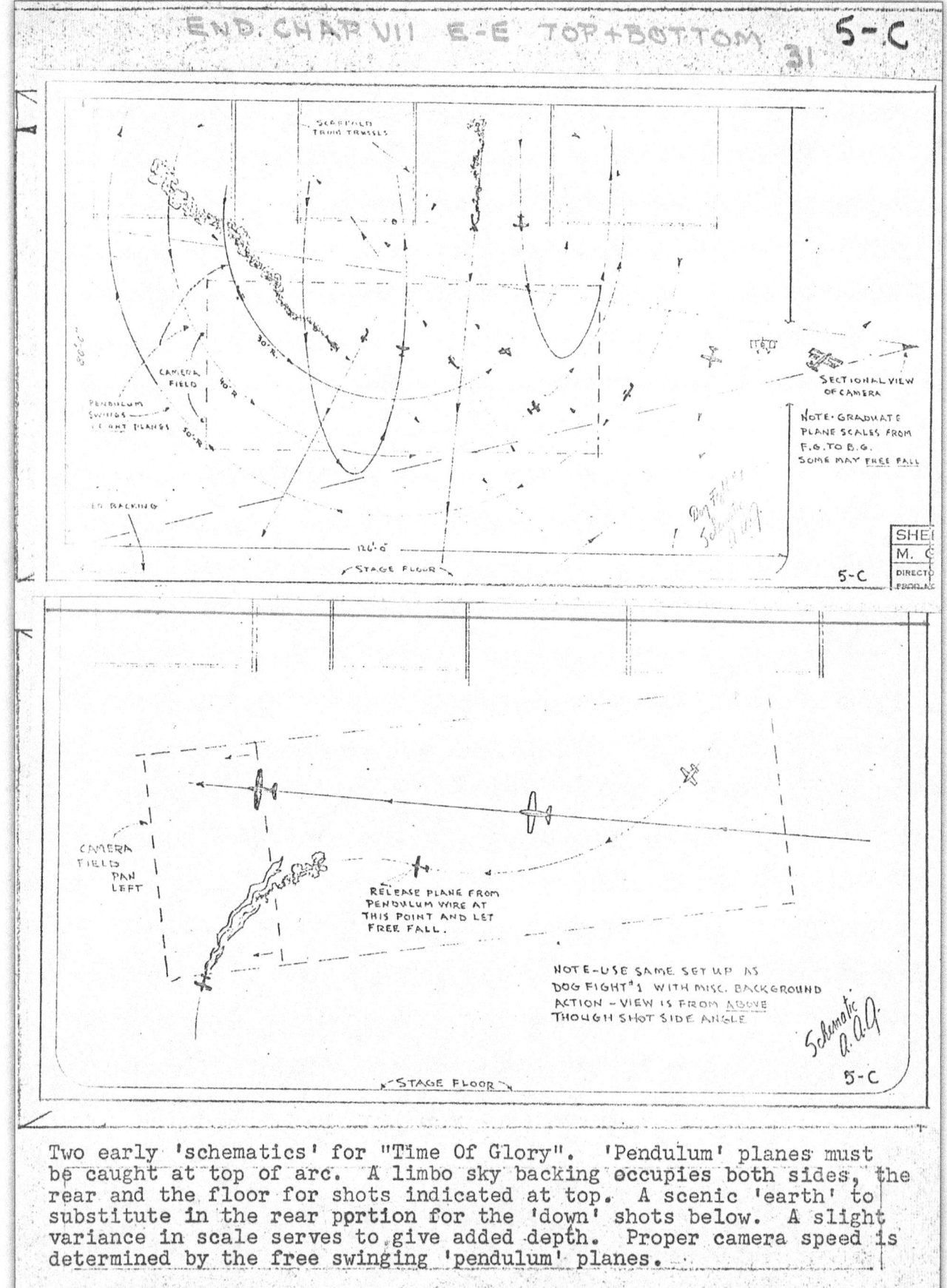

Two early 'schematics' for "Time Of Glory". 'Pendulum' planes must be caught at top of arc. A limbo sky backing occupies both sides, the rear and the floor for shots indicated at top. A scenic 'earth' to substitute in the rear portion for the 'down' shots below. A slight variance in scale serves to give added depth. Proper camera speed is determined by the free swinging 'pendulum' planes.

Time Of Glory was never produced. See preliminary breakdown and continuity sketches in chapter five.

```
                    FALLING BODY

          FROM JIM RINDER
          DERRY PARACHUTE SERVICE
          534 W. ARBOR VITAE, INGLEWOOD
          TEL.  OR. 7-6810

SECONDS              ACCELERATION              DISTANCE TOTAL
   1                   16 Feet                    16 Feet
   2                   46   "                     62   "
   3                   76   "                    138   "
   4                  104   "                    242   "
   5                  124   "                    366   "
   6                  138   "                    504   "
   7                  148   "                    652   "
   8                  156   "                    808   "
   9                  163   "                    971   "
  10                  167   "                   1138   "
  11                  171   "                   1309   "
  12                  176   "                   1485   "
  13                  176   "                   1661   "
  14                  176   "                   1837   "
  15                  176   "                   2013   "
  16                  176   "                   2189   "
  17                  176   "                   2365   "
  18                  176   "                   2541   "
  19                  176   "                   2717   "
  20                  176   "                   2893   "

     MINIATURE FIGURE WILL FALL 42' IN 1.35 SEC. + AT 3/4"
     = 1' - 0" (SCALE OF MIN.) 42' REPRESENTS 672' F.S.
     OR ROUGHLY 7.25 SEC. OF FALL.

     7.25 SEC ÷ 1.35 SEC. = 5.3 + - CAMERA SPEED FOR 1ST
     HALF OF FALL.

     4 SEC. ÷ 1.35 SEC. = 3 - = CAMERA SPEED FOR 2ND HALF OF
     FALL.

     (THE ABOVE WAS COMPUTED FOR AN ELEVATOR SHAFT FALL SHOT
     IN TWO PARTS, THE UP AND DOWN ANGLES, USING THE SAME
     SET FOR BOTH, WERE 'WEDDED' BY A FAST TILT DOWN 'WIPE'
     IN THE MIDDLE OF THE FALL)
```

(Above) Approximate rate of Full-Sized free-fall per second at sea level atmosphere. Camera speed variances may be computed from this table to fit scale of Miniature.

As an example a 3"=12" scale object must take five seconds to fall the equivalent of 124 feet. The actual fall at 3" scale would be 1/4th of 124 feet, or 31 feet, which would necessitate a four times normal camera speed. Though absolute accuracy is not claimed, it is sufficiently close for most problems.

(Right) An elevator shaft for *Uncle*. One miniature 'victim' plunged down this one. Scale 1"-12".

North By Northwest, MGM Production #1743, Released 1939, AAG Contribution: Special Effects.

CHAPTER EIGHT

~

"MINIATURES SANS MUSTACHES"

Lining up a close shot. The "S.S.G." is a garbage truck bed used for fuel in *Too Hot to Handle*.

A crocodile's contribution towards solving a pretty snappy dilemma with which we were faced, will be the lead-off documentation in this chapter. Reference has been made to this scaly creature in previous chapters. True, he was rubber and mechanized but he literally gave his life's blood (his nigrosine dye blood) in such a manner that years later when Atom Bombs number one and number two ~ number one was detonated at Alamogordo, New Mexico ~ were written into our story of Hiroshima, he, old "Crocky," came to the rescue of a bewildered Special Visual Effects "wizard." Wizard? Bewildered? The latter, yes, because this is pretty generally a normal condition, but particularly so in this case, because never had we done an atom bomb. In fact, our whole country with all of its resources and no shepherding budget enforcers, had at this date done only three—the two mentioned and the one at Nagasaki. But sure enough, in M.G.M.'s *The Beginning or the End*, a sort of preachment against playing with this new kind of fire, we were to show what happened to Hiroshima. Not a day or so later but right on the split second of its happening.

As you will surmise, this chapter continues discussions in the Miniature category--a carry over from the last chapter. We certainly intended not placing a solution to this problem within the realm of Full Sized Effects!

So, off again! What to do and how to do it? Picture if you will, the extent of our predicament. This picture was to be <u>made</u>. Actors and director signed, commitments contracted. No one asked, "Is it possible?" No one for a moment (at this stage) even asked, "How much?" Simply a completed shooting script climaxed by Scene 237, or was it 372, which read more or less, "~the 'thing' was dropped thru the bomb bay of the 'Enola Gay,' B29 chosen for this historic mission, as its crew flew it to the predetermined dropzone over Hiroshima. She banked sharply away as Col. Tibbets got her out'a there but fast. In a few seconds the blinding white, unearthly flash, told Parsons, Tibbets and the crew that literally all hell had popped below them. A tremendous concussion wave followed by a second, a third and others, diminishing in intensity, rocked the ship all over the sky. An ominous silence followed as the mushroom, horrible in its sickening, changing colors, grew and churned aloft to thousands upon thousands of feet,"~following which was typed in the script in parenthesis, "(Note, Special Effects)".

Well, we "noted" all over the place and came up with practically nothing except a request for money to start. "Start what?" rightfully asked Cedric Gibbons, my immediate superior. "I haven't the slightest idea," answered a "bewildered" me. "How much money, then?" inquired Mr. Gibbons. "I haven't the slightest idea," I replied. "How can I request an indeterminate amount of money for you to proceed with a completely obfuscated void?" said he. I replied, "I haven't the slightest idea, Mr. Gibbons." And I also had not the slightest idea of what "obfuscated" meant. Nor, I believe, did he. Part of that which made Mr. Gibbons a great executive, as well as the artist and architect that he was, followed. "A thousand dollars, two thousand?" he asked. "I don't know, Mr. Gibbons, but let's start at ten thousand for preliminary experimentation." Up was lifted the receiver of his phone to J. "Judson" Cohn, at that time studio production manager. "Buddy wants ten thousand dollars to start thinking, Joe" ~ pause ~ "Oh, about a bomb." ~ More pause — "No, no ideas. Guess we'd better let him start. I'll sign it, you okay it. "

That was the beginning, and how simple. The problem alone was sufficient without an impossible explanation of "why ten thousand dollars!" Cedric Gibbons understood and so did Joe Cohn. And don't become too overjoyed, Joe, with this and previous plaudits. Eventually I'll probably tell the story of you, a brick wall and Hobart Henley ~ and me.

To shorten the fuse whereby our mental processes finally exploded a respectable miniature atom bomb, I will by-pass two of the three "starts" from which that 'ten thousand' initial grant served as a springboard.

Finding a key to this granddaddy of all puzzlements brought into play one long unused memory cell. When Tarzan did mortal underwater combat with that tail-lashing, jaw-snapping rubber and steel monster in M.G.M.'s huge "dishpan" tank, he, Tarzan, wielded a nasty knife, plunging it repeatedly into the crocodile's rubbery throat, hoping to hit one or more of the sacs of "blood" we had thoughtfully provided therein as targets, the pricking of which would produce gory realism.

This crocodile, by the way, was quite an example of Full Sized Special Effects. Two steel tubes extended, one at a time, through a watertight port into our eighteen foot deep tank. One tube included his hind legs, plus some tail, all the way forward, and the other just aft of his front legs, to the tip of that lashing tail. All of the mechanism was high and dry on the "outside" end of the tube, and if the operators were at all in a choleric mood, they could give Johnny Weissmuller a bad time.

But back to our atom bomb and its strange rapport with a crocodile fight. Well, and please pardon the repetition, up springs the "crazy thinking" department. Thorough cogitation, which brought to mind that underwater battle, put to work a trial and error application of that memory cell and it recalled certain peculiarities of that "*Tarzan*" tremendo.

When Johnny's knife would hit home, out into the water would gush a spurt of crocodile "blood" (nigrosine dye) and it formed, if memory was serving me right, something that looked like a current picture in a newspaper, which showed the actual "mushroom" and its "tails", product of the Hiroshima Bomb. It was shot by the tail gunner in the Enola Gay as she hightailed for home.

So this became Start No. Three, an 'underwater' approach, and we quickly abandoned the first two. It was of course not all that easy ~ puncturing a toy balloon full of dye in a tank. Chemicals of many varieties and colors, and varying in specific gravity, were laboriously accepted and discarded. An ingenious air-mortar, controlled hydraulically, introduced our final formulae with a "whoosh" which immediately formed a perfect white sphere, huge in the center of a painted Hiroshima, thence proceeding to lift and soar, while forming proper "tails," to the equivalent of those thousands upon thousands of feet. An arrangement of individually "switched" flash bulbs and a high wattage incandescence included in the center of this underwater maelstrom, controlled by a rheostat, was devised and helped to add proper visual wallop! Well, we wound up with a pretty good bomb, so good in fact that General Groves, Head of the then secret "Manhattan Project," the group of scientists who held that famous "fission" party in Chicago after which they moved lock, stock and barrel to Alamogordo, New Mexico; so good that the General after viewing the completed production in Washington asked indignantly just why he had not seen this specific film before. And apparently so good that the Military used our shot in their training films for some years subsequently. And much more importantly, the grantors of the original ten thousand "no idea" dollars, who later were called upon for additional grants, let out not a peep.

The "detail of costs thru April 20, 1946" reproduced below may be of interest to the novice in order to show the miscellaneous conglomeration of items and charges which can and do creep into our oft complicated stints. It does not represent the total Effects financial involvement of the entire sequence~only the "experimental" work, which did however produce within this cost, the shots used in the picture of the approach to Hiroshima and the actual bomb detonation.

JOB 99217-1
EXPERIMENTAL WORK DONE IN CONNECTION WITH MINIATURE
ATOMIC BOMB TESTS AND DEVELOPMENTS.
APPROX, ESTIMATE $20,000.00
Per Job Order, this to be Charged to Prod. 1377
"Beginning Or the End"
Job issued January 19, 1946 at request of
Mr. Gibbons
Detail of Costs Thru April 20, 1946

Labor
   Construction (1/14 to 3/15/46)   10,774.56
   Mechanical (1/15 to 3/7/46)   3,132.45
   Painters   151.57
   Storeroom   1.20
   Staff Shop   367.24
   Laborers   994.65
   Mill Carpenters   12.98
   Precision Machine Shop   51.23
   Scenic (1/15 to 3/13/46)   3,573.52
   Background Projection & Miniature 1,491.66
   Cameramen   1,150.41
   Script Clerks   58.32
   Police and Watchmen   78.53
                                    21,838.32

Stores
   Lumber   289.02
   Hardware   209.50
   Electrical   47.16
   Garage   2.80
   Chemicals   31.17
   Arsenal   118.38
   Wardrobe   1.16
   Miscellaneous   178.27
   Paint   152.26
   Precision Shop   .14
   Dry Goods   2.16
                                      1,032.02

Special Effects Dept. Overhead Charges
   2/7/46 Process & Miniature Shot   150.00
   2/8/46   "   150.00
   2/9/46   "   150.00
   2/20/46   "   150.00
   2/21/46   "   150.00
   3/1/46   "   150.00
   3/2/46   "   150.00
   3/5/46   "   150.00
                                      1,200.00

Vouchers Paid
   Agicide Laboratories, Inc.
2 - 100 lb. bags walnut shell flour   3.59
Braun Corporation
25 lbs. 9 mm, 25 lbs. 12 mm, 25 lbs.
   15 mm pyrex tubing   48.43
Herbert E. Britt
5 lbs. Explosive Powder (conflagration) 20.50

Vouchers Paid - Contd.
Cinema Nursery

6 Chinese juniper 4 to 5 ft., 6 pines small needles 6 ft., 6 boxwood 4 to 5 ft. 14 in. Pots	126.08
6 Short needle pines 6 ft.	33.83

Degen-Fiege Co.

2 each of 2 in., 4 in. & 6 in. Hitest chrome cup leathers	5.85

Electric Supply Co.

12 High voltage push button switches #85	18.57

M. Flax

6 bottles (2½ oz.) Textine	1.23

Gough Industries, Inc.

2 cases (240) # 6 G.E. Photo Flash lamps	26.20
4 " (480) #6 "	52.40

Horton & Converse

5 lbs. Benzoyl Peroxide	15.38

The Lighthouse, Inc.

24 SC "H" Sockets	5.90
48 SC Pigtail Sockets	11.81

L.A. Rubber & Asbestos Works

26 2/3 sq. ft. 3/8" soft rubber sheet 66 lbs.	47.36

Special Effects Mfg. Co.

2 Gr, 1 x 4 Dark black smoke pots, 75 lbs. magnesium powder, 20 to 30 mesh, 60% treated	144.53
15 lbs. Flash smoke compound; 75 lbs. magnesium 20/30 mesh, 60%o treated; 15 lbs. magnesium 10/15 mesh; 50 lbs. aluminum powder	221.91

The Wholesale Supply Co.

2 lbs. MCW acid Phthalic Anhydrine 2 x 1#	2.15

Vouchers Paid - Contd.
Pacific Studios

1 - 8 x 10 copy negative, 1- 5½' x 7' Enlargement of 35mm	37.57

Tyre Bros, Glass & Paint Co.

2 Pcs. 1" Plate glass	66 3/4" x 83 3/4"	
1 " 1" "	31 3/4" x 71 3/4"	
1 " 1" "	29 3/4" x 83 3/4"	661.13
		1,484.42

Raw Stock Film

Negative	459.00
Positive	87.50
	546.50

Developing & Processing

Negative Developed	138.98
Positive Processed	144.97
	283.95

Miscellaneous

Stills	1.20
Workmen's Compensation Insurance	131.72
	131.72

** *

Set 71   *

Construction	95.82	*
Total Operation	150.00	*
Operating Costs	25.12	*
	270.94	*
	========	*
	26,518.13	*

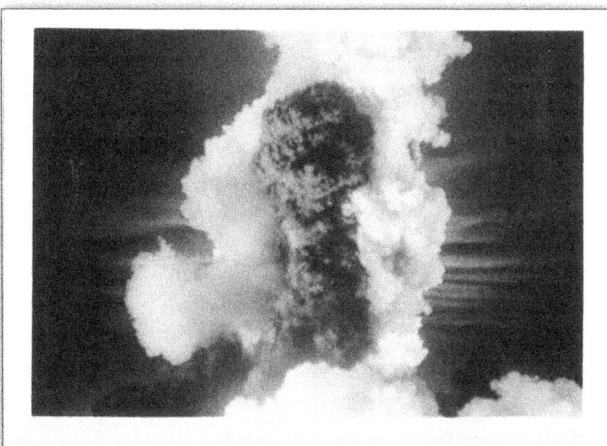

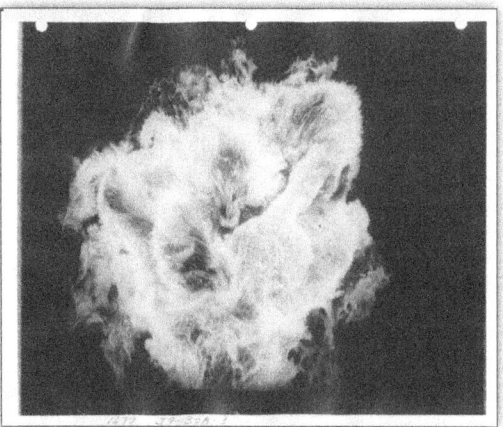
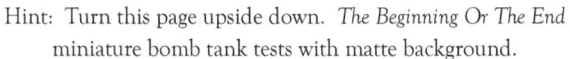

Hint: Turn this page upside down. *The Beginning Or The End* miniature bomb tank tests with matte background.

Tarzan And His Mate - Nigrosine dye bag inspiration.

Right: Photos of flames tests- These effects were part of the initial experimentation. Two of many attempts with various explosive materials shot at high speed during early effect analysis.

These dollars were, of course, 1946 dollars. On today's market that total would be considerably boosted.

One or two sidelights before concluding this episode of M.G.M.'s "crocodile-bomb." First, all information at that time was tightly restricted. Our sole research was that long shot by the Enola Gay's tail gunner which appeared in the newspapers, and some footage of the Alamogordo "tower" bomb. We knew nothing of the shape or size of the bomb itself which was required to be shown in the scenes where Parsons arms it prior to drop. So we "invented" its shape and size, about sixteen feet in length. I could get no aerial photos of Hiroshima from the Air Force, again restricted, but luckily I recalled such a photograph in an early U.S. Camera Year Book and after a diligent search, found it. From this we reproduced our city and environs. What altitude? No one would say, so we "invented" the altitude and came up with thirty thousand feet. Later we were told the "bomb away!" occurred at thirty-two thousand feet.

Lastly, and to me most interestingly, we had very successfully ~ solved a problem which called for gigantic scope, a vast area and a real doomsday holocaust, in a tank of distilled water about four feet by four feet by six feet high. We have discussed "scale" in the last chapter. This one, except for some of our outer space chores, was the smallest scale miniature we had ever attempted.

From crocodiles to disintegrating atoms to whales. This particular species of blubber encased bulk would have truly raised the ire of that horn-rimmed professor who had so thoroughly deflated Mr. DeMille's pomp and circumstance as recounted in the "Neophyte" Chapter. Richard Thorpe, long-time M.G.M. director, was assigned to do *All The Brothers Were Valiant*, a Bob Taylor, Stewart Granger, Ann Blyth vehicle produced by Pandro Berman. The whale turned out to be by M.G.M. in more ways than just building a miniature whale. We designed a brand new specie because Mr. Thorpe felt certain features of all existing whales were not particularly photogenic so we blended together parts of several and came up with a pretty handsome though non-existent member of the order Catacea which we christened "Thorpus Dickus". Sort of a whale of a license we took it might be said (with apologies) but I must agree with Richard that the proper choice, a sperm, for the palm fringed locale of this sequence would have been too bad. A sperm is quite ugly. There were others however, but none tickled Mr. Thorpe's taste buds and as Gertrude Stein might have written, "A whale is a whale is a whale is not a rose." And I might add "A Director's whim is a whim is a whim and <u>not</u> to be trifled with!"

The whaling sequence as finally shot and edited passed with flying colors. The student viewing this "effects-full" portion of the picture will note that three categories, Miniature, Process and Full-sized, were used extensively and particularly in several scenes where all three are combined.

Bob Taylor and his cronies have harpooned their quarry and have been towed for a fast quarter of a mile spin when suddenly, up tail, down nose, the whale sounds. Proper waiting for suspense buildup follows and then with a rush he surfaces and charges the boat and its occupants. His huge flukes lift high out of the water and come crashing down on men and boat, upsetting all into the "salty" deep of M.G.M.'s heated tank on Stage Thirty. Method? As follows! Long shots of whale and boat and people, (Straight Miniature). Close shots of real people and a hydraulic ram controlled boat in water (full-sized Effects), in front of a Process Screen, upon which are rear projected backgrounds of ocean and whale (Miniature Process Plates). The giant miniature tail raising out of the water to crash our full-sized, peopled, boat was of course confined to the Process Screen and there was actually no contact between whale flukes and boat. However, the prow of the boat close to the projected background was rigged and timed to be pulled down violently into the water as the tail appeared to hit the prow, the stern lifting high and dumping all personnel into the water. Bob, unlike Wally Beery, had no aversion to water and seemed to relish this sort of shenanigan. So we have another example of pooling "three" to make "one."

The scale of our miniature rubber whale was three inches to the foot — one fourth full-sized. Recall we nicknamed him not "Moby" but "Thorpy Dick." "Thorpy" was pulled by cables and powerful winches all over the Lot Three ocean, riding up and over simple ramps to give him "life" and down into the

CHAPTER EIGHT 184

deep thirty foot hole for the sounding scenes. Once he was torn into two halves when a cable slipped off an underwater sheave, the stern half remaining placid while his front half made a sudden plunging ninety degree turn and headed pell-mell towards camera and crew. All was not lost however as the bow wave produced by this 'tragedy' was used in the area of the sequence where he surfaces and charges. Sometimes misfortune smiles.

Maximilian Fabian, A.S.C., A.A.M.C.M.C., another one of those gems to which we are eternally grateful, stands high in my catalogue of outstanding craftsmen. The A.S.C. stands for "American Society of Cinematographers," of which he was an esteemed member for many years. The A.A.M.C.M.C. is of my bestowing. It means the "Absolutely Ablest, Most Conscientious, Miniature Cameraman" and scarcely anyone, I think, who ever had the opportunity of working with Max, would question the deservability of the above title.

Fabian's great forte was miniature photography, but the multiple keys he used to unlock the "impossibles" were just plain <u>Fabian</u>. I can think of no one who has experienced, stored and recorded all of the facets of this demanding branch of cinematography to the extent that Max Fabian has done during his years of association at M.G.M. with his beloved James Basevi, my predecessor and great friend. In the years which followed and during his association with me, I made many attempts at equalling Basevi in Maximilian's affections. Though I am sure I never succeeded, it was a continuing privilege to try. Jim, probably my closest friend, has joined Cedric Gibbons, Don Jahraus, Van Dyke, so many others, on that inevitable trek 'Westward.' His legacy, an enviable one in the field of Art Direction and Effects is exceeded only by Basevi the man. A valorous World War I record, and extraordinary capacity for the accumulation of friends and a lasting respect and affection by all with whom he came in contact.

If Max had a fault it could be classified among those of Bossart, Slifer, Olsson and all the other 'stubborn' ones. A perfect job would rarely be quite good enough. And he refused to follow my pet <u>expressed</u> philosophy of "moderation." He worked <u>too</u> hard. He worried <u>too</u> much about his own efforts. He was overly conscientious. And, selfishly, I thank the stars above that Max was all of those "toos." He was a born artist. A few cameramen are by instinct, artists. Some few acquire this highly desirable talent, and some are good mechanics, beautifully versed in light meter readings and film speeds. Strangely, many know little of vanishing points and perspective relationships between foreground and background. This has, upon occasion, required a guiding hand, particularly in Process and Scenic Backing photography.

A smilingly blunt Irishman, Eddie Hannan, Head of M.G.M.'s Film Library some years ago, said, I quote, "All cameramen are glorified plumbers," end quote. Please remember, he said it, not I. Because I am quite sure all cameraman are not glorified plumbers. Not <u>all</u>! It has been difficult at times however, in dealing with some very few of these gentlemen, to forget Eddie's analogy, although I confess to taking great delight in quoting Mr. Hannan to such good friends as George Folsey, Bill Daniels, Harold Lipstein, Joe Ruttenberg and a few others whom I trust to not hit back. And speaking of cinematographers, probably he who may know little of perspective and vanishing points, but who can determine a leading lady's right side and reproduce its beauty, or perhaps add to it, deserves more laurels than Eddie Hannan's pronouncement would indicate.

Harold Rosson, "Put-Put" we call him, or more formally "Hal", certainly qualifies as one of those above who would not hit back, though like Folsey, his ready vocabulary is never at a loss to express mental counter-punches if and when needled a bit by yours truly. Actually George with his Brooklyn-bred Irish wit is perhaps a faster draw than is Hal. A reference to 'plumbers' by me to either of these two usually leaves me badly bruised, mentally if not physically. Two top cinematographers, Rosson and Folsey and two top and valued friends.

Well, Fabian had no "plungers" in his kit. But he could stretch a lens beyond its manufacturer's specifications, he could "dry-color-pounce" a highlight or a shadow in a miniature set and he could cajole a laboratory technician into obtaining that last ounce out of a deliberately underexposed negative, deliberate because of an "impossible" focus elongation made necessary by ingredients so commonly existent in most miniatures. He could do all these things better and with more consistent success than any cinemaphotographer I have known. Slifer, Harold Wellman, Mark Davis and a few others would measure up to close seconds, but Max through the years, set a mark of perfection which in my opinion remains unexcelled.

One of his habitual immoderations was to visit the laboratory developing crew at midnight after a shooting day in order to check his negative. Otherwise he wouldn't sleep for the balance of the night. Such extreme devotion certainly is not recommended herein, but it serves as an example of the dedication Max wholeheartedly applied to his job.

He was fearful of only two things, I believe. Failure and height. The former seldom if ever occurred and the latter could usually be overcome by a sturdy rope, properly noosed under his arms and attached to a pulley on high from which Max would be upped, willing but unwilling, inch by inch, on a ladder to a platform, sixty, seventy, eighty feet high, upon which Fabian's magic Bell and Howell or Mitchell would be firmly "tri-podded." My gratitude, Max, for those climbs and for the miles of perfect or near perfect film which so faithfully and helpfully recorded our many Special Visual Effects, Miniature Category efforts.

ALL THE BROTHERS WERE VALIANT (1953) PRODUCTION #1614

All the Brothers Were Valiant. 2" scale miniature whaler in the 'South Seas' headed for her quarry.

"Thorpus Dick" (not Moby) harpooned and on his way. Whale scale, 3"=12", about sixteen feet in length.

Headed for the horizon of our Lot 3 'ocean'. Black and white blow-up from Ansco color film fails to show scenic clouds.

CHAPTER EIGHT

35-A

```
FORM 48    Dec. 22-23-26-'52-   Jan. 2-14-15-16-17-'53         END
DATE       Feb. 16-17-23 '53                                   CHAP
                                       Estimated Construction and Special Effects   VIII
PRODUCTION  1614               Detached  Preparation........ 5250.00
                               Miniatures Special Camera
                                        Mounts........ 6500.00
SET        73
                                        Operation........ 7500.00
STAGE   TANK LOT #3
                                        Elect. Operation...1000.00
PICTURE ALL THE BROTHERS WERE VALIANT   Add and Changes...500.00

                                        Total Approp...20,750.00
TITLE OF MINIATURE  EXT. WHALING SEQ    Final Cost    35,372.14
                                                  1 Whale
Details of Min. Set—Area  TANK LOT #3   No. of Buildings or Units 2 Small Boats

Scale WHALE & BOATS  3" - 1'-0"         Day  X   Night........ Dawn........ Sunset........

Backing  SKY - SCENIC
```

REMARKS Straight Cuts and Process Plates of Whales (six). Two
Blowing and Cuts and Plates of 3" Scale Whale towing Boat,
Breeching, Sounding, etc. Separate Tail Built for back-
ground of Tail Hitting Boat. Special Rig Built for Off
Stage Control of Tail. Whale Cast in Rubber and Towed,
Cable, Winch. Pulled into Deep Pit for Sounding Shots.
(NOTE: Whale Tore in Two Causing Shooting Delay).

Dressing and Min. Props.

CONSTRUCTION   Detached
                                  Miniatures   6,761.78
  Total Construction Cost. 4,098.80 Total Special Effects... 4,862.21

OPERATION   **Construction Dept. Daily Cost**
  Average Crew

	Foreman	Mechanics	Grips	Laborers
Morning				
Afternoon				
Night				

  Total Operation Cost...... 18,905.75

ELECTRICAL   Average Load........
  Wind Machines and Fans........
  Average Daily Crew........
  Total Operating Cost........ 743.60

CAMERA DEPARTMENT
  Cameraman....... Fabian
  Extra Cameras... 2 Cameras Part of Shooting Days
  Lens........ Varied
  Speed....... 72 F.P.S. & 60 F.P.S.
  Approx. No. of Feet of Film Printed........

Typical record of a completed miniature job. Note total
appropriation and final cost. Alibi? None, though one
torn whale contributed. Mainly a miss in our guess-
estimate.

35A

34-P Alt

All The Brothers Were Valiant miniature ship and whaling boat. Ship 2"-1'. Used "Nathan Ross" miniature ship as "Martin Wilkes". Set involved sky & water and profile of land split and light house. Shot in tank at Lot 3.

CHAPTER EIGHT 188

Whaling sequence continued. Our MGM bred species sounds. Note water at horizon is 'flattened' by wind machines to reduce 'wave' height. This adds <u>distance</u> perspective.

A quick turn to charge the dory. Plate for full sized Process in foreground.

Process plate showing tail about to smash full sized dory and actors. Separate mini-tail built and mechanically rigged for this purpose.

on. Once firmly implanted at the top, King wished not to descend until the episode was finished. Fortunately only the lunch hour suffered, or rather other than Mr. Vidor, only the lunch hour suffered, and his blacked-out descent began at about three P.M.

Some twenty-seven minutes later an unscathed though probably rear-end bruised Director came in for a safe landing on the solid floor of Stage Twenty-One, arose shakily to his underpinning and headed warily for the washroom.

Control of the elements (again no pun intended) wind, storm, tornado or whatever was discussed to some extent as we delved into the Full-sized Mechanical Effects category. I cannot stress too highly the application of "control" as it affects miniatures. Not just in the elements, but as it pertains to the illusions of scope, particularly from the horizon up. Sky, distant mountains, ocean endlessness, unbounded prairies and most emphatically, day for night photography with a controlled "sky" backing can achieve results in my opinion much more to be desired than "location" miniature shooting.

It seems strange that within the limits of a three hundred by three hundred foot tank with its sixty foot high sky backing, we can generally effectuate an illusion of greater distance than if shooting in actuality with a natural horizon miles away. The trick is in "cloud perspective" and with this sort of control the sky supplied by scenic artists, is "made to order" where nature's effort can often be bald and detailless if not lacking totally a horizon at all due to haziness. If clouds do exist, they change from hour to hour and certainly from day to day, often from clouds to no clouds. Hence an inconsistent sequence. We will gladly accept the limitations of confinement as represented by facilities such as our Miniature Tank, for the overwhelming benefits of controls which beneficially shoot off in so many tangents affecting the many problems at hand.

Some studios are lacking, or have at best very limited, installations such as M.G.M.'s. In which case little choice of how and where is left. And no studio other than M.G.M. has George Gibson. George originally came from a highland or a lowland by a low road or a high road to America from Scotland, not too many years ago (at least by my calendar). His sojourn at M.G.M. was interrupted by a stretch in the Marine Corps, World War Two, and although I feel quite certain that my war, the First World War, was a better war, we have yet to mutually agree on this point of dispute.

George Gibson is tiller man, guiding light, professor and inspiration for the Motion Picture industry's most superlative department of its kind in all of what we figuratively refer to as Hollywood. George is the head of M.G.M.'s Scenic Department and he has surrounded himself with the most adept students, each with outstanding talent in his own right, that it has been within my experience to observe in any departmental branch of any studio. I say "students" because

To digress for a moment, most normal people are height conscious. I am abnormal and love it. King Vidor, famous director and author of that autographed photo of King in his director's chair with my Billy The Kid set in the background, mentioned in the Foreword of this volume, was abnormal in the other direction. Max Fabian was a human fly compared to Mr. Vidor.

A scene in The Crowd called for Jimmy Murray, as a boy, to slowly climb an exaggerated-in-length-and-steepness stairway to his second-floor tenement home upon learning of a serious accident which had befallen one of his parents. The problem was not in our "stylized" set or the added length of the stairs. It was how to get Mr. Vidor to the top so that he could direct this highly (no pun intended) emotional scene. I was the Unit Art Director and came up with a solution that finally was unenthusiastically accepted by King. We built a much longer stairway, longer because it was considerably less steep, up to the shooting platform, from the rear of the set. We enclosed this stairway in a black cloth tunnel from bottom to top and our Director, seated on the first step, his back to the required direction of progress, slowly "sat" his way, step by step by step in an almost totally black void, up and up until his posterior was solidly implanted at the summit. Many helping hands then deposited him into his chair as near to the camera as we dared, and gradually the lights were turned

Gibson's scenic artists, through many years, have learned a technique and delivery resulting in a very high degree of excellence.

Teacher and class travel together a sometimes hectic but always harmonious road of mutual contribution. And may I say with little fear of contradiction that Gibson and his absolutely tiptop people present more consistently to M.G.M., top drawer successful efforts than any other "team" on the lot. The closest approach from a departmental standpoint would probably have been Cedric Gibbons and his group, or from a complete organizational standpoint, L.B. Mayer and his vast stable of talent. Neither, however, in my opinion would very closely approximate the Scenic Department's degree of preeminence.

Several of George's former people are Heads in other studios. The germ of his genius has thereby spread, although Gibson would be the last to claim credit. As a canny Scotsman, however, he must be aware of it. The author being of only half Scotch and half Irish forebears, is maybe only half canny, but sufficiently so to recognize Gibson's really great contribution to his field. And sufficiently canny, shall we say, to have included himself as a cog in the above-mentioned Gibbons machine.

The reader, and particularly the student, will recognize the importance of covering our miniature tank's sixty by three hundred feet of backing so that it "works" properly, fulfilling whatever is demanded of it. Whatever mood, or whatever time of day or type of weather, to give distance, mid-distance, to become integrally a "three" dimensional part of a three dimension miniature so that its actual two dimension execution reads three dimension on film. This and more contributes much towards a "whole" success. The eye is usually more critical than a camera lens, but such is the illusion of reality in planes of depth achieved, that often visitors, seeing one of these scenic backings in relation to a foreground set on a stage, cannot believe or know where one starts and the other begins.

The reference to day for night sequences shot in brilliant sunlight made earlier in this chapter is again an indication of control over the "sky". While much passable day for night photography has been done without this control, through reduced negative exposure and laboratory processing and printing, there are always many limitations. Painting a reduced-in-value, low-key sky, or an out-and-out night sky, and using the sun only as a sort of master electrician, overcomes almost all of these limitations, particularly when the brightness of a midnight fire, as an example, is to be photographed. Or artillery fire, bursting shells, or bombs, or a city at night.

We have never at M.G.M. shot a night miniature at night when the tank and backing area, wet or dry, was available. And strangely, to the uninitiated, hot sunlight is generally needed for top results. Never a dark dull gray overcast day. "Tonedown" painting is usually involved to strike a reasonable balance between foreground and background, but this is a small price to pay for the abundance of light needed for highspeed photography, supplied for free by old Sol.

Though not always predictable, the sun is sufficiently reliable to far overshadow in results as well as economy any alternate method of night for night, particularly when large areas of miniature are involved requiring three to four times normal camera speeds and presenting the problem of those irksome focus stretches. Hardly enough synthetic light in Hollywood exists to practically obtain sufficient exposure and focus depth on many jobs we have done in the past. So, and hence ~ we heartily recommend shooting "night" miniatures in bright daylight, providing facilities which include a backing upon which control through painting can be exercised, exist.

Particularly beneficial in its application to the above as well as the multiple stage uses of scenic backings, would be to have the following credits, or a reasonable facsimile thereof, as prime scenic executioners.

Producer and Director :   George Gibson
Technicians and Cast :
Clark Provins, F. Wayne Hill, Harry Tepker, Leo Atkinson, Ad Helms, Wm. Gibson, Ben Carre, Tommy Duff, Bob Woolfe, Jerry Gebr and a few graduates.

George Gibson is an Associate National Academician in the Aquarelle Division of the National Academy; a past president, as well as having held other offices, of the California Watercolor Society and a member since 1949 of the American Watercolor Society. And he is also a charter member of the "Extolled by Me" Society and has been awarded a Fellowship among my stubborn "greats." I, as yet have not purchased one of his paintings. Perhaps the above may suggest a substantial reduction? Or should I dream when I'm only fifty percent Scotch? Anyway, kilts or no kilts, George, a bonnie high and a bonnie low road to you from here on oot, and may the sight of heather always put plenty of burr-r-r-r- in your brushes.

A miniature is not entirely successful when it is complimented as a miniature! In theory, a lay audience should accept any Effects representation as gospel reality ~ if reality is intended. If a miniature acts like a toy, bobs like a cork, splatters with drops as big as basketballs, if it looks just plain phony, unbelievable and somehow vaguely amiss, the effort has been less than it should have been. Reasons for limiting what it could have been are legion, ranging from time and money to incompetence and, upon occasion, bad luck.

The latter, in this type of work, is a built-in hazard and a high average of its avoidance can come only through thorough pre-planning. Pre-planning? Surely everything in this field is

EXAMPLE DAY FOR NIGHT SHOTS

Random day for night miniatures. 3/4 scale line for *Luxury Liner* (1948).

Operation Malaya (1950) - Sampans in sun reflected 'moonlight'.

'Subic Bay', shot on a bright, sunny day for *They Were Expendable* (1945).

Freighter and tug. A foggy 'night' - shot at 2 P.M. on a clear day.

From *"Strange Cargo"* (1940). Becalmed.

"New Moon", Louisiana coast. Foreground 3" scale. Ships are 1" scale. Note distance achieved by cloud perspective.

pre-planned, from method to scale to camera speed to budget. But the adjective thorough, as used above, is absolutely imperative. It is another of those prized keys and because of the usually small leeway between "it does or it doesn't", exhaustive, tedious, time-consuming pre-planning, which finally includes rehearsal upon rehearsal of crew operation, of cue checking, of programmed split-second timing and a personnel check and recheck to avoid later, "I forgot to pull or push or kick or switch," must be adhered to meticulously. A practice which, if followed, materially lowers the luck factor.

A rather extreme example of the time element that can be involved is that of a crashing B-15 (forerunner of the B-17, World War Two Bomber) which we did for Vic Fleming's Test Pilot. It was in the late Afternoon of the third day that five speed cameras whirred for all of about thirty seconds to record, on five strips of film, the crash. Two and three quarter days, however, of full crew rehearsal had preceded those thirty seconds, cameras and all. The real payoff, of course, was in this case that a very difficult miniature plane crash which had to finish looking like the already shot full-sized aftermath of the crash, was signed, sealed and delivered in one take. Extreme? Not really under the circumstances.

It is much better practice to shoot a crash of this nature in miniature before its full-sized counterpart is built. Matching to the static finish of the miniature is naturally far easier than attempting the reverse.

WHEN READY

I have many times tried to explain the fact that when the order, "O.K., let's roll'em. Camera!", is yelled, usually ninety percent of our work is over. The cameras simply record in a relatively few seconds, all the mixing, cooking and seasoning which has been going on for probably hours, occasionally days, before. And I am not referring to advance preparation, building and rigging which may well have been going on for weeks.

It is a common and accepted practice for tomorrow's "yellow" (now white) issued through the Production Office and applying to a regular shooting company, to read:

```
"Crew call . . . . . . . . . .  7:48AM
Many etceteras . . . .  Varying times
   and
Shooting . . . . . . . . . . .  9:00AM"
```

That is when the cameras are supposed to roll, when John Barrymore's makeup is finished and OK, Angie Dickinson's wardrobe zipped and Jim Garner's dialogue memorized and rehearsed. That is when, by golly, the shooting day starts! Our yellow, (also now white~tradition and sentiment~gone) issued through the same Production Office had always read:

```
"Crew Call . . . . . . . . . .  7:00 AM
A few etceteras . . . . . . .  7:00 AM
   and
Shooting . . . . . . . . . .  When ready"
```

Well, one day an alert Production Office suddenly wanted to know why our orders read, "Shooting......when ready," while all others read, "Shooting......9:00 AM." "Suddenly," in the previous sentence should have read, "Suddenly after fifteen or twenty years," because that's about as long as our orders had been so worded. The reader, I believe, will readily understand the logic of the "when ready" wording after the brief explanation and comparison just given, but not a particular person identified, shall we say, at least in my opinion, as being overburdened at times by peculiar stupidities. He and his cozy associates thought otherwise and we were told to always include a definite time by which the cameras were to have started grinding. So, to avoid unnecessary hysteria, we would specify a time, perhaps 5:31-1/2 P.M. Before long, the "when ready" again became the sensible procedure, though never quite understood by our floor-stomping friend.

Wizard of Oz with Judy, *National Velvet* and little Elizabeth Taylor, *Idiot's Delight*, Norma Shearer, Gable and Edward Arnold -- Garbo and Charles Boyer in *Conquest*, a *Marie Antoinette*, a *Boom Town*, a *Red Dust* with Jean Harlow, Gable,

Gene Raymond and Mary Astor, *How The West Was Won*, a recent one – pictures and people, all interesting, all instructive and too many to choose from. A small slice from as many as possible is my loose format. So now come the locusts of *Good Earth*.

Paul Muni and Luise Rainer starred in this epic of old China which covered many years and a variety of seasons. That peach-pit planted early in the story which had to sprout, survive adolescence, flower and bear was a continuing headache. And Muni's winter scenes requiring exhalations of frozen breath. His dentist devised a tiny container into which bits of dry ice were deposited and which did not make him lisp. We thought of the dry ice and it proved very photographic and reasonably comfortable as long as the inhalation route was through the nose, <u>not</u> the mouth. So much for a cold Chinese winter on a warm and comfortable M.G.M. stage in Culver City.

A movie writer must never say to himself, "How in heck are they ever going to get all those locusts!" He must just think, "To heck with <u>how</u> they get those locusts! I'll write 'em in anyway!" And write 'em in he did.

Now a locust is a member of the grasshopper family, but must have short antennae to qualify. The most onerous ones are of the specie LOCUSTA MIGRATORIA and another particularly ravenous family inhabiting the Rockies is known as MELANOPLUS SPRETUS. The call went out for short antennaed grasshoppers with an appetite and several thousand, by-passing Central Casting, arrived in varying conditions of physical fitness.

We had waived the short "feeler" specification as a not too important refinement. Maybe the thought of playing one of those ravenous destroyers, to a law abiding grasshopper, was a fate worse than death so by the hundreds they chose the latter. We promptly pickled these and daily the pickled population grew. The hardy ones received real tender, loving care except for breakfast, lunch and dinner. When the dinner bell, in the form of a close up camera did ring, and we would throw a few dozen into a confined area of "rice" shoots or young "wheat," no one had to yell "Action!" So much for the insects.

To obtain scenes of people lighting trenches of destroying oil and generally whaling the daylights out of the supposed invading millions, we placed directly in front of every camera setup a "bouncing" machine which consisted of a stretch of taut canvas about fifteen by twenty feet in size, under which rotating cams beat fast tattoos that tended to bounce our pickled actors, augmented by hundreds of small balsa sticks about the size of the real thing and stained locust brown, up to two feet or more so that the cameras always shot <u>through</u> a hopping, jumping, bouncing swarm of insect cadavers intermingled with their balsa counterparts. Beyond this lively mess were visible the supposed destroyers in the persons of Paul Muni and company.

Surprisingly alive these scenes became when intercut with those close-ups of the real, live and kicking little varmints. Coupled with the overall magic of a good film editor's art, we were able to deliver a first-rate locust invasion except for one small detail, long shots of the oncoming swarm.

"Appearing over the horizon, the sky becoming darkened by their countlessness, tragedy and starvation--those harbingers of complete disaster--faced the distraught farmers. The faint, distant hum of the approaching 'cloud' grew to a sickening roar." Thus the writer wrote. So once again loomed a formidable "how" on our horizon. Wow, what a how!

Several "long shots" had been made near a Chatsworth area location, a few miles from Los Angeles, where a bit of rural China had been reproduced. These shots included fields and distant hills with properly wardrobed "farmers," backs to camera, looking off towards a blank sky, into which a cloud of locusts was to appear and approach--by courtesy and design of the Special Visual Effects Department.

Don Jahraus and I tackled this one in our usual independent manner and we both came up with an "in water" method. My inspiration came from stirring a cup of tea and noticing the antics of a few errant bits of tea leaves as they settled to the bottom of the cup. Don, I guess, was a coffee drinker. At any rate, coffee grounds were chosen to become our sky full of locusts. When funneled into the water at a given point which corresponded with the V of distant hills in the previous shots, and photographed with an upside-down camera shooting at about a seventy degree angle up, the grounds sliding down a curved piece of masonite painted white, gave us as they moved slowly at first, due to the more horizontal angle of the curve, and faster as they spread and dropped more vertically towards the camera, a perfect perspective of movement. When inverted and superimposed upon the blank sky of our Chatsworth shots, we possessed a very acceptable answer to one writer who had so glibly intoned, "To heck with <u>how</u> they get those locusts!" Whether the "roasted-in flavor" remained intact I know not. But fresh coffee grounds, in this case, satisfied a lot of people in a manner far flung from any dreamed up by a Madison Avenue dark-suited wizard with his aromatic fullypacked commercials. And as far as we personally were concerned, much, much more satisfactorily.

Now you have been briefed on crocodile "blood" and coffee grounds, as promised in the Foreword. But of flying monkeys, a Kansas tornado and a "sky-writing" wicked witch, you know not. The really wonderful *Wizard of Oz* threw these and many more at us in hot succession. Mervyn LeRoy and Victor Fleming, producer and director; Judy Garland as Dorothy with her beautiful, plaintive resonant rendition of everyone's all-time favorite, "Over the Rainbow," and of course Frank Morgan (what a wizard!), Bert Lahr with mane and a tail, Jack Haley, rusty squeaky Tin Man and Scarecrow Ray Bolger, a limp, triple-jointed, bag of straw. Frank has gone to his particular "Land of Oz," I'm sure a good one, and the others remain active and productive.

My dear "athletic" wife loves to tell the story of Ray Bolger joining a feminine threesome one afternoon on the back nine at Bel Air Country Club. He was alone and wanted company. He, however, was suffering from acute laryngitis and, in a whisper, apologetically asked to be excused from talking. About three holes later when Nell's caddy politely and sympathetically said to her, "Mrs. Gillespie, I'll bet you've hit that ball a million times," Ray could stand it no longer! He gulped a couple of throat lozenges, ripped away a protective silk scarf and wheezed almost violently, "Mrs. G., your stance is OK, your backswing is OK, you keep your head down, you follow through alright. <u>Why</u> can't you hit that ball!!?" He proceeded to jabber helpful advice and questions of amazed incredulity for the remaining six holes. Such is Ray's dedication to golf, which parallels his high standard of perfection in his dancing, that he was willing to jeopardize all of his tonsils in this act of charity. Now Mom, <u>you</u> have told the story—why not I?

I recall that our monkeys, the Wicked Witch of the West's flying troops, were suspended from overhead moving grids, by over two thousand separate lengths of the smallest gauge piano wire made—you remember, a Special Effector's best friend and worst enemy—each length having its own function towards creating the illusion of monkey flight. A tedious and ticklish job of rigging climaxed by the necessity of "invisiblizing" those two thousand plus wires. This latter is done with paint, patience, and light; the patience ingredient being probably the most important.

The first attempt at creating these squadrons of winged apes, by M.G.M.'s cartoon department, resulted in failure. It is seldom that the technique of stop motion, frame by frame animation, either three dimensional or cartoon, will

successfully intercut with reality; live action photography. Lightning bolts, tracer bullets, yes, but rarely anything else, particularly if it is supposed to represent living flesh and blood. So we followed "the yellow brick road to the land of Miniature" to solve this one.

The "sky writing witch" did her flying penmanship in milk! A shallow glass-bottomed tank, inch deep in milk, was supported so that our camera underneath could shoot up into a milk "sky." The "wicked witch" was a flat little silhouette about the size of an old fashioned postage stamp and from the end of her "broom" a tube led up through the milk to a container of blackened sheep dip. All we had to do was write in <u>reverse</u> through the opaqueness of the milk from above, right on the glass by maneuvering witch and tube to produce the ominous warning, "Beware Dorothy! ~ W.W.W.," following which Judy reacted with proper shudderings. Our "Wicked Witch of the West" had delivered her message with the able assistance of the dairy industry, the sheep pest people and fringe benefits which often emanate from border line lunacy on the part of the "loose and crazy thinking department."

Closer shots were made in much larger scale, miniature as she sailed from the tower of her nefarious castle, and actual close shots were made in reality, with Margaret Hamilton, who played the part, riding a full-sized broom against various projected backgrounds. Wind and a smoke pot completed the phantasm. Margaret's broommanship was thoroughly tested upon one occasion when the smoke pot over which she was ensconced erupted in the wrong direction. A very popular tune and dance of the time was titled "The Black Bottom." I am quite sure there was no direct relationship, though there was a similarity as a result of this sad happening. Have you forgiven, Miss Hamilton?

One tornado, coming up! Wholewheat or rye? The cooks went to work.

CHAPTER EIGHT

It seemed impractical to send a crew to a farm in Kansas to await a tornado. And more importantly it seemed advisable to be able to control our tornado. The eventual solution proved reasonably simple although its arrival was preceded by having traversed some rocky roads of doubt and indecision, and was beset with such alarming remarks from the bookkeepers as, "Build a steel gantry to run the length of Stage 14?!!! Are you crazy?!!!" I think we concurred, actually, with this blunt reaction to our proposal because, as always, we were aware of the total absence of that genie, sitting protectively on our respective shoulders.

This was one of those times when invention proved the necessity of a mother, to twist a phrase, and that mother took the form of an expensive gamble in the form of the above-requested gantry. Everyone finally yielded and J.J. Cohn, backed I'm sure by Eddie Mannix, made it official. Consolidated Steel fabricated and installed just below the trusses of Stage 14 this imposing rig. And we built below, a lovely stretch of farmland including the house where Dorothy lived with its barns, chicken houses, sheds and trees and fences in miniature, at three quarter inch scale.

The "tornado" was an elongated canvas sleeve, shaped like the funnel of a real tornado. It was attached to the laterally moving car below the longitudinally traveling gantry so that its movement approaching the farm house could show cross screen travel as well. The tip of the funnel was fastened through a slot to another car beneath the set which followed a predetermined path and contained a dust-making arrangement which enabled a cloud of dirt and debris to be a part at all times of the "bottom," wherever it would go. Foreground moving cotton clouds on glass panels gave the feeling of a turmoiled sky and hid the gantry's structure and seemed to "tie in to" the top of our generously dust-laden canvas "wind sock." Sound, increasing in intensity, and the inclusion of live action, Dorothy in front of a Process Screen upon which various background plates, all shot in miniature, were projected, became the sauce for the pudding in the final editing.

The chef and his able cooks had brewed a dish fit not only for all the "kings," but having sampled its tastiness, they were almost tempted to picket Frank Morgan and proclaim themselves as the real "wizards" of Oz. Not to be self-effacing, of course. A blown horn may not harm the blower if the tone is sweet, and Don and I felt our concoction was pretty doggone toothsome. Seriously it is much wiser to tread not that noisome road named "Egotism." If the job is good, it will blow its own horn. And if bad, the fall will be less gleefully enjoyed by critics than had you chosen the above route.

Vast crowds of humanity can occasionally be simulated by bits of ground cork floating in shallow pans of water shaped to whatever areas the crowd is supposed to occupy, and agitated to give life and mass movement. A mixture of colors and densities for a heterogeneous host of people adds reality, or, if it's a Hitler, screaming from on high to a hundred thousand of his Brownshirts, brown generally would be the color, but in varying shades. We used this method to obtain long shots of the crowds when *Marie Antoinette* arrived at Versailles.

Norma Shearer in this M.G.M.'er, directed by the great mustache amputator, W.S. VanDyke, and co-starring Tyrone Power with Robert Morley, was to arrive by carriage on a soldier-lined road on both sides of which were to be thousands of people.

The viewpoint was to be from on high and a cue as to how we might provide all of those people came from the remembrance of many newsreel shots of vast masses of humanity, indistinguishable individually ~ just a salt and pepper conglomeration of a kind of vibrationary aliveness. Perhaps pea gravel would do ~ but better, why not bits of buoyant cork which could be agitated while floating on the surface of water? Cork, of course, was chosen and it worked beautifully.

Purchased toy soldiers lined our miniature road and we shot the horses and Norma's carriage, full-sized, in the parking lot at the Hollywood Race Track, being careful to choose a

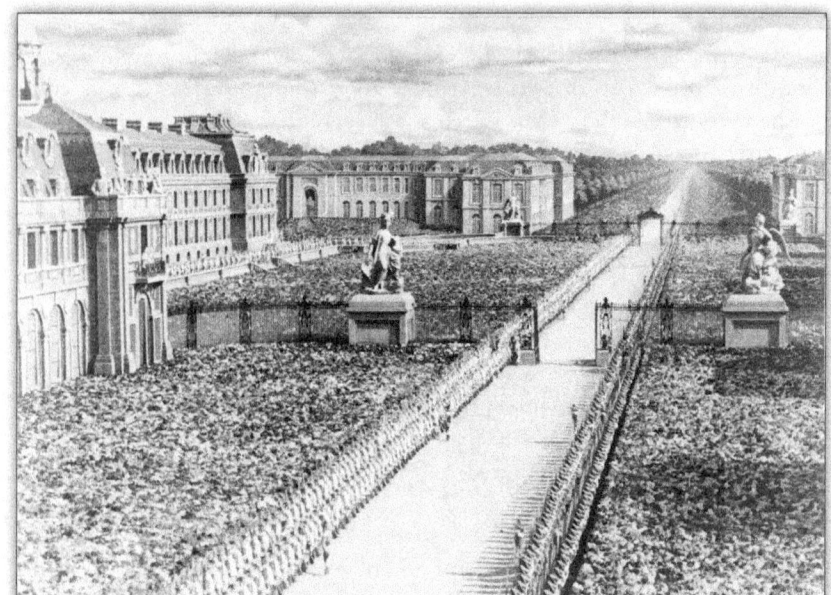

A miniature 'Versailles' for *Marie Antoinette*. Floating bits of cork became a vibrating mass of humanity. Purchased toy soldiers lined the road down which were 'matte printed' real horses, carriages and people.

Center and below. Two enlargements from close shots of 'Rome' burning in *Quo Vadis*. This was a huge miniature occupying almost all of our 'dry' Lot 3 'ocean', 300' x 300'. Scale 1"-12". Controlled 'piped-in' fire and plaster buildings and detail enabled us to burn as long as 'Nero' fiddled, with little damage. This was the job which caused such trepidation in the higher echelon.

CHAPTER EIGHT

Set for Burning Rome for *Quo Vadis* was built in Miniature on Lot #3 shooting against a red night backing. Buildings designed for foreground area of set #70 were duplicated and with few additions were used for remainder of the city. All buildings were cast in plaster and assembled on set. Portions of set were legged up for hilly areas.

Controlled fires were used for Burning of City. Set was divided into sections and each building fitted with fan type nozzels on copper tubing and 1/8" pipe manifolded to 1" pipe supply lines. All manifolds controlled by solenoid air valves wired to single station. Feed lines piped to individual supply tanks installed on sides of tank operating on 80 lb. pressure. Fuel was varied in tanks for effects required. First tests were made with Benzole nearest backing, gasoline middle distance, and a mixture of alcohol with 5 gallons benzole to 50 gal. drum for foreground. Too much smoke developed and final shots were made using alcohol mixture throughout.

set-up which matched the sun's light direction with that of our Versailles miniature. The two were combined optically and were used as both straight cuts and Process plates. So when Process was used, three categories of Special Effects were involved and overlapped to mold a whole ~ Miniature, Optical and Process.

While Nero fiddled and the budgeteers fidgeted, we burned Rome for *Quo Vadis* as Bob Taylor and Deborah Kerr sweet-nothinged to each other. For some inexplicable reason the burning of a Miniature Rome seemed to cause an epidemic of fear and doubt in many areas of M.G.M.'s Culver City lot. We who had to do the burning, were, for an entirely different kind of reason, unfearful, although admittedly somewhat affected by the spread of a kind of contagious nervousness.

The Russian tank chase in *Comrade X* with Gable and that beautiful Hedy Lamarr was certainly high on our miniature problem list. *Valley of Decision*, Greer Garson and Gregory Peck, with its miniature steel mills; *Our Vines Have Tender Grapes* with its dairy farm, fire and floods ~ this one with Margaret O'Brien and Edward G. Robinson; *They Were Expendable*, a P.T. boat yarn in the Pacific with Bob Montgomery and John Wayne; and many more, interesting and challenging, too many to detail within the confines of these pages.

The assemblage of the Dunkerque rescue boats for *Mrs. Miniver* was handled, I believe, uniquely. This Willie Wyler-directed gem, starring Greer Garson and Walter Pidgeon, walked away with most of the "Oscar" honors that year. Our Effects' contributions, while important, were mainly to furnish a background of war atmosphere, over which the story was told. The budget was thereby limited and, as sometimes happens, this very fact served to produce an exciting solution.

The gathering of the craft to effect that gigantic Dunkerque rescue was certainly a case in point. "Hundreds assembled. Boats of all sizes and shapes. They came by river, by canal, along the coast from harbors," the script informed us. And no money ~at least relatively so ~ to provide this picture with such grandiose production. The solution was a mixture of big doses of economy mixed thoroughly with a real "poverty row" approach.

It was decided that four cuts of the gathering of the "clan" would be sufficient. We decided that all of our miniature boats would consist of profiles fastened to the side of a short piece of wood for flotation, upon the end of which was a wire basket into which bits of "dry ice" would be dropped. The latter to form "white water" at the stern to simulate propeller and wake, with the added advantage of the vapor generated when the "ice" is immersed in water. As these "craft" were pulled through water they were exceptionally realistic when viewed from the distance of our camera positions.

Instead of the "sets" bordering the waterways in a conventional manner, we brought them forward quite close to the elevated cameras, thereby reducing their size considerably. The lower "near bank" was built as a three dimensional miniature, the upper "far bank" was entirely in profile and suspended above. The opening between was occupied by the water, some distance away, and our "boats" were profiled at a scale to "tie-in" with the foreground sets. The acceptance of these four scenes by Sidney Franklin, *Mrs. Miniver's* Producer and my good friend, and Mr. Wyler, was reasonably enthusiastic and glory be, the wherewithal was not even too badly dented! As a matter of fact we ourselves thought this rather unique solution was at least adequate and basked in the glory of our own making. Whoa! Get off that road.

And hereby dangles another tip ~ "even we thought the solution was adequate," I have many times asked a responsible party as to how a particular job of his had turned out, and many times has the answer been, "Well, they liked it," or "We sold it," or some other such reply. And just as often I will say, "That's not what I asked. I asked how the job turned out? What did you think of it?" Never fall into the trap of being satisfied just because "they" like it. "They" may not really know, and as pointed out I believe in an earlier chapter, it is often necessary to protect "them" from themselves.

This upon occasion works both ways. "They" may not buy your effort because of a similar lack of knowledgeableness, in which case a long record of honest appraisal of your own work, thoroughly analyzed and judged conscientiously, can often be applied to overcome such acceptance refusals. Over a period of time this straightforward integrity will pay big dividends. Be your own severest critic and when you flop, as from time to time you surely will, just say very simply "I, or we, flopped." Include reasons if you wish but only when they truly relate.

In the same vein it is strange how difficult it seems to be for people to really wipe clean the slate by volunteering, "I was wrong, I made a mistake." Long experience has proven

From *Waterloo Bridge*. St. Paul's Bridge and 'London' (Tower Bridge extreme right) were a small scale single painted profile. The water, shot in much larger scale was composited later. The sky, pure white for swivel mirrors at base to project search lights, was some 100 feet beyond profile. Front projected clouds to darken it.

In *Mrs. Miniver* we process projected three "Waterloo" miniature backgrounds onto a single screen blending foreground clouds to mask top plus added miniature foreground. This in turn became a process plate.

"Miniver's" profile boats. Both upper and lower portions of set were close to camera. The 'hole' between shows water and boats some distance beyond.

the uselessness of defending a miss.

Green Dolphin Street, Lana Turner, Van Heflin, Donna Reed, was filled to overflowing with Visual Effects. It, too, had an earthquake and we drew on our *San Francisco* experience for methods. The principal difference was that of a city's reaction (San Francisco) to this form of nature's destructiveness as against that of a forest populated with giant trees, a la California's redwoods, plus a splitting mountain which released the waters of a lofty lake into a river down which our hero and a few natives rode a log raft to a sawmill on the coast of New Zealand.

As before, we used the horizontal principle of Cal Tech's earthquake table for a "shaking" starter. Our breakaway mountain, some forty feet in height and mounted partially on R.R. car springs, breakaway center part on a cork float, split on cue and "flowing" through the gap, with planned tumultuousness, came Joan Crawford's "water fall." Or rather the same dry "water" method we had used (and have revealed to the reader) in her *A Woman's Face*. As the dry gypsum plunged down the precipitous side of our miniature mountain, creating its own dusty "mist", we released a floodgate behind which an ample supply of real water was stored and timed to come roaring down a dry miniature ravine from which it entered our miniature raft-toting river. Straight cuts and Process Plates were made of this mountain "tidal wave" and It was wedded to the full sized raft with its full sized people through the medium of Process in the following manner.

Upon the Screen was projected our miniature onrushing wall of water, which, when blown up on the Screen to tie into the full sized timbered raft and people, became potently ominous. Timed to coincide with its seeming arrival at the raft, we released several thousand gallons of water from under the Process Screen which was directed up and over Van Heflin and his native "raftsmen." They and their cargo of giant timbers were immediately hydraulically lifted and spilled in various directions onto (hopefully) mattresses which were spread all over the place and out of the camera's range. Three categories were again the ingredients, Miniature, Process and Full-sized Mechanical, which when combined gave us a startlingly real illusion, the only casualties being a bunch of soggy mattresses and a pretty damp star. It took the mattresses much longer to dry out.

Miniatures on this one picture alone included the following.

Listed are the "working titles" of the Miniatures.

1. Ext. Harbor, Ship and Steam Packet - Day
2. Ext. Water Front and "Orion" - Night
3. Ext. Forest - Earthquake - Day
4. Ext. Splitting Mountain - Flood - Day
5. Ext. Creek, Raft, Earthquake - Day
6. Ext. River and Flood - Day
7. Ext. Wrecked "Green Dolphin" - Day
8. Ext, Island - Ship at Sea - Day
9. Ext. "Green Dolphin" and Quay - Day
10. Ext. "Green Dolphin" off Beach - Day
11. Ext. Added High Shot - River - Day

The above of course represents an incredible amount of work, involving a lot of preparation and shooting time and an incredible amount of money - or so said my merry friends the "dollar watchers." Not really at all "incredible" - just enormous - and a bargain!

Torpedo Run was also brimful of Miniatures. This Glenn Ford submarine story really covered the waterfront both above and below - perhaps as much footage in this one as in *Green Dolphin Street*. We photographed Tokyo Harbor, day and night, above and below. We were at sea, we ventured into the Aleutians and torpedoed a Japanese Aircraft Carrier in the waters of Kiska. All in M.G.M.'s Miniature Tank on Lot 3 (our own private ocean) and the below water stuff in a ninety by ninety foot tank on Stage 30.

Stage 30 had been the triumphant climax of a five year campaign by yours truly to convince Management that they needed this stage and the facilities we would design into it with its area and height, for Special Visual Effect purposes, principally and particularly for Rear Projection Process.

Well we finally accepted grateful delivery of this beautiful two hundred and forty by one hundred and thirty-five foot stage, fifty feet from floor to the underside of the roof trusses, ninety foot square tank, ten feet deep and including a twenty foot deeper pit, and we were off to the races, Effects-wise - we thought! But just at that time M.G.M. gratefully accepted delivery of one Esther Williams who also possessed some rather impressive dimensions. She also swam. And where better than in our beautiful ninety by ninety foot Special Effects tank. Swimming musicals! Years later we were able to retrieve Stage 30 for our own purposes at least occasionally and the submarines of *Torpedo Run* frolicked under the very surface upon which and into which Miss Williams had so often and so languorously butterfly-stroked her way about in perfect tempo to a prerecorded rendition of "Swim to Me Darling, Swim Baby Swim" or some such. Dear Esther titillated alluringly in our water.

We depth charged and "sank" one of our subs for this picture in quite spectacular fashion. We jolted all of Stage 30 plus others in the area, in the doing and we praised Corning for the toughness of the glass windows in the caisson from within which we shot. The "ashcans," powder laden, were dropped in from above and were detonated remotely by me when they appeared to have reached strategic positions relative to the submarine and the camera field. Occasionally one of the charges would slant off in a most peculiar manner, up, down or sideways and upon completion of the picture and its showing in Washington, several important Pentagonites wanted to know how M.G.M. had produced "directional" depth charges! Trade secret, was our reply.

Some of you readers (or am I presuming?) of vintage not too recent, will recall a ditty, "I'm Forever Blowing Bubbles, - pretty bubbles in the air, etc." Well this became a despised theme song for us, who, cramped in the narrow confines of that windowed caisson for days on end, would dejectedly watch billions upon untold billions of minute little globular devils, not "in the air," but thoroughly saturating our filtered Stage 30 ocean. A smart Los Angeles smog would have bowed in utter defeat to these little nasties in any kind of a visibility contest. Our submarine would become snow white as legion upon bubble legion would encamp upon every square inch from keel to periscope to bow to stern of her outer surface. Just before shooting, down would go Glen Galvin, one of our underwater prop shoppers, to "dust" our craft. He would fan with his hand the water near the sub and clouds of these pesty beads would be dislodged. If we hurried, we'd get a shot before she became again a snow white ghost ship - boat, I mean. Sorry Submariners! Or are subs now called ships? I think they are.

Having mentioned Glen above, I must report on a strange habit of his while working under water. He would usually forget to breathe. I've seen Mr. Galvin, one of the best underwater men I know, descend to take care of a task and become so involved and interested that it would seem much too long for even one of *Tarzan*'s hippos, except the plaster ones, to remain submerged. And finally, after all of us watching would almost explode, Glen would remember and rise to the surface for a few massive gulps, whence down again to his watery stint. Sometimes he would take an aqualung and tank with him which he would usually lay on the bottom, never use, but always fetch to the surface upon completion of his mission. A halibut may fee somewhere among Glen's ancient ancestors. He was assigned to all of Miss Williams' water movies for those years and at such times as when he would "dust" our submarine, did I see a wistfulness in his eye? - memories perhaps of dusting Esther? Or was she bothered with bubbles?

Glen, a graduate of U.S.C., coached a sort of bush football team on weekends and they were good enough to scrimmage occasionally with the old Los Angeles Rams. Maybe too good for today's. (1965) There'll be a better day Dan (Reeves that is). Just hang on and perhaps take some notes on that Oklahoma City High School, State Champion, 774 points to 13, football team of 1917 about which I have always been reticent to detail in their entirety, those eleven

24-P

TORPEDO RUN (1958) PRODUCTION #1738

Prod 1738 Torpedo Run (1958) Scenes 180 & 182A-1. See diagram in Chapter Eleven for detailed shot layout, 7-C.

Torpedoes "launch" care of three carefully positioned guide wires pulled by diesel trucks on queue. Scenes 256 X1 - 2. See diagram in Chapter Eleven for detailed shot layout, 8-C.

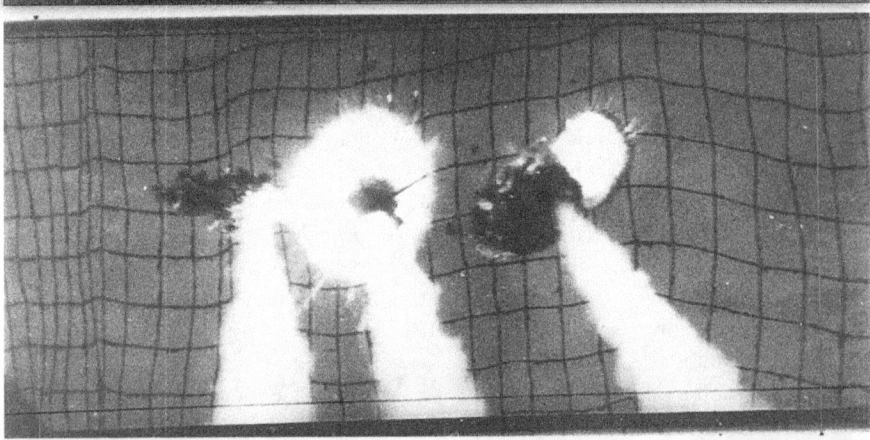

See diagrams in Chapter Eleven for shot layouts and torpedo pull cable method. Scene 258 B-1.

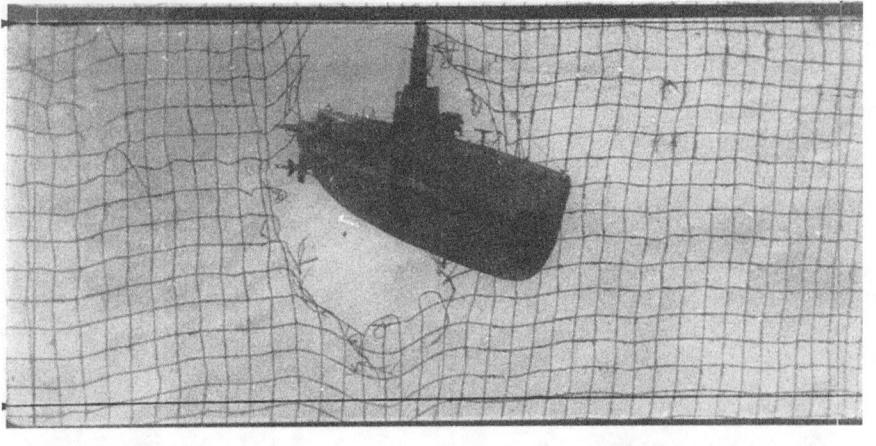

Submarine net opened by torpedo blasts. Scene 264 E-1. See diagram in Chapter Eleven for detailed shot layout, 8-C.

Surface of 'Kiska Harbor' in the Aleutians. Scene 291 A-1. See diagram in Chapter Eleven for detailed shot layout, 9-C.

Shinaru (carrier) heels to port and slides in bow first. She was about 27 feet long at 1/2" scale. Scene 403 C-1. See schematic diagrams in Chapter Eleven 10-C and 11-C.

Depth charges detonated remotely above by the author, providing a good jolt to Stage 30.

straight victories. Isn't that something? 774 to 13 for the season! Eleven straight!

Another real water baby and all-around top person to have as a member of a crew when the going was rough and wet, or dry for that matter, is Chuck Schulthies. What a delight, Chuck. More of a seal than the halibut type, and about as playful. Dead serious however when the chips would be down or about to sink in our unfiltered Lot 3 ocean. Chuck could somehow "see" with his fingers and many a fouled underwater cable or sheave or ship part or whale track, name it, became unfouled through Chuck's adeptness. Good-natured barbs from Claude Williams were fended with equal good-natured adeptness by this happy and capable young man. Claude? A top gang boss with me for quite sometime after Curly Hubbard's departure. Loyal and capable was and is, Claude Williams.

Other equally 'top' – foremen, gang-bosses and crew members, propshop all – would include Ben Cooper, Walter Brown, Hal Dumas, A. D. Flowers, Carl Friend (killed in a powder vault explosion), Roy Cornish (miniature tree maker sans peer), Hal Miller (now Propshop foreman), Andy McDonald (real old timer), Earl McCoy, Tommy Luff, Luther Newman (give him a welding torch, some iron and a problem), Ralph and Walter Winiger, Virgil Beck, Fred Bergams, Lou Erickson, Max Goepinger (glass blower, physicist, wizard), and a host more all under the capable wing of Eddie Stones, Construction Supervisor.

Henry Greutert, modeler, sculptor, plastic expert, sire of our miniature 'people,' of Esther's three-inch scale horse, elephants, whatever – a tremendous talent and quite a 'sire!' Many Effects cameramen who have made non-plumber like contributions; a few not heretofore mentioned. Walter Lundeen, Jack Smith, Mark Davis, Bill Williams. Electricians in addition to "Windy" Joe Regan, Jack New, Perry O'Brien (father to young Perry, Olympic shot-put gold medal winner), Ed King.

Grips galore; the Joes, Haps, Petes — many more unsung leaky-wader-weaving stabilizers of storm-tossed camera tubs, Process manipulators, essential Effects operators (along with propshop men) in all of the categories. Painters and Scenic Artists already mentioned in previous Chapters. Clint Watson, Clarence Albecker, Process projectionists, an earlier Lew Dye and George Brown. With George, in at the birth of M.G.M.'s Process, Merle Chamberlin. Foundrymen, machinists, wardrobe people, sound technicians, still men, laborers, pattern makers, skilled artisans of the 'rubber room' (they cast in rubber and plastics), research librarians, engineers, film lab experts, nurserymen, watchmen, draftsmen; these gentlemen a real godsend to the Effectsman whose rough sketch or audible explanation of the effects conception needs concrete finalizing on paper; workable sets of drawings from which to build. Many too many to name only a few, so we will mention non individually and offend non collectively. Valued fellow workers all, the good ones, and most contribute outstandingly. Our list concludes with estimators and budgeters and yes, even bookkeepers of the unstunted variety. All integral parts of most Effects' results. Whom have we left out? Probably several. One, however really rates high – the chap who signs that weekly check. People and more people representing the whole sweep of many crafts. Our thanks to you all.

Many others too in that Lot 3 crew. How to single only a few! They were all pretty much top cabin as individuals and craftsmen. Have I said this before? Thanks, Gents!

FEATHERED FRIENDS

Some years ago we made a pretty prime and fancy heaven out of spun glass and the white vapor which exudes voluminously from any container of hot water into which "dry ice" is immersed. Our containers were anything but heavenly - old beat-up buckets and garbage cans out of which spread a wall to wall vapory cloud. The <u>taller</u> clouds were wire skeletons upon which skillfully draped globs of spun glass resulted In some pretty fair nebulosities. Altogether a first-rate miniature heaven. Into this we were to optically put Jeanette MacDonald, our Angel. All of this for *I Married an Angel*, with Nelson Eddy who in this picture did <u>not</u> sing, (what <u>was</u> it he did not sing?) - something about "Shortnin' Bread?" He sang many other things however, beautifully and so did she. Wonderful team, those two.

So, we now had a "heaven" and we sent a requisition in for one pair of angel wings because lovely as Jeanette was she of course was not really an angel. The entire facilities of M.G.M. went to work (the angel-wing facilities) and produced the crummiest beat-up pair of appurtenances to be fastened to Miss MacDonald's marble white shoulders that could have ever come out of a wind and floodswept chicken or turkey ranch. St. Peter and C.B. DeMille would have both

CHAPTER EIGHT 206

I MARRIED AN ANGEL (1942) PRODUCTION #1215

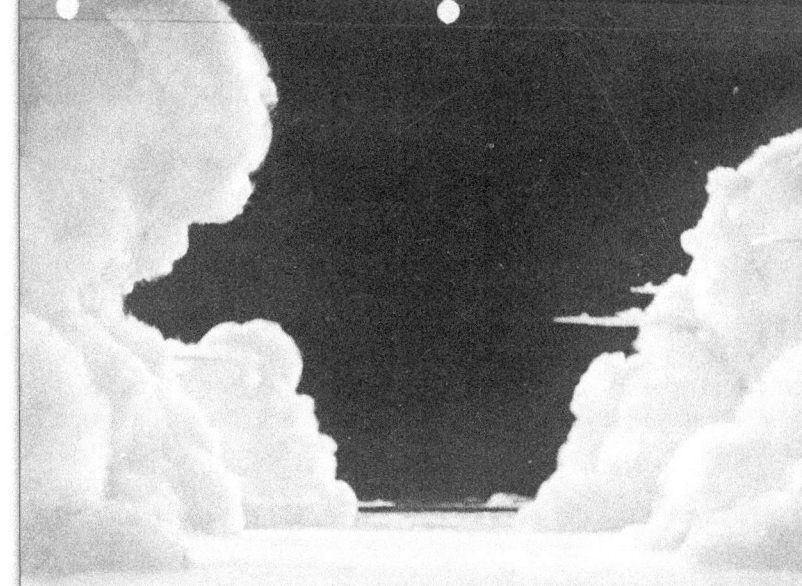

Spun glass clouds for *I Married an Angel*.

"Taxidermist fabricated wings for miniature heaven scene.

Jeanette MacDonald on heaven set, laid vapor clouds against spun glass plumes. Process shot combining the above mentioned elements.

undoubtedly thumbed-down these feathered monstrosities. Feverishly a taxidermist was called in and I am quite sure Westlake Park swans in the wee hours for several nights, were rudely awakened as parts of their plumage was pilfered. Just a feather or two per swan probably to avoid too much swan-fuss. Only a surmise of course but from where else came those many white pinion appendages?

We had attempted, in <u>our</u> wings, to die turkey feathers white and though their final assemblage was terrible, they suffered not too much when compared to this gentleman's effort and I'll swan - ouch! - if these new wings didn't look more like they were well into the last stage of molting than ours did.

Taking a page out of the "modeling-of-clothes-on-miniature-figures" lesson, and once again cogitating in directions sans confines, we decided, why should angel wings be made out of feathers? Why indeed? They were modeled and cast in a pure white plastic and they teamed beautifully with Jeanette MacDonald's alabaster shoulders - and we got on with the show.

Actually, a miniature heaven presents a few problems in execution. Miniature clouds, other than painted ones or fabricated ones, however, can be a migraine. A completely draftless stage with a degree of temperature control is essential. Set lighting naturally generates heat and heat will cause air to move, the currents of which play hob with laid stratus vapor or cumulus puffs. So it is well to 'place' your formation of chemical vapor through the use of fog-guns (air pressured dispensers) as quickly as possible in an unlit, air-still stage, and equally quickly to switch on lights as the camera turns. At above normal speeds, fair amounts of footages may be obtained before complete 'cloud' degeneration.

The Wreck of the Mary Deare, a very much all-at-sea movie, with Gary Cooper (a real top quality gentleman) toothy Charlton Heston and Michael Redgrave, Britisher Michael Anderson directed and the producer was Julian Blaustein. This sea picture was ninetynine and nine tenths percent shot in Culver City (M.G.M. - ville) which is some few miles away from the Pacific not to speak of the English Channel "Minkies."

The Wreck of the Mary Deare was a particularly good example of solving sensibly through the various Effects facets, the problems presented by the story. But not without quite some early sparring with Mr. Blaustein whose faith in Miniatures had been badly shaken by a couple of previous and unhappy exposures to this demanding under-scale Special Visual Effects category. Certainly <u>not</u> at M.G.M.!

The sequence, very briefly, involved the deliberate "beaching" of an abandoned sabotaged freighter, the "Mary Deare," to keep the evidence of some real dirty doings from being destroyed. Cooper and Heston, the latter having boarded her from a salvage tug to claim the derelict for his partner and himself, were the only ones aboard. Much action takes place after she is safely wedged between some of the Minkie rock outcroppings and it was mainly in this part of the sequence that Julian proposed that a full sized ship set, or actual old ship, should be provided and beached on a rocky location if such could be found. Wind and storm, day and night were a few of the script accessories, whereupon, rearing its sage and experienced head, appeared our old standby clincher, "Control" - control of the elements, control of day for day and day for night — control.

During Dutch Horton's Location Department's search for ship and rocks, we were gradually convincing our amiable but dubious producer to go the "control route," Miniature <u>and</u> Full-sized, all within the areas perimetered by the walls and fences of M.G.M.'s dry and dusty Lots - far away from the briny deep and/or shallows.

A further example, this "convincing the producer," of the previously dwelt-upon "sticking-out-one's-chin" department. So to repeat a bit, always and without fear stand staunchly by your method guns if your deep and honest convictions so dictate. Never sit back blandly in these early conferences holding the thought that why should "I put myself out on that precarious limb. Let 'em do it <u>their</u> way." Rather, sell and sell, based of course on some of the points brought out

I hope, in this book, and backed up, we will also hope, by reasonable experience, your recommendations. Julian, with some trepidation, went along with us and I must say he made no bones at the finish of our efforts in showing his gratitude, very complimentarily expressed, and requesting our forgiveness for his early skepticism. We happily forgave.

A helpful sidelight relating to the "Minkies" in our wind-driven, storm-tossed 'English Channel' has to do with 'white water.' The Minkies in actuality are a group of treacherous outcroppings between England and France in Channel waters. Waves or surf, breaking over such impediments, produce 'white water.' It is never sufficient when attempting duplication in miniature to rely solely on wave machine and wind action on water alone. A tried and true way of producing this effect is to introduce water mixed with air through a siphon, exhausted by multiple small nozzles places just below the surface in the areas where white water would normally occur. Many of our Minkie plastic cast rocks housed small electric driven pumps from which copper tubing from manifolds carried the air-water mixture to dispersal outlets nearby. Action of the overall surface from waves and wind tends to break the discharge of 'white' so that a very realistic effect results.

The same principle may be adapted to produce bow wave and wake effects for a miniature ship. Motors, pumps and siphons are carried inboard, tubes running through the hull to adjustable nozzles placed fore, alongside and aft of its exterior. A bit of doing to avoid 'spitting,' but altogether the best way we have found to produce a scale of white water consistent with the scale of the ship.

Ocean going tug, ship, Minkies, storm, the works, were all done in miniature which intercut soundly with a full sized tug and a full sized part of the "Mary Deare," constructed on a Bossart rocker along side Esther Williams' tank on Stage 30, where we brewed up quite a full sized storm to match that of Gillespie's Ocean on Lot 3. "Gillespie's Ocean?" Why not?

Fred Sersen, my counterpart for years at Twentieth Century-Fox wangled a permanent name for his "ocean." They still call it "Sersen Lake." Or did until very recently when it fell victim to the prodigious growth of Los Angeles coupled with the prodigious cost of Twentieth's Cleopatra which prompted a move toward replenishing not only the exchequer but the petty cash drawer as well. Probably there were other considerations too. In any event one huge real estate development known as "Century City," sired principally by Mr. Spyros Skouras, swallowed whole, Sersen Lake. Such can be the fragility of a monument, Fred Sersen was never at M.G.M. which was of course for him a severe handicap - ! - in spite of which he was not only thought of very highly technically and artistically but extremely well liked individually.

While we are temporarily visiting Fox Studio, I will mention a chap now head of their Art Department, who was for years an M.G.M.'er. He was and still is a close and good friend. Jack Martin Smith of the proud and talented Pennsylvania Dutch Smiths. Jack is a top artist, a painter in oils, a watercolorist, an accomplished architect, a polo player, a lousy golfer, owned a six meter sloop once and wheeled a motorbike.

One Sunday, years upon years ago, I made a surprise P.M. call on the Smiths. Phoebe, his wife was puttering in the flower bed as I drove up. "Where's Jack?" said I, noting a bit of pique in Phoebe's pretty face. "In the living room with his Harley Davidson," she responded with charming annoyance. Sure enough, on a spotless rug, albeit covered with old and recent issues of the Los Angeles Times, was Smith's motorcycle in about ten thousand parts. He was cleaning it, he said, and polishing it, and where better than within the aseptisized confines of the living room? Where better indeed, thought I, though I suspect Phoebe and lovely daughter Laurie inclined towards other uses for this particular part of the house. Son Andy seemed to support his Dad. Somehow J. Martin got out of this one and it typifies his ever practical approach to problems. This chapter is about Miniatures. The tangents that do squirm in! So while we are on high echelon Department Heads we'd better mention George Davis, M.G.M.'s present "Cedric Gibbons." George won't resent this reference I am sure. He never knew Mr. Gibbons but he knew of him well, and G. Davis is now enthroned in the same spacious office occupied by Mr. Gibbons for those many years. To M.G.M.'s old-timers, this is a hallowed spot and it is comforting that its occupancy since his departure has been of such high caliber. First, William Horning; serious, scrupulous, high-minded Bill, an absolute authority on an amazingly diversified list of subjects. Bill passed on and we miss him very much - we all know his leaving was far too soon. A young man in his absolute prime, a husband, a father and a good friend. Bill was Mr. Gibbons' first successor and a most worthy one.

Then came George Davis, a newcomer to M.G.M. but not a newcomer to Art Direction. Footballer from USC, sailboat owner and skipper, three grandchildren that he claims are most exceptional (he hasn't seen our eight), a storyteller quite wonderful to listen to if you've fastened your safety-belt. George begins to erupt inside of himself at about the halfway point of a particularly funny yarn. He is, shall we say, not skinny, and the weight of those eruptions as the story progresses would vibrate the pad of a Saturn 5. You can well picture what happens to an ordinary concrete or frame building. Occasionally the final point is so shaken that it seldom registers to his listeners, but this matters not. His mirth alone is sufficient dividend.

George's loyalty to his Art Directors and staunch support of the entire Department is of course laudable. And he can

THE WRECK OF THE MARY DEARE (1959) PRODUCTION #1750

3/4" scale "Mary Deare" in rough waters. See shot schematics at end of Chapter Eleven for scene planning.

Old World War I "Liberty" wind machine mounted on wave machine. Paddle wheel extreme right.

Foreground camera for close shots of the miniature ship.

Thirty-five foot long ship and 'crew'; electric wind machines in background.

"The Wreck of the 'Mary Deare'". Note paint tower, right of backing in top right photograph.

4-P

A few of the 'crew'. Note adjustable 'legs' on camera tub - to rest on bottom or float.

C. Slifer, shanghaied from his beloved printers for a miniature job.

Dump tank on left and miniature 'rocks'. Note black <u>hole</u> cut-outs explained in the text below.

'Black holes' in rear of plastic 'rocks' are access openings to battery driven pumps inside used to mix air and water and produce <u>white</u> water at base through underwater nozzles.

"MINIATURES SANS MUSTACHES"

MUTINY ON THE BOUNTY (1962) PRODUCTION #1769

"H.M.S. Bounty" at scale of 3"=12". See shot schematics at end of Chapter Eleven for scene planning.

Lining up a close shot. The "S.S.G." is a garbage truck bed used for fuel in *Too Hot To Handle*.

Waiting for wind and waves.

Author with Clarence Slifer on right. Part of our three hundred foot 'ocean'.

No 1, 2 and 3 while shooting "Mutiny". Two miniature ships were used. This one hydraulically operated for pitch and roll mounted on pneumatic tired chassis. No. 4, a warm weather operation.

BEN-HUR (1959) PRODUCTION #1724

A.M. preparation for a *Ben-Hur* galley sequence. Two floating camera 'tubs'.

Preparation continuing. Horizon about two hundred and fifty feet away.

Note top of backing upper left. Extreme distant galleys are profiles mounted to move <u>behind</u> horizon.

Cinematographer Harold Wellman securely 'tubbed".

Miscellaneous pre-shooting shots during our *Ben Hur* (no. 2) chore. Scale of galleys, 2"=12".
See shot schematics at end of Chapter Eleven for scene planning.

both flare and weep when the occasion fits. The adult male who cannot choke up or shed a tear is a very unfortunate adult male, Davis can do both.

We are almost daily lunchmates and our coverage of many subjects is extensive as all get-out, particularly (wives please note) when they focus on our respective youngsters and our youngsters' youngsters and when we brag a bit about the little woman (dear Barbara is George's). Men do this, you know. We may clobber each other occasionally about other things but this kind of sparring never really sputters and I am sure George has respect for my viewpoints. It's just that I seldom am able to exhort from him an admission of the infallibility of my more mature position on things. I sometimes have this same trouble with our grandchildren's grandmother.

Also at lunch with Mr. Davis and the "oracle" each day, is a tall dark and handsome Art Director, Edward Carfagno. Eddie was on the U.S. Olympic Fencing team at one time and I think he can still toss a pretty mean epee as well as being no slouch with a saber. He also has some pretty good Art Direction credits, actually too numerous to mention. But three really outstanding credits, produced with the able help of his charming wife Lois, are two really "Wow" daughters, Carol and Linda and a taller darker and handsomer chip off the senior Carfagno block, known as "little Eddie." Little Eddie is well over six feet in his tennis stocking feet and seems to be following his father's architectural career.

A real break in our lunch routine is when any of these three, or George's husky fine son Chris (daughter Karen is married, so we don't get her) joins us for lunch. I must admit my partiality for either one or both of those attractive young ladies as against young Eddie or Chris, for a lunch companion of companions, and I usually burst into a totally mental and silent rendition of "Memories" with its "dreams of long ago, etc.!" At sixty-nine, such lovelies add at least imaginary status - and it is wonderfully warming to have these vital, attractive youngsters friendlily and willingly present. May these reactions of mine, reflexes and ego, ever be thus! And my own sweet Nell, sort of a juvenile grandmother herself, never seems to mind such rapt reveries of mine - I sometimes refer to them as "research." Could it be that she's not worried?!

And while we are on the subject of young ladies who qualify as "wowers!," we have a pretty wow one ourselves. Our daughter Margie, the mother of three of those exceptional grandchildren. Sons Bob and Van complete the family, Van striving for a Doctorate in Psychology and Bob in far away places <u>doing</u> something about world population - Family Planning.

But back to Art Directors and their teamanship with the Effectsman. Others in addition to Davis and Carfagno, are Merrill Pye (half owner of the cow-chased airplane), Preston Ames (a five year student at the "Ecole Nationale Superieure des Beaux Arts" in Paris), Urie McCleary (book collector - accumulator of tremendous library), Hans Peters (pencils always in perfect formation on his desk; he and the author having exchanged opposite-side bullets in World Ware I, mutual armistice long since declared), Randall Duell (has left Art Directing; business of his own, designing and supervising park enterprises throughout the country), Paul Groesse (long at M.G.M., now with Duell), McMillan Johnson (artiste extraordinaire; now heads the Matte Painting Department), Addison Hehr (mechanical and engineering acumen, a plus to his talents as Art Director), Gabriel Scognamillo (chock full of distinct creativeness), Jack Martin Smith (another former M.G.M.'er, now head of 20th Century Fox Art Department; polo player, painter, friend), Eddi Imazu (originally and 'way back, from the shores of Nippon, a 1941 internment having shaken his loyalty to his adopted country, not one whit; capable and loaded with Japanese efficiency, is Eddie), Dan Cathcart (Dan left us some years ago, probably now confabbing with Bill Horning, Horace Jackson, Stan Thompson, on a De Mille super in the realms of St. Peter) and there are more - Leroy Coleman, McClure Capps, Charles Hagedon, Marvin Summerfield, Phil Barber, Jim Sullivan, John Thompson and undoubtedly a few that have been inadvertently omitted, as co-workers, co-helpers (and we might modestly add co-helped) hey all belong, even though too briefly, in this book. Art Direction is or should be a first cousin to Special Visual Effects.

Well, students of Special Visual Effects, take at least some heed of the last few pages. Any direct connection, perhaps not. But <u>people</u> and relationships with them, can provide a richness of comfort and profitableness just as important to you, as scale, or method, or camera speed determinations, in the toughest of miniatures.

This brings us back to the nub of the chapter as well as to an ever-present quandary in the writing of this book. We have scarcely scratched the surface of actual documentation. Such as oil well gushers for *Boom Town* and *Cimarron* - you don't use oil. You may use water. Nigrosine dye (the crocodile's "blood") will do to color the water. Add a thickener for a bit of body, provide a reservoir of the stuff, a husky pump with a by-pass valve and let her go.

If your gusher is supposed to catch fire, as ours did in *Boom Town*, liquid fuel such as gasoline under pressure is fed to nozzles generally through copper tubing and ignited from a pilot light as and when the top banana Effects' Director yells "Camera!"

We used similar copper tubing, much, much, more of it, when we burned Rome in *Quo Vadis* as Nero fiddled and management fretted. For some reason the burning of a Miniature Rome seemed to cause an epidemic of fear and doubt in some areas of M.G.M.'s Culver City Lot. We who had to do the burning, were, for an entirely different kind of reason, unfearful, although admittedly somewhat affected by the spread of a kind of contagious nervousness.

I don't know yet why this particular Miniature caused such qualms. It was big, yes. But it was basic. We knew that construction and materials should be non-inflammable except for planned areas which were to be actually consumed. This, so we could burn and seemingly destroy the city as often as we wished with a minimum of repair and replacement. A tried, and true theory and technique which is practiced in the blowing up and/or burning of ships as an example. Fireproof your ship mate, as much as possible and control your fire. Execute "ons and offs" with the valves which feed fuel to those nozzled copper tubes and have ready extinguishers and hoses to douse residue and incidental burning when cameras and valves are "off".

Explosives always are in protective mortars so that the ship or whatever, actually suffers very little real damage if it is to be blown. We have "blasted" and "sunk," totally "destroyed", a battleship, as many as five times for a single movie and still have had sufficient left to convert her into an aircraft carrier several years later which we also "torpedoed," "blew up," "burned" and "sank" in our Kiska Harbor sequence for *Torpedo Run*. This valiant cadaver's keel and ribs are still ready to rise again from our Miniature Storage graveyard to carry on for dear old Metro. Only a cat has nine lives?

Rome was just more of the same. We cast in plaster, walls and roofs, arches and ornaments, columns and pediments, statues, monuments and all the glories that were Rome. In and around and through all of this assembled conglomeration, systematically placed on the bed of our this time waterless Lot 3 Miniature Tank, copper tubing intertwined endlessly--hundreds of "snakes" with nozzles for heads, their tails caught into a master manifold, each of which had its own valve, adjustable for more or less fueled flame; smoke pots strategically placed, always with wind direction being considered and presto, there lay the Eternal City ready and willing to be thoroughly and spectacularly toasted.

Old Nero could scarcely have resigned his bow with more complacency then was exhibited in our pre-plans, and this attitude probably added to the general questioning dither. An attitude not of deliberate pooh-poohing on our part, but simply that this particular job, though big, was routine. Now that "Bomb" or those *Comrade X* "tanks" or some of the "way-outs" in *Forbidden Planet* - those were the real brow-wrinkling puzzling conundrums.

"Robbie," the star of *Forbidden Planet*, was modeled after an old pot-bellied stove. Robbie was that good-natured, do-it-yourself robot, who was sufficiently straight-laced (or perhaps we should say straight-riveted) that his presence in Anne Francis' boudoir occasioned nary a "clank" or the strain of a fuse, as Anne would perform intimate little girl things like

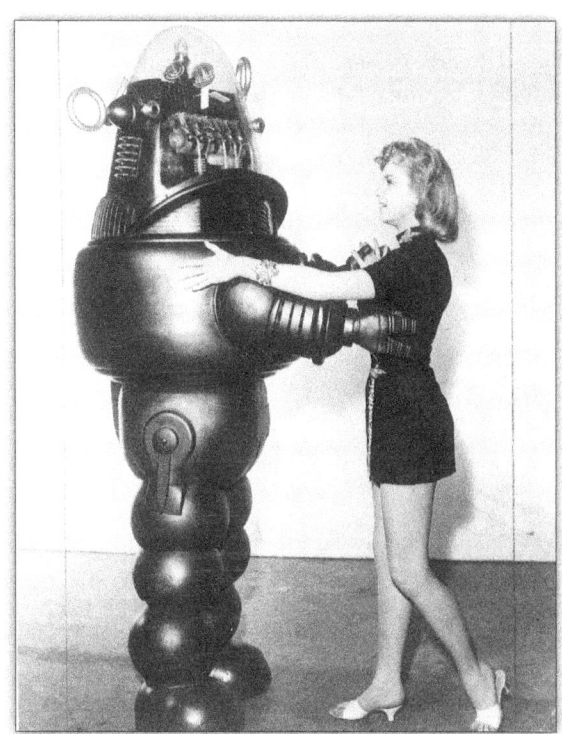

Robby with Anne Francis. Robby always bidding her will.

combing and perfuming, and general dishabille toiletries and robing, as our polished steel and plastic gentleman would solve a stuck zipper problem or fetch a kleenex. Poor Robbie, no fun.

His design idea did come from the aforementioned stove. Who in this generation knows about a pot-bellied stove? Well, we of an earlier era do. We concluded that the trend should be varied~ a robot that didn't look like a man in a starchy aluminum suit. Why not make him look for a change like a good old fashioned country store stove? The kind Norman Rockwell would surround with cracker-box-mounted bewhiskered gents of a bygone era?

So 'twas done, with bits of refinement and a concession or two such as legs and arms. Robbie was just absolutely the best Robot up to the time of his final assembly and for my money he continues to lead the pack to the wire.

He had sinews of steel, polyethylene arteries and seductive little antennae which rotated and oscillated in a most come hither manner. Good thing Robbie <u>was</u> "straight-riveted."

Come to think of it, maybe we should demand residuals. All those toys and TV re-runs! I would certainly include Bob Kinoshita (draftsman) for a goodly share. He helped also to sire Robbie.

Forbidden Planet was jam-packed with effects. Arthur Lonergan the Unit Art Director and I were particularly enthused over the prospects for design-and-effects-fun on this one and we became pretty much the throttle and at times the disc brakes for and to the Producer Nicky Nayfack, and Freddy Wilcox the Director.

One tire-skidding brake job was to get Nicky and his writer to change "exceeding the speed of light" to "approaching the speed of light." We concluded that if our "hyper-power" powered saucer broke that celestial speed limit of 186,000 miles per second, we'd be in a mess, theoretically, at least. How do you see something for instance, going away from you faster than the light it may emit can come back to you? Like the little man who wasn't there, we'd have a photographic problem.

The miniature outer space set through which our interplanetary vehicle swooshed at <u>less</u> than light speed, was composed of a cyclorama of second hand masonite, back side to camera, painted a dull matte black. We didn't even putty or tape the joints. We had dreamed up a new way of showing this jet void, bejewelled with diamond stars and suns, and billions of light-years-away other galaxies with their own myriad stars and suns. We used Scotch-lite, Minnesota Mining Company product which reflects back to the source, any light. Signboards along a highway as well as tape stripped to a rear bumper are familiar examples seen by the night motorist.

Little round Scotch-lite cutouts of various sizes which represented varying star magnitudes were pasted where we wished on our masonite limbo. A new product, Scotch-lite lacquer, sprayed here and there, became distant nimbuses or much more distant outer galaxies and lo, we had produced a real bargain-basement segment of space, occupied and populated by courtesy of Minnesota Mining. I don't recall whether the cost crusaders gloated or not but they should have.

Another method would have entailed light bulbs, of different sizes down to the kind a surgeon may use on the end of a tiny stainless steel periscope when probing and viewing the privacy of one's intimate innards. All we needed was a "horse collar" of photo floods ringing the lens of a camera, which when rheostated up or down, returned to the film via the lens, a bright or less bright vista of our faraway reaches. It worked beautifully and inexpensively.

My association with this picture, sharp-focused a bit of nostalgia and philosophizing, on many warm, starry, August nights, decades upon decades ago, while discussing these things with John. John, a neighbor's English Setter, a constant companion, would listen, as I pointed in various directions. The fascination of the endlessness of space seemed overwhelming to us both.

We (John and I) would discuss at length that if every direction went on forever (Mr. Einstein's "curved" theory notwithstanding), by comparison, our own Earth, got to be pretty small and as for that Oklahoma City patch of Bermuda grass, well it was pretty well reduced to inconsequence. In fact planet Earth dwindled into nothingness materially, as compared to the no-dimension of limitlessness.

So we figured there had to be other "earths," endless other earths "out there", because why should anyone think we were such a much as to be the only earth and the only human beings in all of that vastness. John would offer no contrary argument and for that matter none has been offered to me since that 1908 date, that has ever shaken in the remotest degree a conviction that untold billions of "peopled" planets orbit around their own respective billions of suns within our own galaxy and endless other galaxies.

A by-product of this kind of contemplation was, and is, that stupid little problems, such as the tragedy of income tax or a traffic ticket, should be filed away in their proper area of relative inconsequence. I wish it were possible to always do it. John could. With a gentle poke of his cold wet nose, a wag or two of his plumed tail and a deep satisfied sigh, which seemed to vibrate to his very toes, he would sink silently into the most peaceful and relaxed limpness conceivable.

Dogs really have something~many things going for them. One is instant forgiveness. Often it has been explained to our children the wonderment of this particular canine trait. Inadvertently step on a dog's tail or foot and there follows immediately two reactions, micro-seconds apart. The first, a yelp of pain followed instantaneously by a furiously wagging tail of forgiveness and eyes brimful of love. No malice. No, "why don't you look where you're going, you jerk!" Just honest, affectionate and complete absolution. If the "world is going to the dogs" as is often said, may the Good Lord speed the day.

This book is not about one of man's best friends ~ many other animals are or could be so classified~ so I won't dwell on "Joppa Gate, the Third." Joppa the first and second were snow-white Pyrenees, giant sheep guards used by Italian herdsmen to protect their flocks. These were acquired during the 1920's edition of *Benjamin Hur*. The second Joppa was left upon my departure in the care of Baldo Badalini, my man Friday during those many lovely months. Baldo was more like a man Monday through Sunday and his later letters to me about Number Two (Number One had slipped quietly and peacefully from the view of tear-dimmed eyes) these letters were quite wonderful. "~Your Joppa, he is come along big and beautiful ~," and "~he is miss you very much with tail down, so I tell heem it comes soon to see us Mister Buddy ~ you come?"

The last Joppa, Number- Three, was a St. Bernard and though occasionally inclined towards bringing home the neighbors' porch furniture or their baskets of groceries, was beloved by all with whom he came in contact. He was nursemaid, guardian, traveling companion and my confidant for many years. His picture occupies the highest spot on the

"Robbie," the star of *Forbidden Planet*, was modeled after an old pot-bellied stove. Robbie was that good-natured, do-it-yourself robot, who was sufficiently straight-laced (or perhaps we should say straight-riveted) that his presence in Anne Francis' boudoir occasioned nary a "clank" or the strain of a fuse, as Anne would perform intimate little girl things like combing and perfuming, and general dishabille toiletries and robing, as our polished steel and plastic gentleman would solve a stuck zipper problem or fetch a kleenex. Poor Robbie, no fun.

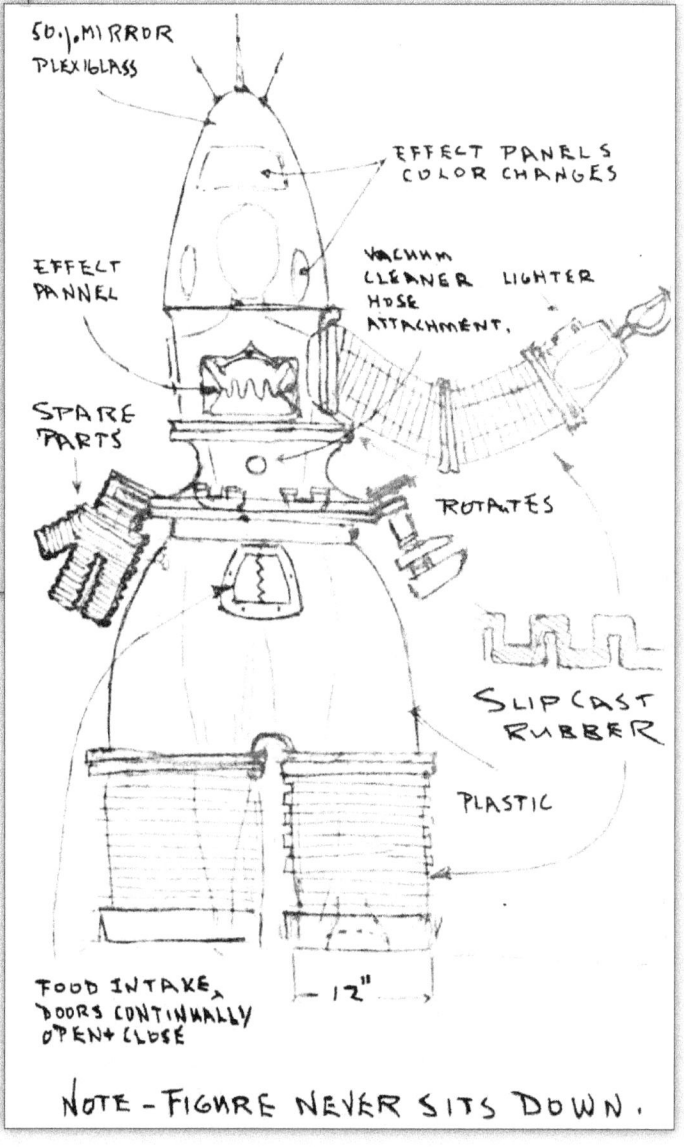

Original Robby design by A.A.G.

walls of my M.G.M. office. Reams could be written about "Joppa la Tirza" ~ perhaps another book, if and when this one ever reaches the finish line. Why and how big dogs were able to squeeze themselves into a chapter on Miniatures must be overlooked and forgiven, please, by the reader. Maybe a Mexican Hairless, yes, but certainly not a four-pounds-of-beef, two-cans-of-broth, one cup-(big)-of-dog-biscuit per day Canis familiaris. No more detours, student ~ at least for the nonce.

One more quick trade secret following which we will sketchily review and conclude this chapter. Lights of a city, such as our Miniature Tokyo Harbor, day for night in bright sunlight, can and were produced by several thousand thumbtacks ~ the convex headed variety. It is possible that this was mentioned earlier, but here are the details. Actual small scale lights at high voltage are an expensive headache to install and maintain. High voltage is necessary to attain brightness competitive with that of the sun, and high voltage means a shortening of a bulb's life. So the thinking department came up with polished convex thumbtacks, varying radii of which would produce larger or smaller reflections of the sun itself, and the sun is about as bright a solution as we could have come up with. We all felt pretty bright ourselves in dreaming up this one. No messy wiring, no continual replacing of small burned out bulbs as well as those dinky ones that can and do infringe from the rear into one's privacy. None of that. Just thumbtacks. Chrome-plating them was not necessary in our case but it is a thought to remember, if additional brightness is needed.

So we conclude with fond remembrances of crocodile "blood" having become an ingredient and inspiration in the production of one of our smallest scale miniatures, the Hiroshima bomb, which depicted such a tremendous area of destruction. We detailed advance Job Number costs of this accomplishment which included from dry goods, to policemen, to powdered walnut shells, to fringe benefits and insurance to etcetera after etcetera ~ all of which good little miniatures are made of. My "cost-cronies" will please note that these requisite parasites lend not one iota of photographable effectiveness though adding materially to the cost.

We "whaled" a bit after originating a new species thereby placating one Director and we illustrated the tie-ins, the intermixing of Miniatures and Full-sized, Process and/or Optical. Again, we talked of many people. It is impossible for me to recall and document even a small number of these past experiences without including associates either directly or indirectly involved.

"Control" was once more reasserted. Particularly as it applies to the confines of a Miniature "Tank," control of the elements and control of the "sky" when using day-with-sun, for night. We extolled a truly Triple A Scenic Department, and broached the subject of luck, good and bad, with stress laid on the only good remedy for the latter ~ thorough pre-planning.

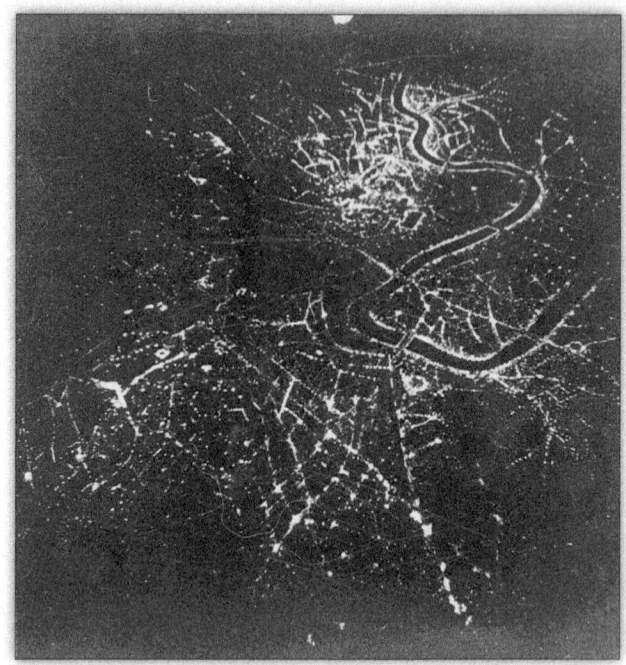

Idiot's Delight air view of 'city'. Opaqued piece of glass, 'lights' etched out, lit from rear.

The advisability of avoiding cart-before-the-horse procedures, when a crashed or exploded Miniature roust in part be duplicated for full-sized action, was outlined. Shoot the Miniature first, and match to it later.

Operational differences between an Effects shooting crew and a regular actor-laden Production crew was exampled and an unkind reference to an individual who either refused to, or mentally could not, distinguish between the two was waggishly underlined.

Paul Muni's "frozen-breath" dental contraption, and an invasion of locusts, both hungry and pickled varieties was chronicled. Bouncing bits of balsa intermingled with those hundreds of grasshoppers who had heeded the call of the Grim Reaper, and a sky full of coffee grounds, were keys to this *Good Earth* poser, rightfully originated and scripted by that writer who showed such a 'cruel' lack of consideration for those of us who occupy those lonely, damp, dark, "grief department" cells.

"Oz's Wizard," a real headachy delight, with its monkeys, its tornado and its black-bottomed witch was lightly sketched and we suggested the limitations of animation, especially cartoon, to the average live action movie. We "sky wrote" in milk and we blew our own horn a few toots.

Bits of cork for people, profile "dry-ice driven" boats for Dunkerque, and a lecture on "how do <u>you</u>, the doer, like it" with accompanying finger shakings, "be your own most severe critic"~ "be honest in self appraisal" and various tidbits as to those "<u>they</u>" people, have been jotted herein. Much unasked for advice about admitting a mistake, "how simple it is to say 'I was wrong,'" was freely given. And then we delved into rural as opposed to urban earthquakes - *Green Dolphin Street* vs. *San Francisco*.

Bubbles, submarines, and Esther Williams' innocent seizure of <u>our</u> Stage 30, hodgepodged with "directional" depth charges which amazed the "Navy." More wonderful people, including some underwater ones and a casual reference to the best football team of all time preceded a treatise on angel wings, a spunglass and vapor heaven for Jeanette, possessor of those white shoulders, after which the subject changed and we patted our own white shoulders when we bragged (instructively I hope) about *The Wreck of the Mary Deare*, in which our old standby <u>Control</u> again starred.

Sticking out a confident chin was again eulogized, and a not too subtle a hint as to rechristening the Lot 3 Miniature Tank was quietly dropped. We moved a bit off M.G.M.'s territory in citing "Sersen's Lake" as food for the above subtlety and we invaded the domesticity of J. Martin Smith, quickly returning however to Leo's lair where more of those impossible to omit associates were immortalized. Which reminded us to tell the student to never underrate the value and importance of human relationships - a real important cog in his drive wheel to success.

Oil well gushers and oil well fires somehow led to Rome's burning for- *Quo Vadis*, when a strange trepidation ran rampant along several studio roads. Which brought up the ever to be followed practice, adherent to any to-be-destroyed subject, of building for Take Two - and Three, and probably Four. Remember that battleship, utterly blasted and scuttled four times, and ditto the same when she became an aircraft carrier? She's still available.

Robbie, the pot-belly Robot, led to general references about a few of *Forbidden Planet*'s other problems. We learned from an inexpensive and effective method of depicting the "fourth" dimension, the no-dimension of space, and we recorded early conclusions of an eight-year-old, substantiated by the wisdom of John the Setter. Some general philosophy about peopled-worlds and dog virtues were expounded.

Thumbtacks, gleaming sun-reflecting polished convex thumbtacks, seen somehow to be a fitting finish to this second chapter on the Third (alphabetically) Category of Special Visual Effects, "Miniatures." A tough one to conclude - a favorite of mine - and an overwhelming sense of not having done justice to this challenging, tough to deliver, medium.

It seems always that at the start of an involved Miniature, your position is located firmly behind a huge eight-ball and that two strikes have already been called. Perhaps this is the attraction. Lining out a bases-loaded homer is the satisfaction while non-emergence from the shadow of that eight-ball, may result in "tears" after well intended "blood and sweat" has been expended. Discouragement, however, should occupy no niche within an Effectsman's mental toolbox.

END OF CHAPTER EIGHT

Nelson Eddy and Jeanette MacDonald in *I Married an Angel* (1942). This set of wings molded out of pure white plastic.

THE BEGINNING OR THE END (1947) PRODUCTION #1377

(Above) *The Beginning Or The End*. Approaching 'Hiroshima' from thirty thousand feet - actually about six feet.

(Below) The 'bomb is triggered. The set, scenically painted was inside a glass tank filled with distilled water.

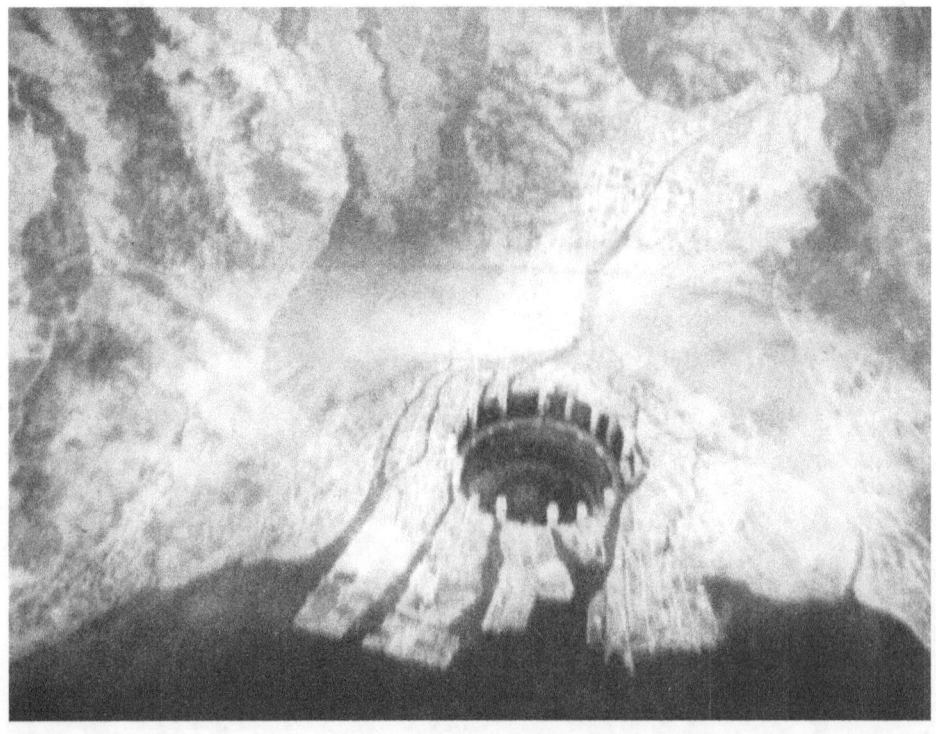

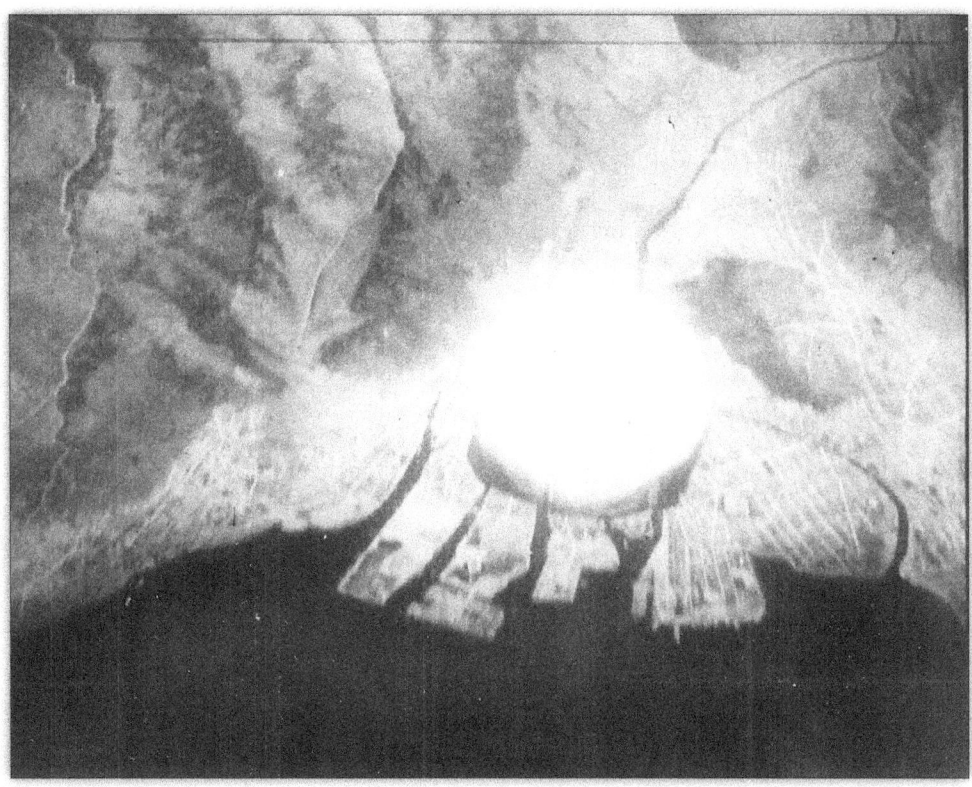

(Above) Size of tank, seven feet deep by four by five feet; the 'mushroom' begins to form.

(Below) The explosion and resultant 'ball' was formed through a piston injection of chemicals in the center of the 'city'.

40-P

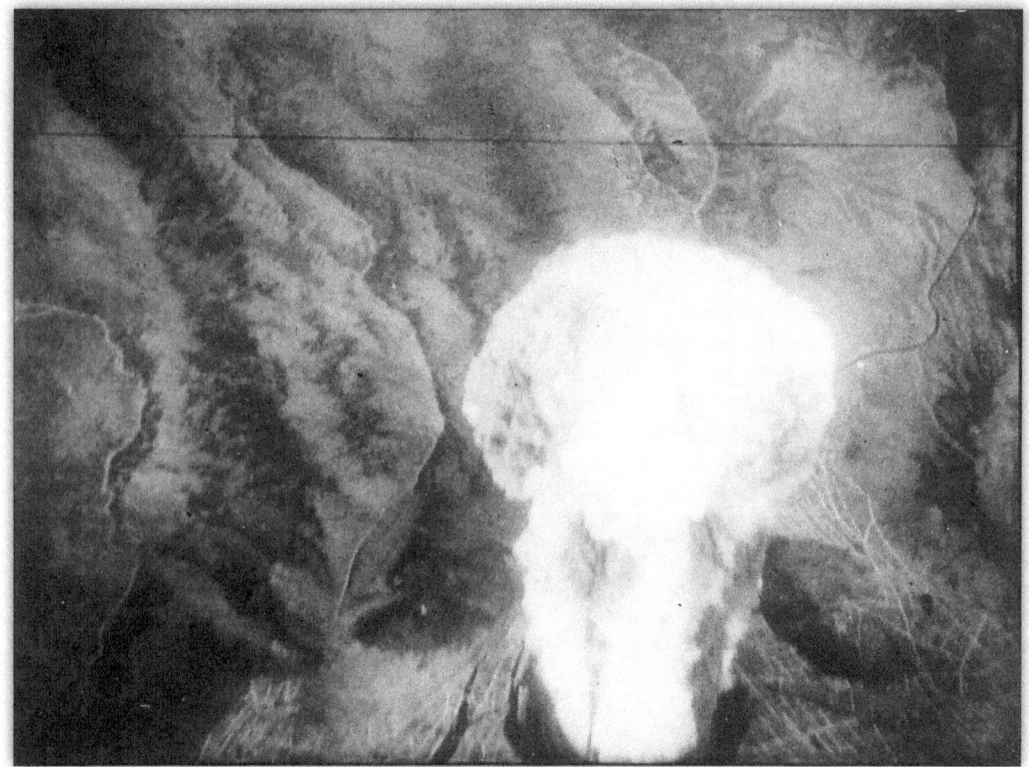

(Above) Camera tilts "up" as mushroom rises. That "*Tarzan*" fight with our steel and rubber crocodile pays off.

(Below) End of the sequence. Note 'tails' from the mushroom Rheostated light and flash bulbs from behind gave added reality.

CHAPTER EIGHT

An ingenious solution in *Young Tom Edison*. The water and center wreckage is miniature. Both locomotives are the same one, shot separately on location. The track, actually undamaged, was 'matte painted' composited into a whole. Newcombe Miniature Matte Painting and Optical Effects were employed.

Used seven agitators and two pumps for water effect. Scale - 1/2 full size.

Here on location, a full-sized trestle and train. Trestle foundations and 'river' are miniatures.

Camera set-up 3'6" above the water shooting up river with matte of trestle on glass 8' from lens. Pier bases set in river to match position on glass.

Used five motor agitators and two pumps for wter. Bulkheads and brush fro river banks. Scale - 1/4 full size.

Salute to The Marines, a 'blown' bridge. 1" scale miniature with distant hills in profile. Shot at Lot #3 in January, 1943.

MAN FROM DAKOTA (1940) PRODUCTION #1124

Arouse and Beware (The Man from Dakota) - CSA Medical Corps wagon crashes off Bridge.

Hospital Wagon without horses as it crashes thru rail of bridge and falls into camera. Wagon and bridge- one third full size (breaking rail).

Shot following wagon as it tears thru rail. Wagon attached to dolly. Fall shot made with two cameras protected by screen netting. Three in. and four in. on dolly. 24mm lens on low setup.

GREEN DOLPHIN STREET (1947) PRODUCTION #1394

Long shot of mountain pre-earthquake from *Green Dolphin Street*. Distant 'cliff' at 1/2"=12" scale. Foreground, 1"=12".

'Earthquake' splits mountain releasing 'waters' of lake. The 'water' is gypsum.

Set built same location as river and raft using same water supply. Mountain sections set on coil springs for quake. Water fall gyp snow on treadmill fed by 3 choppers.

Foreground center section on cork float for earthquake.

Gypsum dust and steam for mist. Real water released from reservoir forms flood.

27-P Alt

Miniature raft and figures. A process plate for full sized foreground raft.

Hit by onrushing water. Used also as a process plate.

Water for river in flood controlled by gate operated ram. Trees from forest earthquake scene. River banks cast rock.

Here it comes. Full sized foreground got doused with water from under process screen.

(Above) "Green Dolphin" forest - pre-earthquake. Excellent detail in miniature trees and foliage. Set built in 3 sectons on car wheels - moved by air rams and pile drivers snubbed by car springs. Lateral movement only. Redwood trees modeled and cast in plaster. Foliage - Virginia cypress and juniper.

(Below) During quake trees uprooted and falling. Set build on 'back-and-forth' 'earthquake table' platform, ram operated.

30-P

Miniature process plate for full sized dory rowing around the "Green Dolphin". Scale 2"=12".

H.M.S. "Orion" at 1 1/2' scale. Foreground craft is 3" scale and town is at 1"=12". Note painted sky perspective.

The "Dolphin" in the 'South Seas'. Our 'ocean' adapts to varied locations.

CHAPTER EIGHT

High shot of lumber rafts before earthquake.

Wrecked on a reef. White water around rocks from siphons and pumps.

1 big pump, 2 smaller pumps, 1 ram to rock boat, siphons for white water around rocks. Liberties and 2 planes on barges.

Close shot. Note miniature figure at extreme left. Scale 2" = 12".

3/4" scale 'Convair' 'flying' in front of a process plate for *Three Guys Named Mike* (1951).

DC-6, profile from photo enlargement. Practical lights behind 'cut out' windows. Process. Also for *Three Guys Named Mike*.

Night landing miniature. *Flight Command* (1941).

A DC-3, hitting high tension lines for *Bad Guy* (1937). Scale, 1 1/2"=12".

Stationary B-29 rolling down treadmill runway for *Above And Beyond* (1953). Slow vertical lift simulated takeoff. 3/4" scale.

Miniature process plate for interior full sized cockpit. One dead engine. *Thousand Cheer* (1943)

Test Pilot (1938) crash landing. Cork and fullers earth on runway. 1 1/2" scale plane, 3/4" scale profile behind. 450 foot travel.

Night shot B-17 base in *Command Decision* (1948). Searchlights moved on backing. Plane scales 3/4" and 1/4".

1" scale 'BT-13' for *Visa / Lady Without A Passport* (1950) against stereo projected sky.

Same plane. Another 'sky'.

Ditto above with third 'sky'. Varieties of cloud formations are simple and inexpensive.

1/4 scale (unusually small) P-38, early Messerschmitt jet and P-51 dive testing against process plate. *Command Decision*.

George Murphy in miniature, test flying our 3" scale idea of a helicopter.

Background full sized process. Foreground building and 'George are miniature. From *Up Goes Maisie* (1946).

15-P Revised

SEVEN BRIDES FOR SEVEN BROTHERS (1954) PRODUCTION #1643

Seven Brides for Seven Brothers - Ext. Avalanche -1/2' scale to match location. Set built on Tank on Lot #3. Plaster rocks skins over wood framing. Dressed with Pyrocel snow. Rocks min. trees and bushes. Painted profile for distant mountains. Avalanche face made of Pyrocel.

Remainder new plastic snow with rock and dirt on 3 cloths belts. Avalanche activated by pipe rods and snow continued on moving belts pulled by rams. 1 Meatchopper, 1 Ritter & small Electric fans used to keep snow dust away from camera.

Falling Mountain scene - Avalanche crashes down the mountain into the river causing it to change course.

CHAPTER EIGHT

```
FORM 48
DATE 11-13-53                                    Estimated Construction and Special Effects
                                                   Preparation........ 11,840.00
PRODUCTION 1643                                  Special Camera
                                                   Mounts.............
SET 70                                           Operation.......... 3,500.00
STAGE Lot #3 - Tank                              Elect. Operation..... 350.00
         SEVEN BRIDES FOR SEVEN BROTHERS
PICTURE SOBBIN' WOMEN (1954)                     Add and Changes......
                                                 Total Approp....... 15,690.00
TITLE OF MINIATURE EXT. AVALANCHE                Final Cost        14,501.14

Details of Min. Set—Area........                 No. of Buildings or Units.......
                                                             Day for Night
Scale     ½" = 1'0"                              Day.......Night..X..Dawn.......Sunset.....

Backing   2 NITE SKY
```

REMARKS   Min. to match location   Set built in Tank on Lot #3
Plaster rocks skins over wood framing. Dressed with
Pyrocel snow   Rocks MIN trees and bushes Painted profile
for distant mountains. Avalanche face made of Pyrocel
Remainder new plastic snow with rock and dirt on 3 cloth
belts   Avalanche activated by pipe rods and snow continued
on moving belts pulled by rams.
Dressing and Min. Props. 1 Meatchopper, 1 Ritter & small Elect. fans used to keep snow
                         dist away from cameras.

CONSTRUCTION   1 Camera   2 Days testing - 5 cameras 1 Day shooting

Total Construction Cost... 12,748.99   Total Special Effects.. 279.75

OPERATION   Construction Dept. Daily Cost   1 Painter
Average Crew | Foreman | Mechanics | Grips | Laborers
Morning | 1 | 7 | 2 | 1
Afternoon | | | |
Night | | | |

Total Operation Cost... 1,228.16

ELECTRICAL   Average Load..........   On day of shooting
Wind Machines and Fans.... 2   added 6 Brutes
Average Daily Crew........ 8   because of weather
Total Operating Cost..... 244.24   forecast   Not used

CAMERA DEPARTMENT
Cameraman........ Max Fabian
Extra Cameras.... 5 Ansco Speed Cameras

After Mt. Slide Set 2"=1' and 3" =1'. Shot in Tank Lot#3 at 84FPS by Max Fabian - 3 Cinemascope- 2 wide screen cameras

58-P Alt

Liberty ship weighs into water in *Meet the People* (1944). Shot at Stage 14. Scale 1"=1'. Backing: Projected Sky and Profile. Cameraman Bill Williams using 40mm lens at normal speed.

White Cliffs of Dover (1944) miniature foreground and background, shot in tank 3. Zeppelins silhouettes pulled across overhead tracks.

The principal signs were of "zeon" in Sweathearts (1938). Camera car mounted 7' high run on track with flanged wheels. Sign backings were white cloth lighted by open arcs and cellophane with a blue black blend.

CHAPTER EIGHT

TARZAN'S SECRET TREASURE (1941) PRODUCTION #1192

Tarzan falling to a ledge and being rescued by Cheeta. Originally planned to be a cheater with part of right bank and ledge modeled and rest of set scenic profiles with a projected sky backing. After 2nd days shooting continued changes were made in set until entire left side was modelled and ledge very much reduced from original.

Tarzan's Secret Treasure, production 1192 - A series of shots and background to cover action of Tarzan swinging across a chasm on a vine- the vine being severed.

YOUNG TOM EDISON (1940) PRODUCTION #1123

Young Tom Edison - Four Seasons Montage. Miniature set consisted of Apple tree, fence walk and painted backing. Set was dressed for four seasons and shot from same camera set-up for each of the four seasons seen out young Edison's window.

McAfee estimates

DATE Dec. 19/39	Estimated Construction & Special Effect.
	Preparation 360.
PRODUCTION 1123	Spcl. Camera Mounts
	Operation 150.
SET 79	Elect. Operation 80.
STAGE 14	Add & Changes
	Total Approp. 590.00
PICTURE Young Tom Edison	Final Cost 564.97

TITLE OF MINIATURE Four Seasons Montage

Details of Min.Set Area   No. of Bldgs. or Units
                                  Day   Nite   Dawn   Sunset
Scale   2/3 Full size
Backing   Painted

REMARKS

   Set consisted of Apple tree, fence, walk and painted backing. Set was dressed for four seasons and shot from same camera set-up for each of the four seasons.

Dressing & Min. Props

CONSTRUCTION

 Total Construction Cost 380. 87 Total Spcl. Effects

OPERATION   Construction Dept. Daily Cost

		Foreman	Mechanics	Helpers	Labourers
Average Crew	Morning	1	3	1 ptr.	1 grip
	Afternoon	1	4		
	Nite				

 Total Operation Cost   154. 62

ELECTRICAL   Average Load

  Wind Machines & Fans
  Average Daily Crew   -5-
  Total Operating Cost   29.48

CAMERA DEPT.

  Cameraman   Fabian
  Extra Cameras
  Lens   40mm.
  Speed   32
  Approx. No. of Feet of Film Printed

HEAVENLY BODY (1944) PRODUCTION #1300

Interior of observatory for *Heavenly Body*. Scale of miniatures, 2"=12". Note fine detail and paint contrast. Shot in June, 1943 on Stage 14.

Straight cuts and many miniature plates for full sized Process.

Telescope was practical to operate during photography. A pierced opaque sky backed by highly illuminated reflective surface supplied the stars.

CHAPTER EIGHT

Another approach from *Heavenly Body*. Exterior comet explosion miniature matte shot.

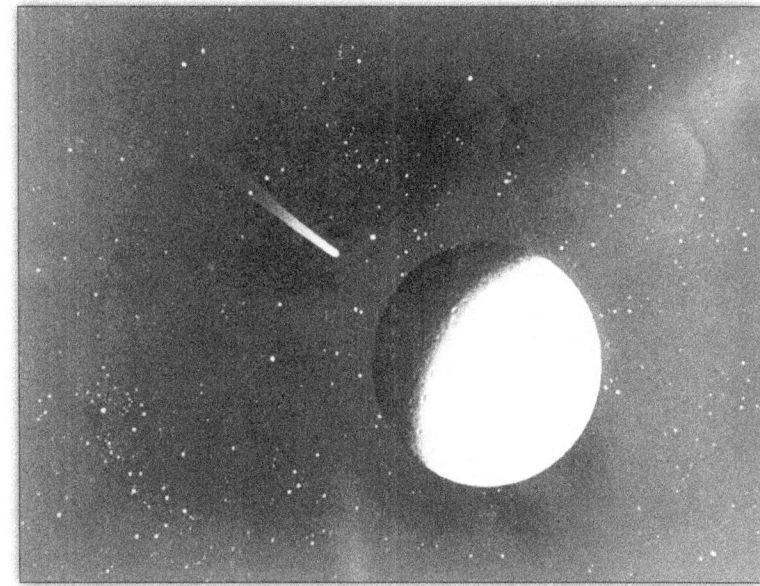

The resultant 'crash'. Also pre-planned.

A bit of diversification. Miniature cars in a *"Caligari"* miniature set. Day for night shot.

The Cabinet of Dr. Cligari (1920) silent German film introduced the jagged set stylization. The 1962 movie with the same title but completely different plot borrowed the stylization for dream sequences.

THE WIZARD OF OZ (1939) PRODUCTION #1060

Wizard of Oz - Tornado approaching Dorothy's farm. Scale, 1"=12". Dust at bottom not yet apparent.

Top of tornado 'sleve' supported by moving gantry suspended from roof trusses hidden by foreground cotton clouds on movable glass panels.

Bottom of tornado with its compressed air dust container moved laterally as well as toward the camera.

Long shot of the 'Kansas farm'. Tornado nearing Dorothy's house. Judy Garland was included in many of these 'plates' through the use of Process.

Enroute to the "Land of Oz". Dorothy and her house inside the tornado. Shot of house falling towards camera, printed in reverse.

Later our 'Wicked Witch of the West', sky writing through a shallow glass bottomed tank of <u>milk</u>.

```
                                              ADDED SET
                                              NO ESTIMATE

                                                              Special
                              Estimated Construction & Effect.
DATE    February 23                     Preparation
                                        Spcl. Camera
                                              Mounts
PRODUCTION    1060                      Operation

SET           84                        Elect. Operation

STAGE         Lot #2                    Add & Changes
                                        Total Approp.
PICTURE       Wizard of OZ
                                        Final Cost            1181.97
TITLE OF MINIATURE   Ext. Witch-Fireball Matte
```

Details of Min. Set Area   No. of Bldgs. or Units
                                         Day   Nite   Dawn   Sunset
Scale
Backing   Black

REMARKS

Shots of fireball position matched to position of
Witch as she throws it.

ONE TEST -- TWO NITES SHOOTING

Dressing & Min. Props

Rig for fireball
Black backing

CONSTRUCTION

Total Construction Cost 346.00   Total Spcl. Effects

OPERATION	Construction Dept. Daily Cost				
		Foreman	Mechanics	Helpers	Labourers
Average Crew	Morning				
	Afternoon				
	Nite	1	3	1 ptr.	1 grip

Total Operation Cost   701.97

ELECTRICAL   Average Load

Wind Machines & Fans   one wind machine
Average Daily Crew   -2-
Total Operating Cost   134.00

CAMERA DEPT.

Cameraman   Fabian
Extra Cameras   Technicolor and crew
Lens   3"
Speed   48
Approx. No. of Feet of Film Printed

1060-84
Wizard of OZ
Ext. Witch- Fireball Matte

Ball of Fire for double printing was made by using a gas
torch fastened to a car travelling a track laid out for correct
path of ball. Track assembly covered with black against black
backing and shot at nite.

Close up fireball matte. Shot cut during final editing.

		Special
DATE April 11	Estimated Construction & Effect.	
	Preparation	
PRODUCTION 1060	Spcl. Camera	
	Mounts	
SET 88	Operation	
	Elect. Operation	
STAGE 30	Add & Changes	
	Total Approp.	
PICTURE Wizard of OZ		
	Final Cost	2105.75

TITLE OF MINIATURE   Ext.=Witch's Castle

Details of Min.Set Area   No.of Bldgs.or Units
Scale   1½" to 12"   Day Nite Dawn Sunset
Backing Painted sky   X   X

REMARKS
        NOTE: See set# 90 -no estimate on above, originally
              planned as Newcombe.

Dressing & Min. Props

CONSTRUCTION
Total Construction Cost 1117.41   Total Spcl.Effects

OPERATION   Construction Dept.Daily Cost

		Foreman	Mechanics	Helpers	Labourers
Average Crew	Morning	1	4		
	Afternoon				
	Nite				

Total Operation Cost   407.27

ELECTRICAL   Average Load
Wind Machines & Fans One electric
Average Daily Crew   -8-
Total Operating Cost   581.07

CAMERA DEPT.
Cameraman   Jack Smith
Extra Cameras
Lens   50mm.
Speed   48
Approx.No.of Feet of Film Pr

CHAPTER EIGHT   246

ATE   March 18--April 11   Estimated Construction & Special Effect.
                                              Preparation
RODUCTION   1060   Spcl.Camera Mounts
                                              Operation
ET   90   Elect.Operation
TAGE   30   Add & Changes
                                              Total Approp.
ICTURE   Wizard of OZ
                                        Final Cost   549.19
ITLE OF MINIATURE Inserts -Sparks from Witch's Shoe

etails of Min.Set Area   No.of Bldgs.or Units
                                        Day   Nite   Dawn   Sunset
cale
acking   Black
EMARKS
        Insert of sparks from shoe for double print.
        Insert of witch's castle at nite
        Retake using stop-motion sparks -Apr. 26-27

ressing & Min.Props
        Spark Gaps
        Witch's Castle

ONSTRUCTION
Total Construction Cost   73.40   Total Spcl.Effects

PERATION   Construction Dept.Daily Cost
                        | Foreman | Mechanics | Helpers | Labourers |
  Average Crew Morning | 1 | 2 | | 1 grip |
                Afternoon| 1 | 2 | | |
                Nite | | | | |

  Total Operation Cost   333.10

LECTRICAL   Average Load
  Wind Machines & Fans
  Average Daily Crew   A.M.--4--
  Total Operating Cost   142.69

MERA DEPT.
  Cameraman   Fabian
  Extra Cameras Technicolor and crew
  Lens   2"
  Speed   24
  Approx.No.of Feet of Film Printed

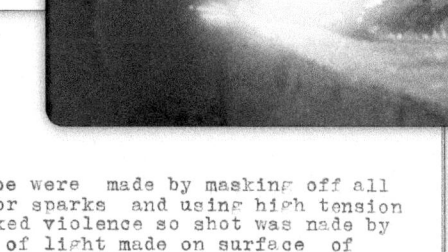

1060-90
Wizard of OZ
Insert Sparks from Shoe

     First sparks from Judys shoe were made by masking off all
but portion of scene required for sparks and using high tension
juice shot at speed. Result lacked violence so shot was made by
shooting in stop motion streaks of light made on surface of
glass painted black on camera side and illuminated by arc from
behind.

```
ATE     Jan. 23-May 1                  Estimated Construction & Special
                                                                 Effect.
                                                  Preparation      400.
RODUCTION      1060                       Spcl. Camera
                                                  Mounts
ET             87                                 Operation        800.
                                                  Elect.Operation  300.
AGE            14                                 Add & Changes
                                                  Total Approp.   1500.
ICTURE   Wizard of OZ                                          *** 6535.55
                                       Final Cost             (see attached
ITLE OF MINIATURE  Ext. Witch Skywriting

etails of Min.Set   Area              No.of Bldgs.or Units
                                       Day   Nite   Dawn    Sunset
cale
acking     Glass tank
EMARKS
           Shots of witch writing "Surrender Dorothy or Die-WWW"
    in sky with smoke from broom. Shot as matte to be printed into
    Technicolor sky.



essing & Min.Props
          6'x6'  glass tank and rigging
          Witch in various angles

STRUCTION
otal Construction Cost  738.66   Total Spcl.Effects
ERATION    Construction Dept.Daily Cost
                        Foreman | Mechanics | Helpers | Labourers
  Average Crew  Morning    1    |    3      |         | 1 grip
                Afternoon  1    |    3      |         |
                Nite       
  Total Operation Cost  3999.55   (Includes fullsize process)

ECTRICAL         Average Load
  Wind Machines & Fans
  Average Daily Crew  A.M.-4   P.M.-3-
  Total Operating Cost  1797.35   (Includes full-size process)

MERA DEPT.
  Cameraman       Fabian
  Extra Cameras
  Lens      25--40---2"
```

```
1060-87
Wizard of OZ
Ext. Witch Skywriting


Jan. 23   -Tests
     31   -  " "
Feb. 1    -Shots-drift corrected
 "   2    -Correction for better letters
Mar. 25   -Retakes new layouts
 "   27   -Retake on R
 "   28   -Corrections SUR
 "   29   -Take of SUR
 "   30   -Surrender Dorothy or die WWW
 "   31   -Retake
Apr. 1    -DOROT toHY
APr. 10   -1½" scale witch on Tower track.
 "   12   -Retakes --entire layouts for white matte
 "   13   - Retakes
 "   14   -  "    "
 "   15   -  "    "
 "   28   -Retakes using first layout
 "   29   -Continuation
May  1    -Test using foreground glass
```

For Witch Skywriting a 6'x6' x4" tank with glass bottom was framed 12' above the stage floor with camera shooting up and thru glass into 2" of white translucent water. The smoke which formed the letters was a black liquid released under slight pressure thru a stylus made with a hypodermic needle upon which a small black profile of witch was fastened. This was moved by operators from above forming the letters required. Wind drift was made by causing slight drift of water across tank. Black and white shots wer printed into color sky.

```
ATE    December and January              Estimated Construction & Special
                                                                  Effect.
                                         Preparation        4400
RODUCTION    1060                        Spcl.Camera
                                         Mounts
ET          77                           Operation          4000
                                         Elect.Operation    1075
TAGE        14                           Add & Changes
                                         Total Approp.      9475.
ICTURE    Wizard of OZ
                                Final Cost                  6990.57
ITLE OF MINIATURE    Ext. Flying Monkeys

etails of Min.Set  Area              No.of Bldgs.or Units
                                     Day   Nite   Dawn   Sunset
cale
acking  Technicolr sky backing
EMARKS
            Shots of Flying Monkeys to be used for cuts and BG's
       for witch's Tower



ressing & Min.Props
       Rigging for Monkeys
       Monkeys in Four sizes
       Backing
ONSTRUCTION
otal Construction Cost  1902.57  Total Spcl.Effects

PERATION    Construction Dept.Daily Cost
                          Foreman  Mechanics  Helpers  Labourers
  Average Crew   Morning    1         4       1 ptr.   2 grips
                 Afternoon  1         4                1 grip
                 Nite
  Total Operation Cost   2424.76

ECTRICAL         Average Load
  Wind Machines & Fans
  Average Daily Crew  A.M. 23---P.M. 23
  Total Operating Cost    2663.24

AMERA DEPT.
  Cameraman      Fabian
  Extra Cameras  Technicolor crew
  Lens    40--50--3"
```

```
1060-77
Wizard of Oz
Ext. Flying Monkeys


Oct.12 -Test of Monkeys and Gauze frames
Oct. 13-Test Modeled Monkeys
Oct.15 -Shot (side angle)
Dec.10 -Tests
Jan.5  -Color shot side angle
 "  7  -Monkeys landing in Forest
 " 12  -Retake approaching Forest
 " 13  - Monkeys leaving Forest
 " 19  -Retake Monkeys leaving Forest
```

   Preliminary attempts to attain side angle shots of monkeys
flying by window were made with profiles in three sizes fastened to
bobinet gauze on frames which were across screen in proportionate
speeds to size of profiles. This assembly was in front of small
painted backing. Profiles were changed to modelled figures but
lack of animation was too apparent. Model monkeys were then cast
in rubber with rubber wings. These were hung by two stationary
wires to head and feet. Two moving wires were fastened to tips
of wings and moved by eccentric in overhead frame supporting
numbers of monkeys in formation. These frames were carried by large
trolley wires and pulled by motor drives. This assembly permitted
a choice of angles. Side angles were shot for BG's for window.
Shots with trees and leaves in foreground were made side, panning
side to 3/4 and ahead for monkeys in Forest.

Wizard of Oz Exterior Flying Monkeys process plate. As seen in the background, outside the witch's castle window.

```
                                              Special
DATE  Feb. 24---25         Estimated Construction & Effect.
                                     Preparation    1600
                                     Spcl.Camera
PRODUCTION   1060                     Mounts
                                     Operation      1000
SET          63                      Elect.Operation
                                                     900
STAGE        14                      Add & Changes
                                     Total Approp.  3500.00
PICTURE   Wizard of OZ     Final Cost              2831.18
TITLE OF MINIATURE   Ext. House falling into Camera
Details of Min.Set  Area          No.of Bldgs.or Units
                                  Day   Nite   Dawn   Sunset
Scale
Backing       White prop sky
REMARKS
             Shots of house falling into camera after it leaves tornado


Dressing & Min.Props
           One house and rigging for same.  Revolving camera rig.
           Rigging for Smoke.  Prop Sky.
CONSTRUCTION
   Total Construction Cost   65.44   Total Spcl.Effects
```

OPERATION	Construction Dept.Daily Cost				
		Foreman	Mechanics	Helpers	Labourers
Average Crew	Morning	1	8	1 ptr.	1 grip
	Afternoon	1	8		1 grip
	Nite				

```
   Total Operation Cost   1940.91

ELECTRICAL         Average Load
   Wind Machines & Fans
   Average Daily Crew A.M. -8-   P.M. -6-
   Total Operating Cost   819.83

CAMERA DEPT.
   Cameraman    Fabian
   Extra Cameras
   Lens     40mm. ---24 mm.
   Speed    24 and 64
   Approx.No.of Feet of Film Printed
```

```
1060-63
Wizard of OZ
Ext. House falling into Camera

    House falling into Camera was made by suspending House
on horizontal shaft ---hung by wires to gantry crane. House
was hung with bottom close to lens, rotated on shaft, and moved
away from camera fast. As house travelled away it was raised
                                            PRINTED
and covered by heavy smoke cloud. This action was/reversed.

Feb. 24--Takes House travelling to Camera
Feb 25 --Correction in direction of travel of smoke
Mar. 9---House falling away agist white ( Stage 30)
Mar. 10 -Correction in clouds, backing and speed.
```

Original title insert test with Wicked Witch of the West's crystal ball as it falls away from camera and bursts onto floor. To be used in reverse.

Large glass ball filled with white liquid with title painted on top surface was dropped from the runway of Stage 14 to the floor covered with black cloth. Effect was ball formed from splash and travelled toward camera coming to stop before lens.

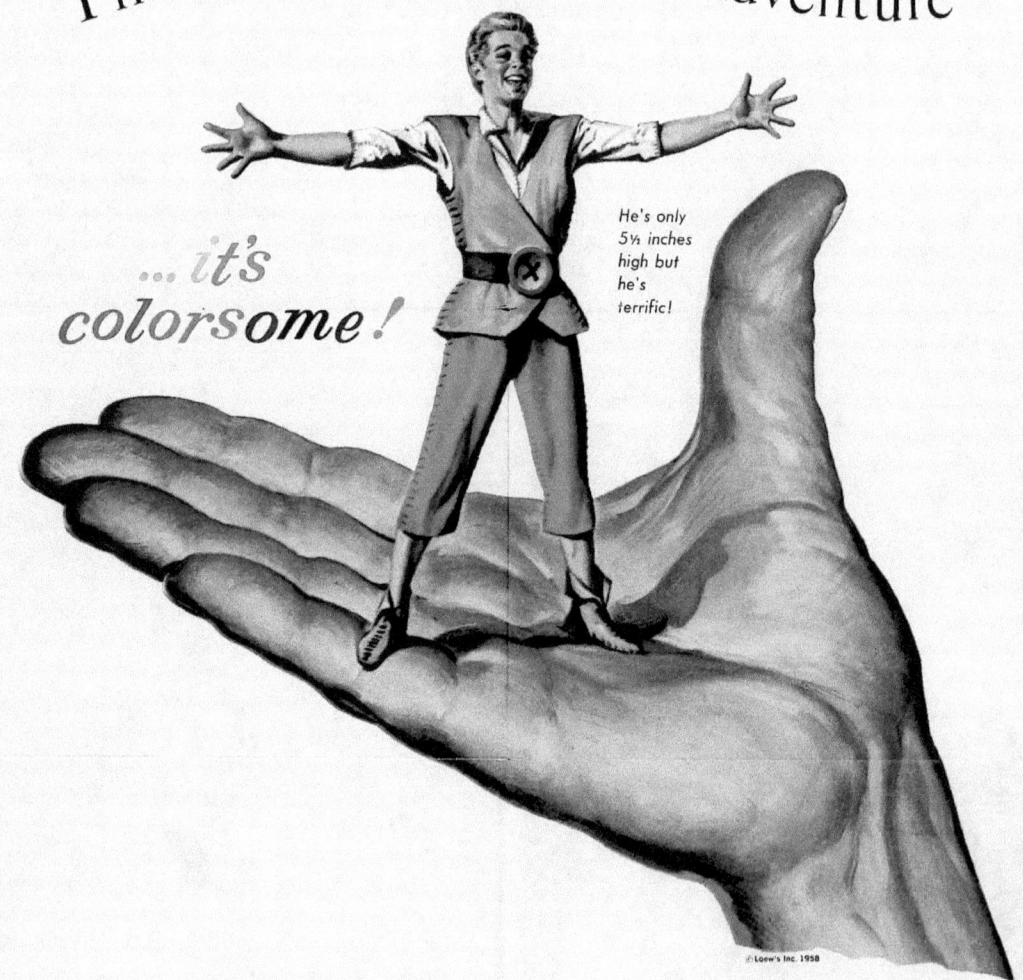

Tom Thumb, MGM Production, Released 1958. Example of Animation Effects.

CHAPTER NINE

CHAPTER NINE

~

"OPTICAL AND ANIMATION"

The ID monster attacks, animated by Disney artist Joshua Meador - Courtesy of Bob Burns.

Optical Effects becomes the alphabetical fourth of the original Academy recognized five categories of Special Visual Effects. A sixth, as you will recall, Animation, was recently taken into the fold although stringently curbed and restricted as to its award consideration eligibilities. This new addition will be discussed and explained later in this chapter.

Optical. A dictionary's definition reads, "constructed to assist the sight, as devices." Another, "pertaining to sight; visual: an <u>optical</u> <u>illusion</u>." The latter, "optical illusion," perhaps exemplifies the most interesting, audience conscious face of this many faceted branch of Effects. Much of a routine, relatively perfunctory procedure takes place in the Optical Department of any Studio. Dissolves, fade outs, dupes, frame holds, skip frames, zooms, wipes, reverse action, color separations, are fairly stereotyped bread and butter activities. Necessary, and done with precision along with a few other chores such as the making of Background Plates for Process - but generally much more mechanical than creative.

It is in the field of "optical tricks" that the men are separated from the boys, so to speak, and a top functioning optical team which can reasonably and consistently turn out acceptable results in these more demanding and more trying fields, is a very invaluable asset to any studio and a necessity often, to men engaged in the other Effect Categories.

If top service cannot be expected when an effect determination overlaps into Optical from Process or Matte Painting, Miniature or Full-sized Effects, that determination will slant towards other methods and choose a different route, by-passing Optical. This situation unfortunately occurs at times and it is a pity because the problem-solvers can be, and generally are, handicapped in varying degrees as a result.

Optical's stumper is mainly due to the fact that tolerances involved are extremely minute. Unless superior craftmanship, with know-how, is tightly welded to a conscientious refusal to do less than the best, these un-met tolerances can and do scream out discordant notes of "Fake! Fake!"

Many times through the years people have asked me, "What Is that line around the people?" (it can be blue or green or black) or, "You could see through him," or maybe, "It wiggled. What made it wiggle?" Or other some such critical observations. Well children, there is seldom a single answer and inasmuch as this category of Optical Effects was outside the perimeter of my particular jurisdiction or responsibility, my single answer has generally been, "It could be any of a dozen different misses." And my own private conviction has usually been, "somewhere along the line, craftsmanship tripped unforgiveably." In this very exacting field, "good enough" is fatal.

I must confess the ease with which we on the outside, not involved in the actual execution of a tight optical stint, are prone to rant a bit over its less than perfect deliverance when such is the case. But frustration over the failure of an important link in a well thought out solution chain, can cause a sweet-mannered Special Effector whose dependence on one part of optical perfection to eight parts of something else so that a perfect or near perfect whole be delivered, to gnash teeth bitterly and think in terms of "relatives dying of snakebite!"

Rarely does the Optical Department actually shoot the material (film) given to them later, although it is usually wise to have a representative present at the time of shooting to double check and approve any technicalities involved. Which means that in most instances the "idea" was born elsewhere and Optical is brought in to service its particular involvement. This of course is as it should be, the "problem" idea coming generally first from the writer and its solving formula from either the Art Director, and/or someone in another category or categories of Special Effects. Occasionally it does originate within Optical itself. The latter applies more often in the great number of optical effects which worm their way into most T.V. commercials. However most generally, dictates of which way to travel, meaning method determination, will come from someone other than the head optical man. At least this has been my experience.

I should perhaps at this early point, temporize any implied criticism in the preceding few paragraphs by stating my full recognition of the difficulties presented in this work by armies of microscopic gremlins which are wont to thumb their unpredictable noses at any and all optical technicians.

But like the Matador who chooses to fight bulls, these chaps have elected to do battle with these mean little devils and I am afraid I have little sympathy with the recipients of either for-real or optical gorings. Now that the wrist of this Category has been soundly slapped, I hereby declare a be-kind-to-Optical-Effects week from here on out.

We will not detail other than the previously referred to "tricks," leaving any run of the mill duties unmolested in their pushbutton mechanically programmed quarters. Very important, this work, and I am sure brimful of snags and barbs, but we are concerned only with "how did they make 'Tom Thumb' little?" or "was that lion really there right next to Hedy La Fru Fru?"

Well, let's talk first about Tom Thumb. A George Pal Production made in England. "Tom" was a real person and he was not just six or eight inches tall. At times he worked in mostly oversized sets with recognizable scale comparison props such as a huge chair which would make him appear tiny. At times he was actually an inanimate "doll," this usually when held in someone's hand, during the kind of action which precluded the necessity of resorting to more sophisticated tricks. And many other times he was a very live and visible part of scenes which included normal sets and normal people. Here Optical enters.

Russ Tamblyn, the athletic young actor who portrayed "Tom," would be photographed separately and matte-printed into a previously shot normal scene. Careful pre-planning of both parts to assure proper "togetherness," with detailed consideration given to such items as corresponding degree of camera tilt, light direction, Tom's "distance" relationship to camera, positioning of "objects" in the "matte set" to correspond with those in the "normal set," look directions of actors in both sets to tie into each other when combined and many other tedious and painstakingly diagrammed and outlined necessities, are all part of the advance layout and shooting procedures which result in two pieces of film being produced and delivered to Mr. Optical Effects to be made into one. It can readily be seen that if the "wedding" fails to come off in this final step, after all of the above, frustration just as readily can really run rampant.

To get along, the Tom Thumb piece of film becomes the material from which a "traveling matte," one of Optical Effects very special, very valuable and vexatiously troublesome tools, is made. What is a "traveling matte?" A term used to designate any piece of moving (traveling) action photographed against a no-detail void or limbo of some kind, which is to be later "inserted" into, and become an integral part of, another scene. Early in these pages "traveling mattes" were sketchily briefed.

In this case and in color, Russ was shot against a blue backings a special blue which has been used for the last few

TOM THUMB (1958)

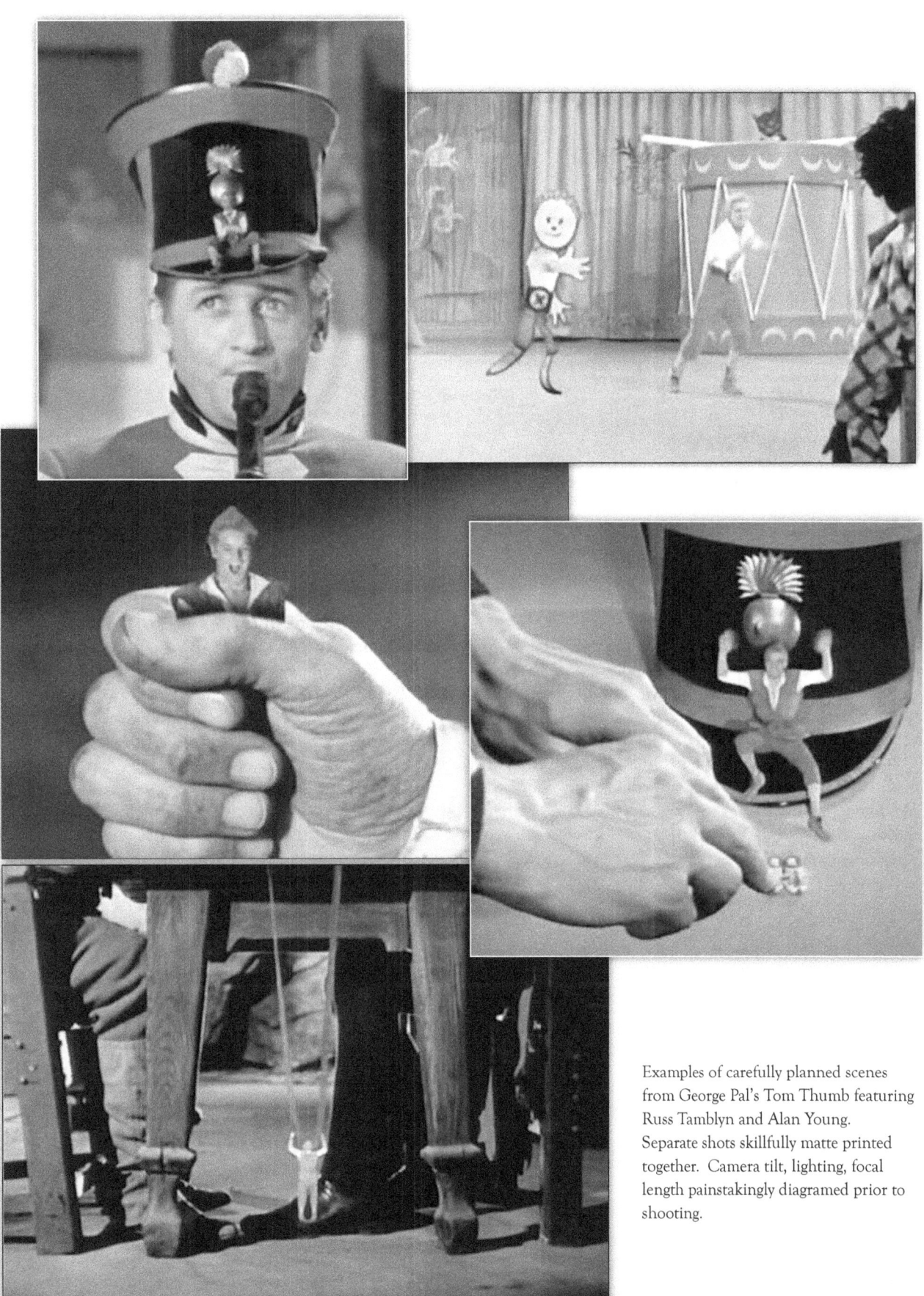

Examples of carefully planned scenes from George Pal's Tom Thumb featuring Russ Tamblyn and Alan Young. Separate shots skillfully matte printed together. Camera tilt, lighting, focal length painstakingly diagramed prior to shooting.

years by most studios when making traveling mattes. There are other methods which combine varying light and different backdrop "systems, " such as Ultraviolet, Infrared, Mercury Vapor and others, all the way back to Frank Williams' process which we mentioned in an early chapter while delving pleasantly into the nostalgia of the first *Ben-Hur*.

So traveling mattes as such are not of recent vintage - only some of the more current methods. A thorough technical perusal of the steps which follow, is available from many sources to the serious student. For these pages a more kindergarten surface description will suffice.

We now have Mr. Tamblyn safely and sharply registered on one piece of color negative. He looks perfectly natural but he is completely surrounded or "backed up" by a sheet of Ultramarine Blue. From this, Optical makes another film strip in which the moving figure of the Tom-Thumb-to-be, has become a high-contrast-to-the-background, silhouette. When this silhouette or "matte" is combined in a printing procedure with the original straight normal set and people, it leaves a blank "hole" which moves about in whatever manner Russ Tamblyn moved as he was originally photographed.

The next and final step is to "fill" the blank "hole" with the figure of Tom Thumb. And hereby hangs the "halo" - those pesky "mattey" outlines of blue, green or black of which people are prone to proclaim critically. If every step is properly executed, our six inch actor will fill and fit exactly into the "hole" of his own making, false halos will be nonexistent as technical excellence produces a true magic.

This is the ABC route that is followed in all traveling matte composites. Film shrinkages, color dupes, all of the other gremlins are always present and it is right smack here that conscientious craftsmanship practiced by a technician who should at all times be stuffed to the ultra 'nth, with the patience of a dozen Jobs, is the only key to consistent achievement acceptability.

There has been considerable use of the traveling matte tool in compositing people into or in front of a previously shot scene, particularly when the mechanics or size of the completed shot falls outside the limits or scope of Rear Projection Process (coming up in a subsequent Chapter).

Such shots as those of John Gilbert in *Rivets*, an early talkie, showing him walking the steel girders of a skyscraper, with New York, far and at an acute angle, below, would not lend themselves to Rear Projection Process because of the steepness of the camera angle. Others such as a long shot of the "Mayflower" from the poop forward, much too much scope for Process, would become traveling mattes in order that the stage ensconced ship set, would, through this medium, "float" on a wet wavy ocean instead of a dry stage floor. A huge blue backing on the floor and the walls of the stage, backed up the deck and superstructure of the "Mayflower" in the same manner as did a much smaller blue backing back up Tom Thumb in order that both "foregrounds" would neatly cohere, dovetail, into their eventual and respective chosen mattes. Hence you will readily recognize a valuable vehicle, this traveling matte device, upon which often happily rides the best of intentions hopefully all the way to a successful terminus. Not always however with the preciseness for which one would wish. Just too tough I guess. I should be more charitable - though I know not why! Gillespie misses (and there have been at least a couple (!) in the last forty-odd years) were never swept <u>beneath</u> and hidden by any carpet of non-criticism that I can recall. Loud wails would issue forth with no regard whatsoever for the tender sensitivity of my epidermis.

The reference above to *Rivets* (it was released as *Fast Workers* if memory serves) recalls a wonderful oldtime director. Tod Browning. Tod directed many of Lon Chaney's (Senior) films. He loved, as did Chaney, the bizarre, and his pictures were usually a steaming brew of freaks and clabber, bearded ladies and sweat, lizards and mystery, photographed through a rancid blue haze, pierced usually by strangled, dying wails or splitting, piercing, neck bristling screams of terror.

I Art-directed a number of Mr. Browning's spine-tingling gems and I have often thought of the completeness of this man's sphere of movie making action. He pushed and shoved from the story's original concept to the final editing. And Tod's able shoulder at the wheel as it rolled over all the rough aspects of movie making, was for years importantly the reason his pictures were successful. A one-man band who drove himself diligently and knew how to accept help. Not like the great U.S.C. football player, (this accepting of help) Aaron Rosenberg, who seemed, as far as my experience was concerned, to shun such idiocy.

I remember of those long gone days when at times a set might fall short of what it should have been, listening to a typical Tod Browning reaction. "Don't worry Buddy, we'll shoot it through a bobbinet. Two if necessary." This sort of reaction prompted of course, extra effort. Lon Chaney was the master of make-up, as you among us who have sampled years of vintages, will know. Too many to itemize here, although one I will never forget, was his use of the almost transparent membrane which encloses the white of an egg next to the shell. This filmy veil he would somehow apply over his own eyeballs to give the effect of stoney blindness. I can still see that wide open cornealess staring whiteness.

True dedication this, which often necessitated Mr. Chaney's arrival at the studio in the AM's wee-est of hours, so that the "shooting at nine" item on those Production Office Yellows, would not be violated. Many actors follow this code - their day starting often with the crow of the first cock. Some don't!

The latter reference to a rare unpleasantness, for no reason at all, brings to mind another irksome yearly event - income tax - as it applies to actors, or prize fighters, ball players or anyone whose period of high earnings is measured by a birth date. Certainly a different computation should be used, one that considers the limitation of a ten or perhaps twenty year stretch of top "incoming" as against other professions which depend not on muscle elasticity, shiny curly black hair or measurements in the 38-21-35 realm.

A bank president of seventy can approve a loan for a paunchy real estate mogul of seventy who has sold a mansion to a wrinkled and active grocery chain head of seventy. They may all even be hairless and shoot in the hundreds, while their amounts of income have usually increased with the years.

I thereby take the stump for my actor friends and propose that Uncle Sam's Collectors pay this some mind. Spread the ten years to twenty - the twenty to forty. Dope out a formula, whatever, but do something. I further hold that taking over 50% of a man's earnings, regardless of the magnitude, is confiscatory and further, economically unsound. A lot of this country's tremendousness is due to individual fortunes, "put to work!" Take half, yes, if it must be, but 60, 70, 90%, no! Like dedicating the subject of "Joppa Gate the Third" to another volume, maybe a future tome will tell those Washington gimme-gimmes just where to head in.

So no more expounding except to hint that this stand of mine may put me back within the good graces of the acting profession. A few members of this enviable group have been gently chastised by me in an earlier chapter because of my own interpretation of "temperament" as a form of dereliction, a culpable neglect of duty and obligation.

On second thought, one more paragraph of expounding. Not having researched the fine print in the volumes of fine print sired by the Internal Revenuers, I may be off base on the 'stretch out' idea of tax payments applying to earners whose top incomes are affected by the ravages of time. Maybe something has been done. But a real pet peeve which has just been experienced by me as an aftermath of my retirement, has to do with Washington's and Sacramento's combined grab of a goodly portion of that supposed hedge against elderliness, a Pension - some 32% of the lump sum flies right out of my Senior Citizen window. Forty-three years of earned salary and investment income payments are understood, and though not always cheerfully paid, the deadline has regularly been met. But to invade this security nest-egg seems to me immoral and corrupt. Income from its investment, yes, but not, gentlemen, the initial sum itself. Think it over. Control by the State of the People through excessive tax squeezing is a dangerous road to travel. Remember that dumped tea in Boston. I know - they wanted representation, but somehow as I review the years we seem to be enjoying progressively less and less control of that representation. Elected officials we have but 'vote-buying' with tax dollars is I believe not what our forefathers had in mind. Another 'seed' planted which I

London After Midnight, MGM Production #330, Released 1927. AAG Contribution: Set Decorator.

sincerely hope may one day sprout and serve to impede the growth of Too-Big-Government. If this sounds like a Scotch Patrick Henry, so be it. I am increasingly aware of the many other 'seed planters'.

Recess is over - back to Optical. The "Matte that Travels" has been given a layman's breakdown, with, I hope, a degree of understandability. The live, well toothed lion, alongside Miss la Fru Fru, will be next for the class.

As almost always, there are several ways in which to achieve such proximities. One is by the use of "Split Screen." Another is through the system of Traveling Mattes, just discussed - the lion or "Hedy" against blue, composited into film strip number two which would include Hedy or the lion - never in actuality, the two together. Another would be the use of Process, with Leo or the lady on the Process Screen while the other cavorts in front of the rear-projected picture. A third could be the use of a Senior Citizen old cat with store-boughten teeth but this hardly seems honest.

Through Split Screen it is relatively a cinch, provided the animal and the actor do not pass one in front of the other. Although this also can be handled. An example (here comes *Tarzan* again) illustrating the mechanics, was a scene in which "Boy," film progeny of Jane and Johnny (without benefit of a leopard-skinned man of the cloth - hm-m-m - never thought of that before) is crawling up a long sloping windfall, the trunk of which is about eight or ten inches in diameter. Following close on his heels, slinks a sure enough lion. No rubber crocodile or plaster hippos here. To do, is simple. Tie the camera, which covers the full scene, firmly down so there is absolutely no movement - use camera jacks to eliminate any vibration or jiggle, and shoot two complete shots. One, of the boy creeping with fright up the tree, followed by nothing. And the other one, the lion slinking up the tree following nothing.

This last sentence could be a mis-statement as it might have been, and probably was, necessary for the trainer to stroll casually ahead of the lion about where the boy should be, with a filet or a chicken or something to start Leo's saliva glands squirting, which hopefully would tempt him to slink up the limb in proper fashion.

The lighting of the set will have remained constant. No wind, no movement of any kind, other than the performers, has occurred and in theory any part of one scene will, through the soft blend "split" technique, match perfectly when printed with the corresponding other part of the second scene. In theory, yes, and practically always in practice, yes, if both "halves" have followed the "fine print" of the specifications.

"Halves" is a misnomer in this instance as the soft split (optical blend line) moved across the screen, close to the barefoot soles of "Boy" on film strip "A" and preceding the lion's whiskers in "B". It would be smart to shoot the King of the Jungle '(fresh out of Thousand Oaks Zoo - some forty miles from M.G.M.) first, as he may be bored and on a diet and take a lot of time. It is always well to shoot the second film part as soon as possible after the first, so that the chances of a perfect match are enhanced. So get the lion first, if it takes two or whatever hours. "Boy" can be depended upon to do his crawl immediately following. I am sure we followed this sequence. In the completed shot, Tarzan's little b__d's part of the film covered the bait toting trainer, or rather substituted for that part of the lion-take in which he the trainer, shows.

An added "extra pair for the price of one" is a choice of variable distances between the pursuer and the pursued, which can fit the whim of the Director or Film Editor (usually the Director's whim becomes enthusiastically the Film Editor's whim). By altering the footage start marks of "A" and "B" forward or backward, the space between "Boy's" feet and lion's forepaws can be widened or narrowed. Sufficient area for the "split" must of course be maintained.

Split Screen is generally used when one actor plays two parts. This can be somewhat more complicated due to dialogue timing and the possible greater amount of time needed between the shooting of "A" and "B", often necessitated because of wardrobe and makeup changes which may be involved in portraying the two characterizations. Talking to oneself in stories of this ilk, is generally handled through a pre-recorded playback and a stand-in may occupy the place of the "real" Joe Doaks so that the eyes of one can follow the actions of the other, etc. The stand-in of course is "split out" (as was the lion trainer) in the final composite.

"Splits" are not limited to just two parts nor are they always top to bottom. Suppose a boa constrictor is stretched on a limb above a jungle trail down which Audrey Hepburn, clad in a 40% cob, 60% spider web, sort of nature's Dior, saunters. A horizontal "split" in this case avoids the possibility of the serpent being tempted. Or if Cheetah had followed the lion that followed "Boy" up the slanting tree trunk, we would have wound up with three parts and two splits - unless maybe the Chimp and Bert Lahr's counterpart were pals, in which case they might work together. This recalls to me a Lion, a Chimp and George Emerson.

George Emerson was our "animal man" at M.G.M. for, how many years. I think it was he who caught that plump little blessed event in the middle of Lake Sherwood which lured Mother Hippo and eventually the others to a hay-filled corral along the shore. I know it was George, who, attired in one of Johnny's cast-off loin cloths, rode Mary the Rhino - the same one which played a one-sided game of tag with me in the lonesomeness of that Lot Two jungle set one quiet summer afternoon.

Mr. Emerson possessed a way with animals while I mainly have only a true love for them and I had no business crawling

TARZAN FINDS A SON (1939) & TARZAN AND HIS MATE (1934)

Tarzan Finds A Son, production 1077, split screen of lion chasing "Boy". Tied down camera ensures exact alignment.

(Above) *Tarzan And His Mate*, production 645- Split screen method of combing Maureen O'Sullivan with hungry lion and tiger.

(Right) Optically combined lion and "African" elephant.

over a stout fence within the boundary of which snorted Mary. I guess I thought she wouldn't notice me, but ladylike, she did. The horn on her snoot is no less deadly than the male, I found out, as she chipped off great hunks of bark from the tree behind which I firmly held my ground. Not often is one privileged to feint and feint to a degree of admitted faintness, with a red-blooded robust adult rhinoceros of either sex, not to mention the "she" of the species.

George maintained a sort of animal warehouse on Lot 3 and Lot 6. Deer, for deer pictures, cows for cow pictures with bulls, a coyote or two, a puma, some long-haired Scotch cattle from *Brigadoon*, and Leo and Cheetah. These latter two spent much time together in the same cage behind the sky backing of our Lot 3 ocean, and George had choreographed a ballet of sorts starring this lion and this chimpanzee. A good act, but the real fun was to stand at other times a few feet away from their common cage and watch.

Leo was the real thing, young and vigorous, but he must have won all lion awards for patience, and for having a good disposition, because invariably when he would slump with a yawn and a deep-throated sigh to the floor for a nap in the sun, Cheetah would start quietly abiding her time. Minutes would pass, sufficient for the transformation from a light snooze to a deep, deep slumber. Then slowly would Cheetah climb to the topmost footing available directly over poor Leo. No one could be more rudely jarred from Morpheus's grip than would Leo be jarred, upon receiving the full dropped weight of Cheetah's fifty or sixty pounds of deviltry.

The chase would commence with ear-splitting Special Sound Effects, the chimp usually emitting the last shrill shriek (of derision) while hanging by all four limbs from the top of the cage, safely beyond the reach of wildly swinging paws. In no time at all it seemed, all was forgotten and forgiven and the two would be happily chit-chatting.

George Emerson has left us and I would feel safe in laying odds that there is a fleecy fenced game preserve up there, around which parades a winged elephant. And nobly astride this most beloved of all his pals, would be George talking softly the same language he used down here, to all of his four-footed angels.

Accompanying George would be Frank Whitbeck, the voice you have all heard for years, narrating M.G.M. "trailers" - the come-ons advertising next week's gigantic. Frank's library of elephant lore was gargantuan and his collection of ivory, ebony, bronze and brass representations of this noble tusked beast, must have excited the envy of the entire Grand Old Party. But politics I refuse to discuss. It's just that all good guys are Republicans (the oldfashioned kind!) In deference to my Publisher, who has some degree of interest in the sale of this book, I confess that there are also a few (good guys) in that other party. And to think I was born in Texas!

Little people, traveling mattes, and split screens have been optically probed. Let's see what's next. The adding of fog or rain or clouds possibly, to a shot already made is a common duty which often to tie critical eye is not too successfully accomplished. Straight superimposition of smoke or mist or rain, which has been separately photographed over another scene, usually fails at least to a degree, due to its transparency and/or lack of atmospheric perspective. Fog "thickness" for instance, that could blot out a street light one hundred feet away, will have very little effect on that self-same light when simply "doubled" over. The "thickness" becomes a transparent sheet and this applies to rain or snow or dust storms, or any "added-to" effect, when superimposed over a scene which has been previously shot and which is lacking sufficient snow, rain, dust or fog. The above "remedy" is often used, I know, and John Q., the ticket purchaser, perhaps will not demand his money back. But to A.A.G., also a ticket buyer, this sort of falsity almost always provokes a wince.

Which is a question in point. John Q. may not know why something looks phony - he may not be a technician - but give him enough of these short cut "conveniences" and he may well develop a perhaps unanalyzed antipathy for the unreality of the flickers, and may decide to deposit his entertainment monies in some other more honest receptacle like a bowling alley or a bar. Certainly commercial soundness and savings, make sense. The lily should not be over-gilded nor, and just as importantly, should it be allowed to tarnish. Don't sell your audience too short.

We have upon occasion added some of the effects in question to a previously shot scene, by projecting in Process the scene, and rephotographing it with rain, fog or snow occurring between the camera and screen. The larger the projected picture, the farther away is the camera, allowing for added "thickness" or depth. Transparency is no problem when following this procedure and indeed with sufficient quantities of the foreground ingredients, the original can be blotted completely out. This would be silly though, wouldn't it? The point is that controllable densities can be used.

Streak lightning is usually added to a scene optically as are tracer bullets and Science and Fiction "rays," good rays and bad rays. These "accessories" are usually created and supplied by other than the Optical Department itself. The combining or compositing however is always theirs.

Another very valuable activity made possible by grace of these optical gentlemen, is the "multiplication of people." Two hundred of Central Casting's extras can become a crowd of a thousand or more. This is accomplished through a well laid out space area plan in which the two hundred occupy in turn each of the alternate areas for sufficient time to obtain the required film footage. Five times two hundred is one thousand, so Optical is given five separate pieces of film which will be put together by them thereby producing in this

instance, a "<u>five</u> pair of pants for the price of one."

And joy is expressed among the greenback guardians. Except they seldom neglect to add, "wouldn't <u>one</u> hundred have been enough?" Might have, for a smaller ultimate crowd, for there <u>is</u> a practical limit to the number of single "parts" which can be combined into a final single whole. Magic, yes - but miracles, not always.

Occasionally individual groups such as the one just described can be shot while occupying one "space" only and optically repeated and fitted like a jigsaw puzzle, producing the final "crowd" through various optical-printer maneuvers of lateral as well as up and down movements, combined with proper and varying degrees of reduction and enlargement. The first method however is generally preferred for simple reasons of perspective and an important plus in quality.

Effects such as "rippling," in and out of focus, zooms and others dreamed up by whoever, become reasonably routine. It is almost always better and considerably safer to put such effects in later rather than attempting to <u>do</u> them during shooting. If done in advance, you are saddled with the result, good or bad. Subsequent application allows for fiddling and changes - so, "letting Optical do it," though at times with guidance, can often turn out to be a decision of wisdom.

High technical proficiency coupled with dedication to patience, are qualities the optical virtuoso must possess, and <u>practice</u>. His thorough knowledge of the many "machines" at his disposal with which he may achieve, in the jargon of the layman, "tricks," should be matched by his determination to wring out the last drop of excellence possible from these highly precision and sometimes temperamental assemblies of glass and metal and electronics. He must be the pilot, engineer and navigator.

The top men in this category of Special Visual Effects deliver a high average of top results. Unquestionably an important contender in the Effects family and a real boon to any imaginative creator.

Because of the advent of Cinemascope, 20th Century Fox's big new "squeeze" play, all studios, or rather most Majors, decided to go it alone brother! Varying aspect ratios were a dime a dozen. Vista Vision, Wide Screen, Wide Scope, Todd-a-o, Panavision and Ultra Panavision, Technirama. Thirty-five millimeter and sixty-five millimeter film were involved, anamorphic lenses (the squeeze family) and the good old-hat standbys, spherical lenses.

Even these latter were affected by aperture mattes placed in the camera, of varying ratios which finally wound up in recent years with a 1.60 to 1 shape which sliced a sliver off the top and bottom of the long-used standard 3 by 4. But hold your horses - the picture was to be released as a 1.75 or 1.85

to 1, so that action had to be framed within those etched-on-the-finder lines so that Yul Brynner's glistening pate be not chopped off, nor the platinum of a Jane-come-lately-Harlow be lost, in a full head closeup. All real crazy, with resultant pyramided problems no end. Competition, I am aware, is stimulating, but all of those better mouse traps! - when the only real tried and true ones are a good or an excellent movie.

This is perhaps as good a time as any to get in my no-holds-barred plug for the individuals without whom those good or excellent movies could not be made. The Writers! I can think of very few exceptions in this case that prove the rule. Included among these non-provers are large groups in other lines of film endeavor who just dearly love to try their hand at "improving" the script.

A great friend of mine, John Tobin, brother-in-law of Eddie Mannix and before his regrettable demise, Plant Manager at M.G.M., once told me, "The laborer who is digging a ditch knows much better than his boss how hard the dirt is." Well there are those in authority who at the drop of a typewriter key, will take over a writer's shovel and dig disastrously, and then perhaps, hand it back with "instructions." Some producers, some actors, maybe even some bookkeepers are gleefully guilty of such unqualified nonsense. They would be much better off tending their own knitting. Exceptions, of course. But seldom.

My doffed hat to the talented among you, scribes, provided your endeavors are sincere and honest.

Now where were we? Oh yes, the shapes and sizes of the Motion Picture. Its effect on Optical has been that of supplying a new, for them, bread and butter chore. Somewhat more refined however than fades, dissolves, step-printing or wipes. Those and others of like status you recall, were not to be included in this treatise. Only "tricks."

A stock shot of Vienna's Ferris Wheel, photographed in Paramount's Vista Vision, is purchased for an M.G.M. Panavision film, along with an old 3 x 4 scene of Lisbon's waterfront and several cuts of a parade blaring down Rome's Corso, in beautiful Technirama. Unsqueezed and squeezed, varying aspect ratios and film sizes, to be "doctored" and made to "fit" a Panavision picture. This, Optical does, with costly lenses, costly machines and "know how". They also provide our Process Plates for two new and vastly improved systems of Rear Projection Process which I, by golly, christened. One is "Laced Process" and it will be thoroughly outlined, trisected and properly credited in an upcoming Chapter. The other and more recent, "Reflex Front Projection."

This particular service of Optical's is demanding, yes, precision, yes, work, as will be detailed later, but the supplying of Process Plates of whatever kind does not in my not so humble opinion, rate as sufficient great shucks in the Special Visual Effect field to warrant equal billing along with another individual whose Screen Credit may be the result of an outstanding creative, ingenious and realistic solving of any of the many documented herein toughies. There are <u>other</u> legitimate Optical Effects which warrant recognition and to stoop to credit, seemingly just for credits sake, seems to me like cheating at solitaire.

The above and the following may be a thought worth mulling by all serious minded students who would prefer that their morning shaves are not marred by having to look <u>away</u> from the mirror.

I nourish a pet complaint re the practice of unearned Screen Credits which from time to time, in my experience, have found their unjustified way into and on the Main Titles of Pictures. I hasten to add in order that possible future libel suits be fended, it is my opinion that some may be unjustified, or at the very least, dubious.

For many years we were granted at M.G.M. the right of credit if we wished it and for many years it was my policy to decline unless I <u>honestly</u> felt there was a sufficient degree of contribution to warrant that credit. Ordinary peanut routine services seemed not to reach that level of importance.

Nor did possibly a gem of excellence qualify, if it would be viewed by an audience for a total of only ten or twelve feet of film. Twelve feet is eight seconds of time which in a six to ten or twelve thousand foot picture hardly deserves, again in my opinion, the name of the begetter being blazoned in equal sized type, in company with those responsible for goodly hunks of footage resulting from the often overtaxed cells which dwell in that corner of the brain peculiar to the adept and creative Special Effector. That particular area is certainly present in most of those who toil in any or <u>all</u> of the five (now six) categories. But when used in a mechanical fashion only, or when quantity is so minute that a head turned briefly to glare annoyance at some nearby noisy popcorn eater, causing a complete miss of the whole of somebody's one and only Effects offering, I say "off with his head," credit-wise at least.

To my annoyance this conclusion has not always been shared by others, and at one time I took counter measures. I accepted Cedric Gibbons' routine organizational request as to yes or no on Screen Credit, regardless of the quantity or gradation or its difficulties of achievement, its excellence or its non-excellence, and I in self defense, relegated deservibility to the locker room in order that if Mr. So and So chose to have his John Henry inscribed, mine would also appear. So "A. Arnold Gillespie," earned or not, appeared on any and all of M.G.M.'s movies when any of his domain of Special Effects was at all involved during this period.

A three week cruise through the Caribbean on the "Stella Polaris" with my wonderful-swing, non-hit, golfing spouse, brought me up sharply on this score one sunny A.M.

This was during the period of my me–too-regardless, credit determination.

Now Mom makes friends easily and charmingly, so out of three hundred and sixty five cruise passengers, only a very, very few, after a very few days, did we not know. The night before this sunny morning, a movie had been shown in the ship's saloon (that's not a bar although saloons are bars - confusing) an M.G.M. movie! - and who should be included among the credits but, you guessed it!

We had not attended and it had somewhat slipped my mind that this particular effort, as far as it related to anything of Effect consequence, was one of those which bore only my defiant name. Well, over three hundred of the cruisers aboard who loved my wife (many, I suspect, at the start of the voyage were undoubtedly under the impression that she was my good looking daughter)- showered me on this bright and shiny A.M. with "Oh Mr. Gillespie we so enjoyed your Special Effects last night! What were they?" Of such is mortification made and of such does justice reap its vengeance. I only wish the ten-second mechanical culprit who was the cause of my folly had been there to explain just why his name might be on an otherwise honest list of those who made the movie.

A few nights later at the fancy-costume Captain's ball, I retrieved my standing somewhat by appearing as Jane Russell, dressed partly in the stateroom's drapes, the bunk's bedspreads and a lovely bra fashioned of bath towels in which were nested two generous porcelain bowls - properly voluminous and fortunately of light weight no slippage. I could not pinpoint within which category they belonged probably that of Full Sized Mechanical Effects minus the "mechanical". In any event they were sort of Extra Special, and my position in this field was restored.

But enough of this self glorification and to further pin-prick any bubble of remaining ego, on that well remembered best forgotten evening, the Captain refused to dance with "Jane" - such Norwegian staidness! And such staidness exhibited all of the next day by, as Ilka Chase would say, my "loved one." Ilka's travel books by the way, are a delight - her, "The Elephants Arrive at Half-past Five" has given me the title of a feature to be written by me which I will call, "The Rooster's Crow at a Quarter to Fo', - in Tahiti" - provided of course, that Publishers, bless them, come knocking at my door.

This Chapter, students and laymen and layladies, in case you have forgotten, had to do with "Optical Effects" with a hint that "Animation" would be briefly diagnosed. Before writing a final "finis" to Optical, I must however, once more mention Cinema-photographer Clarence Slifer. Irving Ries, formerly, and Robert Hoag presently, have headed the Optical Department for many years. Mr. Slifer is a big cog in Matte Painting as you are aware if you minded your P's and Q's while reading the pages devoted to that category. And right at the top of his many outstanding aptitudes is his genius in the realm of Optical Effects.

This talent was lauded heretofore in that one act dissertation, "I Have a Rival," by Mrs. Slifer in which a couple of Clarence's optical printers seemed to vie successfully for his attention, if not adoration.

Upon visiting Slifer's Matte Painting bailiwick, which I do often, I never fail to be bowled over by his tremendous versatility and "stubborn" acumen in this field, in the mastery of those switch laden, dial flushed, precision demanding, machines. This sketchy treatment of Category Four would have been incomplete were I not to have included one C. Slifer.

Animation, though an alphabetical first in my determination of which Category should lead off, is such a newcomer as an Effects contender, and is so limited in its eligibility, that its brief insertion as a part of this chapter, seems fair to me. It could not properly rate, as of now, one of its own. And this conclusion has no bearing on animation as an Art.

I cite Mr. Disney or our own Tom and Jerry or George Pal's Puppets. And talented, now retired Disney's man, Josh Meador, whose contribution to *Forbidden Planet* was so high in importance, as examples of outstanding craftsmen and craftsmanship. But this particular skill has its own niche and with but few exceptions has little in common with the Special Visual Effects definition and breakdown as instituted many years ago by the Academy Committee of the Effects branch. It is those exceptions which prompted this Committee to include Animation (with limitations) as a sixth Category.

Though heretofore included, we will repeat the rules which govern consideration of Animation as an entrant in Hollywood's Oscar Derby.

"Rule Three. - However, animation may only be considered under the following conditions:

(a) Two dimensional animation (cartoon or painting) is eligible only when used as an adjunct to, and included in, live action scenes;

(b) Three dimensional animation is eligible only if its purpose is to achieve a result sufficiently realistic to be accepted as though it were not stop-motion and it must relate to live action scenes or sequences only. Motion pictures or sequences that are principally cartoon or three dimensional animation, are not eligible for this reward."

The above, in a simple nut shell, means that the medium of stop-motion may be used as a method, provided the results are not recognizable as animation. Stop-motion is a frame by frame system of photography whereby "aliveness" is given to a subject as a result of between frames manual movements, either separate drawings (cells) when applied to two dimension, or actual, physical movements given tediously and meticulously (if it is to be at all successful) to a three dimensional subject.

Prehistoric dinosaurs, "King Kong" or Japan's Toho "Godzilla" are examples. An ape must be "flesh and blood," however, and appear not like a jerk - pun intended.

Jerkiness is a noticeable fault which permeates most animation. In a straight animated subject, this characteristic is quite acceptable but we in Special Visual Effects frown deeply upon such unreality. If work of this nature is accomplished in smooth believability, it deserves and gets a shot at those gold-plated bronze statuettes. It must <u>never</u> disclose "animation" as the method used although animation was the method used!

Fairness demands at this point, a word of praise and printed, thanks to M.G.M.'s Barber Shop, or rather its residents. Bob Cox took over from "Slickum" many years ago as custodian of the Shoe Shine Emporium and News Stand. Bob "<u>reports</u>," and if you follow the dictates of wisdom, and open your ears, you will sense the pulse of the entire M.G.M. organization.

'Chief' Bob Crowfoot, <u>Chief</u> Barber, has a tomahawk and teepee ancestry, as his name implies. He fortunately controls any tomahawk tendencies, though at times I am positive it has to be difficult. Chief Crowfoot also reports! Joe Bullaro who crew cuts my grayish, whitish shock, does for me a Michaelangelo-ish job regularly that takes years off my age (it says here) - Joe reports too!

The real dope on all that is pertinent to the studio oozes from this department like a fast leak in the levee - no confidences betrayed, you understand - just the dope. Hence an alert Visual Effects man over- a period of just a few haircuts can generally find out, <u>does</u> <u>he</u>, or does he <u>not</u>!

An ear to the pavement should be at the least, a part time pastime, particularly in a profession equally as full of rumors as those generated in the gents room of a regular army cantonment. Where else would it be more pleasant to find out <u>everything</u>, than in a comfortable barber chair, listening to Joe's fettuccine expostulations, Molly's telephone manicure appointments, Chief Bobs' "Ughs" and "Hows," while getting the fine, fine print from the two gentlemen of the "shiner-shoes" department? Sell not short a studio barber shop, learners. Long live the one at M.G.M.. Through it at critical times I was able to test and determine certain solidities of the ground upon which I at times, was precariously perched.

As has been the custom, our closing paragraphs review sketchily the contents of the previous pages. This Chapter talks again of individuals and makes no apologies thereunto. It delves, in a layman's fashion, into the available benefits of Optical, many of which "fringe" one or more of the other Categories. It holds to the "trick" area and while crediting, it shows Optical bread and butter activities, as falling well outside of the Special Visual Effect perimeter.

Traveling Mattes and Split Screens were dissected and pieced together and we were critically severe and not too tolerant of the bug-a-boo of missed tolerances. Forgive us - We dwelt to some extent on the idea that Optical is often a Service Department for the other Effect Categories, and that their dependence on it is either a God-send, or becomes dark frustrated chagrin when results are found wanting. We mentioned the absolute necessity of utter compliance with conscientious effort in this demanding strata and we apologize for wrist slapping.

"Tom Thumb," "Boy," "Mlle. Fru Fru," and "Leo" were optical subjects. The mechanics of their togetherness has been sketched. A bit of Lon Chaney's makeup crept in and actors received an income tax relief boost! George Emerson's present Heavenly occupation was envisioned and the pal-ship between a chimp and a lion occupied a few sentences.

Then back to Optical; lightning, rays, snow, rain, thickness or not thickness, fog perspective; and when is a crowd not really a crowd.

Once more we stressed "audience." Don't lose them through taking too many economical or technical liberties. And we advised "post" effects, rather than the unchangeability of having included those effects in the original shooting of a scene requiring added effects. Mr. Slifer moved momentarily back in, and all the "scopes" and shapes, squeezes and idiosyncrasies of aspect ratios and their relationship to Optical, were researched.

Writers were placed on a pinnacle, good ones! And interferers were squashed, unqualified ones! Screen Credits, earned and unearned, were thoroughly chewed, the unearned ones spat out! And finally we switched to Animation, only in its swaddling clothes as far as the Effects Family is concerned. Its limited application was stressed.

We concluded with a special reference to the center of all studio news media, the Barber Shop. Which recalls an early tragedy of the writer's while holding down the "bass" position in a high school Barber Shop Quartette.- O.H.S., where else.

The incident has a bearing on the contents of this book because we recognize "audible" effects as of great importance in adding realism to our "visual" effects. A "silent" earthquake would lose its acceptance appeal. <u>Sound</u> is here to stay. It was John Gilbert's high tenor delivery which determined that he was <u>not</u> here to stay. Too bad too - a fine actor.

Our quartette occasionally appeared at luncheons. Rotary, Ad Club, Kiwanis, and we had a ring-ding arrangement of "Yaka-Hula--Hicky-doo!"

On this particular occasion Grant Sinclair, our tenor, blew a modest blast through his pitch pipe so that we would "key" as a team - What we could not know in advance was that the Rock Island passenger train, rumbling to a halt at a block away Depot, would let forth an immodest blast at the identical second of Grant's toot! It shrieked in several keys, none matching that blown by Mr. Sinclair, but regardless, "Yaka" took off - jarringly, in four separate keys!

Recovery, was an instant reaction. As I switched to the baritone's, E-Flat, he chose the second tenor's, E-Sharp while that melody carrier, Howard Main, dropped simultaneously to a C-Natural in time to miss Don Danver's switch to my original D-Something-or-other.

The Rotarians, as is their wont, were charitable, although I recall a few of the more portly, shaking silently behind muffling napkins.

At about the fourth line of the first noise we shin-kicked ourselves into silence, and pitch-piped ourselves off to a new start.

No straying locomotive messed us up this time and applause burst the rafters of the old Skirvin Hotel as we concluded, proving a point.

We as four Visual Effects, fuzzy cheeked with a pimple or two (I am sure) were not such a much. With inadequate sound, by courtesy of a never-to-be-forgiven engineer, we were just beyond terrible. But that second try, with the "audible" hitting harmoniously on all four, saved us from a fate which to the old fashioned teenager was almost unbearable - mortification and hurt pride through failure. Old fashioned? That's unkind and not entirely honest. We had punks too. It just seems in retrospect that the ratio was perhaps less than today's sandled, unshaved, smarties.

In any event, we had a second try. You Visual Effectors may not. So work closely with your Sound Editor, and he with you, so that the roar of a tornado is melodious or at least not out of key with that which it represents. Real good and capable gents, these Special Audible Effects people. I have used them often, as previously indicated I believe, in the Chapters on Miniatures, to help sell a test or a shot of some slam-bang subject which silently shown, would wilt. And they are of course indispensable in the finished, released product.

END OF CHAPTER NINE

Cairo, MGM Production #1248, Released 1942, AAG Contribution: Special Effects.

FORBIDDEN PLANET (1956) PRODUCTION #1671

Int. Cube Vertical-Scale 3/8"=1" - Various materials were used including screen, plastics, glass, wood, met, etc., using various colored lighting effects. A glass and wood energy car moved up and down in a metal track. Various angles were shot and stairs were made for process hots on bridge. The actors were later double printed onto bridge in a metal track. Various angles were shot and stairs were made for process shots on bridge. The actors were later double printed onto bridge.

Forbidden Planet - Approach to Altair four in seven stages from 6" sphere to C.U. of 20' disc. Shot as B.G. for viewscope. Scotch lite used for stars on backing.

Forbidden Planet ship in front of Scotch-lite lacquer sprayed on masonite board for background galaxies. Three space ships made: 2'11" - 4'2" - 8'4".

16-P Revised

Full scale set with painted backing. Ext desert and space ship

Forbidden Planet Space Ship re-used for Twilight Zone episode *Death Ship*. Stage floor painted black with black cloth backing. Scotch light starts. Light ring on camera - F.G. Planet painted cut out. Space ship rigged on mobile car. Filmed with <u>inverted</u> camera.

(Below left) The actual miniature shuttle driven by Robby (Right) Yours truly with the same.

"OPTICAL AND ANIMATION"

20-C (1)

An example of preliminary oddities and diversifications which may fall into the Effects-man's lap, follows. These, picked at random from our "Forbidden Planet" notes, show advance method determinations. The sketches are two of many depicting what an 'Id' might look like and how he would function as he 'swallows' his human counterpart, Morbius. The 'Id' finally selected and shown was the product of Josh Meador, Disney Studios, animated and optically printed into selected scenes.

"FORBIDDEN PLANET"   August 15, 1954
RANDOM NOTES - GENERAL

1. Disposal-Incinerator-Unit appears from floor of wall---
   Demonstrate by tossing dish, stick, rock, etc. Split screen Robby, ordered to hold hand in area, disappears in 24 frames, called back, then ordered to eliminate self, starts to obey. (Makes new hand---stop motion, spin and lap.)

2. Scotch-Lite Lacquer fluid---highly reflective.

3. Garden and birds---erect set early, keep birds in separate aviary attached to set---girl feeds daily in set as birds released to establish rapport. inter-cut close shots feeding---birds must get used to Robby as well as girl. Tiger---split screen (birds and deer have exited) close up contact shots with double. (Sc. 33)

Sample of Special Effects Department notes for *Forbidden Planet* - A.A.G.

20-C (2)

4. Miniature process plates for View Scope, camera stationary---use several plate glass sheets, butt joints 8'0" height---width necessary for panavision---opaque glass with black-purple, scratch stars, provide one sphere (ball-stock) 3", one 5", one 7", one 12", build one 3/4 sphere 6'0" in diameter alta and moons---move alta for ship movement.

5. Landing l.s. from circling to hovering, in reverse, small scale ship---medium shot of landing, larger scale ship---disturbed earth (not dust cloud as from rockets) cartoon or ?, effects from ship to earth. Shoot inside if sky treatment dark. Stars, possibly dots of scotch light reflecting light source at camera.

6. Jeep---3 wheel---Robby in rear becomes motive power, rods from car to Robby---exhaust from Robby---Robby raised and lowered into position---bubble canopy raises, lowers automatically and without visible support.

"FORBIDDEN PLANET"   September 7, 1954
METHODS - 'PLASTIC EDUCATOR'

Sc. 61   Plastic Educator - Altaira appearing sequence--- method.

Split-screen, traveling matte and lap dissolving of separate effect shots

Steps

1. From tied down camera, or cameras, including Morbius and others if desired and allowing in set-up, place for "split" and area to back up "effects." Shoot entire footage required for completed scene. Play light effect on Morbius from glowing panel on table top

2. From same tied down set-up or set-ups shoot
   a. Panel beginning to glow and glowing
   b. Drop from above through funnel small beads or BB shot onto spot where figure is to appear, until considerable pile has formed and spread out to cover portion of table panel. This film to be used in reverse.
   c. Electric impulses from circular area around spot, <u>into</u> spot.
   d. Substitute at center of spot, a small revolving spindle, projecting through table top and progressing up and down from 6" to 18" and to which material is fastened (will experiment) which when axis revolves at varying speeds and heights will change form, density and animation. (Perhaps multi-exposure of two or more of these shots and shapes will benefit.)
   e. Place plastic block or glass globe of sufficient size to encompass 18" figure of altaira and shoot sufficient footage. No effects other than panel glowing.
   3. Shoot Altaira against blue backing. Full figure at angle (degrees down, etc.) matching tied down camera set-ups at plastic educator. Check with optical whether should shoot to avoid reducing.

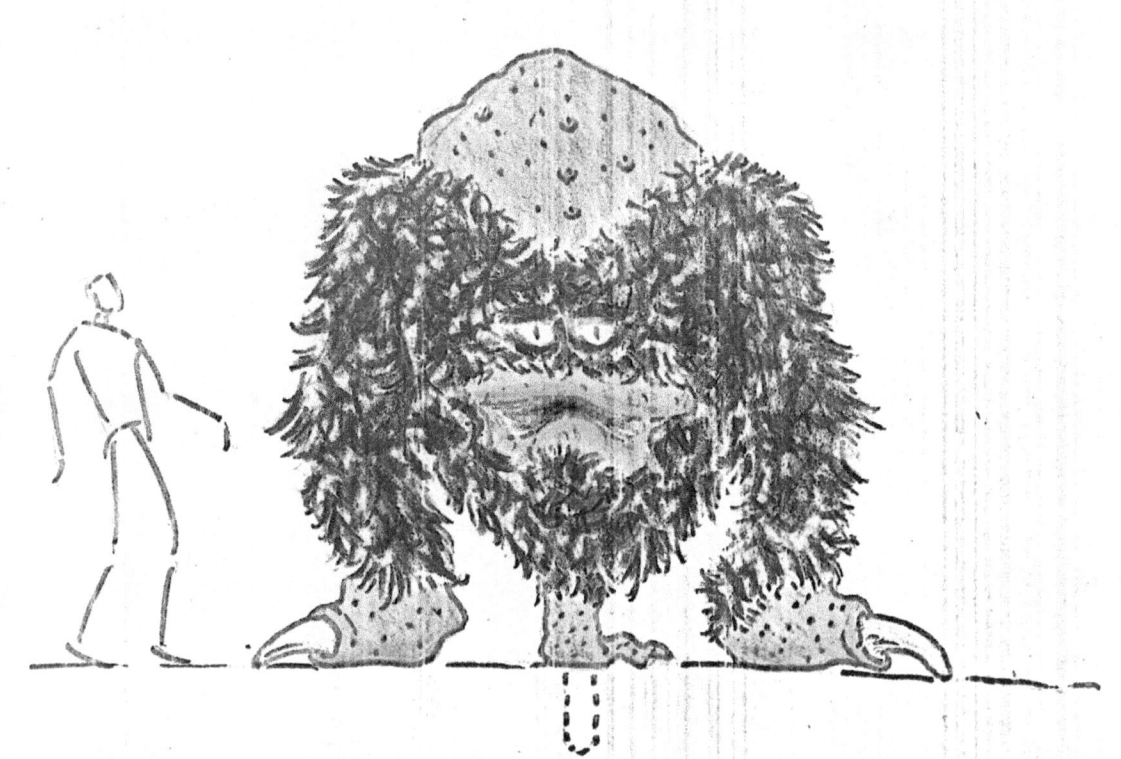

NOTE: 'ID' CHARMS MORBIUS ALL SAME SNAKE — MOUTH SLOWLY OPENS. MORBIUS HELPLESS. SUDDEN LUNGE AND GULP. MORBIUS BYE-BYE! — OR TOAD LIKE TONGUE DARTS OUT, ADHERES TO MORBIUS, DRAWS HIM INTO MOUTH (SANS SALT AND PEPPER)

'ID' SWALLOWS MORBIUS — BOTH DISAPPEAR — MORBIUS APPEARS INERT A FEW SECONDS LATER — MAN INSIDE OPERATES 'ID'

a.a.g.

```
FORM 48
DATE Feb. 14, 15, 16, 17, 21 March 1, 1955     Estimated Construction and Special Effects
                                                Preparation...................................   NO STILLS
PRODUCTION........1671..........                Special Camera
                                                Mounts........................................
SET........Job 99018-1..........                Operation.....................................
STAGE......14 - 12..............                Elect. Operation..............................
                                                Add and Changes...............................
PICTURE....FORBIDDEN PLANET (1956)              Total Approp..................................
TITLE OF MINIATURE   Experimental Work          Final Cost    16,105.60
```

Details of Min. Set—Area..   No. of Buildings or Units.................

Scale...   Day...........Night...........Dawn...........Sunset......

Backing..

REMARKS   Experimental work was done on the Krell Door including various
          materials and light effects   Experimented with holes in the
          backing with a reflected curtain behind also with small bulbs
          and with scotch lite.   Various methods were tried out on
          the Krell furnace   Krell cube and the rigging for the space
          ship

Dressing and Min. Props.

CONSTRUCTION

Total Construction Cost.........................Total Special Effects............................

OPERATION   **Construction Dept. Daily Cost**

Average Crew		Foreman	Mechanics	Grips	Laborers
	Morning				
	Afternoon				
	Night				

Total Operation Cost...

ELECTRICAL   Average Load.......................................

Wind Machines and Fans...

Average Daily Crew..

Total Operating Cost...

CAMERA DEPARTMENT

Cameraman..

Extra Cameras...

Lens..

Speed..

Approx No. of Feet of Film Printed..

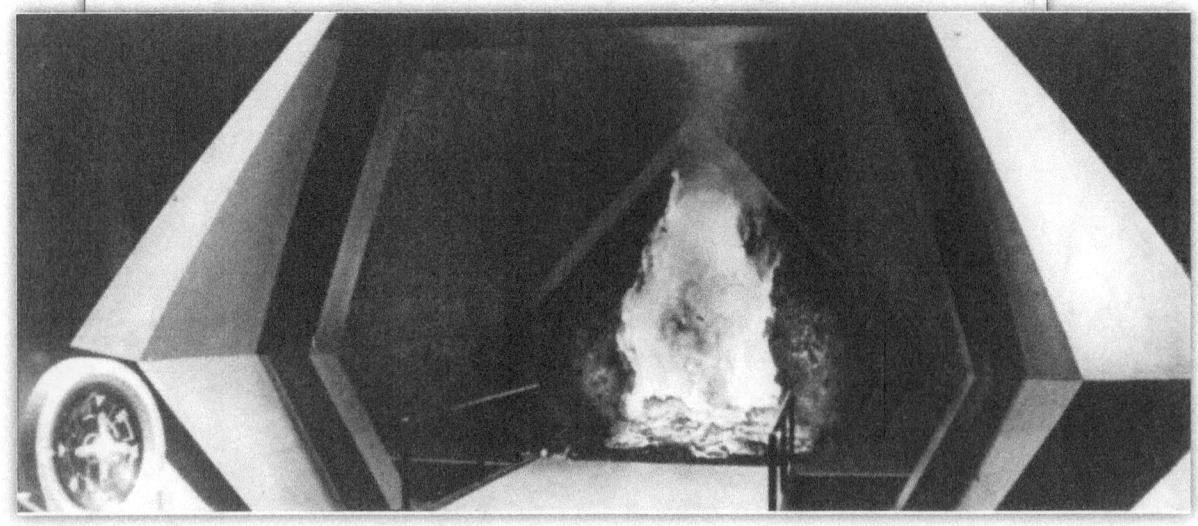

CHAPTER NINE

```
FORM 48
DATE June 30, July 1,5,8,12,14,15,19,    Estimated Construction and Special Effects
                                 1955                Preparation............7950.00
                                                    Special Camera
PRODUCTION........1671................      Det MIN  Mounts............4000.00

SET.................80.................              Operation...........8500.00

STAGE...............14.................              Elect. Operation......500.00
                                             Sp. Eff  Add and Changes.......500.00
PICTURE......FORBIDDEN PLANET....                    Total Approp........21,450.00

TITLE OF MINIATURE  INT. KRELL DOOR TO LAB   Final Cost          10,691.00
```

Details of Min. Set—Area............................ No. of Buildings or Units............

Scale........4" - 1'-0"................   Day.........Night.........Dawn.........Sunset......

Backing...

REMARKS   Various Stages of Door
    1. Rough and smooth plastic panel, rear projected light Effects
    2. Sheet metal panel heated into incadescence with a gas
        and air furnace from behind
    3. 1/2 " zercon metal applied to asbestos board and ignited
        This was done in 3 stages from a solid door to a full
Dressing and Min. Props.   opening

CONSTRUCTION

Total Construction Cost........1,139.00.........Total Special Effects......................

                                                        1 Painter
OPERATION   **Construction Dept. Daily Cost**

Average Crew		Foreman	Mechanics	Grips	Laborers
Morning		1	6	2	1
Afternoon					
Night					

Total Operation Cost..........6,908.00..

ELECTRICAL   Average Load..............................

Wind Machines and Fans......................

Average Daily Crew..............5.............

Total Operating Cost..........2,644.00.....   Plain Door
                                                    Hot steel
CAMERA DEPARTMENT   3 Holes
Cameraman.. Final Stage
Extra Cameras.....................................
Lens..
Speed...
Approx. No. of Feet of Film Printed...............

"OPTICAL AND ANIMATION"

```
FORM 40
DATE    June 6, 8, 1955                              Estimated Construction and Special Effects
                                                       Preparation.............2650.00
PRODUCTION......1671............   Spec. Eff         Special Camera
                                                       Mounts.................125.00
SET...............75..............                   Operation................650.00
STAGE.............14..............                   Elect. Operation.........125.00
                                                     Add and Changes..................
PICTURE.....FORBIDDEN PLANET......                   Total Approp............3550.00
TITLE OF MINIATURE   INT. KRELL FURNACE              Final Cost...............2186.00
```

Details of Min. Set—Area............................ No. of Buildings or Units..............
Scale... Day..........Night..........Dawn..........Sunset.
Backing..

REMARKS   Colored Jells attached to lighted rotating cones, reflected
          onto a translucent screen and photographed from the reverse
          side

Dressing and Min. Props.

CONSTRUCTION

Total Construction Cost.......1004.00........Total Special Effects..........................
                                                                              1 Painter

OPERATION   **Construction Dept. Daily Cost**

Average Crew		Foreman	Mechanics	Grips	Laborers
	Morning	1	5	3	1
	Afternoon				
	Night				

Total Operation Cost............784.00

ELECTRICAL   Average Load...
       Wind Machines and Fans...
       Average Daily Crew.............7
       Total Operating Cost..........398.00

CAMERA DEPARTMENT
     Cameraman...
     Extra Cameras...

CHAPTER NINE   276

FORM 46

DATE June 7, 8, 1955

PRODUCTION 1671

SET 73

STAGE 14

PICTURE FORBIDDEN PLANET

TITLE OF MINIATURE INT. TUBE BACKGROUND

Estimated Construction and Special Effects
Preparation 400.00
Special Camera Mounts
Operation 400.00
Elect. Operation 125.00
Add and Changes
Total Approp. 925.00
Final Cost 1251.00

Details of Min. Set—Area

Scale

Backing

No. of Buildings or Units

Day........Night........Dawn........Sunset

REMARKS Set consisted of a 4'-6" dia. elect. driven, revolving glass painted black with a clear pattern in a spiral design starting from the center This glass revolved in front of a stationary glass painted black with a clear X design approx 3" on the edge dimishing to zero at the center of the glass. The glasses were lit from behind see Enlargement

Dressing and Min. Props.

CONSTRUCTION

Total Construction Cost 814.00 Total Special Effects

OPERATION Construction Dept. Daily Cost
Average Crew

Morning	
Afternoon	
Night	

Total Operation Cost 274.00

ELECTRICAL Average Load
Wind Machines and Fans
Average Daily Crew
Total Operating Cost 163.00

CAMERA DEPARTMENT
Cameraman Fabian
Extra Cameras
Lens
Speed
Approx No. of Feet of Film Printed

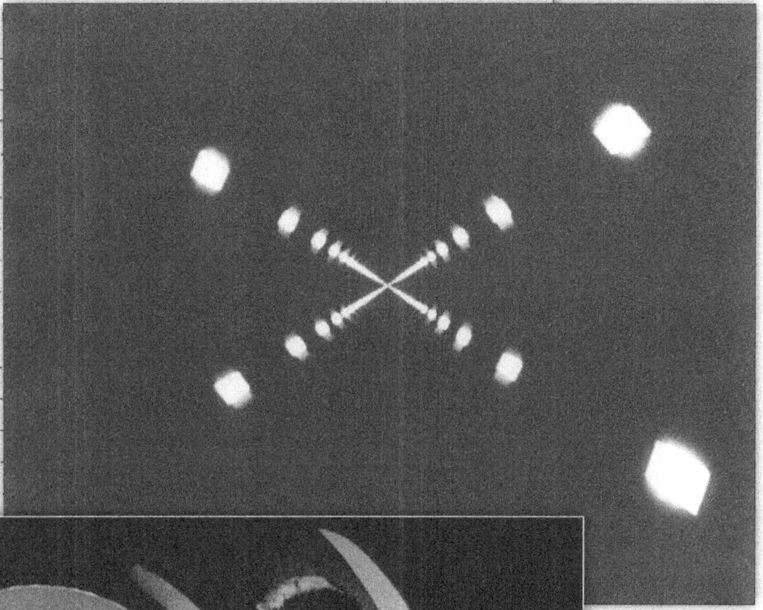

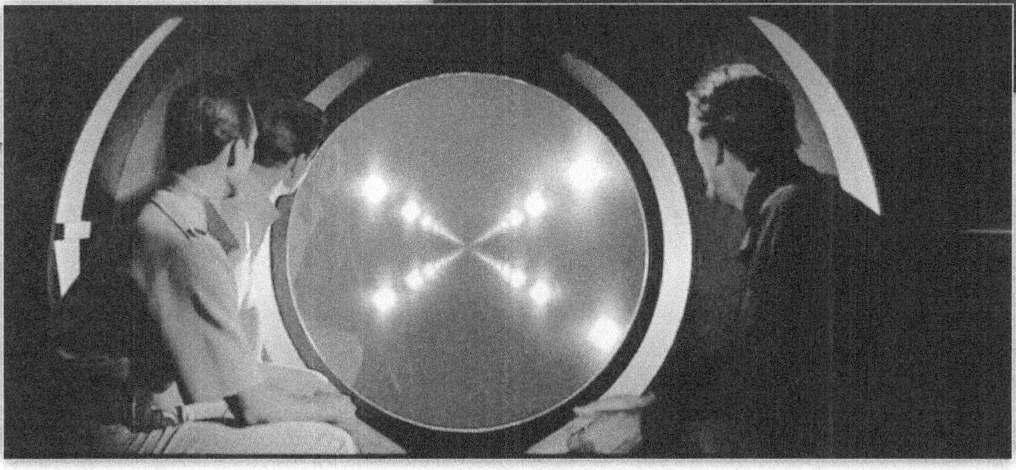

"OPTICAL AND ANIMATION"

FORM 48

DATE May 13, 14, 16, 17, 20, 1955

PRODUCTION 1671   Det. MIN

SET 72

STAGE Lot 3 - Tank
                                   Spec. Eff
PICTURE FORBIDDEN PLANET
                Ext. Altair Ship Landing
TITLE OF MINIATURE Dust Backgrounds

Estimated Construction and Special Effects
Preparation............13,450.00
Special Camera Mounts............6500.00
Operation............4000.00
Elect. Operation............200.00
Add and Changes............350.00
Total Approp............24,500.00
Final Cost............29,859.00

Details of Min. Set—Area............   No. of Buildings or Units............
Scale............   Day............Night............Dawn............Sunset............
Backing............

REMARKS Set in Tank. Painted Sky Backing Foreground set raised
Dressed with Staff Rocks Background staff rocks and
painted profiles ship hung on wires from overhead
carriage remotely controlled Jeep pulled over ground with
wire in tubular track. Backgrounds were made against
backing and F.G. moving rocks on cars, camera moving in
opposite direction - various cuts dissolved together for
final B.G.

Dressing and Min. Props:

CONSTRUCTION   Det. MIN   410.00
Total Construction Cost......22,610.00......Total Special Effects............

OPERATION   Construction Dept. Daily Cost   1 Painter
Average Crew

	Foreman	Mechanics	Grips	Laborers
Morning	1	8	3	1
Afternoon				
Night				

Total Operation Cost......5,554.00

ELECTRICAL   Average Load............
Wind Machines and Fans............
Average Daily Crew......2 Elect 1 Generator Man
Total Operating Cost......1,285.00

CAMERA DEPARTMENT
Cameraman............Fabian
Extra Cameras............
Lens............

CHAPTER NINE

FORM 48

DATE..	Estimated Construction and Special Effects Preparation............................
PRODUCTION 1671	Special Camera Mounts............................
SET 70	Operation............................
STAGE..	Elect. Operation............................
	Add and Changes............................
PICTURE.... FORBIDDEN PLANET	Total Approp..... 6500.00
TITLE OF MINIATURE SPACE SHIP	Final Cost 3258.00

Details of Min. Set—Area..   No. of Buildings or Units............................

Scale..   Day............Night............Dawn............Sunset......

Backing..

REMARKS   Three space ships made   2'11" - 4'2" - 8'4" included in estimate of Set #72

Dressing and Min. Props.

CONSTRUCTION

                              Detached MIN 3175.00
   Total Construction Cost............................Total Special Effects............ 83.00

OPERATION   Construction Dept. Daily Cost

Average Crew		Foreman	Mechanics	Grips	Laborers
	Morning				
	Afternoon				
	Night				

   Total Operation Cost............................

ELECTRICAL   Average Load............................
   Wind Machines and Fans............................
   Average Daily Crew............................
   Total Operating Cost............................

CAMERA DEPARTMENT
   Cameraman............................
   Extra Cameras............................

```
FORM 48     30 shooting days
DATE  4-8-55 to 7-27-55   1955              Estimated Construction and Special Effects
                                               Preparation............9650
PRODUCTION........1671.........     Det. MIN  Special Camera
                                               Mounts.................1100.
    SET.............71.............           Operation..............5150.
    STAGE...........14............            Elect. Operation.......1250
                                              Add and Changes........7675.
PICTURE........FORBIDDEN PLANET               Total Approp...........24,825.
                    Ext. Outer Space Ship
TITLE OF MINIATURE  Altair #4                 Final Cost.............46,134.
```

Details of Min. Set—Area.............................. No. of Buildings or Units...............

Scale.. Day.........Night.........Dawn.........Sunset......

Backing..

REMARKS   Various shots of space ships against outer space backing
          using 2'-0" & 4'-0" ships in various attitudes with and
          without spheres. B.G's for viewscope Approach to Altair
          four in seven stages from 6" sphere to C.U. of 20'-0"
          disc. shot as B.G's for viewscope Altair Sun, eclipse &
          explosion of Altair four for viewscope Scotch lite used
          for stars on backing

Dressing and Min. Props.

CONSTRUCTION

Total Construction Cost......7056.00............Total Special Effects.........73.00........

OPERATION   **Construction Dept. Daily Cost**   1 Painter

Average Crew

	Foreman	Mechanics	Grips	Laborers
Morning	1	6	2	1
Afternoon				
Night				

Total Operation Cost..........24,501.00...............

ELECTRICAL   Average Load...
Wind Machines and Fans..................................
Average Daily Crew..............6 Elec..........................
Total Operating Cost............14,504..........................

CAMERA DEPARTMENT
Cameraman.......Max Fabian - 1 Operator - 2 Assts.
Extra Cameras...........................
Lens...................................

(Above) The 'United Planets Cruiser C-57D' set reference still. Photo courtesy of Bob Burns.

(Below) Funeral scene matte painting layout. Photo courtesy of Profiles in History. (Bottom) Final composite scene.

"OPTICAL AND ANIMATION"

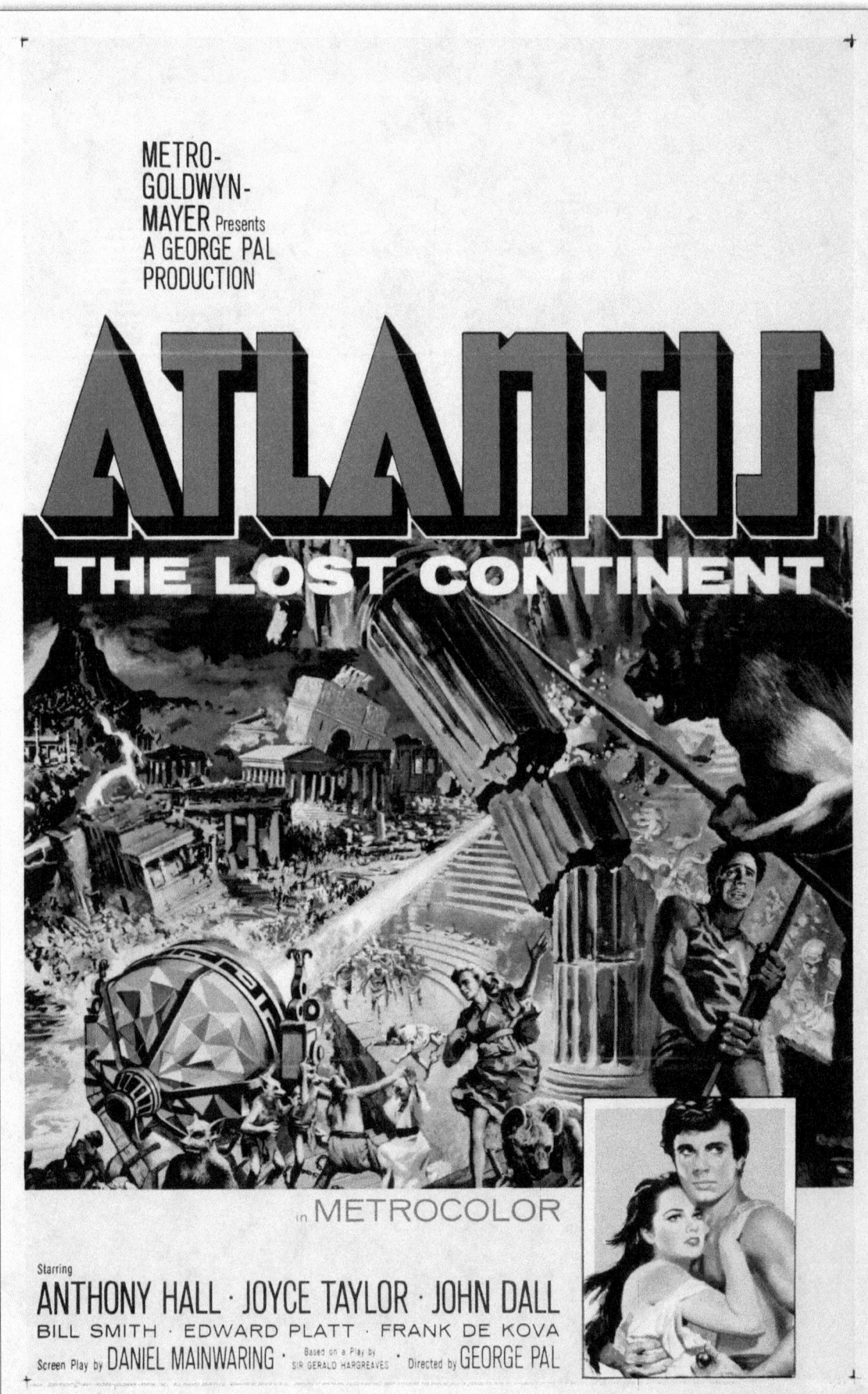

Atlantis, The Lost Continent, MGM Production #1767, Released 1961, AAG Contribution:. Special Effects.

CHAPTER TEN

~

"PROCESS THE WHYS AND HOWS"

One of many *Tarzan's Secret Treasure* Process shot setups. Note the cautionary statement as screens have been previously marred by the arrant fling of a paint brush. Courtesy - The Academy Margaret Herrick Library.

An old nursery rhyme, "Ten little Indians standing in a line. One went home and then there were nine." seems to me to be an appropriate way of introducing our last little Indian, "Process."

A research reference into "Stokes' Wonder Book of Mother Goose" in order to double check a childhood memory of those little "Indians" uncovered the startling fact that it originated as "Ten little Nigger boys standing, etc.," a word now frowned upon and rightfully so. I am sure however at the time of its writing, none other than respect was intended. But that's what Hell is reported to be paved with, "good intentions." What a pity is this racial turmoil and what a pity we can't speed evolution. Legislated cures, rightly or wrongly, are difficult for many well meaning people to swallow. Prohibition was legislated, remember? Some day, I hope Reader's Digest will carry one of their "Most Unforgettable Character" articles, entitled "Jimmy Walker," authored by this writer. Jimmy was a man who could neither read nor write, but whose remarkable traits of good judgment, intelligence, kindness, loyalty commanded top respect and true affection from all who knew him. Our children adored him and when he left us, it was a major personal loss to all of us. Jimmy was happy and proud of his position, I know, and returned our affection.

He was well aware of his endeared place as a part of our household. It would never have occurred to him or to us, however, for him to have been included as an intimate member of our, or our friends', social gatherings. No conscious lines drawn - just custom and tradition. Time and time only, not laws, will change the deep down chemistry of many people's innermost feelings. I think mostly this becomes a two-way street, though agitators as well as some really conscientious do-gooders, would have us believe otherwise. Christianity must, of course, prevail but so must freedom of choice. Jimmy Walker would understand this and so would thousands of others of his wonderful ilk. I spoke of "moderation" early. Let us pray that this philosophy, as well as patience, also becomes a two-way street.

Rear Projection Process, the last of our five-plus-one, Special Visual Effect Categories, is another form of composite photography. As in Traveling Mattes, a foreground and a background are combined into one completed whole. But unlike the "matte" procedure, the wedding is instantaneous. Very simply, and at least sketchily known to many, a previously photographed scene is rear projected onto a translucent screen and re-photographed from the front of the screen which includes whatever foreground set and action is required.

Perhaps we should lead off with a report written to Robert O'Brien, President of M.G.M., addressed to his New York Office early in 1962, as a result of his inquiry, "Just what is this 'Laced Process' I hear about?" And preceding this, portions of a May 1953 communication to various people at M.G.M. who rub shoulders with, or might be directly involved in, this useful tool, "Process." The 1953 epistle relates particularly to Color Process, though its application to all Process is obvious.

5-16-53   A. A. Gillespie

Notes on Rear-projection Color and Black and White Process. For the consideration of all studio personnel directly and indirectly involved in the problem.

Foreword

The purpose of this letter is two-fold. First, to familiarize the reader with the overall problem, and second to stress the necessity of adhering as closely as possible to each "step" involved.

Certainly a more thorough understanding of this medium plus all-out cooperation from every department related, will greatly improve the ultimate results.

1. The Problem

The background becomes a dupe, the foreground is original negative — the original is combined with the dupe in the finished Process shot which can and does accentuate the "dupe" quality of the background. While this applies to black and white Process, as well as color, the problem in color Process is infinitely greater.

2. The Answer

To obtain acceptable Color Process results, the following "steps" must be adhered to by every department and individual involved. If there is a miss in any one or more of these steps the result suffers proportionately.

3. The Steps

(A) The original background must be photographed properly — sufficient light and proper light direction — exposure — focus — lens selection — setup — clear foreground — etc., are even more critical than in straight production shots. Backgrounds must not be shot "when we get around to it," but should be given every preference possible because of the "dupe" problem stressed in Paragraph #1 and the requirements listed above in this paragraph.

(B) Laboratory — Negative development and Background Prints of proper density, contrast and color. If negative is not within the proper range, exposure-wise, it must be so reported as soon as known so that background may be reshot. Background prints made from acceptable negative must fall within extremely small tolerance as to the type of print required for best color reproduction.

(C) Process Projection — Critical focus and superimposition — amperage within specified range of carbons — no arc flicker — absolute maintenance of this precision piece of equipment to avoid production delay and insure best possible projection.

(D) Process Cameraman — Responsible for combining photographically, foreground and projected background. Light balance — focus balance between foreground and screen — checks screen focus and superimposition. It must be recognized that in the entire operation of Process, this step is the most difficult, and sufficient time must be allotted in order to obtain the heretofore mentioned "acceptable" result. This is the step which combines original negative with the background which becomes a dupe.

(E) Process assistant — To pre-line when possible and test when necessary — responsible for effect equipment being on set and its operation — to assist Director in all ways possible,

> segregation of backgrounds, instructions to camera operators as to camera movement, advising Directors as to limitations of the Process medium — to facilitate the operation of the Process Departments' functions and contact all other departments related to the operation — to work in close cooperation with the Production department as to schedule, stage space, etc.
>
> (F) <u>The Director</u> — Should thoroughly understand the purpose and the limitations of Process, and avoid violations of those limitations. Should weigh the alternate method of obtaining his shots (attempting to do them in reality) as to cost, time and possibility, against the cost, time and practicability of Process, in order to more thoroughly accept the time required and technique involved in shooting Process.
>
> (G) <u>Art Director</u> — Responsible for Process lay outs and all sets involved, which include car bodies, correct painting of mechanical horses, etc., etc., or proper layouts when no foreground set is involved — will check with Process department at layout stage for correct lens combinations and throw — should include on layouts and cover costwise, any effect equipment required — responsible in conjunction with Process department for advance layouts and information pertinent to the shooting of the original backgrounds.
>
> (H) <u>Production Department</u> and all Production personnel — Must be thoroughly familiar with the problem of Process and facilitate at all times procedures in line with the above-listed "steps."
>
> (I) <u>Studio Management</u> — Assistance as to equipment and the mechanical and physical phases of Process from Projection Booth to Camera.
>
> 4. Conclusion
>
> Paragraph #1, The Problem, and paragraph #2, The Answer, cannot be too strongly stressed in order that a clarification of the steps involved and the results expected, be thoroughly understood by those actively connected to any phase of Process and those who normally only view the results. It must be realized that, presuming <u>all</u> steps have been properly fulfilled, the net result will approach perfection only to a limited degree. Although it is repetitious I wish to again stress in conclusion the basic reason for the problem. It is simply that the background becomes a dupe and the foreground becomes original negative, the combination of which, causes the background to degenerate somewhat in color quality. It is, however, reasonable to expect that within this degree of limitation, and provided all "steps" are effectively followed, a satisfactorily acceptable result will be obtained.

Years before this date, the old Black and White three by four aspect ratio Process had reached a very sophisticated level of use and excellence. Mickey Rooney had "*Andy Hardy*-ed" through many of those highly successful vehicles, which often contained several thousand feet of Process. A "*Test Pilot*-ing" Clark Gable flew the "Drake Bullet" all the way to Kansas through hellish weather, when a forced landing on a lovely lady's daddy's farm, resulted in his introduction to Myrna Loy — all on an M.G.M. stage, This particular movie was crammed with Process, its use, enabling shots of tremendous importance and consequence to the story, to be obtained practically and safely. Some of these will be detailed later in this chapter. Most of them dovetailed with one or more of the other Effect Categories.

Further analyses of the "steps" outlined above from (A) to (I), follow.

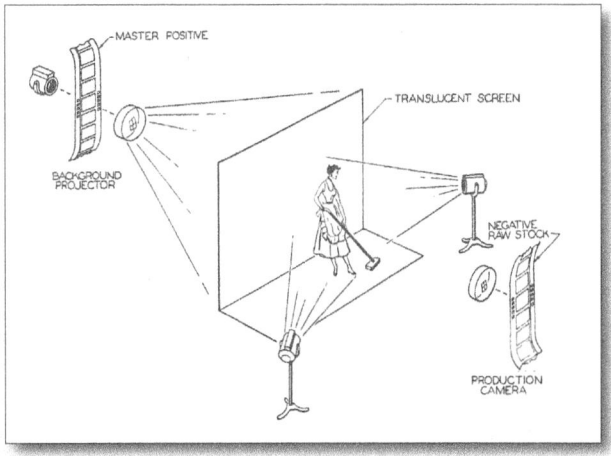

Diagram of the projection background process. Journal of the SMPTE Volume 63; Principles of Special Photographic Effects.

> (A) The original Process background, or "plate" as it is sometimes termed, must be photographed properly. Just what does "properly" mean? Focus and correct exposure are of course elementary. Certain mechanics, however, should be stressed and they are plainly stated in our M.G.M. "General Procedure" instructions that are distributed to all units assigned to the job of "shooting" Process backgrounds. They are reproduced below for the reader's edification.
>
> GENERAL PROCEDURE
> PROCESS MOTION PICTURE BACKGROUNDS
> AND STEREO SLIDES
>
> <u>1. MOTION PICTURE BACKGROUNDS FOR STANDARD 3 x 4. WIDE</u>
> <u>SCREEN AND 35mm CINEMSCOPE OR PANAVISION PICTURES.</u>

A. LIGHT DIRECTION

Front or front cross light is essential for all backgrounds day or day for night. Exceptions - Effect shots such as sunsets, moonpath on water, etc.

B. LENS

For Standard 3 x 4 or Wide Screen Pictures

50mm wherever practical, particularly on architectural subjects. Exceptions side and three quarter angles for moving backgrounds, car, train, wagon, horses, etc., should be shot with a 40mm or a 35mm lens. Also subject matter which is countryside, ocean, sky and clouds, etc., may be shot with 40mm or 35mm if 50mm lens is not practical.

For 35mm Cinemascope or Panavision Pictures

Long focal length anamorphic lenses, 75mm, 100mm and 150mm wherever practical. Exceptions — side and three quarter angles for moving backgrounds, car, etc., should be shot with no longer focal length lens than a 75mm. Shorter focal lengths of 50mm or 40mm may be used if the subject matter is countryside, ocean, sky, clouds, etc., and, though not by choice, also for vehicle backgrounds if narrow roads present a lack of sufficient 'clear foreground'.

C. LENS HEIGHT AND TILT UP OR DOWN

Height depends upon requirement. Normal level modern automobile backgrounds 4'6" from road bed. Vary height depending on vehicle used, lower for small car, higher for trucks etc. Horse backgrounds approximately shoulder height of rider above ground.

In the event tilt up or down is required, drop lens height when tilting up and raise lens height when tilting down. Best practice is to set Background camera with actor or group as intended to shoot in Process at studio, visualizing imaginary position of screen. Move people out and shoot. Degree of tilt up or down should be noted on slate and background report.

D. CLEAR FOREGROUND

In every instance relationship of background to foreground shot in Process at Studio should be considered. Nothing should be closer to the camera when shooting backgrounds than the imaginary plane of the screen. Exceptions — Certain types of backgrounds may be shot when an object, such as an approaching train, may come beyond the imaginary screen plane. These individual cases should be discussed with the Process Department.

E. CAMERA SETUP

In all cases a rock steady setup. When on camera car or dolly a smooth road or track is necessary. Avoid vibration by using jacks on camera. Watch tire air pressure when using camera car. Low pressure smooths "bumps."

F. CAMERA SHUTTER

For pan, tilt or moving shots do not cut camera shutter unless otherwise instructed.

G. GENERAL NOTE

Until further notice, or unless otherwise directed, all backgrounds for 35mm Cinemascope or Panavision productions will be shot with a Cinemascope or Cinemascope-type lens on the camera. For Standard 3 x 4 or Wide Screen Pictures, the old 3 x 4 Process Background Procedure is to be followed. 65mm backgrounds, straight or anamorphed, may be substituted for the above but only on direct orders from the Process Department. Traveling Matte or Blue Backing backgrounds should be shot in whatever medium is being used on the picture for which they are shot.

2. STEREO SLIDE BACKGROUNDS

A. Rules applying to Motion Picture backgrounds as outlined in paragraphs A, C, D, and E above, apply also to stereo slides.

B. Camera and Lens - Use a 4x5 camera with an 8" lens for any architectural subject. Shorter focal length lenses may be used for general subjects but avoid shorter focal length lenses where architectural subjects are involved whenever possible.

C. Film - At present - 4x5 Ektacolor negative is to be used.

D. Shooting procedure — Each stereo slide background will be covered by shooting three negatives. Two normal exposure and one exposed, one stop over. Include in one of the normal exposures an 8 x 10 inch gray card in a representative light. These cards are standard Eastman items and may be purchased at Eastman Kodak stores.

GENERAL NOTE:

Both Motion Picture cameramen and still cameramen should meet with Process Department, Production Department, Art Director, and First or Second Unit Director before going out to shoot slides or backgrounds, to thoroughly understand and review the above-listed procedures.

So much for the shooting of Process backgrounds. There are always those exceptions, the ones which prove the rule, but general adherence to these procedures will pay consistent dividends. The choice of lenses suggested does not necessarily apply to "Laced Process" as will be seen when this revolutionary system of "background" and "foreground" merging is elucidated.

The above "background plate" practices, and the preceding list of instructions, cover the (A) step in our "General Notes" and "Steps."

Step (B), Laboratory. Very little to add to tills "B" note. Top lab procedures again are elementary, except that in the case of Process plates the tolerances of steadiness, cleanliness and evenness, are much more stringent. Faults of any nature in a background print, are magnified out of acceptable proportion when rephotographed in the final welding of "back to front." A scratch, possibly passable in a straight cut, will likely glare at the viewer in Process. Dirt can become a "snow storm" as can excessive grain. Uneven laboratory processing delivers a much more noticeable, annoying fluctuation on a Process Screen than in a straight cut, particularly as it contrasts with the to be expected evenness of the "foreground." Hence just good housekeeping is not enough – wives from Holland should be imported, the kind who could serve completely asepticized meals on their door stoops without fear of any soiled little bacteriums intruding. Let the White Knight on his White Charger point his White Lance to no avail, within the confines of the Process plate department of all laboratories.

Color distortion of color plates is of equal importance. The formula is determined usually through a trial and error series of tests. A different breed of gremlins than those heretofore mentioned, delight in squirming their rainbow-hued selves into Color Process. A knowledgeable filter-pack "chooser" in a laboratory is a must if these active little imps are to be even moderately squelched. Process systems, projectors, screens, optics, light sources, contribute their own peculiar palettes which vary widely as the ingredients vary. The color temperature when read through lenses of different manufacture with a constant light source, may and probably will show a different reading on a Kelvin meter. And different readings through Process Screens of diverse manufacture will also result.

A particular studio's equipment will have its own characteristics ~ hence the unscientific stumble and recover method of try, try, again. Once reasonably established, that key-gentleman in the lab will compensate for equipment idiosyncrasies by color distorting the backgrounds which will, in theory, "flit" all gremlins. Make a bosom pal of this technician, students buy his coffee occasionally and send him Christmas cards, but, and seriously, work together with him and everything else being equal, you may yet wear limousines.

(C) Process Projection. Precision Equipment ~ precise and devoted handling. Microscopic misses enlarge to mountainous megatheres. The whole works can really be messed through bad projection, which is the reason our remarks in "C" paragraph seem so kindergarten ~ "absolute maintenance of this precision piece of equipment" ~ of course! Fortunate indeed is the Process operation on any Lot which includes a dedicated, clear-eyed Head Process Projectionist who is as enamored of his Projectors as is Slifer of his Printers.

Clint Watson has been ours for many years and he has had expert "back-ups" operating each individual booth. He knows the anatomy of our machines from toe to smoke stacks as effectually as anyone in the business, A steady and speedy trouble-shooter whose diagnoses are generally bull's-eyes, and speaking of eyes, most always clear-eyed! Thanks, Clint – you're good, and there have been others of close adeptness and loyalty, George Brown (long, long ago), Lew Dye, both at one time Process Projection Heads, and many of their compatriots, who share my gratitude.

And now with this well-intended and sincere boost, may I suggest that traits of temperament occasionally flare in occasional individuals in this profession, which would rival a Tallulah Bankhead tantrum. Just suggest on a Monday morning that someone could focus faster and better, or inject a bit more speed into threading or trimming, and a cold – cold? – frigid glance of scorn may icicle its way right through your questioning eyeballs. Not always – but on some Monday mornings and occasionally after a modest lunch.

While on the subject of lunches, I am dead against the saturated variety. One martini, two martinis – much, much better, no martinis! Reserve the cocktail hour for home relaxation after a fruitful day's work. This is not a "prohibition" speech. It just makes sense. And if your particular chore has to do with the exactness which relies on the precise functioning of two clear orbs, teetotal while working, student, teetotal!

(D) Process Cameraman. Re-read this paragraph in the series of lettered "steps" and you will note, "It must be recognized that in the entire operation of Process, this "step" is the most difficult and – " we might add, "demanding and frustrating."

Dear old Harold Marzorati, one of our Process cinematographers for many years, eventually "traitored" out and became a regular production cameraman. He remained mad at himself ever after for not having chosen that route instead of Process, early in his career. "This is a cinch, Buddy," he would say to me, "don't ever try to get me back in that noodle-swamp!" Harold Lipstein, another of our former long-time Process cameramen has voiced like opinions since his very successful switch to production.

A great deal of credit is obviously due the cinematographer's "specialist" who is able to strike the fine line of light, focus, and color balance, which produces a harmonious Process composite. Don't overly rush this man. He is a valuable asset. The "mixing" of his original negative, "sore-thumbed" onto that which becomes a dupe (the background) is a demanding business. If unharried and unhurried, his hits will far outdistance his misses. And he becomes experienced only through "experience." Not meant to be cute, this last. Testing and more testing of the more involved types of Process is a steady "man-assignment" to this very difficult photographic component of Rear Projection Process. Such men were "Lippy" and "Marzi" mentioned above and several others — not too many. Max Fabian, though primarily a photographer of miniatures, could do an excellent job of Process, as could Jack Smith (not the Art Director) and Walter Lundin, both long gone, but not forgotten. Harold Wellman would qualify and in recent years, Ed Snyder has been our man. Ed, I believe, rates not one rung below the very top rung of this ladder.

Snyder was at Twentieth Century-Fox for many years before going into partial retirement. We were most fortunate in obtaining a "handshake" first call for his Process services. No contract, no written tie-down promises. There has developed a genuine mutual regard between Ed and M.G.M., which applies to his fine capabilities and his agreeable personality on one side, and his admiration of, and attachment to, our Process management, on the other.

He has been of distinct help in the early development of our "Laced Process" system, as well as having handled the camera end of its use almost entirely since its inception. There are several production cameramen, the gentlemen responsible for the entire picture photographically, who seem to resent outside help. They should welcome the services of a "specialist" in this marginal field of success or failure. Fortunately, by far the great majority of them do. The others, with few if any exceptions, wind up cabin class if not missing the boat entirely, as far as Process is concerned.

Hence this step, which can be such a valuable picture-making ally, is mandatorily essential. Any major studio should develop and retain a top-rate Process facility and though it may grieve some overhead watchers, the cameraman whose responsibility mainly consists of getting it on film, should be a fixture — not as some have suggested, "let anyone do it." This thinking pertains particularly to Color Process of scope.

Step (E) is headed "**Process Assistant.**" This perhaps should be modified to include anyone who runs the Process show. He may be an assistant, as it was my good fortune to have had, or he may be the Head himself. In either event his duties are quite adequately briefed within the "E" step.

If one line in that paragraph should be accented above all others, it would be, "~ to assist Director in all ways possible, segregation of backgrounds, instructions to camera operators as to camera movement, advising Directors as to limitations of the Process medium ~." Chiefly this quote refers to the actual stage operation, the day a Company moves in to shoot Process.

Suppose we assume all "steps" to this point have been adequately performed — the plates well-photographed, proper prints from the Laboratory, the Art Director's Process set ready and workable, all tools in tiptop shape, actors properly wardrobed and the Director straining at the leash. That "yellow" Production Office edict, "shooting at nine," will be adhered to much more successfully if one capable individual who is well versed in all the details, wields his authoritative mace. Such should be the Process Assistant.

Carroll Shepphird at M.G.M. has been that individual for quite a spell, a loyal and able helpmeet, a dependable and valued individual whose speciality has been Process. Shep has devised, supervised and directed miniatures and has contributed to other Effect Categories, but his principal activity has been in the Process field. Membership in the Director's Guild has entitled him to direct second units involving people and he has shown laudable aptitude and sensitiveness in his handling of actors. Upon my retirement, he has been made the top Process Supervisor at M.G.M.. This task coupled with his adroitness and full-scale knowledge of many of the tangents of Effects generally, places him in an enviable position of being able to deliver diversified Effect solutions.

The almost endless areas to which Process may be applied imposes a lot of know-how in the intelligent use of many effect accessories. The bounce of an automobile in front of a Process Screen which should vary in intensity depending on the simulated road condition, or the speed the vehicle is supposed to be traveling, is a simple example. How much wind, the passing of shadows which would fall in reality if the car were actually moving along a tree-lined street, the bump of a sudden stop or collision; dust, rain, snow or sleet, the glare of approaching headlights or passing street lamps when the scene represents night; a wild skid which may involve a full 360° turn — car mounted on a turntable for this — all of these and more, to lend realism, is within the realm of the Process "Chargé d'affaires" stage duties.

Automobile Process, limos, taxis, convertibles, trucks, represent this medium's bread and butter means of livelihood, and more often than not, involve very rudimentary procedures. Many TV cameramen shoot their own Process and do an acceptable job in such relatively uncomplicated uses of this category. As color TV grows and scope increases, their problems will pyramid and the "specialist" Process cameraman should enter.

A further very important function of Mr. Process,

Process plate and set composition for *Our Vines Have Tender Grapes*, Production 1342.

Much ado even on a small Process Set. "Shep" discussing it with Ed Snyder, Process Cinematographer.

"PROCESS THE WHYS AND HOWS"

whomever he may be, is early contact with the Art Director in the planning stage of sequences involving Process. Working drawings should include all information as to projected picture size, choice of projection and camera lenses, uncluttered room needed for lighting and effect-equipment and camera mobility; the entire space area required for an efficient stage operation. Only the proficient Process man is able to look over a Process layout and give correctly, answers to the above essentials. He should also be privileged to "throw out" background plate material at the time of original viewing, if it is found sufficiently wanting. The "chain which is no stronger than its weakest link," certainly has close affinity to, "Process is no better than its worst 'step'"

In line with the above reference to "poor plates," upon numerous occasions through the years, we have been forced to use backgrounds of varying inferiorities. These may come from the stock library, and when inferior, the results invariably skid. Economy is of course the moving factor in these decisions, but the question of when it is false economy, must be intelligently judged. Who better to appraise, than the individual who through experience has been trained to juggle all phases, all steps, which contribute to Process excellence, or at the very least, adequacy?

The reference to "stock" film is not meant to be derogatory. The Film Library is a veritable gold mine of very usable footages. Stock film examination leading to acceptance or refusal as far as Process is concerned however, should be judged by a technician well qualified to assess the whole Process gamut and final result.

Although having noted above, only a few of the stage supervisory chores which are inherent in the shooting of automobile Process, those chores multiply into a manifold complex of dump tanks and wind-driven spray for ships in a storm - remember Spencer Tracy on the poop of the "Mayflower" when hit by our miniature Process background of a "giant wave" — or controlled fire as in *Boom Town*'s oil well fire; foreground dumping of debris as in avalanches, earthquakes; the manipulation of cue-lights or time devices used to put into action hydraulic ship rockers or airplane mount maneuvers, to coincide with pre-planned Full-sized Effect gymnastics, many of which have split-second tie-ins with their projected Process backgrounds. Endless and imaginative devices usually dreamt into workability by co-workers in other Effect fields, such as engineers (Bossart) "crazy thinkers" (all good effects men) "sane thinkers" (all good effects men) from whatever source, but all played with the exacting finesse of an organist. The Process "foreman," with able propshop personnel assistance, can be of immeasurable help to Director, camerman and shooting crew, if he is at all worth his salt. Shep, to this grateful writer, was.

Step (F) The Director, needs little augmenting beyond the paragraph devoted to this "step." One line however,

"—Should weigh the alternate method of obtaining his shots (attempting to do them other than in Process)—," deserves the inclusion of an actual example.

The opening day of Process on Victor Fleming's memorable picture, *Captains Courageous*, (it was also the first day of production) could hardly have been termed a totally successful one. And that is a sad understatement. If much more technical miserableness had occurred, breakdowns, delays, confusion, dismay; one more broken caster, or misplaced wind machine and we of genus Process would probably have thumbed a ride to the nearest ocean (the one nearest Culver City is the Pacific) and waded in, sans waterwings, headed non-stop for any point west.

Enough did happen, may it herein be recorded, to move dear old Vic Fleming to angry tears of decision. "No more Process!" he growled, "We've got that schooner down at San Pedro - brought her all the way from New Bedford through that blankity-blank canal to San Pedro!," he further growled. "Tomorrow we go to sea!," third growl.

Thirty-six hours later, Vic, Lionel Barrymore, Spencer Tracy, Mickey Rooney, Freddie Bartholomew and sundry cameramen, make-up artists, wardrobe people, prop men, et.al. - the whole crew, were back on Stage 12, subdued, humble and more than ready for the trials and tribulations of that beast , Process.

Stage 12 didn't rock or roll so no one became sea sick. At sea there existed rock and roll. Cameras on a camera boom on the stage floor gave our ship set a synthetic, though realistic, up and down movement, which in conjunction with the shot-at-sea backgrounds, simulated a believable at sea illusion. She "floated." There was room and solid space on and around our Stage 12 replica.

At sea, nothing was very solid except the rail which was a popular and overcrowded spot as yaw and pitch took over with ever increasing vehemence. And there was little room for dressing rooms, grip equipment, film and camera paraphernalia. There was no land-locked 'head'. And you couldn't 'turn on' the sun. Just a few of the elements which oftentimes become, lets-do-it-in-reality, headaches. Sufficiently so, in this case, to reverse Vic's well meant proclamation of "We'll go to sea!"

Several salutary bits of wisdom can be gained from the above recital. Equipment breakdowns, costing in delay far above whatever monies their avoidance would have entailed, is an important and obvious one. Locking the barn door after old Dobbin has cantered, is still a state of mind to be avoided. The jolt of that opening day, did produce a few dividends; among them, new casters for our Process platforms that were designed to roll more easily and carry loads far above those normally expected. A many months' old requisition for these,

94-P Alt

Carroll Shepphird and single-head elevating Process Projector.

Mervyn Le Roy, at right, top old time young director, with author, in front of MGM's unique "straight ahead" triple-head Process Projector.

"PROCESS THE WHYS AND HOWS"

was hurriedly signed on the day following that woe-ridden opening day. A few silver lining equipment benefits, yes, but costly ones.

Perhaps the main lesson, however, was that which laid emphasis on method determination – the careful weighing of all the pros and cons. With whatever limitations, whatever seeming delays, Process was without question, in this case the sensible and economic answer.

Similar past instances could be quoted to further verify like situations. The point I believe is clear, and I make it with the hope that a more tolerant appreciation of the time and techniques required, be recognized by some 'time-keepers'. And balance well the alternate, Mr. Director, Mr. Unit Production Manager, Mr. Producer.

The **Step (G)** paragraph on **Art Directors** is quite inclusively detailed. Working as a harmonious team, Art Director and Process Head, can devise and design a correct and fruitful use of this serviceable tool. A really effectual and beneficial overlap of 'togetherness' between these two production activities, is to be desired.

The **(H) Step - Production Department**, its attitude, its help or its hindrance, has formidable bearing on the successful or less rewarding operation of Process. Thorough understanding of its built-in technical and photographic snags, should influence this 'schedule-and-money-watching'-department, towards enthusiastic acceptance of the many entries to be expected in the asset column of its ledger. Simple arithmetic considerations of any alternate, if sincerely analyzed, will do much to alleviate the natural pain generated if and when fifteen minutes is used to move a wind machine, or if the time consumed by a cameraman in achieving his fine-line light and focus balance seems exorbitant. Further, a broken water line in a Process projector, rarely will cause delays comparable to the many that may occur when a shot that should be Process, is side tracked to an "easier" way.

A Production Office can, and should be, the heart of a well functioning studio operation. Not necessarily the creative heart but certainly the organizational one. A thorough ken of all the "steps" briefed in the early pages of this chapter with emphasis particularly on "stage operation" as well as a sympathetic attitude towards conditions which should always prevail during the preliminary shooting of background plates, is imperative. Those conditions of proper and sufficient light, road smoothness when a camera car for moving plates is to be used, coupled with the Production assignment of a 'know-how' crew to shoot Process plates, are all decision elements that lend importantly to the degree of success or failure which this link in the chain entails. Never short change any of the 'steps' and the average of results will largely eliminate expensive retakes. May all Production Departments and their representatives lend capable and understanding hands so that

this category of Special Visual Effects flourishes. It is a handy and worthy implement.

The **(I) Step** refers mainly to all of the 'Steps' enumerated, and more specifically to the "mechanics" of Process. **Management** from the top level through all the chains of command, should favor top maintenance of the precision appurtenances involved in Process, and yield not to departmental 'savings' if and when a paper reduction of overhead adds an indirect, and often difficult to determine, unproductive cost to production.

New developments, new or advanced equipment, new methods, should be intelligently open-armed by Management, with funds made available for all-inclusive investigation, thorough testing, and when warranted, adaptation.

This premise is naturally applicable to all of the physical phases of film production and we at M.G.M. through the years have been reasonably blessed in this area. A qualified Plant Manager is a good buffer for the myriad 'all-cure' contrivances and methods which shower from many sources during any given year. Wise and open investigation by this individual should determine the advisability of his pressing a higher authority for a preliminary or complete go-ahead. We have had at times such men; John Tobin in the past and our present, as of this writing, Tom Curtis. Both with engineering backgrounds, both willing and able to comprehend, and both clear-eyed analysts.

So much for the preceding more comprehensive digest of the Problem and Answer Steps, with their stressing of many of the more critical essentials.

Before delving into M.G.M.'s "Laced Process" a few do's and don'ts follow, accompanied by an assortment of 'tips' which have been garnered over a prolonged period of practical experience in the use of Process. Much will seem obvious and possibly old hat, to current Process people. Their value to the student and their interest to the lay reader, however, will I believe, be of some consequence.

The goal of he who conceives and executes Miniatures is to achieve a result which looks like anything but a Miniature. Process, as do all of the Effect Categories, attempts to follow the same road of 'reality'. Hence many times, as in Vic's day on the briny, we think in terms of the difficulties which might be encountered if location, rather than Process shooting, is broached.

Suppose that a wild automobile chase in and out of a city's traffic, or on a winding mountain road, wherever, were the scenes to be shot. Attempts to obtain individual close ups of the participants from a speeding, alongside-camera-car, would be loaded with ins and outs, camera misses, speed variances, a camera operator's headache. The position relationships between the camera in one vehicle and actors in another, would be anything but smooth or constant and add elements of danger to cast and crew if attempted in actuality. A certain 'realness' however would result. A sequence of this nature to be shot in Process should introduce some of these difficulties deliberately, in order to achieve that selfsame 'realness'.

Camera movement, as it relates to a set in front of a Process Screen, is an important 'do', an elementary and generally known and used tip number one. Variances and types of movement, naturally depend on the subject at hand. A slow moving top-down convertible, meandering down a moonlit lane in the Spring, with a young man's fancy as one of its passengers, would entail a gentle, hardly perceptible, in and out, pan and tilt camera movement. Just enough to 'un-glue' the Process convertible from a stage floor. The chase example mentioned above, would necessitate much faster and more erratic movement. Additional maneuverings of the set itself, car, ship, train, airplane; also add to the illusions of reality. Car bodies, spring mounted, provide bounce. Car bodies on casters allow for lateral movements and skids, and as previously noted, turntables upon which a car may be mounted enable an actor to 'lose complete control' on an icy road, or in an Indianapolis 'race' with no more danger present than that to which he might be subjected, while seated in an ordinary swivel chair.

Within these procedures of set and camera movements, lie the available keys to audience acceptance, their unanalyzed belief that they are viewing authenticity. Provided, of course, and in addition, that all other "Steps" have been meticulously trod.

Process ship sets, or small craft sets, mounted on rockers, 'float' in front of a projected sea background plate, and as alluded to heretofore, the illusion when augmented by a restless camera on a restless camera boom, can be startlingly 'bona fide'.

As a matter of record, the inclusion of rockers or other mechanical devices, may often be eliminated as unnecessary, in order that a solid unmoving deck, anchored to a stage floor, be made to 'come alive.' A boom-mounted, ever-shifting camera, intelligently maneuvered usually can supply sufficient sea action to satisfy the saltiest of audiences.

Gimble camera mounts should be used with quite some discretion, primarily because side camera tilts often spell fake, through the simple fact that standing or walking, people (and actors <u>are</u> people) are usually perpendicular. A level 'un-rockered' deck, made to 'slant' by throwing the camera sideways from vertical, will result in a human 'Tower of Pisa', or 'Pisas' if more than one of a ship's company is aboard. A gimble, mounted on the end of a boom, may add dividends to a stage bound ship 'at sea'. But again, only if

Boom Town Process shot. Courtesy - Margaret Herrick Library.

used with discretion.

An obvious component of this number one 'movement tip', is to always consider the overall bulk of your set subject. The "Queen Mary" will roll in a slow, massive manner. A canoe in a rapids will bounce and tilt and flit with the timing of a fast tempo, frugging go-go girl. A lazy moonlit wooded lane, and the slam-bang of a cops and robbers chase are opposites. Fit your rhythm to the sequence's intent. Otherwise, "Mary" may appear to bob like a cork and the 'chase' will be robbed of suspenseful excitement.

I shudder at shots I have seen in the interior of a "depth bombed" submarine. Healthy, ill-advised, shakes of the camera are often so overdone, that this tremendous mass 'moves' with much too violent rapidity, hence destroying all sense of weight and size. The sudden force unleashed at the bottom of an outer-space rocket, millions of pounds of thrust, triggered in a split second, barely moves those giants for the first few seconds. And yet one "ash can" can induce some cameramen and some directors to 'shake' willy-nilly - a submarine that in weight alone, may exceed that of a fully loaded, fully fueled, ready to blast off lunar vehicle, by about twice. Rather, it would be better for these gentlemen to vibrate the camera, timed to coincide with the mythical depth bombs, or optically vibrate the scene later. A minimum poetic-license jar to the camera could be condoned, and if possible, a sudden impact to the sub set Itself from an air ram or other source, a high-lift or jamming truck, would help, but never, never a terrier shaking a rat. Use some conservatism and take no undue liberties with impossible actions and reactions — audiences are not that stupid.

An excellent exemplification of camera movement technique, was that used in the previously mentioned cross country record attempt by Clark Gable in *Test Pilot*, who "flew" his 'airplane', the "Drake Bullet", through a storm ridden hell and high water, about fifteen feet above the floor of Stage 15. Lightning punctuated cloud backgrounds, shot in Miniature, were Process-projected on a thirty-four foot screen, in front of which a Bossart designed airplane mount carried the "Bullet". She could bank a full 90°, either to port or starboard, and at times she was pelted with "sleet and snow", (driven <u>puffed rice</u>, wind and shredded asbestos) and obscured at times by close proximity "clouds" (wind driven jets of steam) located near the camera.

Picturing to ourselves the type of photographic coverage an accompanying camera plane would have registered under such storm conditions, we determined to deliver a similar brand of camera work. A fast traveling, up-and-down camera platform, riding a vertical column which in turn was mounted on a forward and backward husky dolly, enabled us to assimilate rough air and storm conditions. At times and by design we would 'air-pocket' drop the camera, cutting 'Pilot' Gable partially or completely out of the picture, then swoose back up — in, out, up and down, varying ins, outs, ups and downs to avoid mechanical repetition.

Vic Fleming, the Director, loved it and complimented our temerity in 'chopping' Mr. Gable's head off occasionally in the interest of portraying reality. And Clark loved it.

Test Pilot was a Special Effector's bonanza, principally within the over-lapping range of full-sized Mechanical, Miniature and Process Categories. We mentally contrived one dilly, a looping and rolling airplane (full-sized) in front of a Process Screen, knowing that John Bossart and our prop shop and mechanical departments would devise a physical answer. In fact, his and their answers to all of the varied airplane mounts needed to tell the story of *Test Pilot*, were top contributions.

One sequence had to do with the Thompson Trophy race, a fixture in those days of the National Air Races, held for many years in Cleveland and also in Los Angeles. We determined to cover this closed course, three (or four?) pylon event, as though a camera plane were above and to the <u>rear</u> of the racers, shooting down at a 45° angle.

Now Process normally is a level operation, although we have handled tilts up or down considerably off the horizontal. Forty-five degrees, however, is a bit much, so we placed our racers on 45° mount and shot level. The projected background plate having been shot at this corresponding angle down, resulted when combined with our tilted foreground, in a perfect illusion, though we were actually photographing our Process composite, in the normal level manner.

Supplying the backgrounds for this sequence brought forth the use of an unusual piece of equipment — a wheelbarrow! The Thompson race is flown right down on the 'deck', extreme low level, and an added method of obtaining the needed plates, came from a golf course! Wheelbarrow, golf course? Well, upon occasions when playing this wonderfully frustrating game of golf, I had formed the habit of 'polishing' the underside of my 'woods', by pushing them along the fairway while walking, head down, discussing with myself as to why my head had not stayed down at least through impact. While glaring at the business end of this laminated, obnoxious golf tool, I would become fascinated by the blurred changing patterns of the fast passing sod. An ordinary walking pace, yet the grass seemed to flow by my driver or brassie with amazing speed. Coupling this 'astute' observation with the later need of down angle backgrounds for speeding airplanes, two and two became four.

The next move towards attainment produced a long strip of canvas, scenically painted with blobs of green fields, grey roads, squares of off-white 'houses', brown 'plowed' fields ~ roughly executed with little detail. This constituted our terrain.

'Crazy-thinking' begat a wheelbarrow, as the simplest way of passing a camera over this very small scale, abstract 'countryside'. A 45° tilted-down camera, clamped over the single wheel of this unique dolly, enabled Bill Foxall, camera operator for Max Fabian way back when, to stroll across the 'landscape,' pushing his wheelbarrow briskly to the imaginary first pylon, at which spot he would bank in a 180° turn and retrace his steps to 'pylon' number two, another bank, and he would mosey back to number one, which now became number three, and on and on for as many laps as needed, or when Bill yelled "Uncle!" The 180° turn, which in reality would have been 90° or 120°, was a liberty which proved not apparent and which added glee to the bookkeeper's oft unhappy existence, because of the fact that <u>one</u> strip of canvass, instead of three or four sufficed.

I really should stop needling these worthy gentlemen. The great majority have been and still are my valued pals. There have been a few, however, hard to forget!

Our racers, on their 45° mount, would bank in unison with Bill's wheelbarrow background plates and we had the makings of a thrilling, authentic appearing, race. The same plates were used to obtain longer shots, which included several miniature planes jockeying for position and moving in relationship to each other, all in Process.

This 'tip', roughly outlined in the last episode, explains a simple though limited method of being able to shoot acute up or down angles, beyond the practical limits of high or low angled Process Projection, with the correlative use of tilted screens. Simply <u>lean</u> your foreground so that it matches the angle of the originally photographed plate.

An actor, standing alongside, or leaning over, a parapet

(Above) Process unit at work. Reading left to right, at right, grip Howard Bradlet behind boom, Max Fabian, camera, Director Bundy Marton, Carroll Shephird, Dan Powers, Electrician Jack New.

(Below) Canoe at left mounted on hydraulic ramrocker. Process screen out of picture to left. From *The Wild North*.

(Above) Set-up for *Million Dollar Mermaid*. Note small process screen at right center. Water in foreground reflects background projected water and 'ties' the two together. Mervyn Le Roy in the Director's chair.

(Below) Another water to water 'tie-in', this one rough. Boat is hydraulically rocked. Note edge of projected plate on extreme right.

or window sill in which the street far below is visible, perhaps almost straight down, can often be shot in <u>level</u> Process, by 'laying back' a foreground set and supporting the prone or partially prone actor on an 'ironing board' contrivance. If the scene dictates that a high sky from "whence cameth his health," is to be included behind him, necessitating an up angle, just reverse the position of his "board", and lean him <u>towards</u> the Screen. The limitations are obvious; he or they cannot walk around or move beyond the zone of their support. If action of this mobile nature is required, another category is paged, Optical, and a traveling matte procedure, would probably be in the offing.

The advantage of 'elevator' Process Projection booths, has proven of value in being able to handle lesser up or down angles. An important additional asset, is the ease and speed with which they can adjust to varying heights for straight level Process as well as the tilt up or down feature. Our projectors travel vertically in a range from a five foot six inch lens height (stage floor operation) to twenty-one feet on our Triple Head and eighteen feet on our Singles. The elevators are an integral part of the units and after some twenty-five years of use, this feature would definitely be included were we to design and construct brand new ones today. They are completely mobile and are used on many of M.G.M.'s stages, on concrete or wood floors. So 'tip' number three could be ~ 'elevatorize' your Process Projectors and design Process Screen frames so that they slant to a sufficient degree that they may be positioned, at right angles, to the line of projection, for those occasional departures from the horizontal.

A fourth quick 'tip' involves the desirability of including two or three gloss finish Screens in your 'screen stable'. The basic Process Screen is a clear, transparent sheet of some material, usually one of the 'polys', which must be spray treated in order that the projected image be 'stopped', at and on the screen surface. The general manufacturing procedure is to apply 'frosting' to both sides of the basic sheet, the <u>back</u> or projection side lightly sprayed to avoid light 'bounce' from the projector, while the camera side of the screen constitutes the major image-stopping surfacing. By omitting this light spray application to the back of the screen and substituting a gloss finish, a screen is produced, one side of which is photographically impervious to water. By reversing its normal use, placing the gloss side to the camera, effect water in a rain or storm-spray sequence which may splash or be wind driven onto the screen, will not be visible. This does not hold true if water should contact the surfaced side of a screen. Hence, unwanted, wayward water, need not be a problem.

Another, at times, very handy little stunt, is that of placing a screen at other than right angles to the line of projection. Not particularly recommended except in cases of stage emergencies. Mr. Director may wish to shoot his action further aft or forward in an automobile as an example, than that of the background plate angle for which the background was originally shot. By moving the 'plan' position of the Screen at a slight angle to the projection center line, a three quarter back plate can be made to appear to have been photographed for a seven-eighths back, or a five-eighths back shot. A useful trick whereby happiness for the Director is brought to pass and a merit mark for the Process Department is gained.

Dogs often run with their hind quarters slightly to the left or right of their forward line of progress. Automobiles shouldn't. It is imperative that a Process car body be properly adjusted to the direction of a moving background, to avoid disturbing, dog-like, characteristics. Camera position can also affect this elementary rule. It is possible in spite of correct placing of a vehicle to that of the projected plate, that it sometimes doesn't seem to 'fit'. An up or down change in the camera location as it relates to said vehicle, will correct this situation and remove any illusion of skidding. The "elementary, Dr. Watson!", reaction to the above rudimentary 'tip' by old hands, is fully expected. I include it for the uninitiated and because I recall that from time to time even 'old hands' may forget their A-B-C's.

Gilbert and Sullivan's quote from "The Mikado" ~ "Let the punishment fit the crime," is analogous to "let the aspect ratio of a background plate fit its use," regardless of a possible differing aspect ratio which may apply to the ultimate movie or T.V. product. Again, venerable ones, I hesitate to include this bit of counsel. But sometimes, the D-E-F's also occasionally take a holiday and for this reason, lend an ear.

Almost invariably the 'shape' which exists through the windows of a closed car, a bus, a train, a ship's bridge, becomes an elongated rectangle. Quality is gained when this 'space' is more efficiently covered, by choosing and projecting a 'shape' (aspect ratio) background plate which closely 'fits' the to-be-covered 'rectangle' or Process area. Hence, a T.V. shape which has a more nearly square aspect ratio, may beneficially use as a plate, one which has been shot in Cinemascope or Panavision, if the foreground set is a car, bus, train or whatever may require a more rectangular Process coverage. By the same token an anamorphic 'squeezed' production, one in either Panavision or Cinemascope, should choose an old 'unsqueezed' three by four shape background if the Process area more nearly approximates a three by four shape, such as a three by four or thereabouts, window.

The important point is to use as much of the projected background as possible. This automatically increases the usability of available light at the Screen as well as adding materially to the overall quality of the composite.

To further stress this very fundamental rule of hoarding every last lumen of light projected on to a Process Screen, and to illustrate resultant gains in Process excellence, as well as observing a basic perspective and scale 'don't', the following account of a pleasant and educational tiff in the early days of

Process, may serve to clarify the above maxims.

In those days, Process was extensively used in the Andy Hardy series produced at M.G.M. George Seitz directed many of them and as was typical of many Directors of that period, certain inherent limitations of the medium were not always fully understood. George at times, would insist on dollying forward from a long shot to a close-up while shooting Process. Though quality loss was pointed out (the enlargement of grain and other possible plate defects such as 'dirt' or minute scratches) he at times felt the value of the camera moves was of more importance to the scene than any defect consequences. This was a reasonable but debatable premise. In due time, however, we were able to show Mr. Seitz that he could have his cake while also partaking of the last crumb. By lap dissolving during the first three or four feet of camera progress towards the Screen, to the last few feet into a close-up, the desired effect was obtained, smoothly and with an actual saving of film footage. Our difference was that we were able to reduce the size of the projected background for the close-up finish, which meant simply that camera coverage of the projected screen image continued to include nearly the total background plate. No grain-size increase, no defect enlargement, profit to all.

Out-of-proportion 'scale' increase as a result of such undesirable moves in Process, aside from quality loss, was also sometimes a stickler to explain. Until, in discussing the subject with George one day, the moon came to our rescue.

"Suppose," I said, "we should drive twenty odd miles from downtown Los Angeles to Santa Monica. In the western sky is a full moon. Upon arrival in Santa Monica, the moon has remained in size, the same as it appeared twenty miles away. Right, George?"

"Right Buddy," replied he.

"What happens, Mr. Seitz, if we project a 'moon' background onto a Process Screen and then proceed to move a camera towards the Screen for twenty feet ~ not twenty miles — just twenty feet?"

No pondering by George on this one. "Oh, yes, h-m-m-m, yes, of course. It would get bigger, wouldn't it?"

So we established with this fine gentleman a pretty thorough knowledge of 'growing' moons as well as other right routes to be pursued in all phases of Process, and we have often used the above illustration to good avail, with new and younger 'George Seitzes,' even as of today.

Specifically, this exhortation on the perils and pitfalls of indiscriminate camera wanderings, applies mainly to 'open screen' Process ~ that which involves no set as such ~in which, foreground action is backed up only and entirely by a background plate. The camera field must stay closely within the limits of a background plate's perimeter if the potential is to be realized.

Less restricted camera movements are quite acceptable in a situation whereby the area of the Process portion of the overall field covered by a camera is but a part of the whole, such as that of a four or five foot window, backed by Process, in a twenty foot wall. The camera may move towards the window from a full long shot of the wall without degrading the quality of the background image — but progressing not through the window, in which case, shooting too far within the projected image, enlargement of grain, possible defects, and 'scale' fallacies, can be expected.

There are many such combinations of 'set' and Process which allow added freedoms of camera movement. In all cases however, either 'open screen' or 'set' Process, one rule does hold about 99% constant ~ that of adhering closely to the 'center line' of projection, A big and elementary 'don't', is, stray not to the left or right of this center line. A contradiction to this rule (the remaining 1%) is the exception that proves it.

A particular background because of its nature, can be photographically improved by moving the camera off center, if more or less light on one side or the other, or at the top or bottom, is desired. Dropping below the horizontal center line of a landscape plate which contains an objectionable 'hot' sky, will reduce some of the projection 'heat' and glare. Or, if more brilliance will help the right half of the Screen subject, a camera position to the right of center will improve the ultimate result, and vice versa. Generally however, hew close to the line (the center line) and let the frustrated chips of he who wishes to violate, fall where they may.

A further mild contradiction to the previously admonished 'dolly-not-towards-the-screen', is the limited liberty that may and should be taken, in the wild and wooly species of Process uses, such as Mr. Gable in his storm-tossed "Drake Bullet" or Captain Bligh's "Bounty" crew taking in sail while precariously perched on a weaving, bucking, yard arm, high above a gale activated, raging, Cape Horn sea ~ said sea having been provided through the courtesy of the Miniature Department, said yard arm rocking contentedly on a wet, windy, M.G.M. stage. In and out, as well as rise and fall movements of the camera, necessitate a wider margin between the camera 'field' and the background's outer edges if the lily is to be gilded. Gained audience reaction to this type of delivery, however, far overshadows such reasonable violations which may borderline quality loss. But only when a degree of violent action is the order of the day.

To digress a moment from Process, but related to 'camera movement,' we unequivocally advocate the use of a camera boom when photographing the interior of a ship. This axiom of ours has produced at times howls of dissent from a director or two and a few cinematographers. Their argument is reasonably valid. "If," say they, "we were aboard a liner at sea shooting scenes in the Grand Salon, our camera would be placed on a normal mount on the floor, and other than pans and tilts or perhaps dolly moves, that would be it, brother!"

Well, that probably would be it, but we have employed a bit of open-minded subterfuge which to date has brought not one letter of pain from any viewer anywhere. A subtle rise and fall of the camera with a slow tilt-down during the rise cycle and a like tilt-up as the camera lowers, has accomplished a sense of actually being at sea. As mentioned previously in discussing similar camera movements, the anchored-to-a-stage-floor set, deck or Grand Salon, 'floats'. No analysis by an audience — just a subconscious, worthwhile reaction of reality. So even though it may be quite true that observing a budding shipboard romance which may blossom to the point of, "let me take you to my Casbah, little one," is far more intriguing than why does the camera go up and down, I hesitate not one whit to proclaim that the ticket buyer will more definitely accept that the 'Casbah', (Suite "A", Promenade Deck) is on a 'live' ship, than if we were to follow the dictates of some inflexible individuals who never condone license of this order, poetic or otherwise.

TIPS, DO'S OR DON'TS

Any more 'tips', 'do's' or 'don'ts'? Probably many which have momentarily escaped our memory. The most valuable all-inclusive one however, yet remains the same one so often alluded to in these pages — thoroughly digest all Effect problems, both sanely and crazily, invent, contrive, take conservative liberties; but plan always towards supplying those extras which usually spell the difference between a 50-50 result or an outstanding achievement. The added cost of a camera boom? Well, a miss can really be a mile in this profession; one dollar saved on an eleven dollar job may quite often be a very expensive dollar. Judgment, good and experienced judgment, again rears its hoary head.

The next page or so has absolutely nothing to do with Process, so unless you are in the mood for a practical joke breather, skip it. A pipe has been a trademark of the author's, since the initial purchase of a French briar in World War One days. That one pipe has multiplied to over six hundred as the years have passed. The proper place to carry a pipe is between the upper and lower dentures of the owner, and one or another of this group of six hundred, like Jeff Smedley and his mouth full of nails, was from post-breakfast to pre-bedtimes always firmly clenched just there. Hence, the reference to 'trademark'.

A trip to Tahiti in 1934, with a brand new wife, followed a previous trip (the Van Dyke 'mustache' one) in 1928. Unbeknownst to your pipe smoker, Ulrich Busch of the beer Busches, our Unit Production Manager, radioed ahead to Tony Bambridge, one of Papeete's important citizens, a

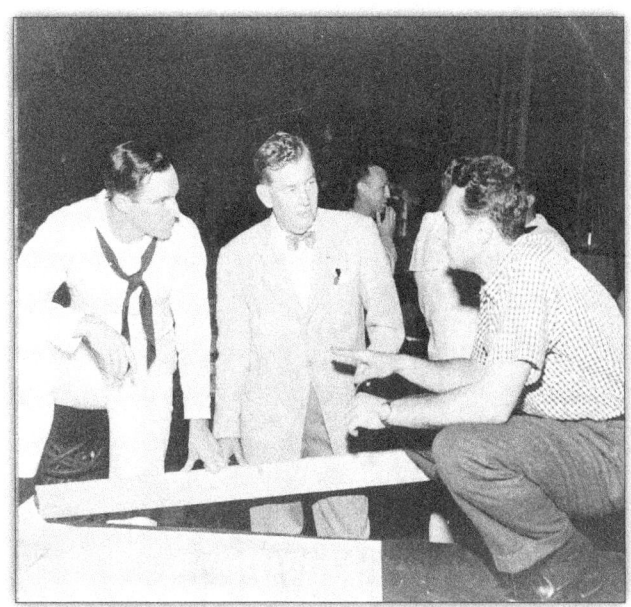

Gene Kelly, and Stanley Donen. Stage conference *On The Town*.

fiendish order. Round up all youngsters of proper age, said it (H-m-m, that would be 1934 minus 1928 minus 9 months) and buy them pipes.

At pier-side, the morning of our arrival, forty (40!) six year old little Tahitians, all with a pipe in their little mouths, greeted the ship's docking, with enthusiastic cries of, "Where's Daddy, where's Daddy." In unison and individually the "Where's Daddy" reverberated in shrill sopranos from the steel plates of the "S.S. Tahiti" to the green clad slopes of Tahiti's highest peak. Upon finally spotting my identifying puffing accessory, they dutifully changed to, "There's Daddy, there's Daddy!"

Tony had followed his instructions well. Three words in English had he taught them, 'where', 'there', and 'Daddy', and the merchants of this South Sea Paradise had been momentarily denuded of pipes. The word 'paradise', as it applies to all south sea islands, was somewhat dubiously questioned by 'some-of-us' aboard. Soon after the "Tahiti" sank. If Caruso's high "C" could shatter a goblet, is it possible that those shrill "Daddy's" could have loosened her plates?

Tony Bambridge was my Tahitian 'Tito Neri'. Our friendship ripened in 1928 during production of *The Pagan* in Tahiti. This present 1934 stint of his, as an 'English teacher' and pipe purchaser was quickly forgiven by the victim, but Budweiser, for many months thereafter, seemed to contain audible 'guffaws' among its foam topped ingredients. My good pal, Ulrich Busch! By the way, what a compliment! Forty little pipe smokers!

When Judy Garland bowed out of M.G.M.'s *Annie Get Your Gun*, Betty Hutton was being seriously considered to take over the title role. Though a decision of this nature had

nothing whatsoever to do with any of the Effect Categories, I managed to nose-probe into this affair. It was none of my business (a continuing weakness of mine) and I rather vehemently objected to the casting of Miss Hutton. I had never met Betty Hutton ~ but within a very short period of time, I did!

She was given the part, and after I had viewed the first few day's 'rushes', my reaction was one of complete reversal; she was just super as "Annie." I mentioned this change of heart to Bill Ryan, the Producer's Associate. And one morning when Betty was morose, Bill told her the story in an attempt to cheer her somewhat. He told how a gentleman on the lot had protested loudly as to her qualifications, type-wise, and in every other way, to play "Annie." And further, how the same gentleman had become an enthusiastic convert.

That morning, the company was shooting in Process and some problem developed that required my presence on the stage. Arthur Freed, the Producer, was present, Cedric Gibbons my immediate boss was there, and the entire "Annie" shebang was there, watching our serious little group out in front, 'in conference'~and Betty Hutton was there! Well, Mr. Ryan had succeeded in cheering Miss Hutton quite somewhat. I was pointed out to her by 'dear' Bill, and suddenly became aware of the success of his morale building tale, by receiving in the seat of my pants, in front of the entire assemblage, a kick which would have done justice to Lou Groza, outstanding place kicker for the Cleveland Browns. Attacked from the rear and in the rear by the Star! A split-second, red-faced reflex, spun me 180° to face the grinning face of Betty Hutton. "That is your deserved receipt," she murmured, "for those unkind advance notices, Mr. Gillespie." And then, clad in among other things, fresh makeup, she planted lipstick-red onto various areas of my crimsoning visage with a, "And these are for your wisely changed current feelings, Buddy." The red of her lipstick was for the moment scarcely noticeable ~ an almost perfect match for the hue of me. A sudden thought as I write this~ the L.A. Rams should seriously consider drafting Miss Hutton and billing her as the 'kissing kicker'. I have researched both talents and can vouch as to their effectiveness.

Back students, to the text book.

Laced Process was a departure from the tried and true since the inception of Process. It came into being as a result of an idea for an improved three-projector theater 'Cinerama' type presentation, which involved breakdowns from an original 65mm anamorphed negative, into three extracted prints, each one of which covered one third of the whole. This conception came from Douglas Shearer and in discussing the idea with him early in the 1950's, the thought of its possible application to Process was suggested by the writer. Doug immediately concurred.

Many years previously in the '30's, we had tested an idea of 'spread' Process Projection to increase and more evenly distribute light from the projectors, at the screen's surface. Within certain 'keystone' limitations, we accomplished just that. From two projectors, some twenty-eight feet apart, we superimposed two identical background plates, onto a twenty-four foot wide screen, using four-inch projection lenses.

Matching of the superimposed background plates was obviously not exact, because of the slight keystoning due to the 'spread' position of the two projectors. However, certain subject matters such as clouds or seascapes, became quite acceptable, and we found that we were able to increase the size of the Process area considerably. Within these limitations, spread projection became a practical technique. I believe this was the first time multi-projection of the superimposition-ilk, was used, and certainly the innovation of 'apart' positioning, was a first.

In any event, the basic concept of three thirds from one negative, for theater triple projection, coupled with those early 'spread' tests and uses, gave birth to a new approach which we dubbed, "Laced Process." The name was inspired by footwear of the non-loafer variety. Two parts 'laced' together to become 'one'. The optically unsqueezed-thirds, were slightly wider than true thirds, allowing for an overlap which became the 'lacing' area.

As in many inventions, time passed until necessity became the mother ~ in this case, *How the West Was Won*, an M.G.M. Cinerama biggie. Mr. Shearer's theater exhibition concoction, unfortunately became the victim of Cinerama's decision to eliminate two of the three theater projectors, and never got beyond the proving ground. On the other hand, early testing of the idea's adaptability towards an improved Process, both in scope and quality, was established. And this we were able to do with existing equipment, with the addition of two rather crude 'lacers.' Then for eight years, we were laid to rest. It was the Process problems we faced in "West," which re-injected life blood into this long dormant, but not forgotten, idea.

A new regime at M.G.M., included Raymond Klune as General Manager. The suggestion that Laced Process would probably solve the scope needed for many of the contemplated Process shots was made. With little hesitation Ray gave our Department the green light. Your acumen Ray was beyond reproach, for which, our gratitude. We designed proper 'lacers' and tackled the chore.

The preliminary testing of years before became the foundation upon which our structure was built. 'Bugs' were squashed, one by one. Balanced color-and-density prints, were provided by Optical and the starting gate flew open.

Our long shot entry started well, but came a cropper on the back stretch. (Thanks Malcom and Phoebe Shelton of Amarillo, Texas, for my acquaintance with racing terminology. The two dollar windows, however, often proved expensive). No form sheet, no bloodline and an apprentice jockey up.

Mutiny on the Bounty needed large scope Process, and though inadequate time had been allotted for final tests, we plunged into 'Lacing' as the hoped-for answer. *How the West Was Won* had been delayed, so "Mutiny" was our debut. Several early additional 'croppers' excited some harsh observations from the Producer. I presume 'twas ever thus. We certainly were not looking for sympathy. We were looking for an answer. Why at times did it work beautifully and then nose-dive?

Fine-tooth-comb investigations uncovered nothing of consequence; all of the obvious requirements, balanced prints, balanced projection and positioning of the 'lacers', continued nevertheless to lead us up a hit-or-miss alley. Fortunately, before too many days had elapsed, the dawn came. Perhaps the most obvious condition of all had eluded us. A simple drafting-board plan view of a typical 'lace' set-tip, thoughtfully analyzed, supplied the cue to the riddle.

The two outside 'spread' projectors of the system, had remained at a predetermined distance apart. As projection lenses were changed to produce a larger or smaller image on the Screen, we had failed to consider that the 'spread' projectors' light intensity at the critical 'lacing' points, would increase or decrease. The needle in a haystack, grew in a relatively few minutes of cogitation, to a dimension at least as big as the haystack itself.

The principal of off-center-line camera shooting, as earlier described, to increase or decrease light, well known to us, served to spatter many eggs over many of our faces.

The dilemma was over. The key? We now had three instead of just one, center-lines to consider; the conventional middle one, and the two outer ones. It was immediately apparent from the drawing, that two additional imaginary lines, drawn from a camera location through the center of the overlap) 'lacing' area, mandated that the positions of the projectors be equidistant from these lines, if light from the projectors was to be of equal amounts, at the 'lace'. Re-page Dr. Watson, and this time request that he bring his needles with him.

A 'guide' chart was mathematically and graphically formulated and through this simple little way-shower, our 'plates' became a 'stakes winner'.

With no further ado, we include as part of this text, a substantial portion of a paper presented in April of 1964 to the Society of Motion Picture and Television Engineers, printed in their Journal of November, 1964 as well as in several other trade papers.

After a few introductory comments about Process generally, the article entitled, "Laced Process - A New System of Rear Projection Process," continues ~.

```
    "When new aspect ratios such as cinemascope and the various new wide screen "shapes" were
introduced, Process received a severe new challenge. We at M.G.M. recovered somewhat by being
able to superimpose anamorphed background prints on the process screen, thereby using the
full available projected background image, with resultant quality improvement. Much still was
to be desired, however, including the need for greater expanse which required larger screens
than the present existing factors of limited light and only fair quality allowed.
    Laced process has proved to be our answer and as a dividend, solved completely important
Cinerama sequences in How The West Was Won, as well as many other productions in both ultra-
Panavision and Panavision.
    "Laced Process" is so named because it involves the 'lacing' of three extracted
deanamorphed prints from an original anamorphed 65 M.M. negative, into a single
```

photographable 2.95 to 1 process background. The gain in all aspects of the process medium is enormous and it has enabled us to deliver shots to current pictures heretofore impossible of attainment.

The accompanying diagram will explain graphically the system as it compares with the use of triple-head process projectors now used in all of the studios and will we believe, be more readily understood than will a word description. The big advancement is in the scope and quality of the composite results and in the physical layout of shooting process which enables us to save greatly in stage space on both the projector and camera side of the screen. As an example it is possible for us to produce a 21' - 0" picture with a projection throw of only 40' - 8" and with a constant 62' - 0" throw we can range from 32' - 0" to 10' - 9" picture widths. A 76' - 6" throw gives us widths from 13' - 4" to 40' - 0".

This very startling space saver has an even more important pay-off in light gain due to the much closer proximity of the light source coupled with the new 'spread' positioning of the projectors.

Briefly we use three single-head process projectors, each projecting a print of slightly more than one third of the original negative so that two "overlaps" occur and these are blended or 'laced' together with instruments of our own design and construction which we call "lacers". Further, we have placed the two 'outside' projectors "A" and "C" at some distance from the center line upon which the center or "B" projector remains constant. This distance changes with varying picture sizes and in stage operation we are guided by a table or chart of our own development. The positioning described above, which is totally unique in its adaptation to process, coupled with the reduced circle of light which ensues when each machine projects roughly only one third of the whole picture, has enabled us to collect light at the camera in far greater quantities than with the old system although the individual light sources (projection lamps) remain the same and actually produce no greater quantity of light than before. This gain has given us a greater "F" stop with a very desirable increase in focus depth.

A later application of the original laced process system (now referred to as "Tri-Lace") has given us a "Dual-Lace" system which works generally the same as our 65 M.M. anamorphed Tri-Lace system, except that our backgrounds can be obtained from an original 35 M.M. negative, either anamorphed such as Panavision or Cinemascope, or in the old three by four full-aperture flat unsqueezed aspect ratio, or from a 65 M.M. spherical unsqueezed negative. Two projection prints are extracted from the original negative, each constituting one half of the original plus the overlap area. The procedure from then on follows that of the original invention except that we lace two instead of three to make the whole. The same 'spread' projector idea is of course followed. Basing the following opinion on results to date, the 'lace' method of rear projection process as it applies to any of the wide aspect ratio pictures, has given us a vastly improved process system. This can alter production planning in many cases which at present requires that principal actors and first units be on costly locations with the usual hazards of weather delays etc. It is hoped that further refinements and equipment improvements will be implemented which should add even additional scope to this very valuable tool.

The original idea for the laced process of background projection came from the writer and Douglas Shearer and forms a part of Mr. Shearer's Patent No. 2,920,526, owned by M.G.M. Other recognition should be given to: Carroll Shepphird, Process Assistant, Ed Snyder, Cinematographer, Robert Hoag, Optical (Background Extractions), Clint Watson, Process Projectionist, and Joe Gabouri, Process Grip.

In conclusion may the fact be stressed that this system is totally new and unique, including its use of 'spread' projectors. In the 30 odd year history of rear projection process, this is the first and only radical departure from the here-to-fore accepted 'center line' method.

Following is a list of productions which have used laced process.

Mutiny On The Bounty	Tri-lace
How The West Was Won	Tri-lace
Billy Rose' Jumbo	Tri-lace
It Happened At The World's Fair	Dual-lace
A Ticklish Affair	Tri and Dual-lace
Wheeler Dealers	Dual-lace
The Prize	Tri and Dual-lace
Viva Las Vegas	Dual-lace
The Greatest Story Ever Told	Tri-lace
The Unsinkable Molly Brown	Tri and Dual-lace

Thank you for your attention - we will now view some early and more recent tests and examples of laced process from some of the above productions."

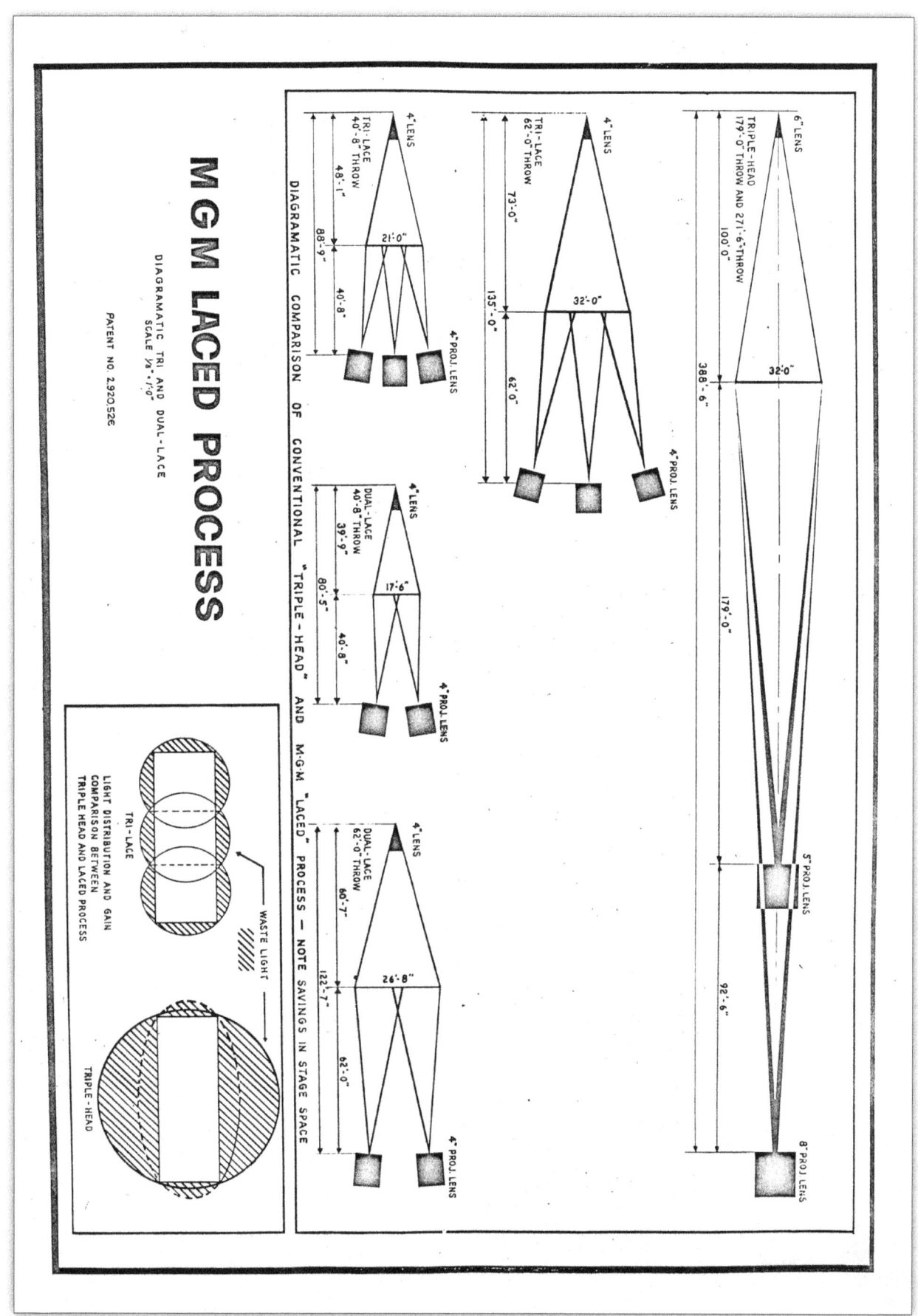

Published in Journal of the SMPTE, Volume 73, November 1964, pages 947 to 948.

The diagram should be self-explanatory. It represents only a few typical picture widths, the varying of which is accomplished through the use of projection lenses which, may range from 4" to 12" focal lengths, or more, plus the lateral position adjustment of the "A" and "C" projectors, as previously explained.

Joe Gabouri, our head Process grip, has thoroughly schooled himself in the 'floor layout' of Laced Process and methodically 'tapes' in advance of shooting, on the stage floor, all likely booth positions, marked and identified by the focal lengths of the selected projection lenses. Joe's teammate is usually Elbert 'Slim' Neill, and their combined proficiency in this and all other Process 'grip' work, has been of continuing and reliable comfort to all of us. In fact at times, trepidation has nudged our sense of 'comfort' because of Joe's adroitness. He might well replace the so called 'upper echelon' with whom he works. So we try to retain a few of our secrets, though I suspect without success. Thanks Joe, and thanks Slim, and thanks to others in this important stage-operation group who have become so thoroughly, well-grounded in their Process duties. The list of 'Steps' narrated early in this Chapter should include an additional one, 'Step 2.' "Develop and maintain a top Process crew," from the rear of the booth to the back of the camera. And maybe it would be wise to ignore the above reference to "secrets." There actually should be none, in an efficient, harmonious crew working with each other, rather than for each other. A repeat, this last? Yes, but one which bears repeating. If there has been one attitude, and certainly it has been an honestly endeavored one as far as my experience is concerned, it accents that type of relationship with fellow workers and has gone far towards filling an ever receptive personal container labled, "Help Needed."

REFLEX PROCESS

A very recent and exiting development which has greatly increased the scope of Process, is a front projection system known as "Reflex Process". Not a totally new concept but made possible through 3M's (Minnesota Mining and Manufacturing Co.) refinement of their Scotch-lite product and an improved projection and photographic arrangement. Much of the latter, a highly precise and controllable unit, was developed in our British studio under the guidance of Tom Howard. It was successfully used in Stanley Kubric's *2001 – A Space Odyssey*.

The system is relatively simple, consisting of a single projector, lamp, and taking camera, mounted on a common base, the camera at a 90° angle relative to the projection unit. A 50% transmission mirror is place at a 45° angle to both camera and projector. The mirrored surface of the glass faces the projector and reflects the projected image to the 3M screen from which it is returned directly to the light source within the projector. This characteristic of light reflection is basic in Scotch-lite. Roughly 50% of the returning image passes through the 50-50 mirror and is registered on film within the camera, the balance returning to the projector. The extremely high gain achieved, 400, 500, 600 to 1, allows much larger areas to be covered than heretofore possible. Laced Process, as an example, is limited to probably a 50-foot-in-width-screen. Reflex Process has had successful results (in 2001) up to 100 feet and there seems to be no reasonable limit to acceptable results; perhaps in excess of 200 feet.

The mirror transmission ratio may be varied from 50-50 depending on subject matter. A low in value background may require a 55-45 or a 60-40 ratio of reflection and transmission or perhaps the reverse on high key bright background material to be projected.

Glass upon which the mirror surface is applied must be optically near perfection and free of any color distortion. The mirror frame must be absolutely free of jiggle or vibration so that the projected image remains steady and constant.

A rudimentary question has been asked, "what happens to the projected light on foreground elements of the composite, people, set, etcetera?" Well, just don't be concerned. Foreground lighting, even at low key, completely eradicates any possible background image. As a matter of fact the high reflex properties of the screen totally overpower photographically any background image pick-up when there is no foreground lighting at all; foreground elements become simply silhouettes.

It is obvious that people or objects being photographed will intercept the projected image, leaving bland areas or "holes" in the background. Proper alignment of camera, mirror and projector is essential in order that "rimming" be avoided. Foreground should and does precisely "fill" these blank areas provided meticulous attention to alignment is practiced.

Uses of this relatively new adjunct to Process are legion. It doe not necessarily supersede Rear Projection Process in run-of-the-mill process demands which fall generally in the category of its past application. For scope, however, and imaginative adaptations, Reflex Process is a very valuable tool. A simple illustration. An actor whose costume has been partially or wholly covered with patches of 3M material, matching that of the background screen, will be photographically invisible in the areas covered by Scotch-lite. The projected image, supposedly "behind" him, reflects back to the camera as though his body or parts of it, were totally transparent.

Within fairly generous limitations objects covered with this reflex material in planes considerably closer to the camera than that of the basic background screen will react in their image-return as though only one surface were serving to reflex. Balancing the neutrals may be necessary due to the closer proximity to the light source (the projector) and resulting added brightness, when such treated foreground areas are a considerable distance from the screen. Depth of projected image focus will also govern object placement or live action limitations in such instances.

Too numerous to mention and other adaptations, such as "walking" on water (?), or in musicals, dream sequences, science and fiction effects or straight large scope composite photography. The reader will readily see the value of this added tool in the process kit – Reflex Process.

CONCLUSION

In concluding this last Category, Process, a brief review of its contents, follow. Somehow we started with a nursery rhyme which drew us into expressed hope that a speeded-up-evolution would bring racial harmony. Jimmy Walker was eulogized. Then we buckled down to the subject at hand, Process. Elementary descriptions and procedures followed, with reports, instructions and 'Steps' detailed. The promised report to Mr. O'Brien was waylaid, principally because it was covered in essence as an integral part of the "paper" presented to the Society of Motion Picture and Television Engineers. Studio 'instructions' to be followed in the shooting of background plates, preceded the all-important 'Steps' list, which were then more comprehensively defined and stressed.

The advisable and varied use of camera movement, the intelligent handling and supervision of related Effect mediums while shooting Process, were exemplified with hypothetical and actual examples illustrating. Close teammanship with the Art and Production Departments was decreed and the desirability of qualified judging of 'stock' film took its place as an important 'sub-Step'. Dollars saved which can become 'expensive dollars,' was underlined and 'control' was again included as one of the Effects-man's 'ten commandments'.

Actuality versus Process was cited in the paragraphs devoted to Victor Fleming's "at sea" edict and will serve we hope, to promote thoughtful consideration of all alternatives, in determining available methods of solution. New and long-sought adequate casters were part of this cloud's silver lining and we suggested that the ear of management be sympathetically and understandingly tuned towards legitimate requests for proper tools. We hastened to 'gold-star' M.G.M.'s management for its past record of mostly 'now', and occasionally 'eventually'. Only a few times did the barn door remain unlocked after the horse was stolen.

Legitimate stage 'delays' and the allowance of sufficient time needed to achieve Process adequacy were accented. 'Know-how' crews and the need of proper conditions, carrying the blessings of a Producer, a Production Department, and the overhead watchers, were hopefully propounded. 'Do's', 'don'ts' and 'tips' were freely offered and 'open-mindedness', as it relates to 'liberties and licenses', was advised.

Techniques involving the purposeful inclusion of difficulties encountered in 'real' location shooting, when Process becomes the alternate, were proposed. The 'unglueing' of a ship's interior was explained and recommended. We explained that 'rockers' may at times be dispensed with, provided a camera portrays proper movement, and judicious use of a 'gimble', so that 'leaning towers' do not result, was given utterance.

Variance in the violence of camera movements between wild and wooly, and serene scenes, was thoroughly defined and in this vein we chastised those who 'shake' a submarine beyond physical possibility. We 'amputated' a star's head in *Test Pilot* and we included some new and workable airplane mounts. A wheelbarrow was enlisted as an answer to banking-and-straight-run race backgrounds, and we told of our inspiration for the low-level race course, having come from a golf club. 'Leaning' foregrounds, sets and people was illustrated as a 'sometime-answer' to steep-angle projection, and elevating booths for lesser angles was extolled.

The inclusions of gloss finished Process Screens to better cope with wayward water was mentioned and screen frames adjustable to selected degrees of slant were recommended. Off center-line camera positions to gain or reduce light, and the angling of the 'plan' position of a screen to obtain other than the angle for which a plate was originally shot, was timidly suggested. Not good general practice, but a good emergency maneuver. Lining camera, vehicle and screen, to avoid dog-like askew skidding was a 'tip'.

Many recommendations relating to aspect ratios and their possible intermingling to better cover the projected screen-image field regardless of camera field, led into a foreground and background 'scale' relationship discussion, in which the moon became a factor. We also rang the tocsin forewarning against moves towards the screen which would result in the enlargement of grain and possible background plate defects, and offered a substitute to Mr. Seitz. Forty small Tahitians dressed in forty pipes and a well aimed kick, forcibly delivered and salved with kisses, was documented to show that extra-curricular happenings can and do occur in the field of Special Effects.

The birth, development, and use, of "Laced Process," described and diagramed, brought us pretty well to the finish of Process as a subject. We then added a 'Step' to our early list, which preached the value of developing and maintaining a hep crew from whom no 'secrets' should remain under wraps. The loyalty and added efficiency of a 'with' crew instead of a 'for' crew was praised and advocated. And that's about it except for some further ramblings and a few randoms in the concluding Chapter to come.

The following pages include diagramatic drawings of some of M.G.M.'s mounts and rigs used primarily for Process shooting and generally for comparatively small units. The "mechanical horses" are adjustable for various gaits. Speeds are controlled by a rheostat, The treadmills are also similarly controlled and may be tilted for up-hill or down-hill action.

The airplane mount (showing a small plane) is one which enabled us to "fly" full rolls in front of a Process Screen. An adapter to this mount, supporting the airplane at the wingtips, gave us full loops.

The "jeep" coil-spring car mount is used mostly for rough-going simulations. It has also served for high speed motor boats "in" choppy water. The ski-rig, snow or water (reverse for water) rests the "ski-slats" on shock-cord at one end. They are hinged at the other.

Many others, not shown, include various race car mounts and motorcycle mounts with underslung counter weights. These, as well as some of the car mounts, are designed to allow for "banking" on turns.

Often, in spite of our large stable of mounts and rigs, new gimmicks must be contrived and no long periods of imaginative dormancy can be condoned. There is much more to Process than just photographing a foreground against a projected background (Process Plate) and the development and design of mounts and equipment constitute an important facet of Process activity.

END OF CHAPTER TEN

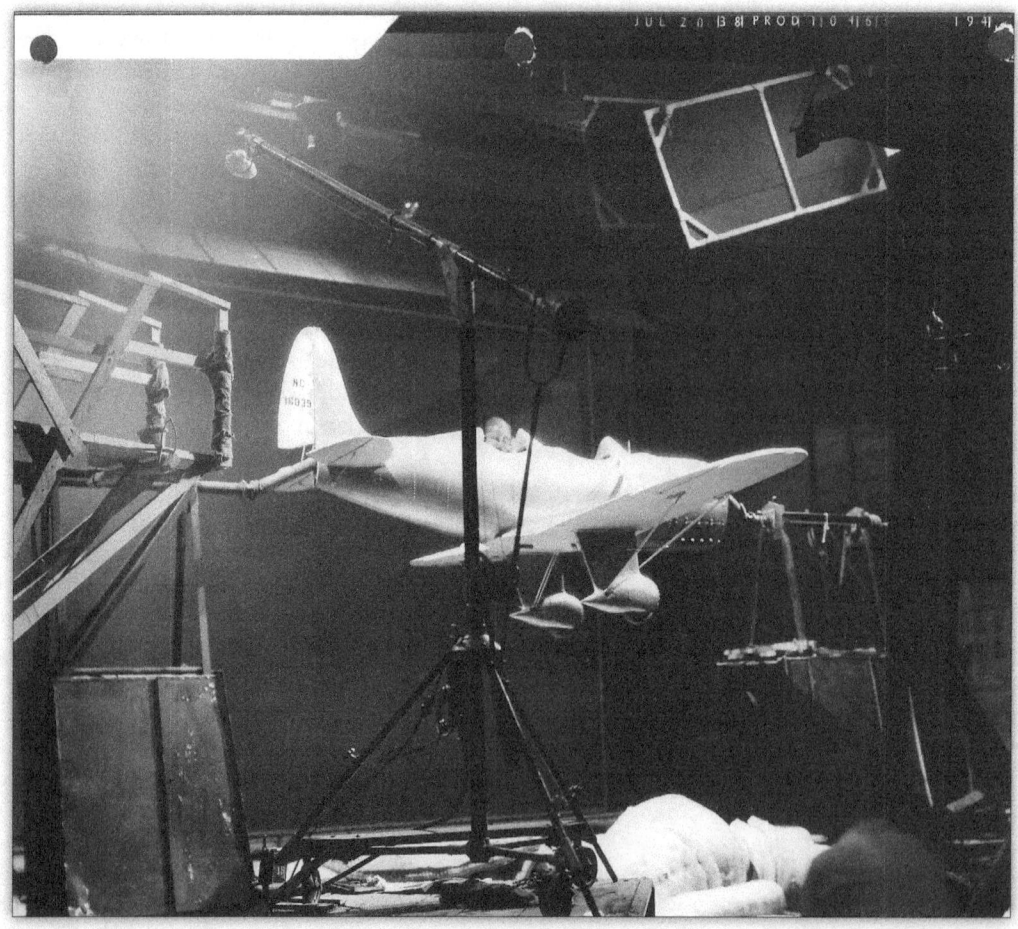

(Above) Airplane mount for *Too Hot To Handle* contrived by John Bossart and our prop shop and mechanical departments for looping and rolling airplane (full-sized) in front of a Process Screen.
Courtesy - The Academy Margaret Herrick Library.

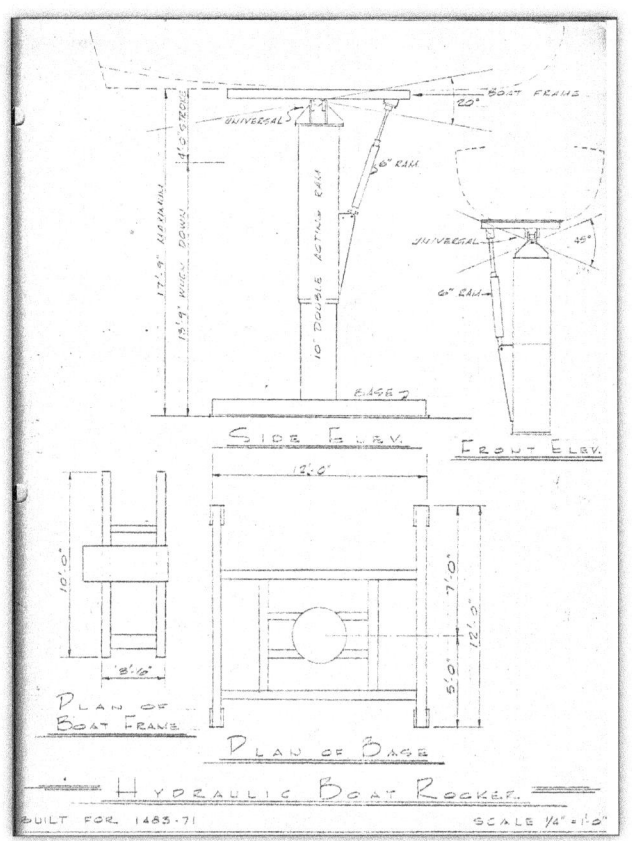
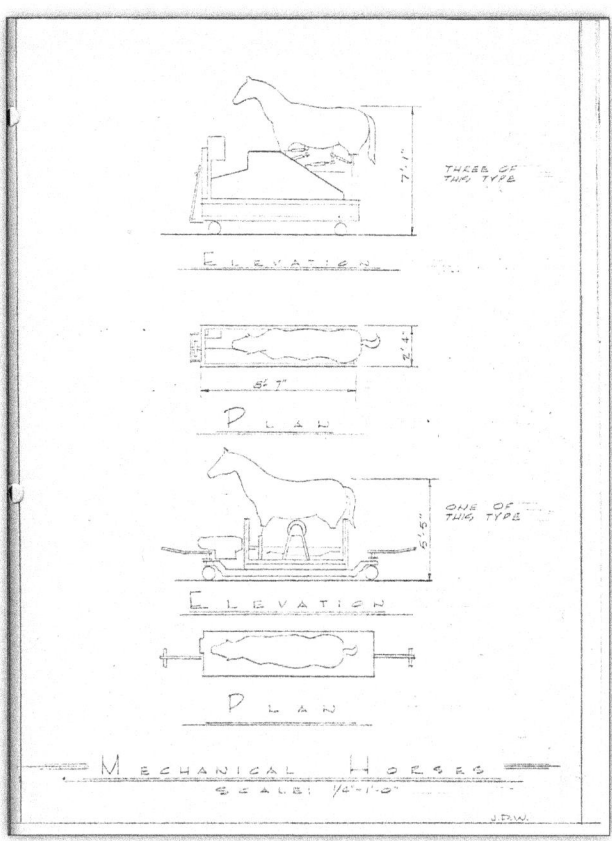
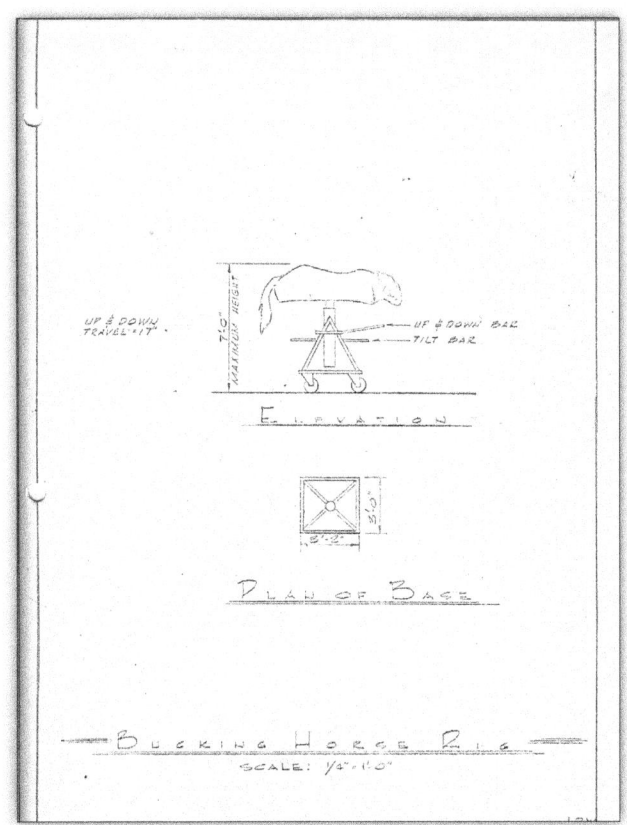
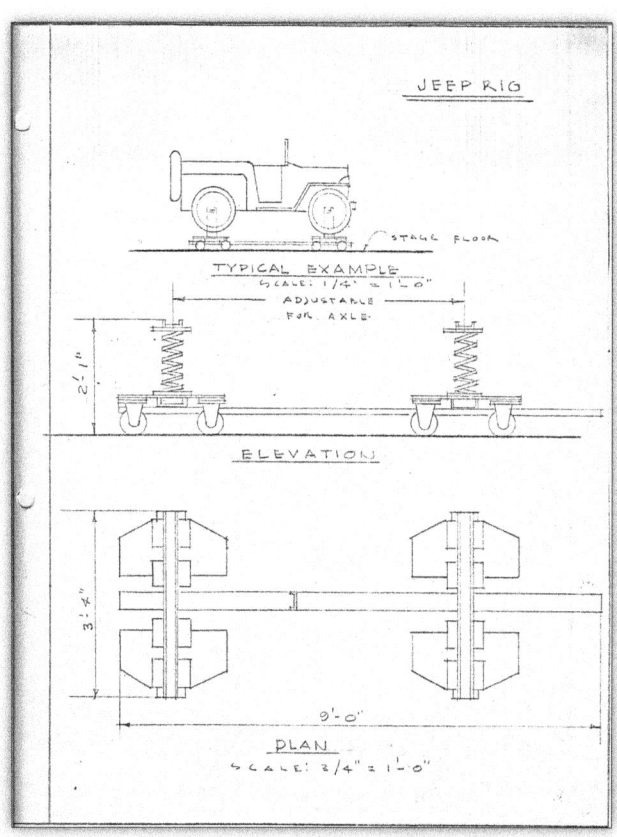

90-P

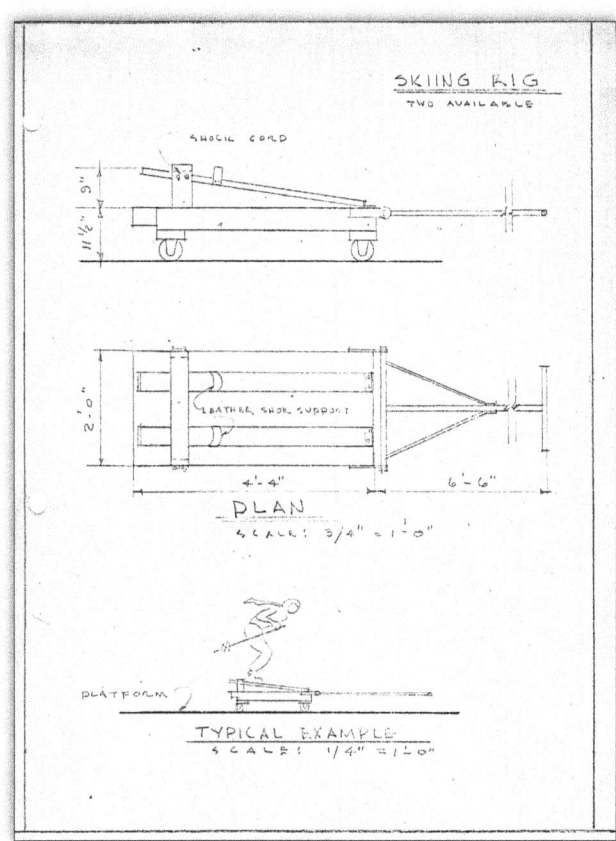
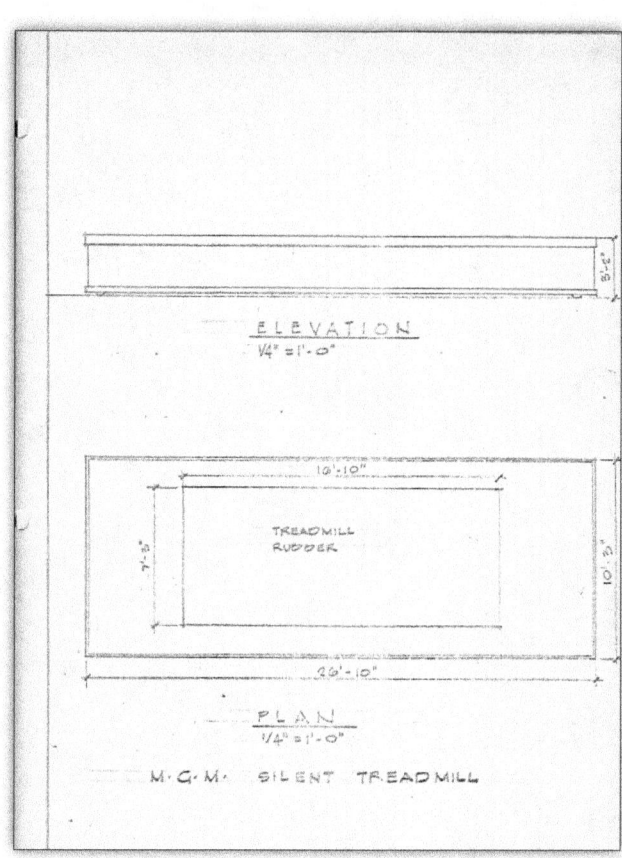
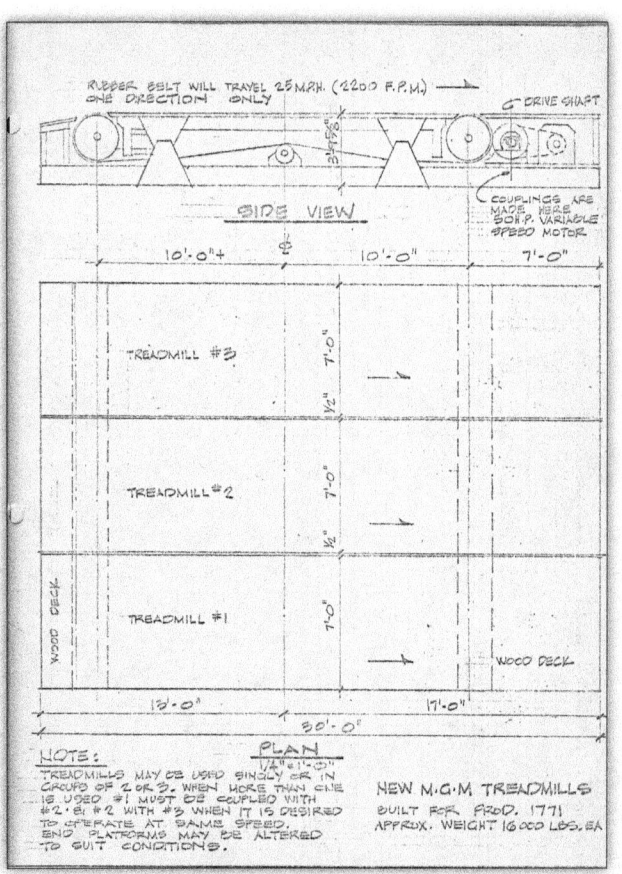
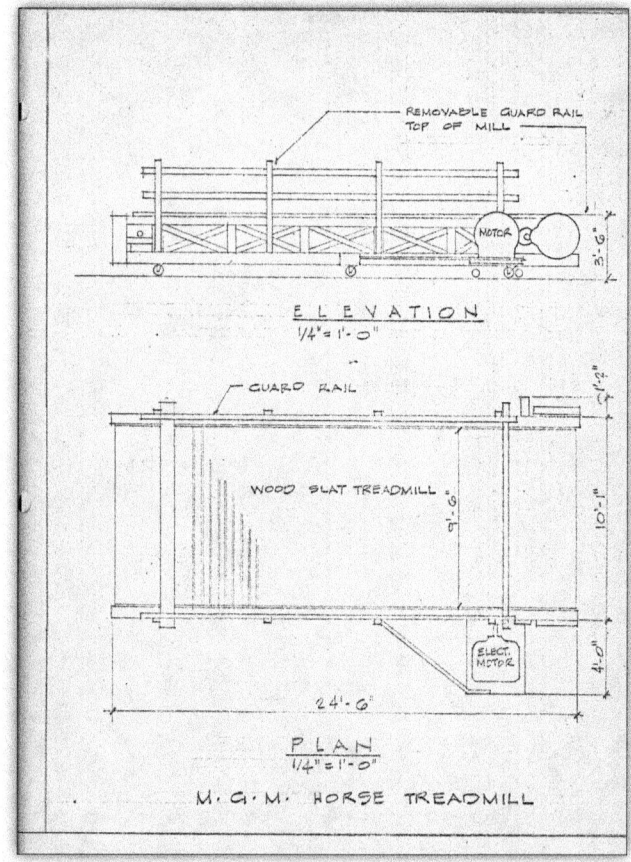

CHAPTER TEN 308

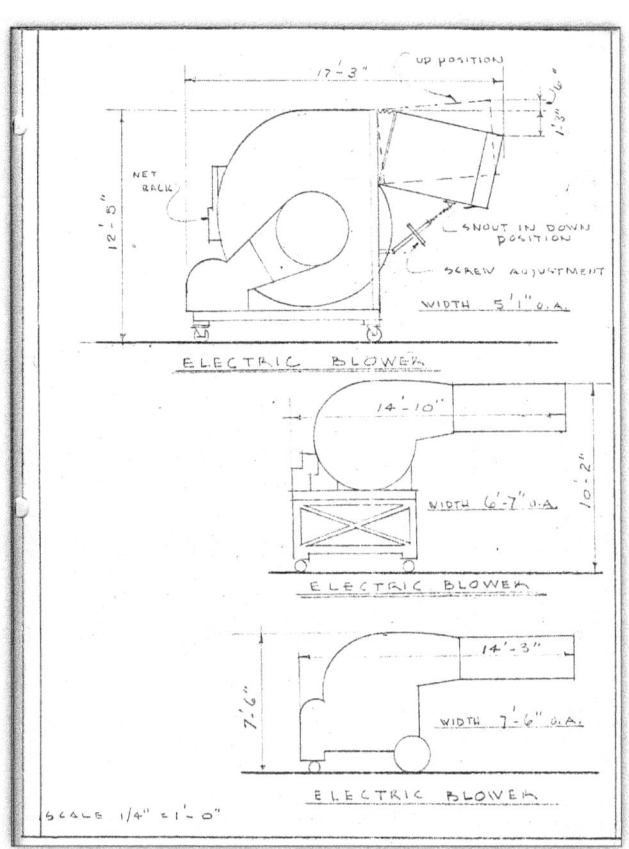
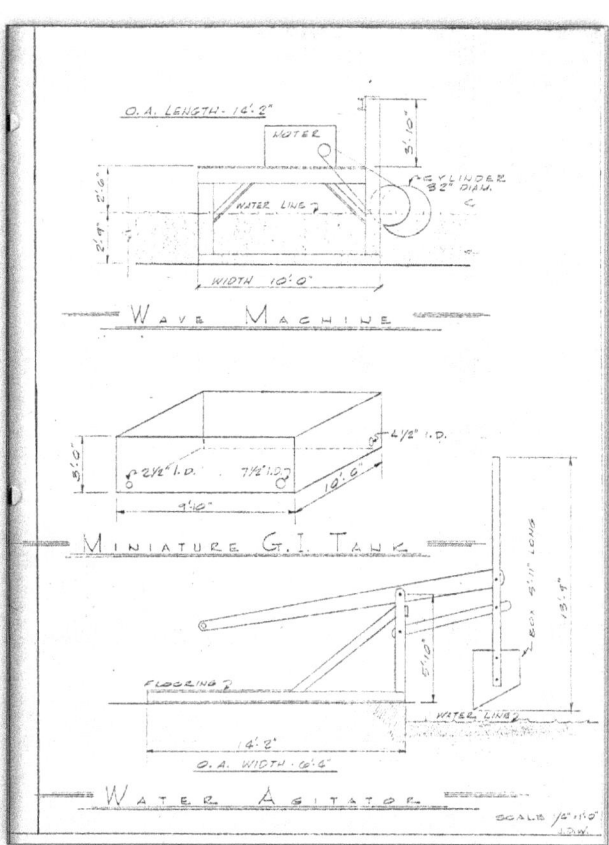
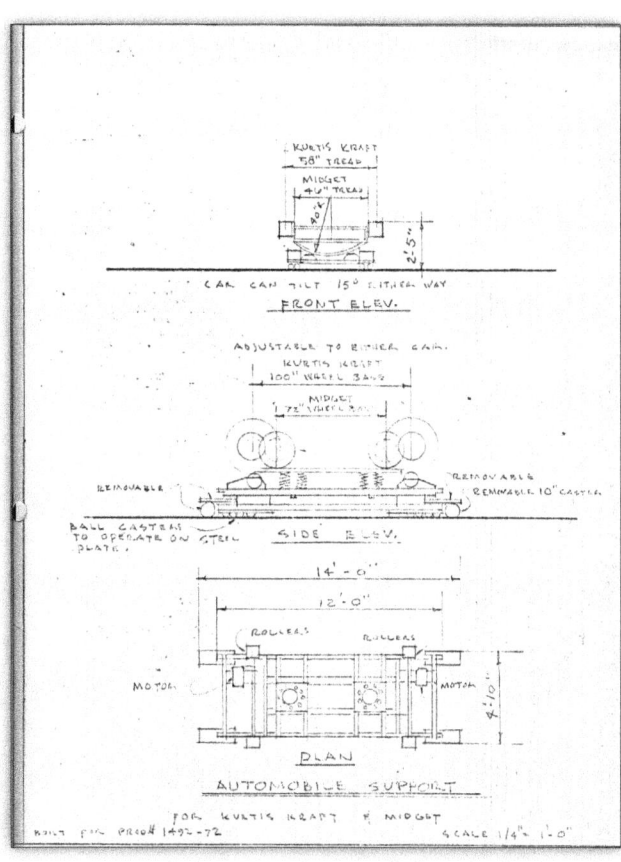
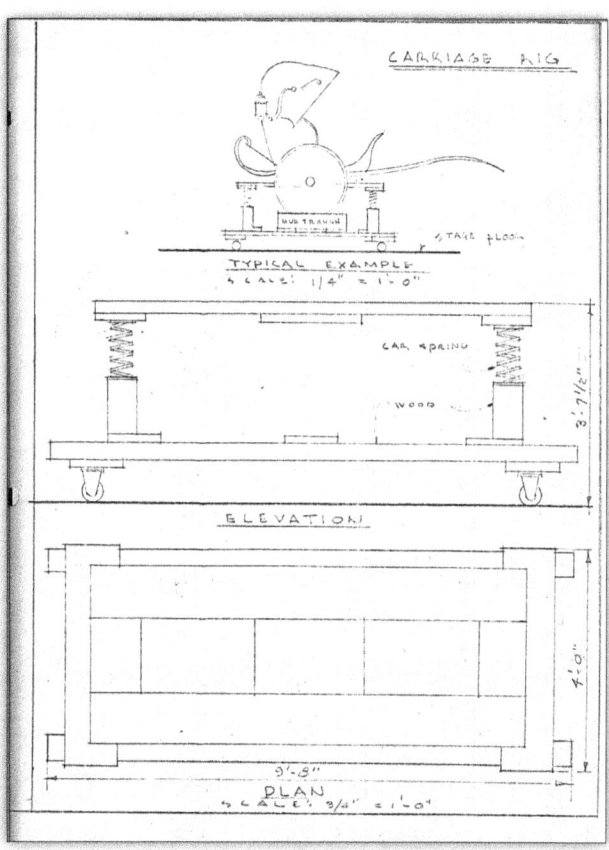

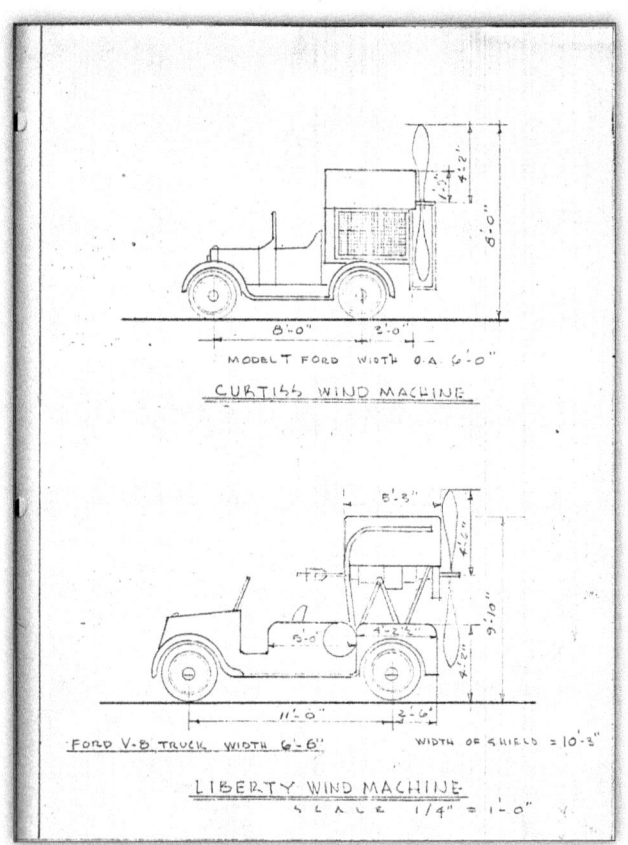
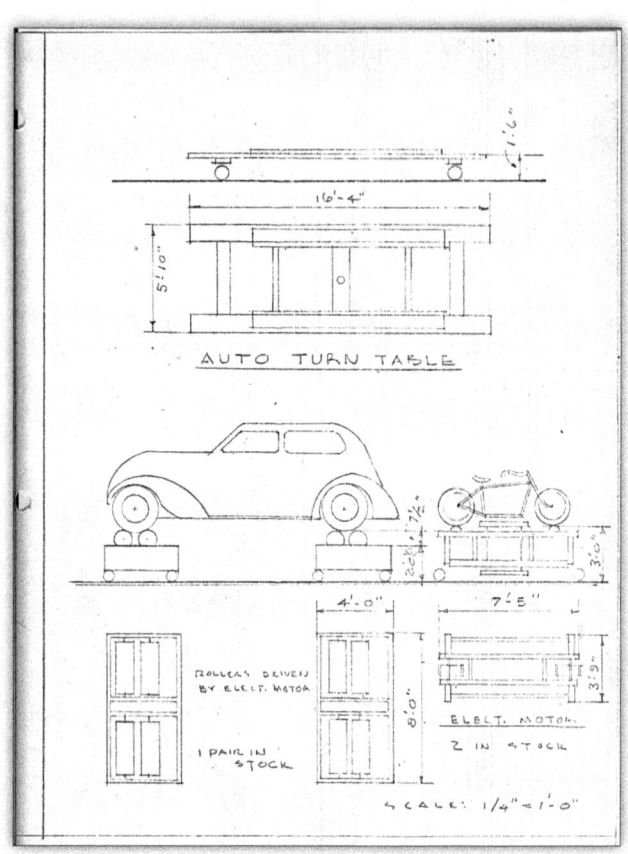
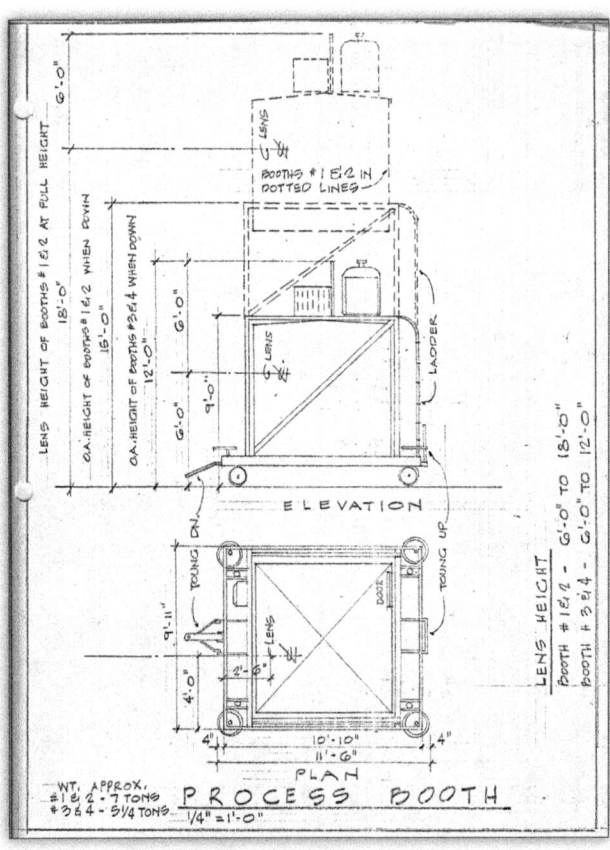
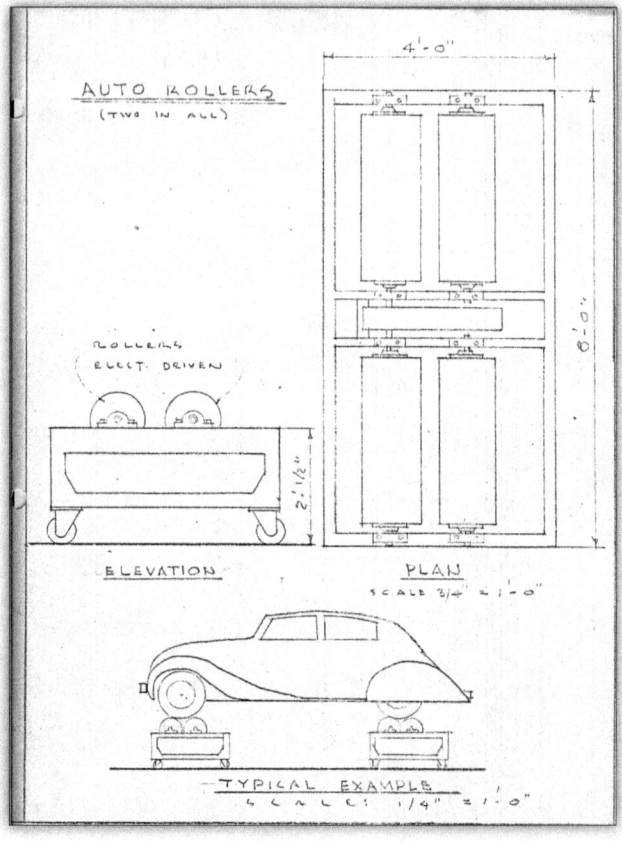

CHAPTER TEN

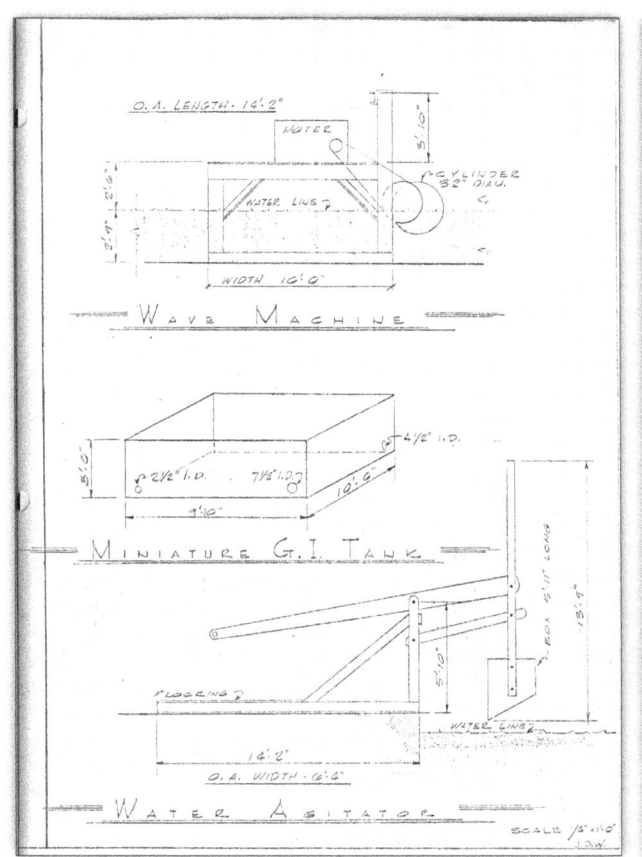
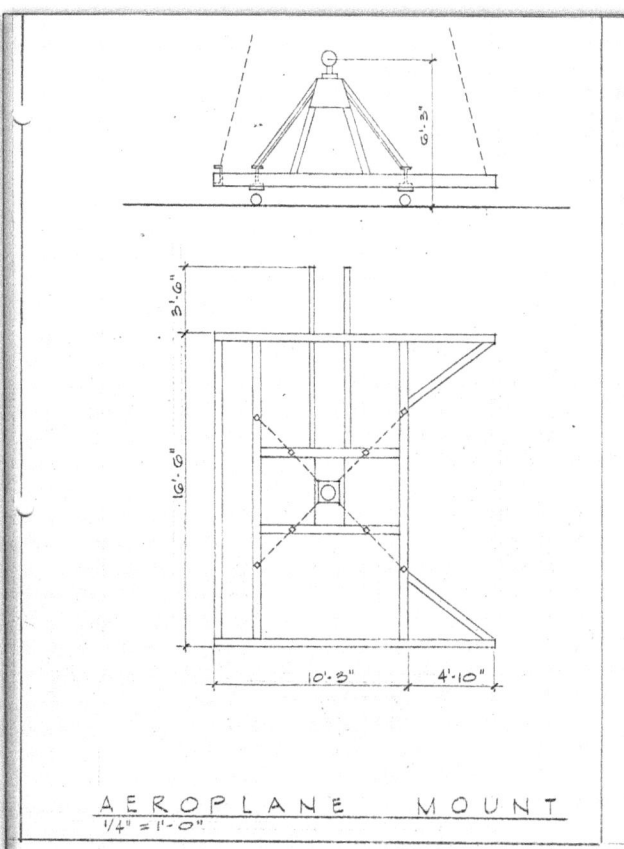

Captains Courageous - Motorized auto roller for car body and boat. Process screen in background.
Courtesy - The Academy Margaret Herrick Library

BOOM TOWN (1940) PRODUCTION #1138

Boom Town - Scene 128X8 Process Shot. Stationary B.G. for two johns in group. 2 Johns enter scene from Left after having been wrapped in burlap. Shield is brought to them from right. . . They are wet down and exit left with shield, starting into fire.

Boom Town - Scene 133C, 134X5, 132 B-2. 75mm lens. Trucking background straight ahead and straight back for 2 Johns planting shield and retreating. Aperture pieces selected for matte shot of 2 Johns as they retreat after having planted shield and then nitro. . added mattes.

Boom Town "Beautiful Betsy" #2 oil derrick 1/4 full scale. B.G. sky and plain for well and tent. Newcombe top. B.G. for tent and table with derrick. Nigrosine dye colored water as oil substitute.

Liquid fuel routed through copper pipe in bottom of miniature oil well. Used for process plate. Rigging for fire, rotating nozzle for gasoline under pressure-smoke on wells, steam, water, oil and air on engines and boilers.

Ext. "Beautiful Betsy" #2, 1/3 scale derrick. Used for backgrounds and Mattes, dolly shot for fire sequence. Rigging for gusher, 10,000 gal pump, pipes, sump, and hydraulic valves and boilers.

Boom Town - Beautiful Betsy #2 just after she blows. Miniature shown on previous page. Two Johns exit tent hearing rumbling of oil derrick. Scene follows long shot of Beautiful Betsy #2 1/4 full scale shot.
Courtesy - The Academy Margaret Herrick Library.

Boom Town - Cyclorama background and F.S. oil derrick for McMaster's oil field shot, scene 187. "Oil" recipe 1/2 drum oil, 10 Chunk resin, 1 gallon turpentine, muric acid, 1 lb carbite, 3 to 4 square sponge rubber.
Courtesy - The Academy Margaret Herrick Library.

Below - Clark Gable and Lionel Atwill, oil promoter, stand on bridge over pool used for temporary storage.
Courtesy - The Academy Margaret Herrick Library, John Francis and Shirley B. Gibson.

Additional *Boom Town* Process shots - Scene 128X8 Process Shot close up set and Process background. Stationary B.G. for two Johns in group. 2 Johns enter scene from Left after having been wrapped in burlap. Shield is brought to them from right. . . They are wet down and exit left with shield, starting into fire. Courtesy - The Academy Margaret Herrick Library

Below - Spencer Tracey and Clark Gable wrapped with water soaked burlap. Era 1921. Before asbestos suits.
Courtesy - The Academy Margaret Herrick Library, John Francis and Shirley B. Gibson

Boom Town Process shots - Scene 166, Fire Sequence set and Process plate on right.
Courtesy - The Academy Margaret Herrick Library.

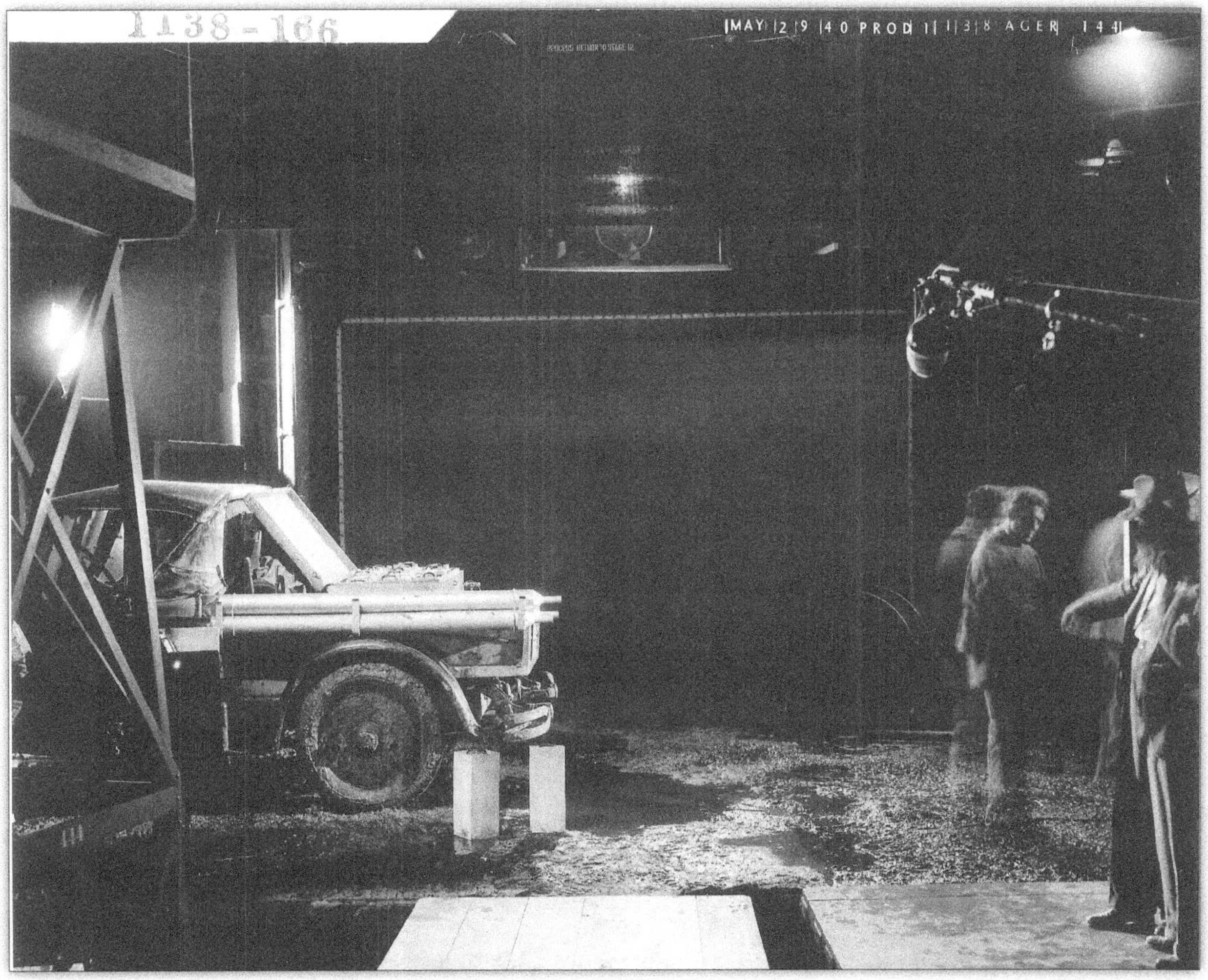

"PROCESS THE WHYS AND HOWS"

Night Flight, MGM Production #677, Released 1933, AAG Contribution: Special Effects.

CHAPTER ELEVEN
~
"RAMBLING RANDOMS"

Idiot's Delight, MGM Production #1056, Released 1939, AAG Contribution: Special Effects.

A general summation at this point of each category into which Special Visual Effects is divided would be repetitious. This has been attempted at the end of each chapter - a brief review, designed to serve as a 'reminder list' of that Chapter's subject. Tedious details have also been omitted. They are infinite in number and I believe would have little instructional value. Rather, an overall 'surface' picture has most generally constituted the book's contents.

The thinking behind this conclusion is the old, "can't see the forest for the trees" observation, or "a nose much too close to the grindstone". The use of competent and diversified talents to handle much that must be engineered, invented, contrived - allows for a less restrained approach at the outset of a problem, in determining methods and in removing 'detail' obstacles from the freedom of creativity. Practical concessions may come later, but a successful Effectsman will always start with the ideal, and pare it only when practical or economic necessity dictates.

Now, as indicated at the end of the last Chapter, we will proceed to 'ramble'. Repeats may occur, but if so there is probably a wish to further accent certain ideas and possibly a criticism or two. Of the latter, a constructive one, I hope, will serve as a kick-off.

KNOW-IT-ALL

There are those people in many walks of life, certainly a few in our business, who consistently refuse help, or at least the acknowledgment thereof. The 'know-it-all' individual who cannot be told, builds for himself a stupid stockade, through which beneficial ideas originating outside of his thinking realm will gradually cease in their efforts to penetrate that realm. He will in time thicken the skin of his well-intentioned benefactors and, of course, he becomes the loser. Curious, this phobia, and harmful not only in closing the tap through which helpful information would flow, but much more seriously, such an attitude weakens, rather than strengthens the imagined position of the offender. A person, especially if he is the boss, a department head or a top executive, who cannot say, "Thanks - this I did not know. It's a whale of an idea!" Or perhaps a "Of course, of course! I know about that. Why didn't I think of it?" is an unfortunate individual. Born perhaps of a deep-seated sense of inferiority or worse, ego, this attitude should be 'garbaged'. Your underlings and your overlings will respect you infinitely more if you don't <u>always</u> insist upon having <u>all</u> the answers. The successful leader will add to his stature by adopting this simple frame of mind in all of his dealings - "Let's call in so-and-so. He probably knows more about this than I do." Such admissions do nothing to detract from his supervisory standing. Rather, he gains by it. So one and all, forget this not.

DIPLOMACY

The fine art of 'diplomacy' should be cultivated by each and all, and at times it can become a real asset in controversies with many of the personalities with whom an Effectsman comes in contact. One day during the shooting of *How the West was Won*, Henry Hathaway, Director, threatened the equanimity of our lunch period by descending rather wrathfully alongside our peaceful commissary lunch table.

"Buddy", he expostulated, as only Henry can expostulate, "you said I should 'this' and I should 'that' in shooting Laced Process, and you're wrong, Mr. Gillespie, Wrong!"

Well, who hasn't been wrong, once, twice, many times. In this case, however, I felt there was some deviation between my actual 'do this'es' and 'do that's' and Henry's interpretation of same. You don't say to Mr. Hathaway, "You misunderstood, Henry," unless you are prepared to absorb a minor or a major tirade, delivered with or without tongue in cheek. At this luncheon interruption, Henry's cheek was not bulged. The straw I grasped at this moment of potential drowning was one labeled "diplomacy"

"Mr. Hathaway," soothed I, "if my remarks were as you say, I'm sorry. But surely a man of your <u>technical astuteness</u> would have known much, much better than to have followed such instructions, Mr. Hathaway."

We had an audience, my lunch-mates. All was momentarily quiet in the immediate area and a slow grin replaced the glare on Henry's visage as he departed. So tact, a soft answer, and that out of the blue inspiration, "a man of your technical astuteness –" served to turn away wrath. Seldom will such a soft-soap rebuttal come to mind, but diplomacy as such may win the battle, if not the war.

The entire association with Henry on this top M.G.M. Cinerama epic was a delight. He is technically astute and a very capable director, and though upon occasions he erupts with his own convictions of righteous indignation, our experience on "West" was mutually harmonious. A worthy team-mate. Diplomacy.

The use of very long focal-length camera lenses, mounted on a geared pan-and-tilt, or a free head, may be of value in obtaining moving side-angle background plates from a <u>stationary</u> position. Ski backgrounds for close up Process shots, are often difficult to attain from a moving 'snow vehicle'. Earlier, I believe, we mentioned this problem as it pertained to shots needed in *Duchess of Idaho*. A location in 'ski country' was found which enabled us to place a stationary camera several hundred feet from, the imaginary 'run'. The camera operator simply 'followed', with a long tilting pan, an imaginary skier as he sped down the slope. The small field covered by the long focal-length lens in the close vicinity of the 'skier' served to produce the needed plates quickly and far more smoothly than had we attempted them in some other manner. The obvious requirement is that no obstructions exist between the camera and the path of the 'run'. We have used this method to obtain Process plates for close-ups of surfers and in other instances where conditions are right (obstacleless foregrounds) and where it is not practical to provide for a moving or dollying camera. Such plates for surfboard riders, as an example, may be photographed from a pier, the end of a breakwater, or any properly located solid spot. They should be shot from a reasonably high set-up, perhaps twelve to twenty feet, which will necessitate a slight tilt-down of the camera, and the position selected for the camera should be so that the 'face' of the breaker during its progress shoreward is included. Background plates for short close-ups of a speeding racer, such as on the salt flats at Bonneville Flats in Utah, or for a <u>circling</u> airplane against a cloud-studded sky. Many more, but <u>always</u> with nothing interrupting the space between camera position and the immediate area where action is to be later placed in front of a Process Screen, and always with lenses of the telephoto family.

MOVING WATER

In *Cairo*, an M.G.M. 'oldie', a shot from on high of a soldier-laden troop ship passing through the Suez Canal was required. A miniature ship and canal was determined as the sensible method. But what about the troop-littered decks? We were too close to fall back on the floating bits of cork bit, used at Versailles in *Marie Antoinette*, and the troops were too loosely strewn here and there and about to not be individually distinguished. Their action precluded the use of mechanized miniature people, which by the way is generally the poorest of practices as well as expensive to manipulate even <u>badly</u>. So full-sized flesh and blood people must somehow be optically printed onto the decks of our <u>moving</u> miniature ship. No brain-racking solution here if the ship had been static. Just photograph an assortment of soldier-wardrobed

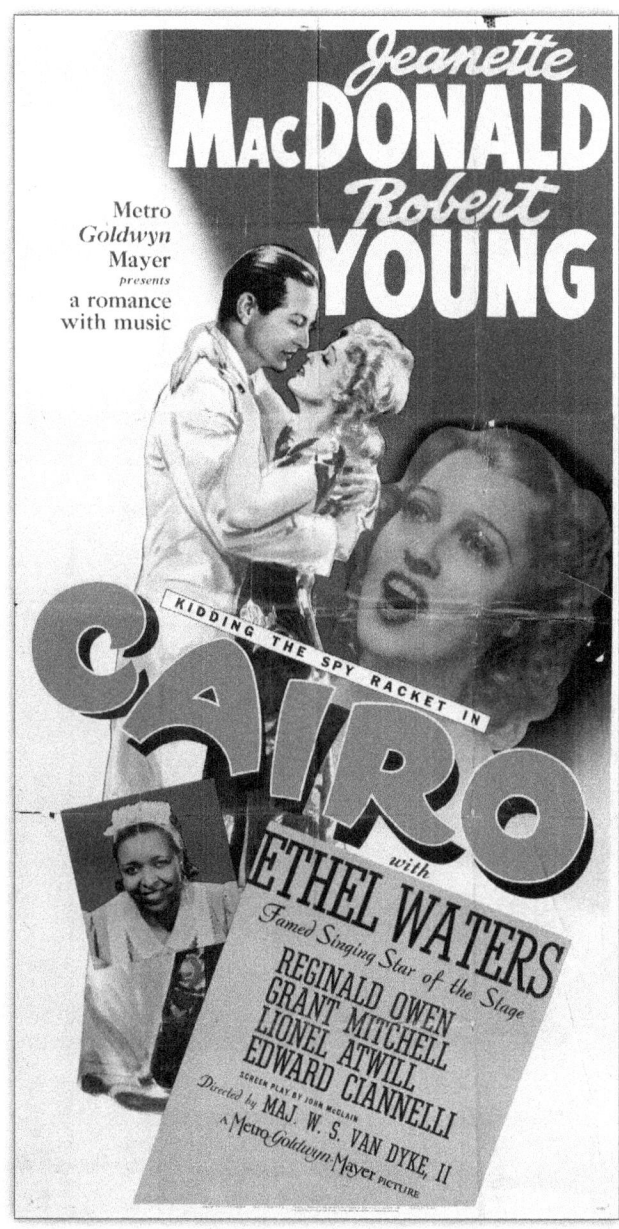

extras from a stationary camera position and optically reduce and fit within the confines of the deck areas of a stationary ship. But our vessel must move, albeit slowly, through the Suez. The answer? Rudimentary, and don't smile, ye of well-foundationed Effects' wisdom. This tome is for the perusal of the student, the layman, and just possibly also for "ye of wisdom". We simply put into motion, at the desired ship 'speed', our canal, the bordering banks, everything within the camera's range and shot an immobile ship. Later, active people photographed from stationary cameras were printed aboard. To further gloss the completed composite, that final pinch of paprika, we later optically moved the ship within the frame lines of the original 'field', thereby removing any sense of static deadness that might have remained. So often there are more ways than one to skin a cat.

UN-UNIONS

Recently, in discussing a certain individual with his department head, I was driven to the unearthing of another bone to pick with Unions. The chap in question possesses outstanding talents, a craftsman of exceptional value to his department, a man highly desirable to retain as an employee. But his arrival in California and his employment by M.G.M. was of recent date. That automatically placed him on the "number two" list according to his Union rules, and in the event of a slack-time lay-off, he qualified as the first to be fired, whereas his actual qualifications merited and should have dictated his being perhaps the last. The only alternative to this kind of a situation is for the 'boss' to retain the whole string of those doing the same type of work, and this at times just doesn't make economic sense.

Where is the reward for the years devoted to costly study and training which, when combined with an inborn ability of such an extraordinary degree of excellence, regulates that person to "list number two"? I am quite aware of the stock 'organized' answer, and there is some justification to it.

"We must protect and give seniority to our long-time, dues-paying, members." Not a very satisfactory one, however, to a man who excels, nor to his superior who is powerless to keep him under such conditions. As exemplified earlier in these pages, something is radically hay-wire in Denmark when impeding blocks, regardless of their well-meaning, are thrown across a man's road to success and achievement and retention.

COW HERDING

In a lighter vein, and instructive only if you are not cognizant of the fact that cows are curious and have an appetite for airplane 'dope', the following account of a game of 'cow-tag' may be entertaining.

Early in 1928 a small group at the studio formed a flying club and, strangely, we all learned to fly, or at least we were able to take off and return our powerful sixty horsepower flying machine in one piece. Doug Shearer, Ray Binger, Bill Daniels, Jimmy Manatt, Merrill Pye and yours truly were charter members.

Upon completion of a first solo flight each of us were obligated to be host for a quiet evening, celebrating the event. Quiet? Well, that was the intention (?). Most of these get-togethers seemed to accumulate more dangers as the evenings progressed, than the actual solo flights themselves. Actual structural failures were rare though wrestling and show-off gymnastics at these soirees did occasionally result in bruised landing gears and sacroiliac damage to our respective fuselages.

Some years later, I having acquired half of a two-cockpit biplane (Merrill owned the other half), the adventure with the cows took place. A big shindig at the Albertson ranch, not far from Tarzan's 'Hippo' Lake, was to take place on the coming Sunday, and I thought it might be appropriate to arrive by airplane if a suitable place to land could be found.

CAIRO (1942) PRODUCTION #1248

FORM 48

DATE May 19, 21, 22, 23 '42

PRODUCTION 1248

SET 79

STAGE 14

PICTURE Cairo

TITLE OF MINIATURE Ext. Troopship in Canal

Set & Plane Rigging $2000.
Camera $150.
Sky $75.
Spec. Effects $75.

Estimated Construction and Special Effects
Preparation 2300.
Special Camera Mounts 1300.
Min. Operation 1600.
Elect. Operation 600.
Add and Changes
Total Approp. 5800.
Final Cost 2843.79

Details of Min. Set—Area .... No. of Buildings or Units ....

Scale 3/4 .... Day .... Night .... Dawn X Sunset ....

Backing Projected

REMARKS

Straight shot of troopship in canal with Spy Plane diving and exploding.

B.G. shooting down on deck of troopship. Ship and camera stationary so that people could be printed in.
Water and Canal bank moved to give progression to ship.
Forward progression given by optical printing.

Dressing and Min. Props.

Background Long shot for spy plane diving on Canal and Troopship. Used scenic drop with camera on gantry crane moving through clouds.

CONSTRUCTION 711- 556.63
              713- 442.67
Total Construction Cost... 999.30 .... Total Special Effects 80.63

OPERATION   **Construction Dept. Daily Cost**

Average Crew

	Foreman	Mechanics	Grips	Laborers
Morning	1	6		2
Afternoon	1	6		1
Night				

Total Operation Cost... 1,215.20

ELECTRICAL Average Load ....
Wind Machines and Fans ....
Average Daily Crew 12
Total Operating Cost 248.66

CAMERA DEPARTMENT
Cameraman Fabian
Extra Cameras ....
Lens 50 MM - 40 - 35
Speed Explosion 5&16 Other 48 - 32
Approx. No. of Feet of Film Printed ....

Cairo's optically printed soldier-laden troop ship passing through the Suez Canal. Correction, the Suez Canal was passing by the troop ship.

Myron Albertson, his uncle's nephew, accompanied me in the front cockpit. We found Uncle Albertson's house and what appeared to be a likely spot close by upon which two wheels and a tail-skid could be safely and softly brought to earth. There were numerous oak trees and a herd of fifteen or twenty cows peacefully off in one corner of our selected field, chewing their noonday cud in the shade of one of them. No problem and we landed.

A few minutes of chit-chat was interrupted when Myron, having turned from the fore cockpit to face me in the rear, gulped a sudden "Look!" I turned aft and looked, and there, within a hundred feet or so of the spot where we had come to rest, came loping several yearlings, a purposeful bull and his many wives. Then I found out that cows are curious. What I did not know was that they also relished airplane 'dope', the stuff applied to a fabric-covered plane, or that its aroma could be wafted a breeze some distance. They were down wind, and their sensitive nostrils had apparently received the come-on. Fortunately we had not cut the engine. Handcranking a propeller can consume time, and time we had not. So with no more preliminaries a new game, "Cow-tag", was launched.

Taxiing hither and yon, in and among those sturdy California oaks, leaving behind tail-skid and wheel marks in the fresh green of that pasture's grass, herding and escaping, escaping and herding, a group of obstinate and persistent cows, in an attempt to maneuver all of them so that we might clear several hundred straight yards of take-off space, occupied a lonesome pilot carrying a laughing passenger for the next twenty minutes.

Note to the publisher: Here's another long sentence - my apologies - but it scarcely does justice to the interminability of that twenty minutes. We finally made it and we attended next Sunday's party by automobile.

Much fun, those early flying days, which included as a trophy a triangular shaped, baby-blue painted, wooden 'medal', the recipient of which was forced to display it in a prominent place until the next boo-boo was committed by another of our club. Though it changed hands with quite some regularity, three 'wins' entitled the 'winner' to perpetual ownership. It is among my treasured permanent possessions.

FILTER ME NOT

Never putting off until tomorrow what you can do today has at least one glaring exception. I mention it because continually through the years the question of color-distorting a scene or sequence arises. "We'll shoot through a red filter, or orange, blue, or whatever," is often volunteered by someone. Don't! As in the 'over-shaking' of a camera, you are saddled with the result, good or bad. Let Optical or the Laboratory handle desired color effects after normal shooting, thereby allowing for any post-corrective changes which may be desired. An elementary 'do' this, but well worth remembering.

BULLETS AND BANGS

Bullet holes in glass are often 'effected' by the use of an 'air gun' firing pellets full of a light-colored 'grease', which may be mixed with a coarse powder such as salt. Should the scene be through a windshield, photographing straight ahead into a Process Screen, the problem of lack of space within which to place and fire the 'gun' or 'guns', has been occasionally solved by us through the use of a piece of clear plastic attached to the windshield's top. Spring-hinged, bullet effects pre-prepared and out of sight, it snaps down when wanted against the glass with sufficient speed as to be unnoticed. Proper sound administered later, audiblizing the 'spats' of multiple bullets or the 'pow' of a single one, completes a very realistic effect. In cases of a curved windshield, this method becomes more complex, requiring a molded plastic sheet to snugly fit whatever form is presented. A simple solution, however, for flat, small glass areas, and one which contains the added advantage of more realistic-appearing 'holes.' If they are artistically executed.

Another uncomplicated and safe gadget with which large expanses of glass can be cracked and shattered, is a 'ball-bearing projector'. *Idiots' Delight*, a Norma Shearer, Clark Gable, Edward Arnold starrer included as one of its many Effect sequences, the lobby of a large mountain hotel under bombardment. Full of expansive picture windows and housing expensive stars who detest cuts or abrasions from flying glass, we were confronted with the necessity of bowing to this latter understandable reluctance. With the cooperation of the Plumbing Department we appropriated several lengths of 1/2" and 3/4" pipe, into which we fitted wood dowels. Short lengths of shock-cord attached to one end of the dowel provided enough propulsive force to plunge the dowel to its length limit through the plumber's pipe - a sort of 'cross-bow' weapon. The ammunition consisted of ball bearings of analogous diameters.

Several of these placed within a pipe would fly in a reasonably confined pattern towards the target, upon releasing the shock-cord taut 'piston'. A bit of testing determined just how much propulsive push was needed to shatter but not penetrate or 'fly' the glass. As a consequence, 'bomb concussions' did our picture windows in, visibly as well as audibly, and though ball bearings caromed here and about, their force was spent. No bandaid requirements from the distinguished cast, nor whimpers. And none from Clarence Brown, the Director, and few complaints from the cost accountants - the bearings were retrievable.

Again, why do we seem to be continually jabbing at these 'money' gents? Un-Scotsman-like behavior for a Scotsman, to be sure. Perhaps a clan existed at one time whose kilted members' motto read, "We Nae Dinna Pinch a Penny", and though most of my unappreciative friends may disagree, the Gillespie Tartan could have been woven by a bonnie lassie of that now probably extinct clan. Or is it possible that the expenditure of just 'other-money', such as M.G.M.'s pains me not? So gather ye, all unintentionally maligned budgeteers and penurious Production personnel — accept my apologies. And bring with you those few 'deserving' cinematographers whose feelings may have herein been bruised. Time heals all wounds, imagined or real, and I find few remaining scars, most of which probably belong in the former 'imagined' category. You're all forgiven!

COLOR OF FIRE

Fire sequences are as varied as the faces of the Moon and when people are a part, it can become a major headache. And people are usually a part. Long focal length lenses may be used to foreshorten the spread between foreground and background of a set. Hence fire near the camera seems much closer than it actually may be to the conflagration raging in the rear and the reasonably safe area between, planned and used for an actor's histrionics, will appear due to the lens, much less open and safe. Or the major back part of the fire may be projected onto a Process Screen or combined later with actors and front fire by resorting to a 'traveling matte' (optical). Choice of method will depend on careful analysis of the physical action requirements.

Control is always a must. Advance rigging and installation of protection measures and fuel source and flow needs careful doing. Copper tubing tipped by brass spray nozzle fittings, carry the fuel from a safely distant manifold at which each tube has its own valve. The manifold in turn is fed from a large pressure tank which contains a cheap gasoline or possibly a more exotic mixture. Pilot lights, usually old film cans or some such container filled with kerosene and a wad of asbestos for a wick, are placed at the nozzle end of each tube. They may be ignited manually, or with a squib, electrically. Regulation at the individual valves, controls the desired amount of fire and they can be 'played' up or down during a scene and cut completely at its finish. Fireproofing may be applied to slow or partially protect surrounding areas, and often flammable debris, liberally sprayed with gas or kerosene just before ignition, is place near a nozzle but sufficiently distant from the pilot so that pre-lighting doesn't set off the whole caboodle.

Separate smoke generators, ordinary smoke-pots of varying colored smoke, tanks of burning crude oil and rubber, and live steam or chemical vapors when 'white' is needed, are often employed to augment a fire effect. Prevailing wind direction should always be considered, the control of which may at times be implemented through judicial placing and low R.P.M. use of wind-machines. Swirls of smoke opaqueness blotting from the camera's view a fire spectacle, is hardly desired film fare.

The wide range of fire effect demands is limited only by a writer's imagination, though the budget at times may become a quickly efficient extinguisher. If a simple campfire is to be shown, or perhaps a romantic twosome lazing in front of a flickering (plaster) log fire in a fireplace, sans chimney, smokeless piped-in fuel such as 'photoflame' is available. Bits of 'smoke-cloth' may be added if desired, and through this control we avoid a stage full of unwanted smoke which would normally result were the fire actual. "Where there is smoke there is fire" does not necessarily always hold true in the movies.

The 'tie-in' or matching of foreground fire to corresponding 'fire' which may be projected onto a Process Screen, presents a ticklish problem of attaining color sameness. A 'warm' background print to the eye always looks warmer on a Process Screen than it photographs. We have made the mistake of 'warming' the foreground in attempting to achieve a better color balance and to generally create an amber or reddish hue, supposedly reflected light from the fire itself. In spite of its eye appeal and seeming correctness, it can easily become much too 'red-hued' in the final composite. An ultraviolet 'bluishness' creeps into Process projection which is quite invisible, and the completed results may tend towards a 'cold' fire and reflections <u>on</u> the background, when the foreground is printed for the desired 'less warm' effect. A closer final merging of the two will result if studied attention is given to this criterion and advance testing is heartily recommended. A top Process camera 'specialist' will know of this, but there have been instances when such photographic combinations have been victimized by over-zealous use of those amber filters in the foreground - once, I recall, by a top Process camera 'specialist', no less.

TREE MOVER

A daily 4:00 P.M. coffee-break, a sort of ritual, attended by a group of four or five of us, often brings forth days-of-yore recollections. Preston Ames, long time M.G.M. Art Director, Huey Hunt, longer time M.G.M. Set Decorator, Merrill Pye, Carfagno and the writer, make up this little band of 'memory-reminders'. There was this time, recollected someone, when a rather exacting Director insisted upon moving a tree four feet, three inches to camera right, to better accommodate his selected camera position. Sufficient time for the proposed replacement existed, as several days in advance of the scheduled shooting remained. On the following day the Director revisited the set, re-studied the 'moved' tree and, calling for his Art Director, apologetically informed him that he had changed his mind and to please move it back to its original location. Unsmilingly the Art Director agreed, and later when the set was shot all was satisfactorily rosy. The punch line point to this little episode was that the tree had never been moved at all. Our exacting Director to this day knows it not.

MILEAGE

We recalled a bit of by-play involving Lou Strohm, former Head of the Location Department, who had just purchased a new Volkswagen. Lou would boast about the phenomenal gasoline mileage he was obtaining on his many location treks, and we decided to provide additional material for his boasting. Our 'additional material' was composed of many gallons of gasoline which we surreptitiously added to the Volk's tank over a period of many weeks, allowing for only an occasional legitimate filling by Lou so as to make our hoax somewhat more acceptable. Well, Lou's cheery round face sported a growing grin as the days sped by.

"You just won't believe it, you guys, but that car just doesn't use hardly any gas at all!" he would chirp. "Forty, fifty miles to the gallon'."

At about eighty M.P.G. someone came up with the heinous thought of reversal, and we immediately began to gradually cut down our donations to the point of none - whereupon a siphon was requisitioned to further the dirty work. A full tank would become half a tank - a half of a tank, a quarter tank. Lou's mileage deteriorated alarmingly and Lou's visage became increasingly serious. A hurt frown replaced that boastful smile. His little gem became a beast and worried silence completely muted former prideful utterances.

Just short of an impending breach of German-American relations, we confessed all. His reaction was a heterogeneous mixture of relief and not too well camouflaged pique, capped finally, however, with an honest and hearty laugh. Good old Lou Strohm, long time fixture at M.G.M. We miss you, Lou.

DUCK DIVER
Rotund Huey Hunt who can character-dress a set as well or better than anyone in the business, is a wonderful story-teller. And his contributions to our daily soirees are backlogged by many true and amusing tales. Preston Ames supplies the culture - five years as a student at the "Ecole Nationale Superieure des Beaux Arts" in Paris. The initials D.P.L.G. may legitimately kite-tail his moniker, so I am informed - something to the effect that he may practice architecture in France, (Who wants to practice architecture in Paris?) His coffee-break problem is in gaining even one of the eight ears present, excluding his own two. But somehow our appetite for the enriched and elegant amenities of mind-improvement at 4:00 P.M. is dulled by the sometimes earthy tales tilled by we other tellers. Like Mr. Pye's recital of ducks who had not been taught to swim. Watery, this one, not earthy.

It seems, according to Merrill, that a hurry up last minute call for swans, geese or ducks, engineered by Production Manager Joe Cohn about ten minutes before Director Bill Nye was to start the day's shooting of "Mr. Wu" (Lon Chaney was 'Mr. Wu') so that his, Pye's beautiful wisteria-lined pond would have some live floating atmosphere, was put into speedy motion. "Take ten or even fifteen minutes, Merrill, but get 'em," said Joe.

For the Head of the Production Department to endorse a fifteen minute delay, devoted to the obtaining of lovely ducks to further enhance a lovely set, would normally be classified as a sort of millennium. In fairness to Mr. Cohn, however, he quite often violated his own long-standing "don't open a can of beans" proclamation.

A nearby market supplied two crates of ducks some thirty minutes later. Within another ten minutes they were led to water, but like the horse who wouldn't drink, they wouldn't, or couldn't, swim. Now at this assertion of Merrill's, I interrupted and scornfully questioned, "Who ever heard of a duck that didn't take to water - much less not be able to swim?" With matching scorn he retorted, "Their mothers never taught them. They had never seen water. They were for roasting, not swimming."

So, though all of the hurry-up acquisitions were dumped in with the hope that a few at least had taken an aquatic course, they all promptly wended their downward way to Davey Jones' locker.

It was now ten minutes after ten, and the very photogenic slanting rays of the nine o'clock sun slanted no more. One photographic bonus gone. But, as we say in show biz, it, the 'show', must go on, although minus the rays and minus the ducks. Or so the waiting assemblage thought. Because from that first 10:20 A.M. moment of "Action, Camera!" unexpected 'pluses' popped to and upon the surface of this dream pond in the form of upside-down ducks, their stiff webbed feet pointing in reproving admonishment towards all present. Pitifully, many seemed to be pointed towards J.J. Cohn, Production Manager of M.G.M. Studios, Culver City, California. At 11:30 A.M., by hasty count, the last pop-out occurred, was retrieved, and the cameras rolled.

I cannot authenticate it, but rumor persisted that duck in any form was scratched from the Cohn household menu for months to come. Not so the crew. Water-logged roasts were plattered on many tables for the next few ensuing days. I have several times asked Mr. Pye to explain just how a mother duck teaches her ducklings to swim, and his reply has always been, "She simply teaches them, Buddy, by the latest approved method, you feather-brain," and deep hurt clouds his countenance at my questioning the veracity of his story.

In a like situation I am sure we of Special Visual Effects, we of fluid mind, would have devised some sort of water-proof remedy, such as perhaps twenty scuba divers swim-finning below the surface, each one supporting one or two land-loving ducks at the proper water-line level, or perhaps a diet of ping-pong balls would have been prescribed. A ping-pong ball filled duck will, I believe, not sink. Or perhaps duck stilts, or a false bottom upon which the ducks could have safely waddled. Many solutions, Mr. Pye, for the 'thinking man'. Certainly, if we were able to eventually handle disappearing hippopotamuses you should have been able to keep a few measly ducks from submerging.

LAVA LAUGH

Then there was that instance of the Great Lava flow. Quite an extensive set had been constructed which was to be inundated by rivers of 'lava'. The site of the set was alongside a series of long steep flumes, each about six feet wide and perhaps forty feet long, at the top of which were enormous dump tanks. A gooey mess, sufficiently liquid to flow, had been brewed to simulate lava and each dump tank was filled to the brim with this smoking (chips of dry ice) concoction. Cue lights were to trigger each tank in turn, controlled from below, to fit the action requirements of the Director.

The day of shooting this well-prepared depiction of nature's fury arrived. Explanations to the Director of the hows and whens of the dumpings convinced him that he should be the one to press the button that would start the 'lava' onslaughts. Each press would release in rotation a tank containing many hundreds of gallons of this sticky, slimy amalgamation, and in a last minute review of what was to be, Mr. Director walked into the set, carefully rehearsed his action, explaining to all that when he pressed this button - "this one here", he said, "down will come the 'lava', and you must run for your lives."

Just why, no one knows, least of all the holder of the cue-button, but he demonstrated - and down came Number One! In split second frantic reflexes he repeated his presses, thinking perhaps to stop the descending cataclysm. Each press cued another dump. Our propshop 'tilters' above were doing their job well. "When the cue-light goes on, dump!" they had been told, and dump they did.

Well, Full-sized Mechanical Effects should have been proud. All worked to a 'T'. The 'lava' snaked beautifully over, in and around the entire set. Cameras of course, were not turning. They should have been in order to have preserved for posterity a spellbound, out of character costumed individual, caught momentarily to his knees in and at the foot of the avalanche. Then he ran, or rather sloughed his way, hither and yon, gesturing and shouting frenziedly to "Halt! Stop! Desist!", all in vain as his push finger worked automatically. The actors, well rehearsed, had "run for their lives", adding unrehearsed roars of laughter as they 'escaped'. There's probably a lesson here somewhere.

The depiction of 'lava' is always a toughie. The "gooey mess" which filled our smoothly operating containers mentioned above (though I recall no the exact recipe) was probably a mixture of sawdust, shredded asbestos, pebbles, possibly oatmeal, water having been added to the whole to insure proper consistency.

Generous last minute applications of chipped dry ice and liquid smoke (Titanium Tetra-chloride) supplied the illusion of heat. When color is a factor, which was not the case in our director-engulfing black and white flow, the problem mounts. Quantities of 'hot' colors, oranges, reds, yellows (powdered dry mixture) will produce a fair substituted for the real thing. If possible, and in small areas, molten 'dirty' metals, mixed during the melting process with asbestos chips, small rocks, bits of clay and sand, will serve realistically. It supplies its own vary photogenic heat and will ignite on contact in flammable set appurtenances, so planned and placed in its path. Cooling and hardening occurs quickly, the choice of the use of molten metal hence should be judged with film footage in mind - and discretion.

MCCLEARY'S PENNY

Urie McCleary, another veteran M.G.M. Art Director, used to join our afternoon tete-a-tetes 'until the price of coffee was raised to a dime. Mc's smiling barbs re moths in my purse have many times been firmly imbedded into my undeserving skin. So hereby, in print, I counter-attack. If I, as a Scotsman, squeeze a copper, Mc exerts all of his one hundred and eighty pounds, perhaps thirty pounds of which are muscle, the balance Mc, in closing a well-geared and powerful vise, on his. Strangely, if a book is involved, that self-same vise pops wide open. He has accumulated one of the finest libraries of which I know, and if brewing his own coffee will contribute towards the pittance required to purchase this volume, thereby making his fabulous collection complete, I commend his thrift. Also I must reluctantly admit that his fine family seems not to have suffered from malnutrition, in spite of the pangs of pain which must wrack Mr. McCleary to his toes upon being compelled to choose between a six dollar roast and a thirty-five dollar de luxe edition of a cook book within which are recipes for its roasting. A real good friend is Mc, pleasant and entertaining and always enthusiastically willing to accept an invitation - to dinner. Touché, Mc?

TRAIL OF NINETY-EIGHT

One more reminiscence and we'll return to the more mundane sphere of Effects ramblings. This will appeal particularly to Mr. McCleary as it involved the freezing of many of those reputed 'moths' of mine.

In the early heyday of Hollywood premiers, the grandiose opening nights were aflutter with gorgeous gowns on gorgeous ladies, arriving in gorgeous limousines, often escorted by pudgy but solvent industry potentates. Criss-crossing searchlights sought, searched and found, as they do to this day, these titillating bits of escorted fluff, as they exited their limos, gyrating slipperily towards a waiting microphone to purr, "Oh, I know the picture is going to be just glorious! I just adore Rodney Dare! I just think he is so marvelous! I just - " whereupon the harried interviewer at his mike may interrupt with a, "And here, ladies and gentlemen, comes 'Rodney' himself. Thank you, Miss er, Miss — Oh, yes I - Miss Oo-la-la Voluptuous — Oh, hello, Rodney!" A tug from Daddy, and 'Oo-la-la' petulantly glides into the theater. Thousands of cheering onlookers - a heady few minutes for any participant.

Well, Nick Grinde, former Director, and yours truly, both at that time bachelors, decided to mingle with all these V.I.P.s and partake of a share of this glory by attending the Grand Opening of *Trail of Ninety-Eight*. We would do it in frilly and impeccable style, sparing neither expense nor preparation. First and excitingly foremost would be our dates. A degree from nursery school was not even demanded so long as we could find physical and tangible assets comparable to those which clothed Miss 'Oo-la-la'. We hoped that ours would also put their very best front forward.

The chauffeur-driven limousine presented no obstacle. A friendly studio driver promised a shiny vehicle for the evening at rates which made me question the sincerity of his professed palship. But we had determined to open our wallet gates - whole-hoggedness crowned our every pre-Premiere preparation. Good enough was not to be good enough. The Wardrobe Department fitted our two lovelies with fetching, if somewhat startling, glamour. Mine scintillated in clinging gold lame, well air-conditioned, and Nick's filled generously a something or other which must have been sewn on with care and patience. Readers, we were set.

The well-thought-out plan of our procedure was to join the ladies with sufficient time for casual cheese and crackers and then on to Grauman's Chinese Theater for the big splash. The big <u>expensive</u> splash, McCleary. We determined not to arrive too early. All of the ultra-ultras seemed always to turn up at these affairs about curtain time and always curtain time was delayed. So we cheesed and crackered until the propitious moment of departure. After tenderly assisting our two starry-eyed, tightly gowned enthrallers into their costly transportation contrivance (it <u>did</u> shine), we left. And then we arrived! - to a silent, dark, depopulated area of voidness.

For the first time in history (radio commitment or something) The *Trail of Ninety-Eight*'s gala premiere was on time. Searchlights neither criss-crossed in the sky nor searched the parade of emptying vehicles. There was no parade, the temporary bleachers of applauding fans were empty, the interviewer and his 'mike' had vanished, the picture had started and deep gloom descended. And Ah, what price that gloom. Our two stunning creatures were in a tearful state of 'stun'. Nevertheless, they bravely undulated from car to theater entrance, accompanied by two deeply distraught escorts. We both unbelievingly kept looking at our watches - wordless. As an old golfing partner of my father's used to say, "Some days you just can't lay up a cent."

TABLE TOP TOWERS

During the early days of Special Effects we stupidly exercised the prerogative of secrecy in our contacts with other studios. An idea, a solution, an invention which turned out well, was guarded meticulously. In recent years, largely, I believe, because of the Academy, a committee within which was composed of fellow Effectsmen from all the studios, a gradual departure from this short-sighted practice developed. A closer friendliness soon unlocked our little individual 'safes' and a sensible exchange of ideas, tried and untried, successes or failures, established a mutually valuable rapport. An exception or two, but by and large mostly all-inclusive. Seldom were our methods and determinations too radically different from those practiced on other lots, and if we did occasionally come up with a gem, the odds-on chances of our benefiting reciprocally paid profitable rewards to both.

May I at this point pay tribute to other supervisory industry members of our tight little group and to the vast numbers of those individuals in the various crafts at all studios whose contributions to the Effects' Categories so importantly spell successful achievements. We have confined our documentations mostly to within the boundaries of M.G.M., but endless examples of top proficiency and creativeness belong to many outside the hearing-range of Leo's roar. Our hat is doffed to you, gentlemen, in fact, many times we have felt gratefully relieved that your 'solvings' of real sticklers were destined to be yours, not ours.

The utilization of old, battered, rust-covered-and-impregnated sheet metal with which to make miniature mountains, boulders, sheer cliffs, was an eye-opener upon a recent trip to Japan. Visiting a studio in Kyoto, I saw a remarkably true depiction of a snow-clad valley, bordered by steep scarps and ranges of snow-capped peaks. Upon contoured framework of this rather expansive Miniature set, was fastened and fitted and hammered bits and pieces of this crinkled, rusty scrap sheet. All vertical or near vertical surfaces were so covered, and the effect and scale of rugged granite was beautifully represented, A 'thrown' application of dry 'snow' (perhaps gypsum or salt) to these surfaces further enhanced the sense of absolute reality. Each crack and crevice, each minute outcropping and ledge, retained its proper amount of 'snow' whiteness, the sharp and irregular detail of all flaked surfaces resulting in a very true depiction, scaling down to extraordinary fidelity. The thought occurred to me that Detroit might be represented here - some of the residue of those shiploads of crushed automobile body scrap which we so generously paraded to Japan pre-World War Two. Clever, these Japanese, and a far better usage of this old beat-up material than that to which it was formerly allocated. Altogether a very unique and effective solution.

In Tokyo I also visited the Tojo Studios as the guest of Mr. Fujimoto, Production Head, and Mr. Tsuburaya, their Miniature Effects entrepreneur, both of whom had spent a few days in Culver City a year or so before, during which they gathered Special Visual Effects honey wherever it would drip. In return they hosted us royally, which included a night on the town. A lovely evening, pregnant with delectable Geisha accessories and other tidbits of less consequence, such as excellent food and soothing libations. My Geisha was particularly adept at making birds and ballet dancers out of cigarette paper, and thinking to rise to the occasion as the evening progressed and the libations continued to be libated, I plunged into my one social proficiency, 'Table-top-towers'.

This has long been the source of horrific reactions from my wife, and occasionally her difficult to understand trepidation has resulted in nervous shakes, seismograph readings unrecorded, which have tended at times to topple tower, social prestige, et al, into a jumbled heap. Moisture sometimes would impregnate this litter, if, as was usually the case, a full glass of liquid crowned the glory of my Pisa-like creation.

On this memorable night I performed. Mom immediately and hurriedly left to pay call on Miss Ladies-only-san.

She returned just as the crowning glory took its rightful place, balanced perfectly on a box of matches, which rested on a beer bottle, seated in an ash tray (with chopsticks projecting like antennae), which surmounted another beer bottle upon another beer bottle and upon still another beer bottle, the whole rising majestically and resting securely on top of a little flat-topped ivory Buddha who sat sublimely on the top of the table, contemplating. A deep hush over all of this Tokyo equivalent of a late late spot was broken only by the "Ohs" and "Ahs" of my tissue paper virtuoso. <u>She</u> was appreciative.

Mrs. G. nearing the scene of my triumph, reflexed violently but the floor was solid and she had not yet gained her seat. The structure remained intact and stood securely in noble defiance until a kimono clad young lady from a nearby group of play-boy-sans squeeked in perfect soldier-English, "Oh, lookee, boy geisha!" The usual motivation for my dear spouse's tremulousness was changed in a spark to lady-like quiverings of mirth as she sat, but alas, <u>these</u> jouncings would have really taxed the most rugged of seismographs!

Tenderly, albeit with polite giggles, did our hostesses of the evening clean up the mess. The one male entertainer had been the recipient of the full foamy brown contents of a substantial fraction of a Koku of that 'crowning glory', well-brewed Japanese beer, in his lap.

A modern warm-air blower-dryer in the Papa-san room eventually pretty well dehydrated one pair of pants, one pair of shorts and a drenched shirt-tail. Japanese-American relations had been fluidly cemented. Mr. Fujimoto's gracious roars, coupled with Mr. Tsuburaya's complimentary remarks, "Never I see sootch Effect!" served to speed jovially the remainder of the night. To this member of the party, however, thereinafter addressed as "Boy-geisha", the hours dragged as dampness of spirit and underpants persisted.

EXPERIENCES AND TRAVEL

A few words on the value and edification of Travel may properly follow the above comments. Any creator benefits. Earlier it was suggested that many advantages may be pocketed through traversing all avenues of escape from the humdrum of routine. Travel can really be a gold-headed cane, and if at all possible (it never is, but make it so), gather yourself together, hie hence and reap the rewards offered.

Broadening experiences can lurk up many dark alleys. Wide open eyes and tuned ears will directly or indirectly amass for you a storehouse of useable ideas and associations. A further important asset to be gained has to do with contacts and dealings with Studio personnel. To be able to say to a Producer or Director whose script embodies a Nepal or Bombay, Ceylon or wherever, locale - "When I was there - ", is often a very useful lever with which to pry open his confidence.

The cost of extensive trips is considerable, but the many business bonuses that accrue as a result are well worth while. And though the boys in Washington on April 15th are inclined to take a dim view of such travel deductions, they are valid. Yes, even tabletop gymnastics should fall in this category, though such allowances may depend solely upon the reasonableness, if not the sense of humor, of your tax-paid employee, the Internal Revenue Investigator.

In any event, launch a 'trip-savings-account' and let not extracurricular temptations invade it until its total has grown to provide the wherewithal for a two or three or more months' journey to distant lands. Interim ramblings while your fund swells, to spots near at hand, will almost always supply <u>something</u> of value, provided that alert eyes and ears hold attentive sway. "Go West, young man", or North, South or East - but go!

QUIET ON THE SET!

Unwanted noises generated from Effects equipment should never curtail the attainment of those effects. To sacrifice an 'effect-need' because its din may interfere with the recording of dialogue, is tantamount to the expensive 'savings' of a dollar, illustrated in another application of this principle in a past chapter. True, it may be necessary to re-record or dub or loop (our Sound gentry call it "post—synchronization" - high falutin', our Sound gentry) the dialogue. Your effects suffer not, however, if this post-procedure is followed.

Some reticence to this practice may crop up from any of various sources, but if a lot of wind is too noisy, or an earthquake battering-ram disturbs a tender "Fear not, fair one, I'll save you", stick to your wind and battering-ram guns and recommend "post-synchronization." Certainly at times compromises may be in order. A give and take relationship with the objectors. A sensible balance between the obvious advantages of straight recording, if accompanied by not too great a diminution of the effect or effects, makes economic sense. This attitude of cooperative willingness on the part of the Effectsman will serve to strengthen his case upon occasions when his effects should be dominantly important.

PIANO WIRE

A sequence in *Command Decision*, starring Mr. Gable, Walter Pidgeon and Van Johnson involved a 'talk-in' landing of a B-17 upon its return from a 'bombing raid' over Germany. The pilot killed and his co-pilot badly wounded, the controls were supposedly taken over by a non-pilot member of the crew. Our problem was to bring the big bomber in, somewhat erratically but to a 'safe' landing. Whereupon, so the script dictated, the port landing wheel was to collapse and it was to skid the equivalent of several hundred feet to a grinding ground-loop stop. And then within seconds disaster was to strike.

An overhead trolley with a 'guillotine' control from which our 3/4" scale miniature B-17 was suspended, enabled us to 'fly' it erratically. Forward progress was achieved by two invisible nose wires fed through two split brass tubes from the 'stop' spot to the point of initial ground contact and on up to the approaching airplane. This was tied into a pull wire system which activated the overhead 'trolley car' so that all movements would be synchronous. The master pull was manual, compounded two to one.

The airplane was rigged with a self-contained 'breakaway' wheel device and wing-tank explosives, both individually and remotely to be triggered. Auxiliary high pressure gasoline was piped to the 'disaster' spot. And this is the crux, students of the above detailed recital. Weight was lessened – wire gage reduced.

Our old friend, piano wire, has of course a weight limited tensile strength - the smaller the gauge, the less in load capacity, but the more easily it becomes to camouflage or invisibleize. We were able to materially save a big portion of the B-17's heaviness by supplying fuel at the scene, rather than transporting all of it within the miniature itself. Therefore smaller wires could be used with the resultant simplification of 'losing' them photographically. The plane's eventual arrival at the exact pinpointed area, however, was mandatory and this was the purpose of those two split brass tubes, imbedded at the surface, the wires through which could not fail to convey our skidding, disabled ship to its final terminus. A few rehearsals with a 'dummy' plane determined the walking speed of the pullers, which was to be slowed at the end of the run, but paced sufficiently so that a half ground-loop would occur at its snubbed limit of travel. Everything functioned in applepie order, climaxed by its spectacular flaming finish, and the shot was successfully delivered. Not at all new or unique, this approach and method determination. But for the tyro, a cue which may be of value to him when confronted with a similar quandary.

Its application to a tumbling automobile, either full-sized or miniature, exemplifies a good utilization of this method, provided contours are such that the car will deposit itself exactly where a pre-prepared fire and/or explosion has been located. *The Postman Rings Twice*, which teamed our former Hollywood High School 'sweater girl', Lana Turner, with John Garfield, had such a scene. With no guiding 'nose wires', directional contouring solved the planned route her free falling vehicle was to take - to its doom. Our miniature Lana was somewhat singed.

The 'flying' of miniature aircraft is often a stickler. Seldom have we used radio controlled flying miniatures because of certain limitations. Against a natural sky for straight flying and maneuvering, O.K. But as they must be lightweight to fly under their own limited power, added weight needed for possible effects installations, such as a blow-up in mid-air, make them impractical. Also a deliberate crash of any nature lacks sufficient force to make it appear real with too little weight to deliver that force.

We suspend from above our 'wing-wire' fly our aircraft, almost entirely. Free gravity falls and pendulum swings, revolving boom suspensions and traveling car rigs, such as the aircraft carrier launching described in the "Tokyo" episode, are additional choices dependent upon the problems to be faced.

A "dog fight" may use combinations of all of the above. Diagramatic schematics at the end of this chapter shows typical preliminary thinking for such a sequence.

Miniature aircraft suspended in front of a Process screen upon which are back-projected actual or miniature flying backgrounds is a simple solution for shots photographed theoretically from an accompanying camera plane. Hung from above the Process camera's field by three fine piano wires or three of the new plastic filaments which travel over sheaves to a 'T' control, manually operated from below, the 'airplane' will seem to 'live' as it banks, climbs or loses altitude by simple manipulations from the 'T' operator. Current, activating small electric motors, supplied by batteries within the craft or from off stage through extremely fine copper conductors, rotate propellers, always flat pitched, or actuated retracting landing gears, bomb-bay doors, or whatever. Weight, or rather a minimum of it, enables application of finer gage supporting wires, always difficult to completely camouflage from the camera's all seeing eye. As previously mentioned, paint, light and patience are the ingredients to be mixed here so that suspension supports and current carrying filaments 'disappear'.

'Wing wires' for long straight travel of a miniature plane, one port and one starboard, pass through a tube extending from the leading to the trailing edges of each wing sufficiently outboard to obtain lateral stability and to clear propellers.

COMMAND DECISION (1948) PRODUCTION #1425

Nelson's approach and crash - 3/4" B-17 makes erratic approach in *Command Decision*. Distant landscape is scenic profile.

B-17 hung from overhead trolley system with guillotine control for height, wings and trim. Manual pull - 2 to 1 compound. B-17's taxi controlled by 2 split brass tubes in runway. Breakaway wheel, wing and tank. Explosions built into plane. Auxiliary high pressure gas fire piped to crash location. 3 cameras used and previous tests mad for positions.

'Pilot' and 'co-pilot' hors de combat. Invisible wing wires from backing to landing area.

Pulled by nose wires to 'ground loop' spot of explosion and fire.

She burns. Fuel piped to pre-planned crash spot. Six background B-17 are 1/4" scale. Shot on July 19th, 1948 on Lot #3 by Max Fabian.

A GUY NAMED JOE (1944) PRODUCTION #1291

Early German Aircraft Carrier and Destroyer at 1/2" scale. Note 'white water' from self contained siphon pumps.

The production, *A Guy Named Joe.* She's hit. Explosion care of Primacord.

The B-25 that "bombed" her, also comes out second best.

(Jet aircraft simplify this problem.) The tubes, copper or brass, may be refined at both ends by inserting a tightly coiled inch or so of piano wire to insure a smooth entry and exit of the wing wires as the miniature plane, propelled usually by a nose pull-wire, swooshes down or along their length. A degree of banking can be had through manually or mechanically throwing one or both wing wires alternately out of level parallel. We have at times used a single wire through the fuselage to depict a laterally out-of-control plane, or by adjusting its ailerons, the air acting on these parts as it 'flies' along, will cause it to roll.

The student will choose a "sauce to fit booth goose and gander" (to originate and old maxim) in his solution arrivals. "Originate?" Well, though the somewhat distorted quote above is not a direct-from-the-shoulder piece of mantel acumen, "origination" may be the key thought here. Ever will a new approach be found necessary when previously tried and true methods draw a zero, so your thinking and your listening becomes a sensible prerequisite. A doffed hat is due the author for his having learned to listen to men like Glen Robertson, Bob McDonald, Jack Gaylord and many others. He in turn doffs a most grateful hat to them.

EXPLOSIONS

Explosions, like those Riviera bikinis, are of all shapes and sizes. Their attainment, however, involves many more types of 'sewing machines.' The may be activated by mixtures of powder or dynamite and dynamite caps, "Primacord," compressed air, gasoline filled Christmas tree ornaments or old light globes or open containers filled with an explosive fluid; the material to be chose are multitudinous. Your expert prop shop powder man will be consulted profitably in any blowup procedures.

Mortars are pretty universally used as billets for these pre-prepared destructors and to direct their forces. Properly scaled debris, dirt, cork, bits of balsa and heavier objects, to produce 'force lines,' top off the mortar's content. Inflammable chunks of material such as gasoline soaked asbestos fragments and the addition of flash powder will materially help to produce a photogenic blast. Detonated electrically (if the quick action valves may be also opened and closed electrically) in individual or multiple or in series. The control may be a simple manually operated 'wipe' board, contact spacings of which will give desired timing, interval and pre-planned location. Or a more sophisticated mechanical contact apparatus may be devised, pre-set to split seconds - perhaps for a sweeping barrage entailing a hundred or more individual explosive effects.

A point should be made here regarding a too literal depiction of a miniature explosion's full –size counterpart. It may usually be exaggerated in order to deliver the 'message' within short film footages. A film editor's scissors should always be borne in mind when preparing such Effect. The total 'over-length' of a completed motion picture is an ever-present problem. Cut here, cut there - down to the minimum. Quite often only the kernel is left and a quickly passing few seconds may be all that is allotted to the effects of an important 'blockbuster'. Hence those few seconds must impart to an audience the degree of magnitude that fits whatever effect is desired, and pictorial overstatements often the answer. Make that block-buster throw up perhaps half again as much in height and debris quantity as would be normally correct, so that its few seconds of viewing will deliver the message. Good judgement will dictate the limits of such multiplication. Otherwise an eruption may become ridiculously out of scale. But the point of on-and-quickly-off shots of this nature should be always carefully entertained.

Primacord, (trade name for a kind of cordite) instantaneous and potent, has served to produce excellent water explosions when coiled on a heavy steel plate a few inches below the surface. Little if any smoke is visible and an impressive column of white water results. Handle it delicately and with respect. Yellow phosphorous, intermixed with explosives in a mortar, will add a bit of pyrotechnics and may be used here and there to relived the monotony of a series of straight H E explosions. Also the inclusion of white smoke, or yellow, or red, used judiciously will vary pictorially the usual preponderance of black smoke. This will apply to a city on fire (the burning of Rome in Quo Vidas) as well as a bombing or a barrage. Live steam has also been employed for 'white relief or contrast.

The student will see from the immediate above that a dose of variety may spice an explosive or conflagatory sequence. A degree of artistry in a holocaust is of value.

BLACK AND WHITE NIGHT

Here is a real quickie for the Process gentlemen who may be confronted with the need of a night storm background plate for a color picture. None in color may exist in the film archives of the Stock Library - only some in black and white. With no hesitation whatsoever, choose one if it fills the bill otherwise. Process project it onto a screen sans tinting, sans blue filters, just straight black and white, and when re-photographed with its composite foreground in color, the results will not only be acceptable, they will usually result in a very definite plus.

Subject matter must of course be considered, but we have found pretty generally that normal laboratory printing on the 'blue' end of the spectrum, which all night scenes receive, bestows enough night hue to such a storm sky, or for that matter, sky and water, as to make it completely suitable, whereas an original color plate may possess an overabundance of 'blue' in the completed composite. We have followed this reasoning upon occasions when shooting day for night out-of-doors miniatures, in color, on our Lot 3 'ocean'. An existing black and white scenically painted storm sky has often sufficed beautifully. Day Process backgrounds are another matter, although within subject matter limitations, some in black and white may at times be tinted or color-filtered satisfactorily.

READY EXAMPLES

Demonstration reels of past work in all of the Effects Categories should be assembled and updated when a goodly assortment of examples have been accumulated. These can be of real value in 'selling', and oft serve as memory jigglers. Periodically an authoritative gentleman who has perhaps had a wry experience (not at M.G.M., naturally) may be difficult to persuade as to a particular Effect. Break out the reel or reels that are pertinent to his problem and if the examples are good to excellent he will usually follow your proposed method. It goes without saying that ours have always been either exceptionally good or exceptionally excellent, excluding, of course, the ones he never sees, which we cannily omit. If confessions are good, our soul is hereby benefited.

The reader will recall an exhortation in an earlier Chapter re the entertainment, hence box office value, of well executed Special Effects, to a movie. 'San Francisco's earthquake,' one of many example of potent audience reaction obtainers. Certainly in this field the job should be done well or not at all. Eliminate rather than cut seriously a realistic Effects budget. In a Life Magazine Movie Review of October 21, 1966, by Richard Schickel, the above admonition perhaps applies. We quote the first paragraph of this review:

```
        "The High Cost of a
          Paradise Lost.

              HAWAII
         With Julie Andrews
         And Max von Sydow.

    After years of effort and the expenditure
of many millions of dollars, HAWAII turns out
to be one of the strangest motion picture
enterprises for which anyone was ever asked to
reserve a $4.25 seat.  Usually when the prices
are high, the screen wide and brightly colored,
and the running time close to 3 1/2 hours, one
can expect some sort of large-scale action -
fires, floods, earthquakes, maybe even a volcanic
eruption.  Not so in HAWAII.  Except for an
all too fraudulent storm at sea, an indifferent
riot, the tiniest of hurricanes and an epidemic
of the measles, this film contains less of what
you have probably come to expect for your money
than any film spectacular in recent memory."
```

The underlining is the author's, not Mr. Schickel's.

If there were but two messages to be stressed in these pages, one would be to heed well the value of a slam bang, Effects sequence, and two, to provide and accept the necessary wherewithal. Of the latter, and I quote from above, "After years of effort and the expenditure of many millions of dollars ~," an oft times quandary is entailed. We do not know the details of this particular picture but we do know there is often a tendency on high cost pictures to 'save' dollars budgeted for strictly physical sequences. We feel strongly that along with unhesitating provision for high priced stars, writing, directorial assignment and schedule, recognition of another high priced star or stars, as it or they may contribute to overall movie excellence a hurricane, an earthquake, a conflagration, should be of equal budget consideration. If not, write 'em out!

PLANNED OPPORTUNITIES

Continuity sketches and schematic shooting layouts of an involved Miniature are highly recommended. Both apply to almost any ' physical' sequence, and the latter should be a must as a guide and time-saver in shooting an extensive and scene-laden Miniature. A plan view layout of an entire miniature and immediate surrounding area, usually available from a working drawing which along with detail drawings serves construction, may be used as a key. Transparent overlays, as many as required, will serve to spot camera positions and lens selections, equipment locations such as wind and wave machines, or dump tanks, paddle-wheels, rainpipes, fire control panels, mortars - the myriad out-of-camera effects paraphernalia necessitated by the sequence's requirements. Action within the camera's scope is carefully plotted on these overlays; ship movements, an airplane's path, a sweeping barrage, the locomotive and its cars approaching a bridge to be blown; whatever those Effects-conscious writers have concocted can be analyzed, progressively diagramed, timed and thoroughly programmed in advance on a drafting board.

These 'schematics' generally serve dual purposes. The obvious one is organizational. They become the rigging and advance preparation Bible, from which crews go to work <u>after</u> overall construction is completed, or nearly so. The extra and very important bonus which may also be derived, in addition to the above, is in the field of 'ad-libbing'. Hours of concentrated 'schematic' table work devoted to fully covering all of the Script requirements, will generally bring to mind a few unasked for, unthought of, 'tidbits'. Many times this extra icing to the cake produces the difference between a good or an excellent result.

Within the bounds of good judgment, 'ad-libbing', generally practiced, can become well worth while.

We have talked to many Second Unit Directors who have been assigned to handle sequences in a picture ranging from 'thrill' episodes to run of the mill prosaic shooting. Quite often in answers to our questions as to "why didn't you <u>also</u> do so and so?" The reply has been, "They didn't ask for it." Sad. Our advice has always been to never miss any opportunity to put on film <u>good</u> ideas if and when they unfold, as they most generally will during the planning and shooting of almost any sequence, particularly the thrill ones. Top echelon men whose work falls in this often difficult and always important subdivision of movie making, for the most part follow this precept, and though initial criticism may shower upon them during the shooting phase, final editing usually sprays the aroma of roses on their 'stubborn' and capable shoulders.

Henry Hathaway, shooting his own 'second unit' in *How the West was Won*, the train episode and wreck, is proof of what we say. Violent objections by a segment of Management rained on Henry to no avail during his actual photographing of this thriller - "what does he think we are, Ft, Knox?". He was well aware of the sequence's audience appeal and value to the entire production, and his deaf ears absorbed the entire impact of such non-creative onslaughts. In fairness to Management as a whole, he must have had their blessing - 'twas only that small, untutored, though perhaps well meaning group of watchdogs, who failed to understand that Henry had a job to do and was going to do it. In this case it was their judgment against Mr. Hathaway's in a field creatively foreign to their thinking. Peep into the other man's backyard, yes, and certainly be aware of his doings, but allow him at least a reasonably free rein in achieving what he thinks, through experience and closeness to the problem, is best. Should any individual miss too often, someone else will fall heir to future handlings. But give your well foundationed man leeway. If he is adept and when necessary can adopt Mr. Hathaway's 'hard of hearing' technique, his extras, his ad-libbing, will likely pay off handsomely.

MANAGEMENT

As I near the close of this final chapter, an additional word or two re Management's rightful place in the sun, is gratefully acknowledged. These often maligned 'bosses' would not be bosses, I presume, if they were not 'often maligned'. Second guessers inhabit all realms of life and the Studios contain their share. Saluting the uniform and griping in 'the latrine' is a good old American and probably universal custom. But let us give the great majority of those 'uniforms' their just and deserved due. A few minor pip-squeaks are hereby exempted from these plaudits. The others particularly in top Executive positions, merit a better fate than being so often the recipients of critical barbs. Responsibilities of varying degrees weigh heavily, and daily problems and decisions about which we underlings may know nothing, must be faced by these gentlemen. Misjudgments will occur which are generally pounced upon by second guess 'experts' like a starving dog thrown a savory bone, while correct and profitable moves are seldom applauded.

Big business is big because it is successful, and the many contributions of those beneath, duly recognized and rewarded, is a very integral part of that success. Though there will be instances of top level injustices, the average 'boss' is well aware of the foundation upon which his well-being is based. And if he is to flourish, a minimum of personnel faux pas is to be expected. In any event he is at the helm and petty criticism should be ruled out. Let loyalty far over-balance, if any legitimate fault appraisals do occur, and try always to realize that your own position in an organization is dependent on the fact that there is an organization. Executive administrators are mostly dedicated to keeping it intact - for their benefit as well as yours.

The many years of my being a somewhat cog in M.G.M.'s wheel of operation has left me convinced that loyalty is truly a two-way street. I am grateful and appreciative and by the same token I have expected and, I believe, received a fair measure of gratitude in return. There was that time when Henry Henigson made a salary survey of the Studio, however!

THE WALL?

And perhaps we <u>should</u> tell of J.J. Cohn, Hobart Henley and a 'brick' wall. Not too earth-shaking a finale for these pages but quite possibly a smile will come from its telling, and I will be repaid for one morning's excessive wear of shoe leather.

The era was during my early activities as a Unit Art

Director and the situation was this. Mr. Henley picked a camera set-up for his first shot of the day which necessitated the addition of a twenty foot 'brick' wall. An old M.G.M. 'New York' street was the set. His newly located camera position had been a last minute change, and we Art Directors had been well schooled as to last minute changes. An approval from the Production Office was the ordered routine and I so informed Mr. Henley. He understood. Available were several stock 'brick' walls (plaster 'brick' on fairly light wood frames). I hightailed it to Mr. Cohn's sanctum sanatorium for an official consent.

"Did he not see the set last night?" was Joe's first remark.

"He did, Mr. Cohn," I replied.

"Did he not OK everything? Did he ask for a brick wall?"

"Yes, he did. No, he didn't," I answered to both interrogations.

"You go back and tell him he can't have it. We're going to stop these delays!" fumed Joe.

The distance from the Production Manager's Office to our New York street was about one sixteenth of a mile, so I had covered a full eighth upon my return to deliver Mr. Cohn's edict to Mr. Henley. A large shooting crew and a host of extras were waiting.

"Now," I was informed by Hobart, "you just go back and tell Mr. Cohn I won't crank a camera until I get my wall."

I scooted to report and was shuttled immediately back to Mr. Henley with a rather fervid admonition from Mr. Cohn. "Will you explain to Mr. Henley that he should have thought of any additions to the set before, not at shooting time. No wall!"

The Director's controlled reply upon my return was a request for his wood and canvas director's chair upon which he sat. "Explain to Mr. Cohn that I am quite comfortable and willing to wait," said he.

After several more laps of message carrying, hence the reference to shoe leather, I finally prevailed upon Mr. Cohn to pay Mr. Henley a visit in person. The following conversation took place.

"Good morning, Hobart." Joe's inner-office fury had changed to happiness and a smile. "What seems to be the trouble?"

"Good morning, Joe. I need a brick wall," volunteered Hobart.

"Can we supply Mr. Henley with a brick wall?" said Joe to me.

"Yes, Mr. Cohn," replied I.

"Well, that sounds reasonable. Suppose you get it. How long will it take?" he pleasantly questioned.

"Ten or fifteen minutes, Joe," I rather flabbergastedly replied.

"Fine, Hobart. Hope all goes well today. Ta ta," and dear Joe departed.

No moral to this story. Just a foot-weary, slightly dented morale, suffered by one bewildered message-toting Art Director.

Long ago this happened, and the dialogue may not be verbatim but in essence, if Joe Cohn's memory serves him right (mine does), this little by-remote-control skirmish is pretty validly chronicled. Joe's generosity and valued long-time friendship leaves me in little fear that its perusal by him will generate the same sincere smile with which he greeted Mr. Henley at the finish of my two mile or thereabouts hike.

We sincerely hope that the written, diagrammatic and photo contents of this book have given helpful aid to all who may contemplate a journey into one or more of the fields of Art Direction or Special Visual Effects, and indirectly to those in all other branches of Studio endeavor as they relate to these fields. Its writing has been particularly rewarding to the author in the recalling of the past - usually pleasant, often amusing, occasionally sad. For the lay reader well, you are now an authority! And invariably people have entered, the most valuable commodity of all.

So we conclude with multiple salutes to all of our assistants. They range from the lofty pinnacles of Management to the deep and valued valleys of we lesser people - all directly or indirectly contributing in their big or little ways towards a happy and satisfying "Forty-two six Years at M.G.M.".

The Greatest Story Ever Told, MGM Production, Released 1965, AAG Contribution: Special Visual Effects.

STAND BY FOR ACTION (1943) PRODUCTION 1237

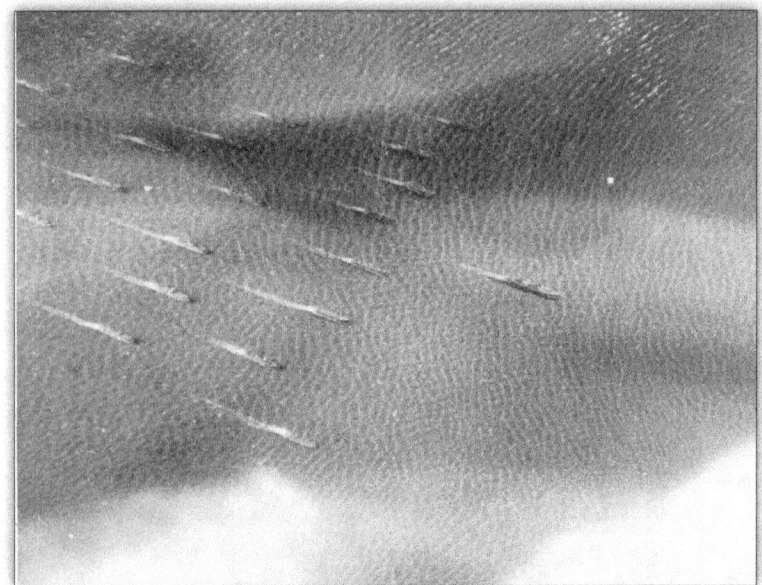

Stand By For Action sequence. 8" to 10" ships. Painted cellophane 'wakes'. Water 1" deep. Foreground clouds on glass.

Long shot, convoy 3/4", 1/2" scale ships and profile smaller scale ships.

#2 and #3 were process plates for full sized destroyer "Warren". Note foreground, white water from "Warren".

Straight cut of miniature "Warren", scale 3/4"=12". Note bad adjustment on bow 'wave' nozzle.

Convoy under attack. 1/2" scale cruiser hit astern. Foreground freighter is 3/4" scale.

Miniature attacking plane. Binocular matte added later.

"Stand By" sequence continued. Anti-aircraft 'bursts' plotted to path of plane.

Attack plane speed and attitude manually controlled by overhead wires hung from trolly.

"Bursts" plotted and timed for cross screen plane path, matted in later.

Shell shots created by dropping balloons filled with powerder on floor of stage 14. Shot downwards on white B.G. Printed into shot afterwards.

'Shell' from "Warren". Destroyer foreground 'bow wave' produced by outboards on camera raft.

Direct hit. Break-away plane powder loaded, detonated remotely.

The "Warren" starts laying protective 'smoke screen'.

She continues. Smoke was from tanks of burning crude oil. Recall reader, lessons learned about making smoke during "Too Hot to Handle".

"Stand By" continued. "Warren" turns. Note white water from self contained siphons and pump.

She emerges through 'screen' to attack.

The target. An early 'Christmas Tree' Japanese battleship.

At close quarters. Used as a process plate for crews at torpedoes.

She launches two.

Straight cut of both 'ships' and first hit.

Our 'World War I' four stacker, scores. 'Torpedo' hits were mortars attached to hull of battleship.

Fired remotely they were followed by mortars aboard.

Her 'magazines go'. No serious damage to the miniature. Several 'takes' actually were shot.

49-P Alt

Long shot, convoy, point of view.

The Warren in rough weather.

Day for night. Shot in bright sunlight with a night 'sky' and a black "Warren".

"RAMBLING RANDOMS"

(Above) *Stand By for Action* - Safely home. 'Golden Gate' Bridge. Near ships are 3/4" and 1/2' scale. Distant ships are profiles that move slowly behind our miniature ocean's horizon.

(Below) Mission completed, she heads westward. We used two "Warrens", one 3/4" scale and one 1/2" scale. Again note seeming distance to horizon through scenic sky perspective.

Production 1291 - J4 - 26B-1 *Guy Name Joe* (1944). Filmed on Lot 3, airfield crash landing. 1/2" scale miniature.

Production 1291 J4-26B-1 *Guy Named Joe* (1944). 3/4" scale plane "flown" by three guide wires.

An Egyptian dawn with front projected sky, profile Pyramids, three dimensional foreground for *Cairo*. A miniature in three scales.

A "PBY" forced landing in *High Barbaree*. Note miniature 'people'. Scale 1"=12".

A 'parachute' sail is rigged. Now becalmed, we later sank her.

CHAPTER ELEVEN

Son of Lassie miniature village absorbing an air raid. Distant mountains were painted on the backing, one end of which shows on lower right photo. Wooded hills are profiles. Village scales 1"=12".

Shooting Schematic in "Tokyo Harbor" for *Torpedo Run*. Note use of 1/2" and 3/4" scale miniature 'ships'. The 'city' was a profile in front of 'lower sky'. Convex thumb tacks for lights.

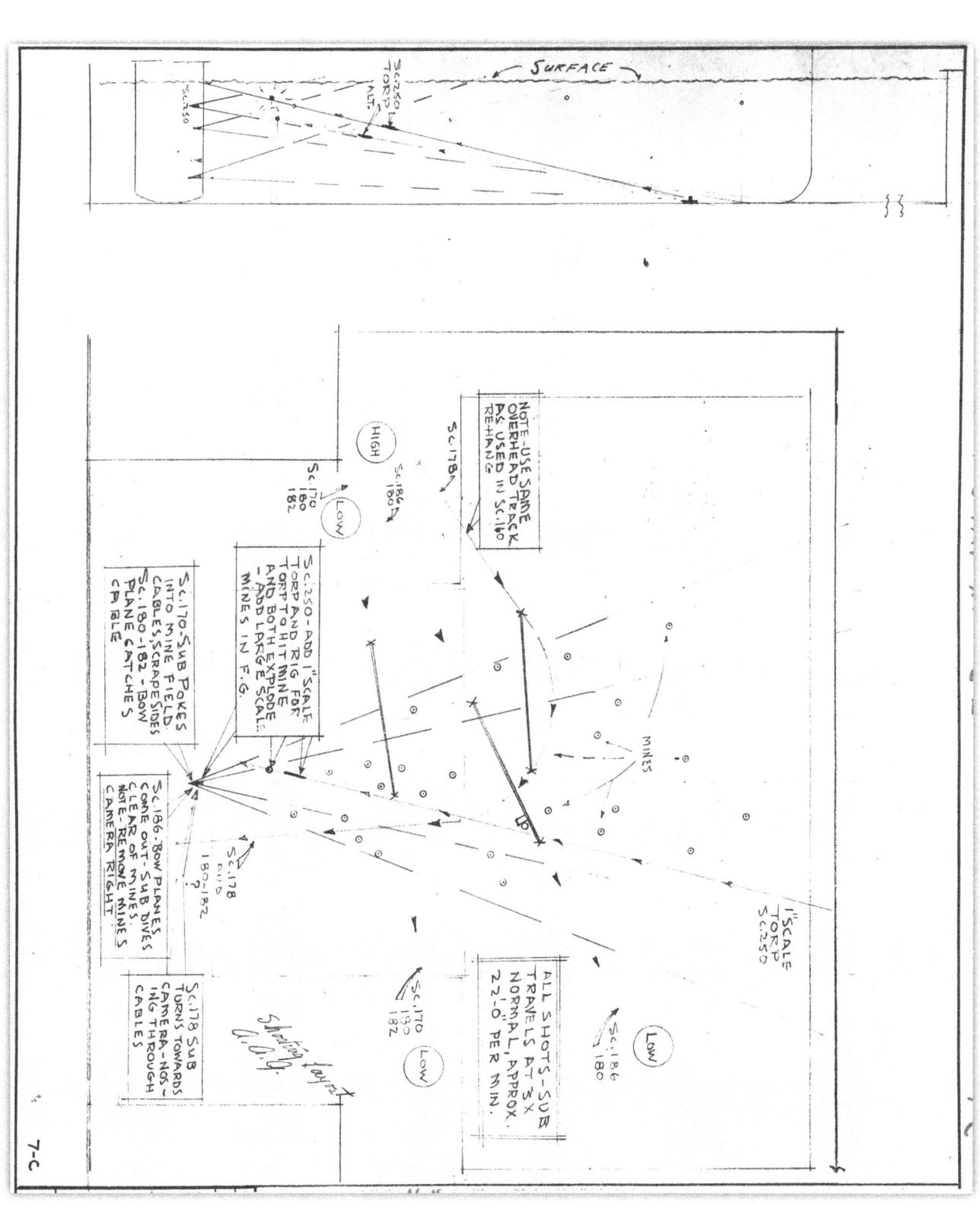

Underwater Shooting Layout for submarine inching through 'mine field' and firing torpedoes to detonate one. 'Tokyo Harbor' for *Torpedo Run* submarine 1/2" scale.

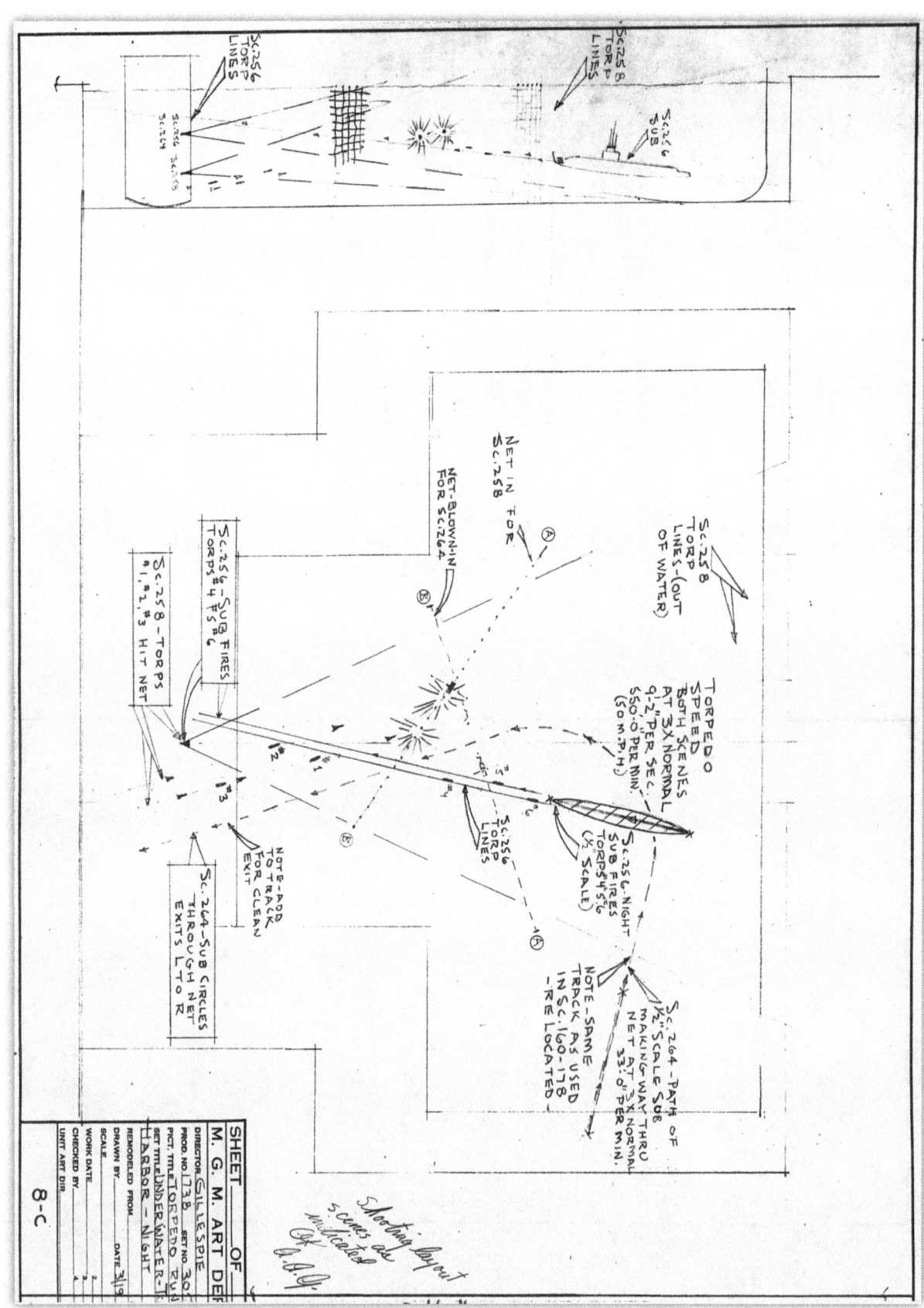

Underwater Schematic showing harbor submarine net which torpedoes blast. Sheep dip for torpedo 'wakes'.

CHAPTER ELEVEN

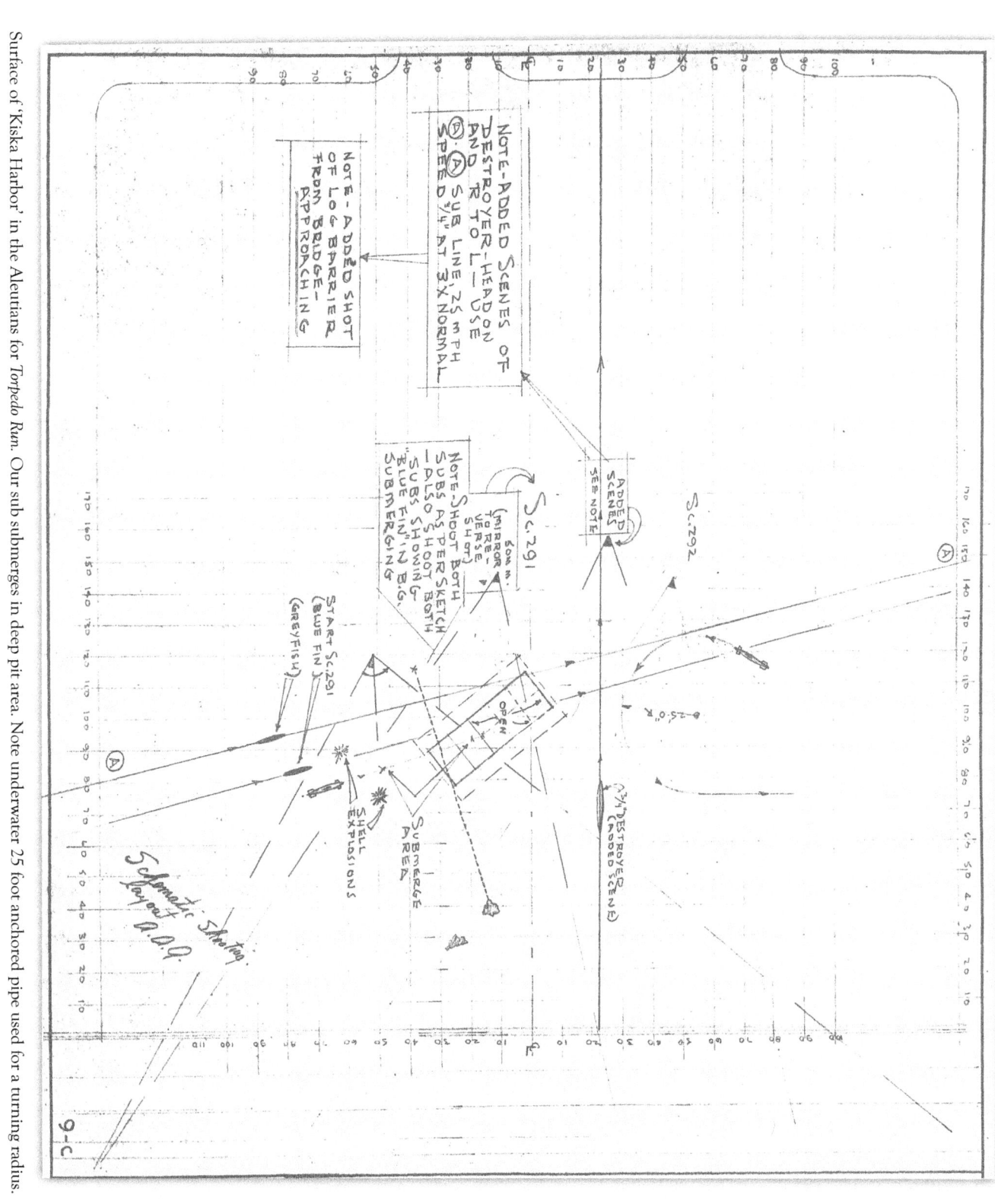

Surface of 'Kiska Harbor' in the Aleutians for *Torpedo Run*. Our sub submerges in deep pit area. Note underwater 25 foot anchored pipe used for a turning radius.

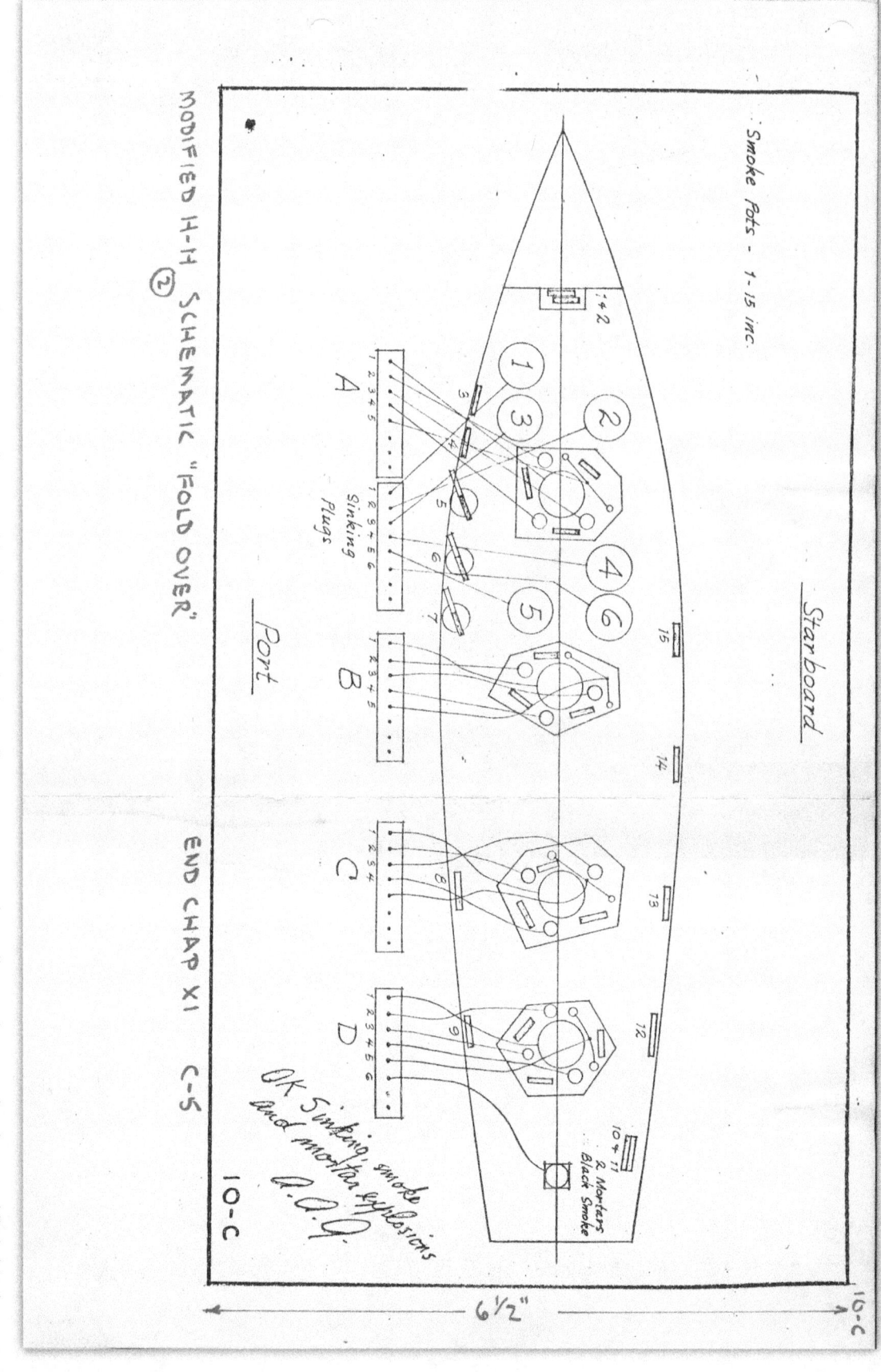

Firing diagram in sequence for smoke pots, mortar explosions and 'sinking plugs'. The latter allows water to enter the Hull in pre-determined and prepared 'holes' facilitating her bow-first pull down into the deep pit of our Lot 3 ocean. This was a 1/2" scale Japanese Aircraft Carrier for "Torpedo Run". Firing was done electrically from shore.

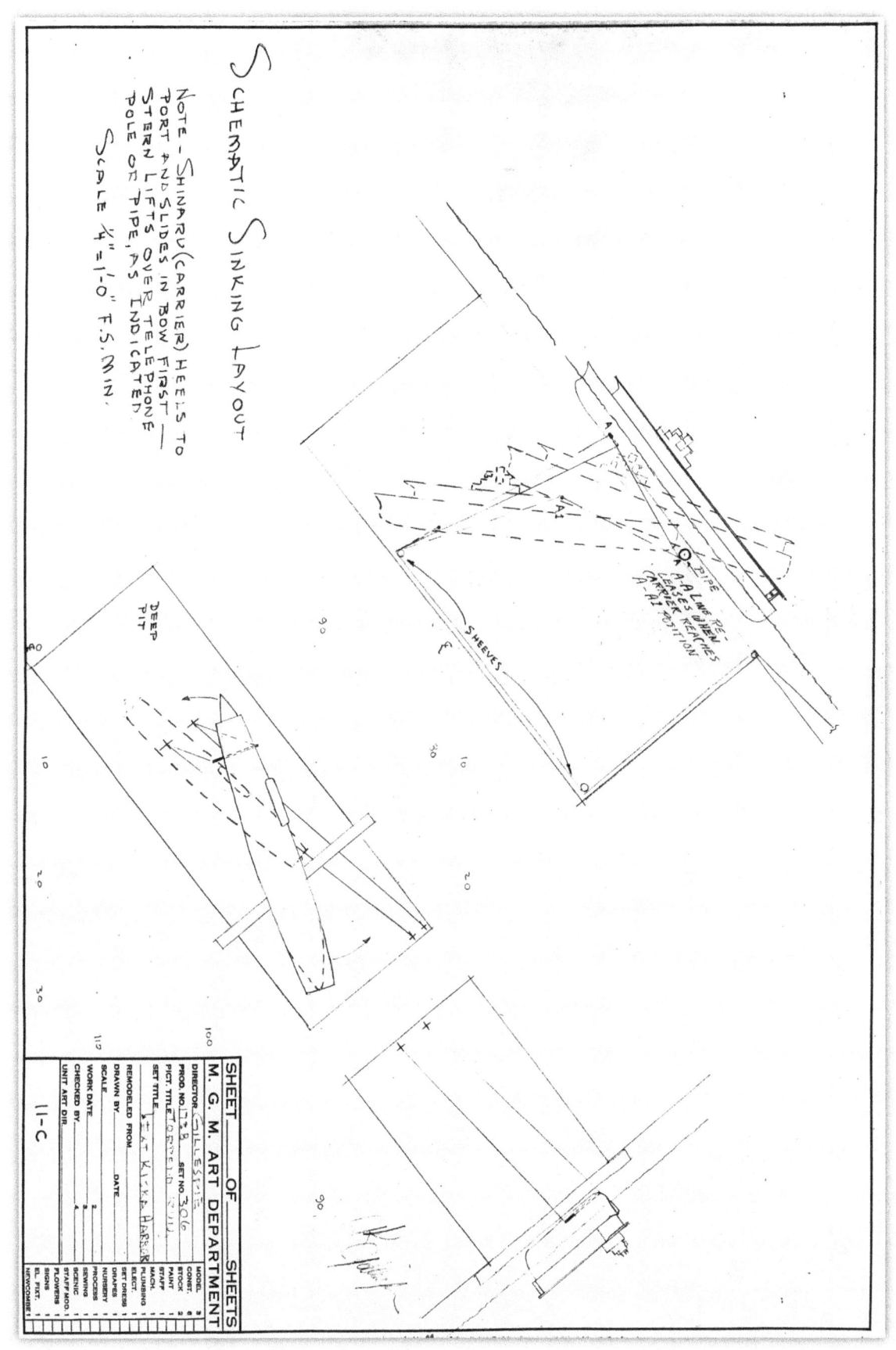

Schematic method of 'sinking' carrier into deep pit. She was about 27 feet long at 1/2" scale. Cable winches were used to sink her.

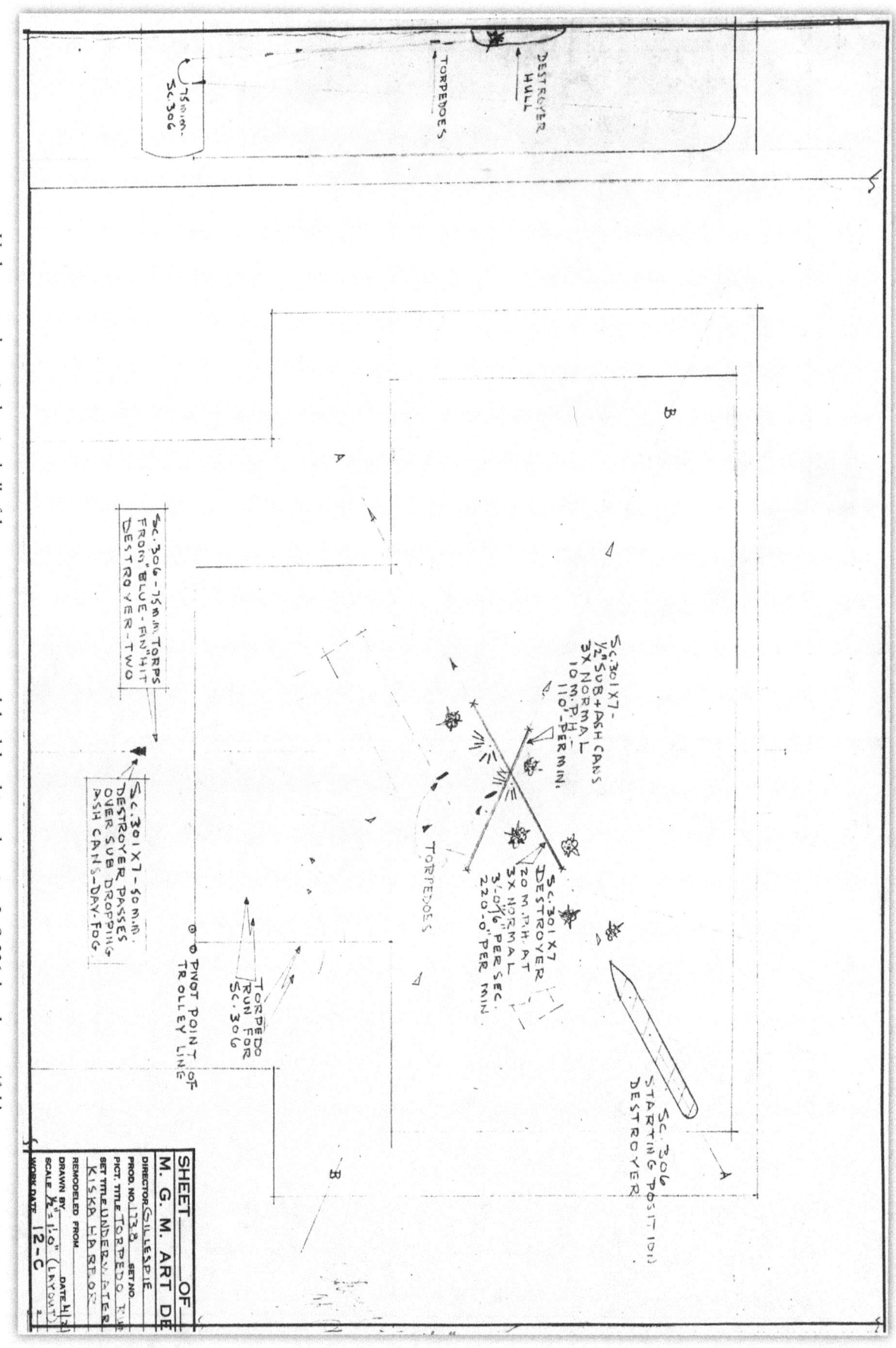

Underwater schematic showing hull of destroyer passing over and depth-bombing submarine. In Sc306 she takes two 'fish'.

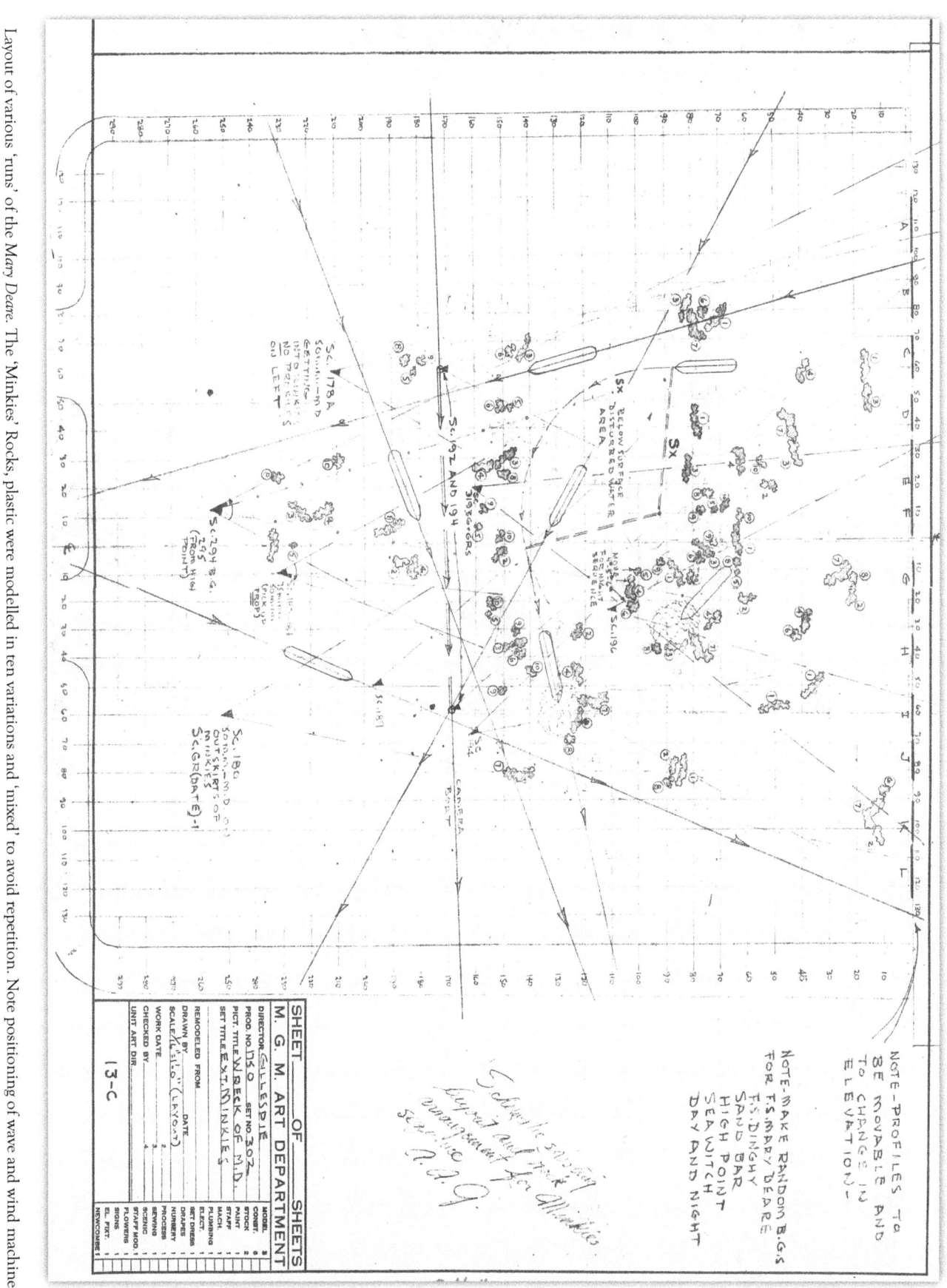

Layout of various 'runs' of the *Mary Deare*. The 'Minkies' Rocks, plastic were modelled in ten variations and 'mixed' to avoid repetition. Note positioning of wave and wind machines.

"RAMBLING RANDOMS"

The Wreck of the Mary Deare (1959) Tank Lot 3.

CHAPTER ELEVEN

14-C

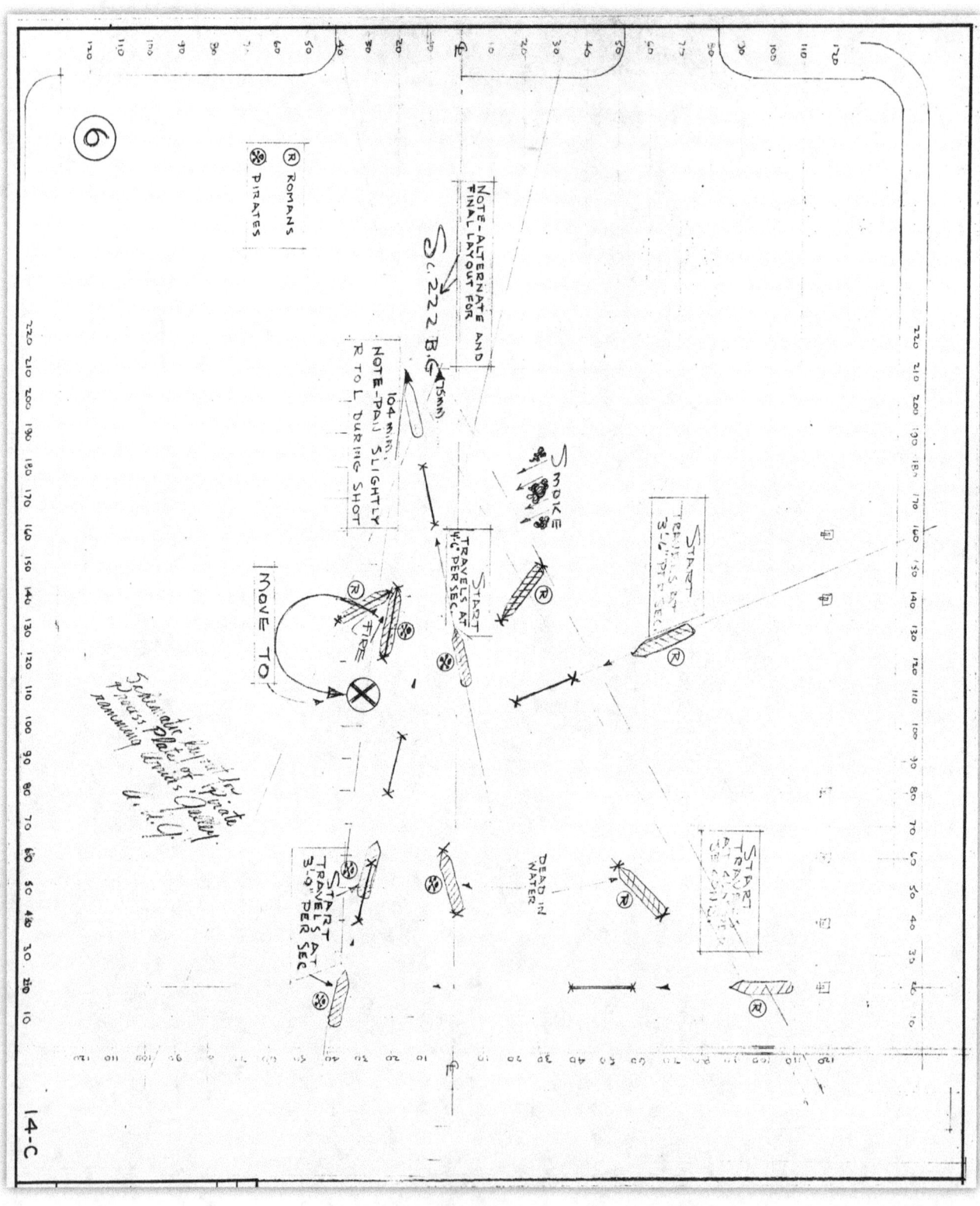

One of many *"Ben-Hur"* miniature galley sequence schematics.

CHAPTER ELEVEN 360

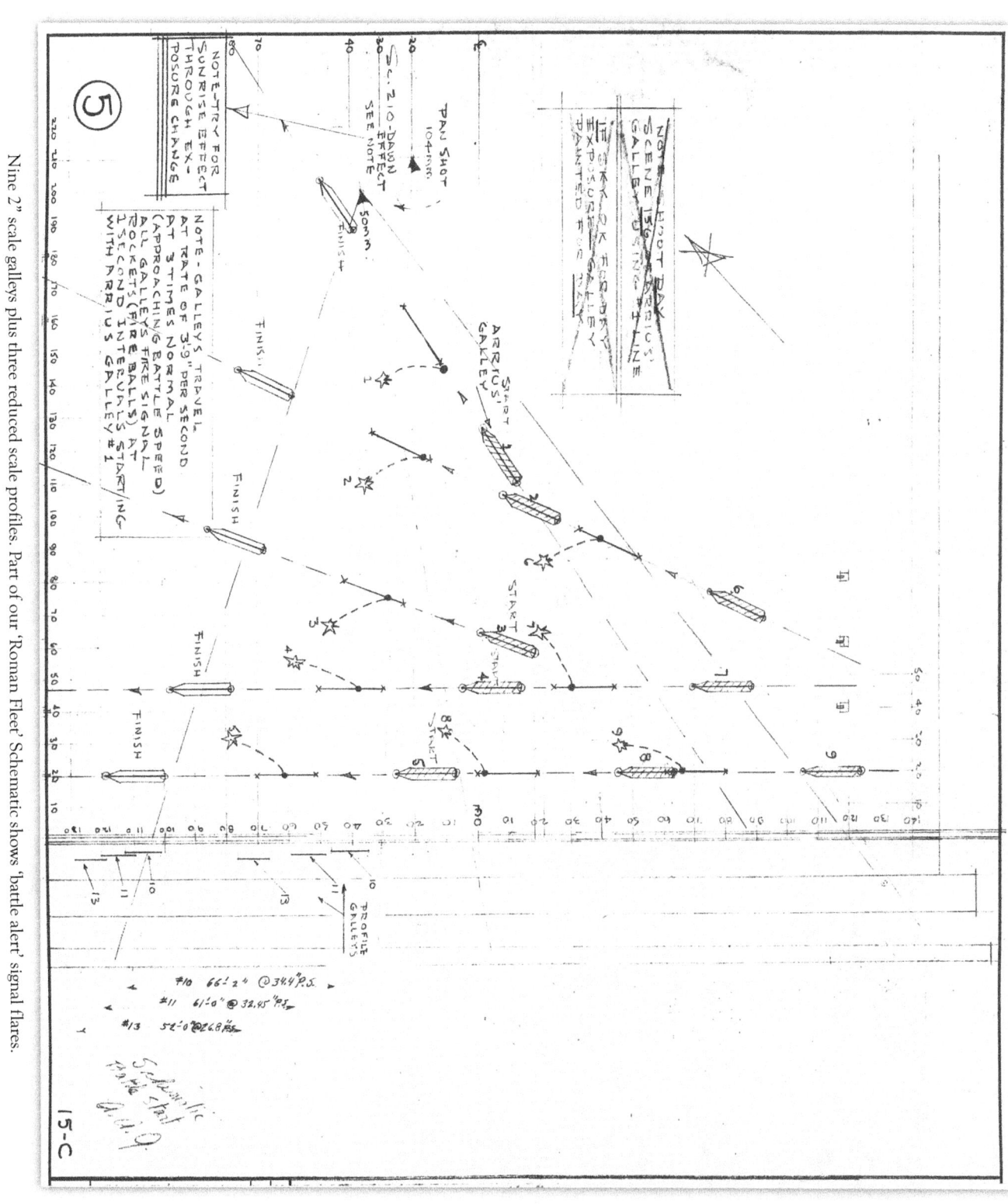

Nine 2" scale galleys plus three reduced scale profiles. Part of our 'Roman Fleet' Schematic shows 'battle alert' signal flares.

"Ben-Hur" 1959 galley sequence left side of Lot 3.

CHAPTER ELEVEN 362

"Ben-Hur" 1959 galley sequence right side of Lot 3.

Another "Ben-Hur" Schematic. Profile galleys #1 to #7 were made from photos of the miniature galley as per 'schedule' showing proper angle and height so that they 'tie in' with the three dimensional 'ships'.

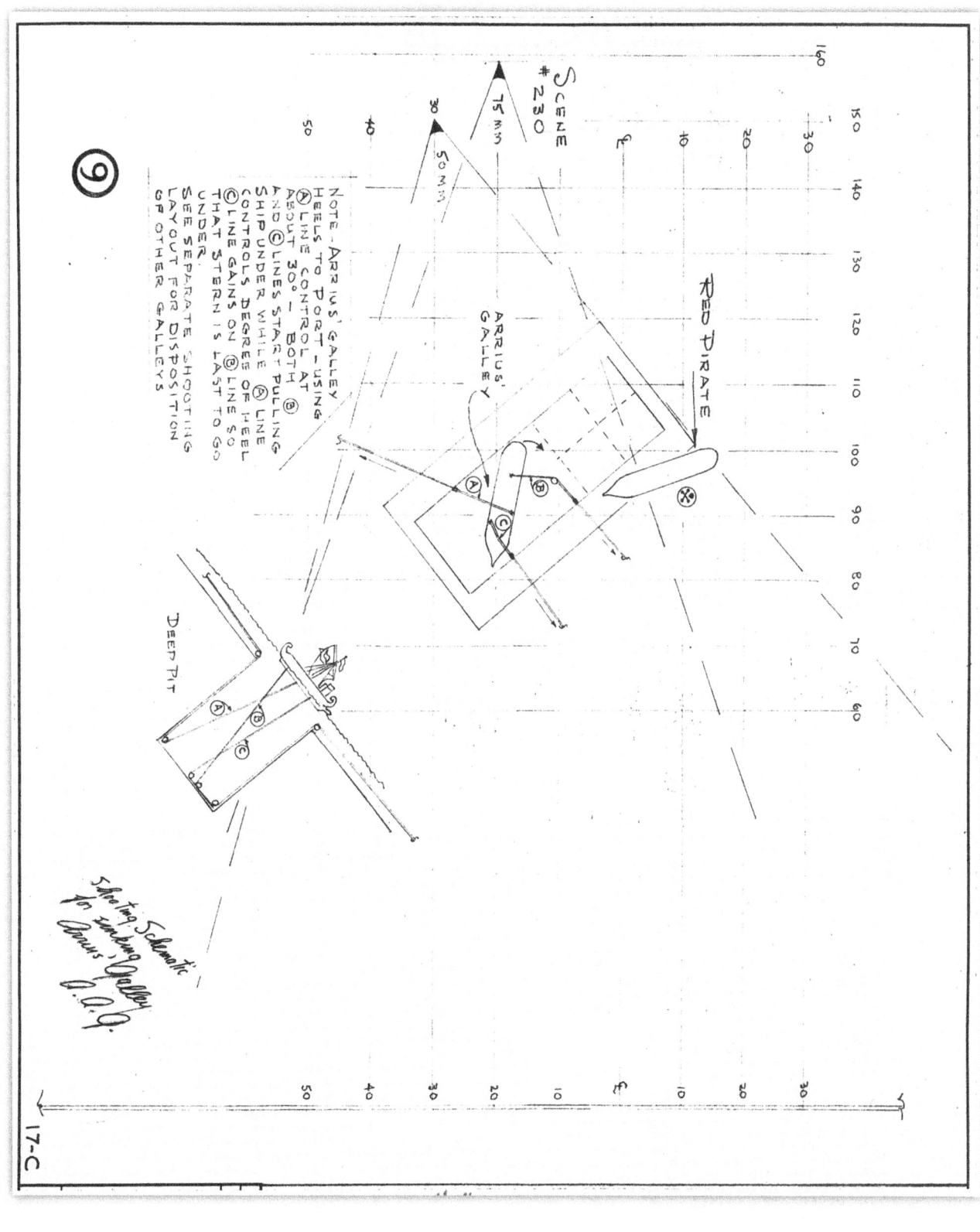

Schematic Layout of "Arrius'" blazing galley. Schedule of 'cable pulls' resulted in a photogenic sinking.

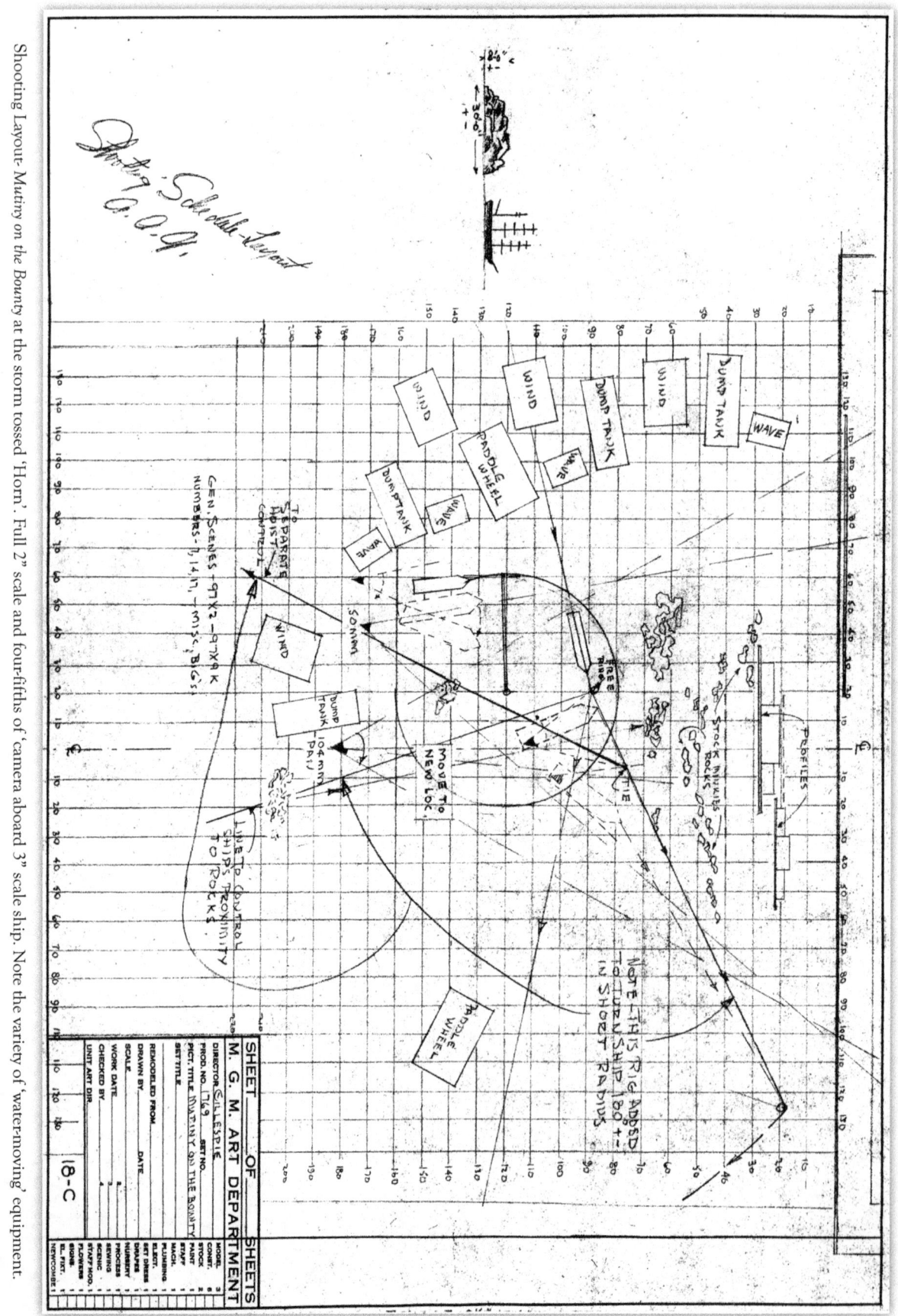

Shooting Layout Mutiny on the Bounty at the storm tossed 'Horn'. Full 2" scale and four-fifths of 'camera aboard 3" scale ship. Note the variety of 'water-moving' equipment.

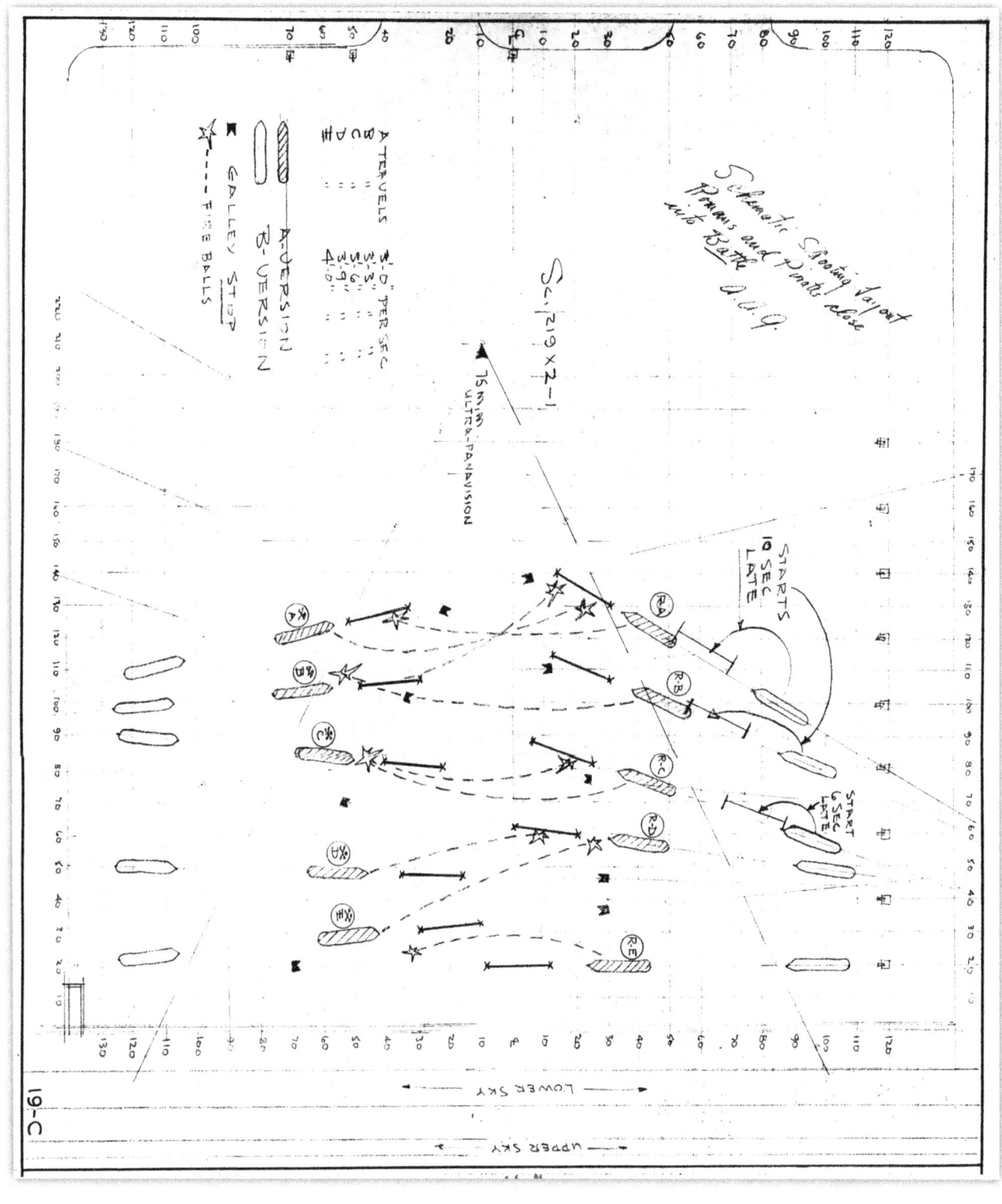

The start of *"Ben-Hur"* miniature galley 'battle'. All ships were 2" scale.

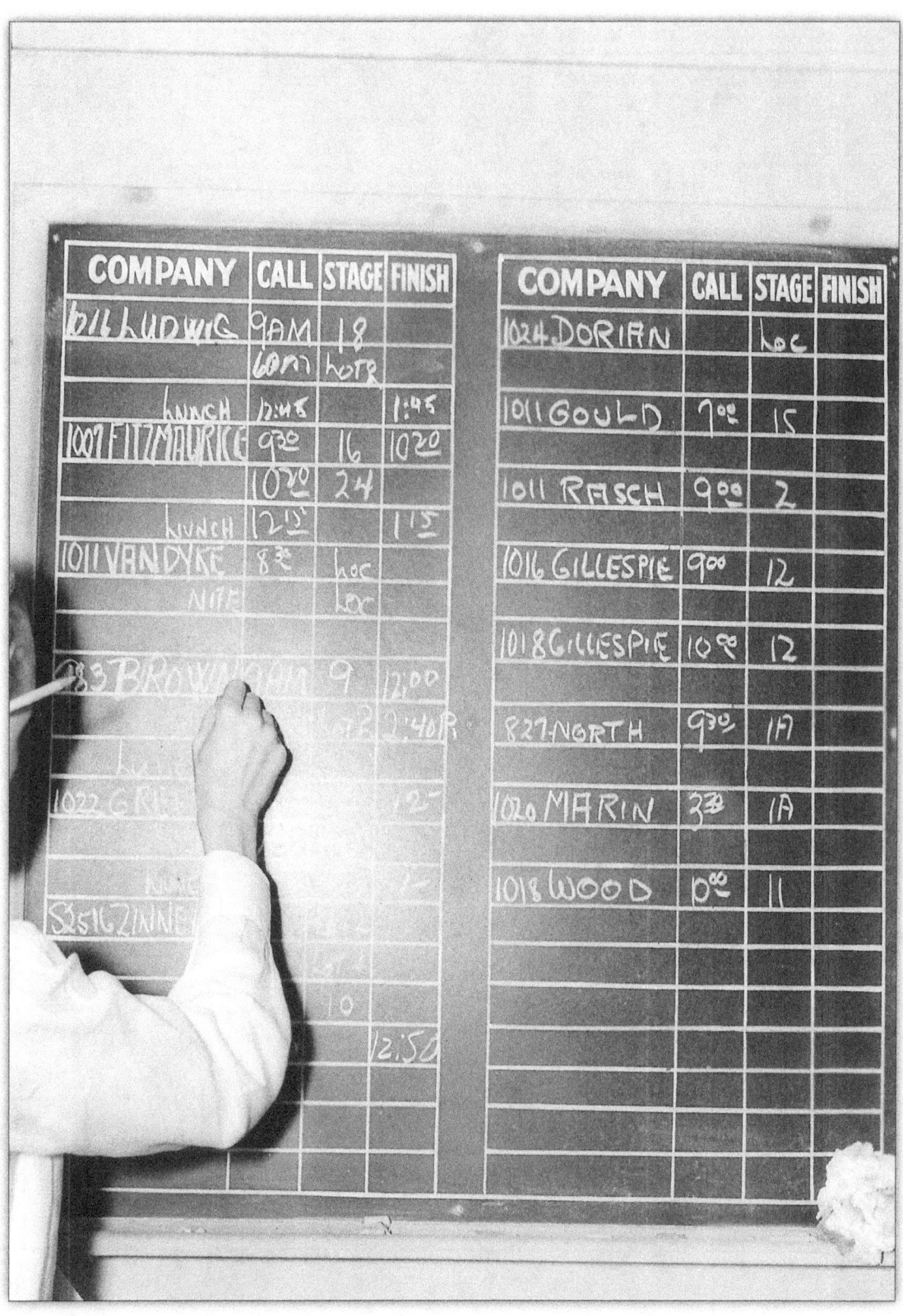

MGM Call Board circa 1937. Production 1016 is *The Last Gangster*.
Production 1018 is *Navy Blue and Gold*.
Courtesy - The Academy Margaret Herrick Library, MGM J. Real Neth collection.

FILM CREDITS

FILM CREDITS

Special Effects
1961 Atlantis, the Lost Continent (special effects)
1960 Cimarron (special effects)
1960 Bells Are Ringing (special effects)
1960 The Adventures of Huckleberry Finn (special effects)
1959 The Wreck of the Mary Deare (special effects)
1959 North by Northwest (special effects)
1959 Green Mansions (special effects)
1958 Torpedo Run (special effects)
1957 Don't Go Near the Water (special effects)
1957 Jailhouse Rock (special effects)
1957 Until They Sail (special effects)
1957 Tip on a Dead Jockey (special effects)
1957 Gun Glory (special effects)
1957 The Seventh Sin (special effects)
1957 Ten Thousand Bedrooms (special effects)
1957 The Wings of Eagles (special effects)
1956 The Great American Pastime (special effects)
1956 The Opposite Sex (special effects)
1956 The Power and the Prize (special effects)
1956 High Society (special effects)
1956 Gaby (special effects)
1956 Forbidden Planet (special effects)
1955 The Prodigal (special effects)
1954 Green Fire (special effects)
1954 The Last Time I Saw Paris (special effects)
1954 Rogue Cop (special effects)
1954 Her Twelve Men (special effects)
1954 Seven Brides for Seven Brothers (special effects)
1954 Valley of the Kings (special effects)
1954 Men of the Fighting Lady (special effects)
1954 Prisoner of War (special effects)
1954 Executive Suite (special effects)
1954 Rhapsody (special effects)
1954 Rose Marie (special effects)
1953 The Long, Long Trailer (special effects)
1953 All the Brothers Were Valiant (special effects)
1953 Latin Lovers (special effects)
1953 Ride, Vaquero! (special effects)
1953 Arena (special effects)
1953 Dream Wife (special effects)
1953 A Slight Case of Larceny (special effects)
1953 Young Bess (special effects)
1953 Scandal at Scourie (special effects)
1953 Cry of the Hunted (special effects)
1953 Code Two (special effects)
1953 Bright Road (special effects)
1953 Jeopardy (special effects)
1953 I Love Melvin (special effects)
1953 Battle Circus (special effects)
1952 Above and Beyond (special effects)
1952 The Bad and the Beautiful (special effects)
1952 Sky Full of Moon (special effects)
1952 Million Dollar Mermaid (special effects)
1952 Desperate Search (special effects)
1952 Plymouth Adventure (special effects)
1952 Apache War Smoke (special effects)
1952 The Merry Widow (special effects)
1952 Fearless Fagan (special effects)
1952 Washington Story (special effects)
1952 Glory Alley (special effects)
1952 The Sellout (special effects)
1952 Lovely to Look at (special effects)
1952 The Girl in White (special effects)
1952 Scaramouche (special effects)
1952 Young Man with Ideas (special effects)

1952 Carbine Williams (special effects)
1952 Talk About a Stranger (special effects)
1952 Just This Once (special effects)
1952 Lone Star (special effects)
1952 Invitation (special effects)
1952 The Light Touch (special effects)
1951 It's a Big Country (special effects)
1951 The Unknown Man (special effects)
1951 Callaway Went Thataway (special effects)
1951 Quo Vadis (special effects - as A.Arnold Gillespie)
1951 Angels in the Outfield (special effects)
1951 Texas Carnival (special effects)
1951 The People Against O'Hara (special effects)
1951 The Strip (special effects)
1951 The Tall Target (special effects)
1951 Excuse My Dust (special effects)
1951 No Questions Asked (special effects)
1951 Go for Broke! (special effects)
1951 Soldiers Three (special effects)
1951 Inside Straight (special effects)
1951 Three Guys Named Mike (special effects)
1950 Pagan Love Song (special effects)
1950 The Magnificent Yankee (special effects)
1950 Watch the Birdie (special effects)
1950 Kim (special effects)
1950 Dial 1119 (special effects)
1950 To Please a Lady (special effects)
1950 Devil's Doorway (special effects - as Arnold Gillespie)
1950 The Toast of New Orleans (special effects)
1950 A Lady Without Passport (special effects)
1950 Crisis (special effects)
1950 Annie Get Your Gun (special effects)
1950 The Reformer and the Redhead (special effects)
1950 The Yellow Cab Man (special effects)
1950 Side Street (special effects)
1950 Nancy Goes to Rio (special effects)
1950 The Outriders (special effects)
1950 Key to the City (special effects)
1949 Malaya (special effects)
1949 East Side, West Side (special effects)
1949 Adam's Rib (special effects)
1949 Scene of the Crime (special effects)
1949 The Secret Garden (special effects)
1949 The Stratton Story (special effects)
1949 The Bribe (special effects)
1948 Command Decision (special effects)
1948 The Kissing Bandit (special effects)
1948 Luxury Liner (special effects)
1948 On an Island with You (special effects)
1948 State of the Union (special effects)
1948 Homecoming (special effects)
1947 High Wall (special effects)
1947 Cass Timberlane (special effects)
1947 Desire Me (special effects)
1947 This Time for Keeps (special effects)
1947 Green Dolphin Street (special effects)
1947 The Hucksters (special effects)
1947 High Barbaree (special effects)
1947 The Sea of Grass (special effects)
1947 The Beginning or the End (special effects)
1947 Lady in the Lake (special effects)
1946 The Green Years (special effects)
1946 Up Goes Maisie (special effects)
1945 They Were Expendable (special effects)
1945 What Next, Corporal Hargrove? (special effects)
1945 Yolanda and the Thief (special effects)

1945 Our Vines Have Tender Grapes (special effects)
1945 The Valley of Decision (special effects)
1945 Son of Lassie (special effects)
1945 The Clock (special effects)
1945 Without Love (special effects)
1945 This Man's Navy (special effects)
1944 National Velvet (transparency projection shots - uncredited)
1944 Meet Me in St. Louis (miniatures and transparency projection shots - uncredited)
1944 Thirty Seconds Over Tokyo (special effects)
1944 Mrs. Parkington (special effects)
1944 An American Romance (special effects - as Arnold Gillespie)
1944 The White Cliffs of Dover (special effects - as Arnold Gillespie)
1944 The Heavenly Body (special effects - as Arnold Gillespie)
1944 Song of Russia (special effects - as Arnold Gillespie)
1943 A Guy Named Joe (special effects - as Arnold Gillespie)
1943 The Man from Down Under (special effects)
1943 Salute to the Marines (special effects - as Arnold Gillespie)
1943 Pilot #5 (special effects - as Arnold Gillespie)
1943 Bataan (special effects - as Arnold Gillespie)
1943 Assignment in Brittany (special effects - as Arnold Gillespie)
1942 Stand by for Action (special effects - as Arnold Gillespie)
1942 I Married an Angel (special effects - as Arnold Gillespie)
1942 Mrs. Miniver (special effects - as Arnold Gillespie)
1942 Tarzan's New York Adventure (special effects - as Arnold Gillespie)
1942 The Bugle Sounds (special effects - as Arnold Gillespie)
1940 Flight Command (special effects - as Arnold Gillespie)
1940 Comrade X (special effects - as Arnold Gillespie)
1940 Boom Town (special effects - as Arnold Gillespie)
1939 The Wizard of Oz (special effects - as Arnold Gillespie)
1938 Too Hot to Handle (special effects - as Arnold Gillespie)
1938 Test Pilot (special effects)
1936 Tarzan Escapes (special effects - uncredited)
1936 San Francisco (special effects - uncredited)
1933 Night Flight (special effects)

Art Department
1937 Captains Courageous (associate art director - as Arnold Gillespie)
1937 The Good Earth (associate art director - as Arnold Gillespie)
1936 San Francisco (associate art director - as Arnold Gillespie)
1936 Speed (associate art director - as Arnold Gillespie)
1936 Small Town Girl (associate art director - as Arnold Gillespie)
1935 Last of the Pagans (associate art director - as Arnold Gillespie)
1935 Mutiny on the Bounty (associate art director - as Arnold Gillespie)
1935 Naughty Marietta (associate art director - as Arnold Gillespie)
1934 Evelyn Prentice (associate art director)
1934 Student Tour (associate art director)
1934 The Girl from Missouri (associate art director - as Arnold Gillespie)
1934 Operator 13 (associate art director - as Arnold Gillespie)
1927 Buttons (sets - as Arnold Gillespie)
1927 Body and Soul (sets - as Arnold Gillespie)
1927 Women Love Diamonds (sets - as Arnold Gillespie)
1927 Altars of Desire (sets - as Arnold Gillespie)
1926 Valencia (sets - as Arnold Gillespie)
1926 There You Are! (sets - as Arnold Gillespie)
1926 Brown of Harvard (sets - as Arnold Gillespie)
1926 La bohème (settings - as Arnold Gillespie)
1925 Ben-Hur: A Tale of the Christ (set designer - uncredited)
1923 Adam's Rib (assistant art director)

Visual Effects
1965 The Greatest Story Ever Told (special visual effects)
1964 The Unsinkable Molly Brown (special visual effects)
1963 The Prize (special visual effects)
1962 Billy Rose's Jumbo (special visual effects)
1962 Mutiny on the Bounty (special visual effects)
1962 How the West Was Won (special visual effects - as A. Arnold Gillespie)
1962 The Four Horsemen of the Apocalypse (special visual effects)
1959 Ben-Hur (special photographic effects)
1958 Run Silent Run Deep (special photographic effects - as Arnold Gillespie)
1945 Keep Your Powder Dry (camera operator: transparency projection shots - uncredited)
1945 The Thin Man Goes Home (transparency projection shots - uncredited)
1944 Kismet (miniatures - uncredited, special photographic effects - uncredited, transparency shots - uncredited)
1944 Maisie Goes to Reno (transparency projection shots - uncredited)
1944 Dragon Seed (miniatures - uncredited)
1943 Cry 'Havoc' (miniatures and transparency projection shots - uncredited)
1939 The Wizard of Oz (visual effects supervisor - uncredited)

Art Director
1934 Tarzan and His Mate (as Arnold Gillespie)
1934 Laughing Boy (as Arnold Gillespie)
1934 Fugitive Lovers (as Arnold Gillespie)
1928 The Latest from Paris
1927 The Fair Co-Ed
1927 Heaven on Earth (as Arnold Gillespie)
1927 The Demi-Bride
1926 Upstage
1926 The Road to Mandalay
1926 Memory Lane (as Arnold Gillespie)

Set Decorator
1928 The Crowd (settings / as Arnold Gillespie)
1928 The Divine Woman
1927 London After Midnight (settings / as Arnold Gillespie)
1926 Tell It to the Marines (settings / as Arnold Gillespie)
1926 Lovely Mary (settings)
1926 The Blackbird (settings / as Arnold Gillespie)

Self
1980 Hollywood (TV mini-series documentary)
- Trick of the Light (1980)
- Autocrats (1980)
- Pioneers (1980)

Archive Footage
2009 To Oz! The Making of a Classic (video documentary short)
2004 Cecil B. DeMille: American Epic (TV documentary)
1990 The Wonderful Wizard of Oz: 50 Years of Magic (TV documentary)

The complete list of credits exceeds 84 titles for Art Direction, and 329 for Special Effects.

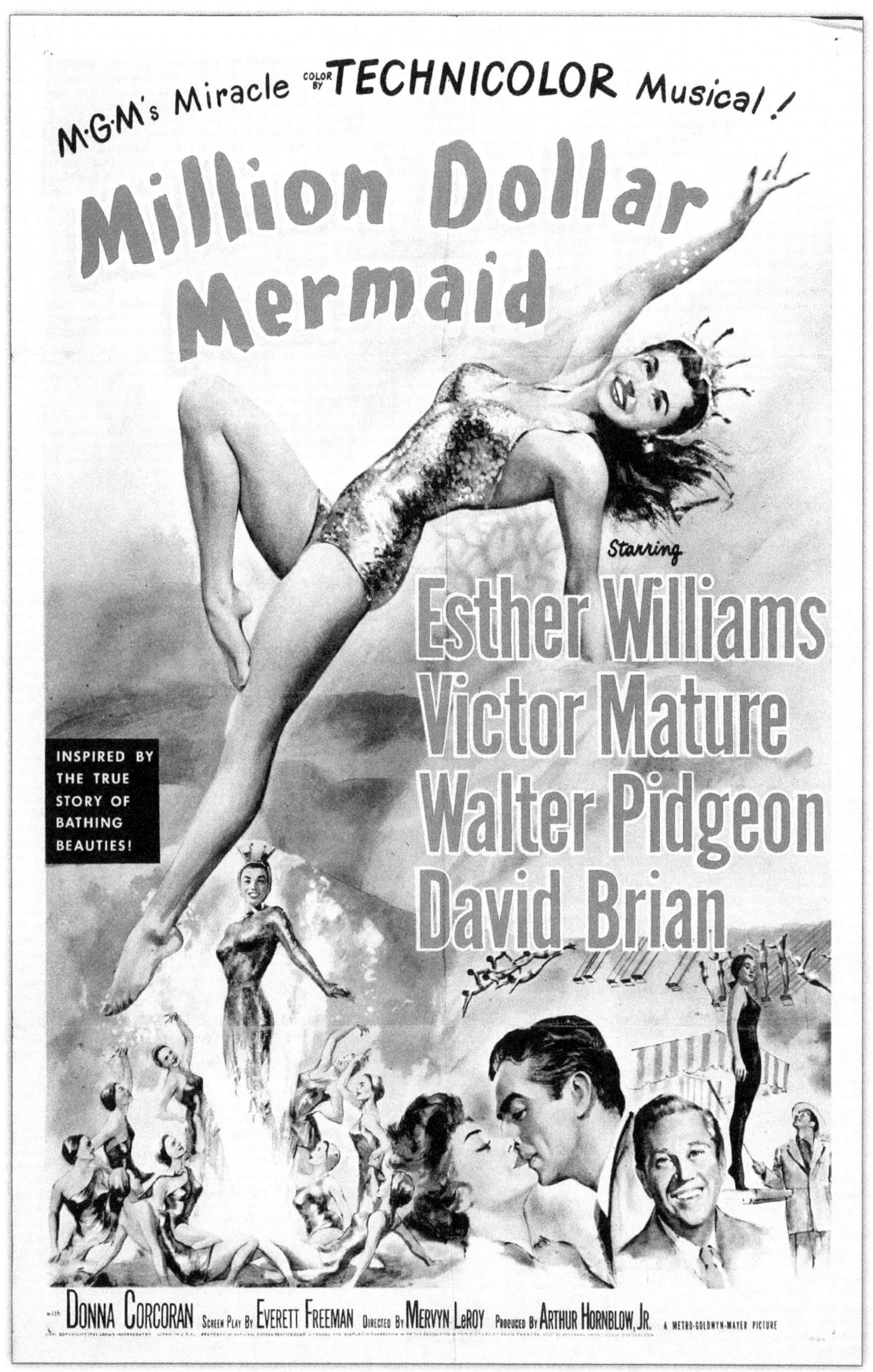

Million Dollar Mermaid, MGM Production #1567, Released 1952, AAG Contribution: Special Effects.

NAMES INDEX

Adorée, Renée	79, 148
Albecker, Clarence	206
Albertson, Myron	324
Albiez, Harry	149-150
Ames, Preston	214, 325-326
Anderson, Michael	77, 208
Andrews, Julie	334
Apger, Virgil	4
Arnold, Edward	194, 324
Arnold, Pop	149
Aronson, Al	58
Ashe, Harry	75, 83
Astaire, Fred	77-78, 82
Astor, Mary	195
Atkinson, Leo	191
Atwill, Lionel	315
Badalini, Baldo	216
Baggot, King	77
Bambridge, Tony	299
Bankhead, Tallulah	287
Barber, Phil	214
Barrymore, John	194
Barrymore, Lionel	17, 127, 290
Bartholomew, Frederick Cecil	17, 127, 290
Basevi, James	97, 185
Bauchens, Ann	22
Beaumont, Harry	77
Beck, Virgil	206
Beery, Wallace Fitgerald	12, 17, 71-72, 140, 158, 184
Bell, Kenneth	4
Bennett, Enid	31
Bergams, Fred	206
Berman, Pandro	184
Binger, Ray	83, 321
Blaustein, Julian	208
Blyth, Ann	184
Bolger, Ray	196
Bossart, John	59, 71-72, 78-80, 82, 104, 111, 137, 144, 185, 209, 290, 294, 306
Boyer, Charles	194
Boyle, John W.	30
Brabin, Charles	77
Bradler, Howard	295
Brando, Marlon	106-107, 171
Brown, Clarence	18, 324
Brown, George	206, 287
Brown, Johnny Mack	12, 97
Brown, Walter	206
Brynner, Yul	264
Bucquet, Harry	77
Bullaro, Joe	266
Burroughs, Edgar Rice	149
Busch, Ulrich	299
Bushman, Bruce	81
Bushman, Francis X.	30-31, 38, 81
Canutt, Yakima	49-51, 77
Capps, McClure	214
Capra, Frank	77
Carfagno, Edward	214, 325
Carpenter, Eric	4
Carre, Ben	191
Cathcart, Dan	214
Chamberlin, Merle	206
Chaney, Lon	258, 266, 326
Chase, Ilka	265
Cohn, Joseph Judson	110, 112, 138, 180, 197, 326, 335-336
Coleman, Leroy	214
Constable, Dave	81
Conway, Jack	18, 77
Coogan, Jackie	45
Cooper, Ben	206
Cooper, Gary	208
Cornish, Roy	206
Crawford, Joan	17, 145-146, 202
Creamer, William	4
Crisp, Donald	148
Crowfoot, 'Chief' Bob	266
Cukor, George Dewey	18-19, 145
Curtis, Tom	292
Daniels, Bill	83, 97, 185, 321
Danver, Don	267
Davis, George	209
Davis, Frank	97
Davis, Mark	4, 185, 206
DeMille, Cecil. B.	18-22, 24-27, 57, 184, 206
Dickinson, Angie	194
Donen, Stanley	299
Douglas, Melvyn	145
Dressler, Marie	17
Duell, Randall	214
Dukelski, Alexis	81, 92
Dumas, Hal	206
Dunn, Irene	80
Durante, Jimmy	17
Dye, Lew	206, 287
Dyer, Elmer	96
Eddy, Nelson	70, 206, 219
Edington, Harry E.	30
Emerson, George	260, 262, 266
Erickson, Lou	206
Fabian, Maximilian	4, 172, 185, 190, 235, 274-281, 288, 294-295, 331
Fairbanks Sr., Douglas	51, 60
Fengler, Harlan	88
Fisher, John	24
Fitzgerald, F. Scott Jr.	47-48, 52
Fitzgerald, Zelda	47-48
Fitzmaurice, George	77
Fleming, Victor	18, 80, 127, 196, 290, 305
Flowers, A. D.	206
Folsey, George	88, 185
Ford, Glenn	70, 108-109, 202
Ford, John	77
Foxall, Bill	294
Franklin, Sydney	145
Frank, Melvin	77
Frazer, Harland	81
Freed, Arthur	300
Friend, Carl	206
Fujimoto, Sanezumi	328-329
Gable, Clark	17, 59, 68-69, 72, 84, 111, 194, 200, 285, 293-294, 298, 315-316, 324, 330
Gabouri, Joe	302, 304
Garbo, Greta	150
Garfield, John	330
Garland, Judy	17, 68, 196, 243, 299
Garner, James	194
Garnett, Tay	77
Garson, Greer	17
Gaylord, Jack	137, 333
Gebr, Jerry	191
Gibbons, Cedric	18, 30, 180, 185, 191, 209, 264, 300
Gibson, George	190-191
Gibson, William	191
Gilbert, Jack	148
Gilbert, John	79, 258, 266
Glen, Galvin	203
Goepniger, Max	206
Gold, Milton	4
Granger, Stewart	184
Greer Garson,	17, 200
Greutert, Henry	206
Grinde, Nick	328
Groesse, Paul	214
Groza, Lou	300
Hagedon, Charles	214
Haley, Jack	196
Hall, Dave	81, 118
Hamilton, Margaret	196
Hannan, Eddie	88, 185
Harareet, Haya	103
Harlow, Jean	17, 194
Hathaway, Henry	320, 335
Hawkins, Jack	119
Heflin, Van	202
Hehr, Addison	90, 214
Held, Tom	97
Helms, Ad	191
Henigson, Henry	145, 335
Henley, Hobart	180, 335
Hepburn, Audrey	260
Hepburn, Katharine	3, 16-17, 19
Heston, Charlton	50, 103, 121, 208
Hilburn, Percy	30
Hill, F. Wayne	191
Hill, George	72, 77
Hinchey, John	75
Hitchcock, Alfred	77
Hoag, Robert	265, 302
Horning, William	209, 214
Horton, Dutch	208
Howard, Tom	125, 304
Hubbard, Curly	88, 138, 140, 206
Hubbard, Lucien	88
Hubbell, Eddie	4
Hughes, Howard	58, 74
Hunt, Huey	325-326
Huston, John	77
Hutton, Betty	299-300
Iribe, Jeanie	26
Irebe, Paul	21-22, 24-26
Jackson, Horace	30, 46, 214
Jahraus, Donald	132, 137-138, 151, 185, 195
Janis, Dorothy	148
Johnson, Gene	81
Johnson, McMillan	104, 214
Johnson, Stan	81
Johnson, Van	75-76, 130, 330
Joy, Leatrice	19, 21
Kaplan, Bill	88
Keaton, Buster	77
Kerr, Deborah	200
Kelly, Gene	17, 299
Key, Kathleen	30
King, Ed	206
Kinoshita, Bob	215
Klune, Raymond	301
Kosloff, Theodore	22, 26
Kubric, Stanely	304

Lahr, Bert	196, 260	
Lamarr, Hedy	200	
Lampkin, Ray	80, 82, 137	
Laughton, Charles	88, 110	
Lawson, Ted	72	
Lena, Al	31, 33	
Leonard, Robert	77	
Leroy, Mervyn	75, 77, 196, 291	
Lincoln, Garland	74	
Lipstein, Harold	4, 185, 287	
Lloyd, Frank	77	
Lonergan, Arthur	215	
Lowe, Marcus	45	
Loy, Myrna	17, 72, 285	
Luff, Tommy	206	
Lundeen, Walter	206	
Lundin, Walter	288	
MacDonald, Jeanette	12, 68, 111, 206-208, 219	
Main, Howard	267	
Manatt, S.C. 'Jimmy'	4, 83, 321	
Mannix, Eddie	18, 52, 197, 264	
Mann, Tony	77	
Mantz, Paul	74-75	
Martin, Mary	70	
Marton, Andrew 'Bundy'	49, 295	
Marton, Bundy	77, 295	
Marzorati, Harold J	4, 287	
Massey, Ilona	70	
Mathis, June	30	
Mayer, Irene	46, 80	
Mayer, Louis B.	17-18, 45-46, 51-52, 72, 127, 141, 191	
McAfee, Lew	149	
McAvoy, May	30	
McCleary, Urie	214, 327-328	
McCoy, Earl	206	
McDonald, Andy	206	
McDonald, Robert	137, 333	
McDowell, Claire	30	
Meador, Joshua	255	
Meighan, Thomas	19, 21	
Meredith, Bess	30	
Miller, Hal	206	
Minnelli, Vincent	70-71, 163	
Montgomery, Bob	17, 200	
Morgan, Frank	196-197	
Morley, Robert	197	
Mortara, Dario	82, 137	
Muni, Paul	195, 218	
Murray, Jimmy	190	
Myers, Carmel	30, 47	
Nagle, Conrad	72	
Nayfack, Nicky	216	
Neilan, Mickey	77	
Neri, Corrado	34	
Neri, Ilva	34	
Neri, Tito	5, 30-31, 33-34, 36-37, 39, 41-43, 46, 299	
Newcombe, Warren	100, 102-103, 112, 168, 223, 313	
New, Jack	206, 295	
Newman, Luther	206	
Niblo, Fred	30-31, 33, 45-46	
Nolta, Floyd 'Speed'	5, 75-76	
Novarro, Ramon	30-31, 38, 47, 148-150	
O'Brien, Perry	206	
Oliver, Harry	46-47	
Olsson, Olof	141-142, 151	
O'Sullivan, Maureen	61, 149, 261
Pal, George	155, 256, 265
Panama, Norma	77
Partridge, 'Stan'	31
Peck, Gregory	200
Peters, Hans	214
Pidgeon, Walter	200, 330
Powell, Bill	17
Power, Tyrone	197
Powers, Dan	295
Provins, Clark	191
Pye, Merrill	83, 214, 321, 325-326
Rainer, Luise	195
Randall, Glen	50, 77
Raymond, Gene	195
Redgrave, Michael	208
Reed, Donna	202
Regan, Joe	141, 155, 206
Reicher, Frank	97
Reid, Laurence	27
Reisner, Chuck	77
Reynolds, Ben F.	30
Ries, Irving	265
Robertson, Glen	333
Robinson, Edward G.	200
Robinson, Glen	137
Robson, Mark	77
Rooney, Mickey	17, 127, 285, 290
Rosenberg, Aaron	258
Rosson, Harold	97, 185
Rowland, Roy	77
Ruben, J. Walter	88
Ruggles, Wesley	77
Ruttenberg, Joe	185
Ryan, Bill	300
Saville, Victor	145, 148
Schenck, Nick	52
Schickel, Richard	334
Schreiner, Martin	141
Schulthies, Chuck	206
Scognamillo, Gabriel	214
Sculati, Al	137
Seastrom, Victor	77
Seaton, George	77
Sedgwick, Ed	77
Seitz, George	298
Selwyn, Edgar	77
Sersen, Fred	209
Shearer, Douglas	18, 83, 300, 302, 321
Shearer, Norma	17, 194, 197, 324
Shepphird, Carroll Leethem	288, 291, 295, 302
Shugrue, Frank	4
Sinatra, Frank	17
Simmons, Jean	115
Sinclair, Grant	267
Skouras, Spyros	209
Slifer, Clarence	4, 104-106, 109-110, 112, 115, 143, 185, 211-212, 265-266, 287
Smedley, Jeff	137, 299
Smith, Jack	75, 206, 288
Smith, Jack Martin	209, 214
Smith, Len	88
Snowdrop, Chief	74
Snyder, Ed	4, 288-289, 302
Stahl, John	77
Staples, Bob	82, 137
Stewart, James	17, 70
Stone, Eddie	80, 82
Strickland, Auby C.	72-74
Strickling, Howard	60
Strohm, Lou	325-326
Struss, Karl	30
Sturges, John	77
Sullivan, Jim	214
Summerfield, Marvin	214
Tamblyn, Russ	256, 258
Tate, Cullen	21-22
Taurog, Norman	77
Taylor, Elizabeth	194
Taylor, Robert	17, 72, 97, 184, 200
Tepker, Harry	191
Thalberg, Irving	17, 52
Thompson, John	214
Thompson, Stan	214
Thorpe, Richard	184
Tobin, John	264, 292
Tod Browning,	258
Tomick, Frank	74
Tonk, Ernest	81
Tracy, Spencer	3, 16-17, 19, 59, 68, 72, 76, 80, 127, 129, 290, 315-316
Tsuburaya, Eiji	328-329
Tuch, Freddy	81
Turner, Lana	202, 330
Van Dyke, W.S 'Woody' II	18, 148-151, 185, 299
Veidt, Conrad	145
Vesey, Jim	141
Vidor, King Wallis	12, 97, 190
Vogel, Joseph R.	103
von Sydow, Max	334
Walker, Jimmy	283-284, 305
Walters, Chuck	77
Waters, Johnny	77, 85, 87
Watson, Clint	206, 287, 302
Wayne, John	200
Weismuller, Johnny	12, 51, 68, 149
Wellman, Harold	4, 185, 213, 288
Wellman, William A.	74, 77, 97, 158
Whitbeck, Frank	262
Wilcox, Freddy	216
Williams, Bill	4, 170, 206, 236
Williams, Claude	206
Williams, Esther	138-139, 152, 203, 209, 219
Williams, Frank	48-49, 258
Wilson, Carey	30, 46
Wilson, Roy	74
Winiger, Ralph	206
Winiger, Walter	206
Wood, Sam	77
Woolfe, Bob	191
Worsfold, Dick	105
Wyler, William	103, 145
Young, Alan	257
Young, Robert	72
Yuricich, Matthew	99, 105
Zarubica, Mladin	79
Zimbalist, Sam	102-104
Zinneman, Freddy	77

MOVIE TITLE INDEX

2001: A Space Odyssey	304
Adam's Rib (1923)	20, 22, 24-25
Adam's Rib (1949)	16
Above And Beyond	231
All the Brothers Were Valiant	184, 186-189
America	166-167
American In Paris, An	71
Annie Get Your Gun	299, 300
Atlantis, the Lost Continent	144, 153-155, 169, 282
Bad Guy	230
Balalaika	70, 79
Beginning or the End, The	23, 51, 72, 179, 183, 220-222
Ben-Hur (1925)	18-19, 28, 30-43, 45, 47, 49-50, 58, 99, 258
Ben-Hur: A Tale of the Christ (1959)	2, 12, 19, 50, 99, 103, 116, 118-121, 143, 163, 213, 360-365, 367
Big Parade, The	79, 148
Billy Rose's Jumbo	60, 302
Billy the Kid	12, 97, 190
Boom Town	194, 214, 290, 293, 312-317
Brigadoon	262
Brown of Harvard	54
Cairo	267, 320-323, 348
Captains Courageous	19, 124, 127, 141, 290, 311
Cimarron	108-109, 214
Command Decision	231, 233, 330-331
Comrade X	160-162, 200, 215
Conquest	194
Crowd, The	190
Dawn Patrol, The	74
Death Ship	269
Demi-Bride, The	54
Divine Woman, The	53
Dragon Seed	8, 122
Duchess of Idaho	320
Fair Co-Ed, The	53
Fast Workers	258
Flight Command	230
Forbidden Planet	125-126, 215, 217, 219, 255, 265, 268-281
Four Horsemen of the Apocalypse	70, 71
Girl from Missouri, The	63
Glass Bottom Boat	19
Good Earth, The	12, 23, 151, 194-195, 218
Greatest Story Ever Told, The	302, 337
Green Dolphin Street	59, 202, 219, 202, 225-229
Guy Named Joe, A	59, 80, 332, 347
Heavenly Body	240-241
Hell Divers	72
High Barbaree	123, 348
High Society	113
How the West Was Won	19, 67, 195, 263, 301-302, 320, 335
I Married an Angel	12, 206-207, 219
Idiot's Delight	218, 319
Jailhouse Rock	375
Jupiter's Darling	138-139
Kismet	113
Lady Without A Passport	232
Legion of the Condemned	74
London After Midnight	15, 259, 377
Luxury Liner	168-169, 192
Malaya	192
Man from Dakota, The	224
Manslaughter	19-22, 27
Marie Antoinette	194, 197-198, 320
Meet Me in St. Louis	113
Meet the People	236
Million Dollar Mermaid	296, 371
Mrs. Miniver	145, 200-201
Mrs. Parkington	170
Mr. Wu	326
Mutiny on the Bounty (1935)	56, 77
Mutiny on the Bounty (1962)	19, 51, 59, 77-78, 107, 109, 143, 212, 301-302, 366
My Fair Lady	148
National Velvet	194
Naughty Marietta	55
New Moon	193
Night Flight	318
North by Northwest	77, 178
Our Vines Have Tender Grapes	156-157, 200, 289
Outrage, The	144
Pagan Love Song	148
Pagan, The	148, 299
Phantom Raiders	164
Plymouth Adventure	59, 126, 128-131
Postman Rings Twice, The	330
Prize, The	95, 302
Quo Vadis	98, 154, 198-200, 214, 219
Red Dust	194
Road to Mandalay, The	44
Royal Wedding	78
Run Silent Run Deep	111
Salute to the Marines	223
San Francisco	18, 64, 68-69, 111-112, 202, 219, 262, 334
Seven Brides for Seven Brothers	234-235
Son of Lassie	349
Speed	88
Stand by for Action	338-346
Strange Cargo	193
Sweethearts	236
Tarzan and His Mate	10, 51, 149, 183, 261
Tarzan Escapes	57
Tarzan Finds a Son	261
Tarzan's Secret Treasure	237, 283
Tell It to the Marines	53
Test Pilot	19, 59, 72, 80, 194, 231, 293-294, 305
They Were Expendable	165, 170, 192, 200
Thirty Seconds Over Tokyo	72, 74-76, 130, 133-136
This Could Be The Night	115
This Man's Navy	158-159
Thousand Cheer	231
Three Guys Named Mike	230
Thunder Afloat	164
Ticklish Affair, A	92-94, 302
Time of Glory, A	89-91, 176
Tom Thumb	254, 256-258, 266
Too Hot to Handle	81, 84-87, 179, 212, 306
Torpedo Run	202-205, 215, 350-356
Trail of '98, The	328
Two Weeks In Another Town	163
Unsinkable Molly Brown, The	117, 302
Up Goes Maisie	233
Upstage	54
Valley of Decision, The	172-173, 200
Viva Las Vegas	302
Waterloo Bridge	201
West Point of the Air	72-73
Wheeler Dealers, The	302
Wings	74
White Cliffs of Dover	236
Without Love	152
Wild North	295
Wizard of Oz, The	12, 30, 65, 194, 196, 242-253
Women's Face, A	144, 146-147
Women Love Diamonds	53
Wreck of the Mary Deare, The	208, 210, 219, 357-359
Yellow Jacket	23
Young Tom Edison	223, 238-239

Jailhouse Rock, MGM Production #1719, Released 1957, AAG Contribution: Special Effects.

Books by
Philip J. Riley

CLASSIC HORROR FILMS
Frankenstein, the original 1931 shooting script
Bride of Frankenstein, the original 1935 shooting script
Son of Frankenstein, the original 1939 shooting script
Ghost of Frankenstein, the original 1942 shooting script
Frankenstein Meets the Wolf Man, the original 1943 shooting script
House of Frankenstein, the original 1944 shooting script
The Mummy, the original 1932 shooting script
The Mummy's Curse the original 1944 shooting script (as Editor in Chief)
The Wolf Man, the original 1941 shooting script
Dracula, the original 1931 shooting script
House of Dracula, the original 1945 shooting script

CLASSIC COMEDY FILMS
Abbott & Costello Meet Frankenstein, the original 1948 shooting script

CLASSIC SCIENCE FICTION
This Island Earth, the original 1955 shooting script
The Creature from the Black Lagoon, the original 1953 shooting script (editor-in-chief)

THE ACKERMAN ARCHIVES SERIES - LOST FILMS
The Reconstruction of London After Midnight, the original 1927 shooting script
The Reconstruction of A Blind Bargain, the original 1922 shooting script
The Reconstruction of The Hunchback of Notre Dame, the original 1923 shooting script

CLASSIC SILENT FILMS
The Reconstruction of The Phantom of the Opera, the original 1925 shooting script
The Reconstruction of "London After Midnight" the original 1927 shooting script (2nd edition)

FILMONSTER SERIES - LOST SCRIPTS
James Whale's Dracula's Daughter, 1934
Cagliostro, The King of the Dead, 1932
Wolf Man vs Dracula 1944
Lon Chaney as Dracula/Nosferatu
Robert Florey's Frankenstein 1931
Frankenstein - A play, 1931(editor)
Karloff as The Invisible Man 1932

AS EDITOR
Countess Dracula by Carroll Borland
My Hollywood, when both of us were young by Patsy Ruth Miller
Mr. Technicolor - Herbert Kalmus
Famous Monster of Filmland #2 by Forrest J Ackerman
The Wizard of MGM by A. Arnold Gillespie - co editor with Robert A. Welch

FILM DOCUMENTARIES
A Thousand Faces - as contributor (Photoplay Productions)
Universal Horrors - as contributor (Photoplay Productions)

Mr. Riley has also contributed to 12 film related books by various authors
as well as numerous magazine articles and received the Count Dracula Society Award
and was inducted into Universal's Horror Hall of Fame

A. Arnold Gillespie with co-editor Philip J. Riley working on Phil's book, "The Reconstruction of 'London After Midnight'", a lost film from 1927 on which Buddy was Set Designer. Cira 1973.